Welcome of Tears

Welcome of Tears
The Tapirapé Indians of Central Brazil

Charles Wagley
University of Florida

WAVELAND
PRESS, INC.

Prospect Heights, Illinois

For information about this book, write or call:

    Waveland Press, Inc.
    P.O. Box 400
    Prospect Heights, Illinois 60070
    (708) 634-0081

Maps and diagrams drawn by David Lindroth.

To
the memory of Herbert Baldus
and to
the Order of
Les Petites Soeurs de Jesus

may they long endure.

Welcome of Tears

"*As soon as the traveler has arrived at the* Moussacat *house* (Moussacat *means the household head who feeds the visitor) which he had chosen to be his host, the traveler must sit down in a cotton bed [hammock] hanging in the air and wait quietly for a while. Soon afterwards women appear, surround the hammock, squat on the ground and, covering their eyes with their hands, cry. With their tears they welcome the visitor whom they profusely praise. . . .*"
Jean de Léry, Le Voyage au Brésil, 1556-1558 [1st ed., 1578], 1927 ed., p. 258.

"*When a visitor enters their home, they honor him by crying. As soon as he arrives, the visitor is seated in a hammock; and without speaking, the wife, her daughters and friends sit around him, with lowered heads, touching him with their hands; they begin to cry loudly and with an abundance of tears. . . .*"
Fernan Cardim, Tratado da Terra e Gente do Brasil em 1665, describing the Tupinambá.

"*When any of them or their foreign friends arrive, they immediately offer him a cotton hammock. The women gather around the visitor and with their hands covering their eyes and grasping him by the legs, they begin to cry with shrieks and marvelous exclamations. This is one of the strongest signs of courtesy they can show their friends.*"
Claude d'Abbeville, Historia da Missão dos Padres Capuchinos na Ilha do Maranhão (1614), describing the Tupinambá.

Preface

This was not an easy book to write for several reasons. Yet each drawback seemed somehow to be balanced by a positive factor, which made me determined to tell the remarkable story of the Tapirapé Indians of Central Brazil as I have followed it for over thirty-five years. The greatest drawback is the fact that my basic research among the Tapirapé took place so many years ago. In 1939-40 I spent over fifteen months living and doing research with the Tapirapé. At that time they were isolated in the wilderness of Central Brazil, far beyond the reach of modern communication, and were relatively uninfluenced by Brazilian civilization. Over the years I have written a series of articles on various aspects of Tapirapé culture and on various theoretical and comparative problems based upon my research in 1939-40. I have never organized my data into an integrated book, however. Since 1939-40 I have continued to do research with the Tapirapé by means of short visits to their village and through reports from other researchers. In 1953 and 1957 I made brief visits of a few days each to the Tapirapé, and in 1965 I spent over six weeks there. I was then accompanied by my wife, Cecilia Roxo Wagley, and by David Epstein, who was then a graduate student at Columbia University. During those later trips to the Tapirapé I was able to verify and to add to the field notes I took in 1939-40, and, perhaps more important, to observe the changes that had taken place in Tapirapé society over a considerable period and under new conditions.

But I must say at once that my field notes are "cold"; that is, they cannot be filled in by my memory as is the case with "fresh" field notes and diaries written only a few months or a year ago. As I review them now, they open up questions of substance and interpretation of Tapirapé culture and society which I wish I could pursue, especially in view of anthropological concepts such as structuralism, ethnoscience, and cultural ecology which have appeared or have been refined over the last decade and more. Yet the main body of my data regarding Tapirapé culture and society is essentially correct. The facts are clear, and often repetitive, in my early field notes; and they are frequently confirmed in notes taken later. Moreover, my facts are corroborated by others. Whenever any doubt remains as to fact or interpretation I shall so indicate throughout this book.

Other observers have indeed been of help in my study of the Tapirapé. The Little Sisters of Jesus, an order of working nuns, established themselves among the Tapirapé in 1952. I have had occasional letters from them and during my return visits they have been able to "fill me in," so to speak, on local history. Valentim Gomes was my constant companion and employee in 1939-40, and he became the Indian officer in charge of the Indian Protection Service post, established in the early 1940's at the mouth of the Tapirapé River ostensibly to keep outsiders from penetrating Tapirapé territory. His name appears frequently in this book. In 1953 and 1957 he recounted in some detail the history of the tribe over the years since I had last seen them in 1940. More recently, Judith Shapiro, while a graduate student at Columbia University, made two field trips to the Tapirapé—one from June to September of 1966 and another of one month's duration in August of 1967. Her two highly perceptive articles (Shapiro, 1968a and 1968b) as well as our long discussions have added much to my understanding of the Tapirapé. My wife's diary for 1965 has been especially useful. And in recent years, as the problem of land-grabbing has stirred up trouble on the Brazilian frontier, the Tapirapé have even been the subject of newspaper stories in both the Brazilian and the North American press.

The most important source other than my own field data has, of course, been Herbert Baldus (1899-1970), the German-Brazilian anthropologist. Throughout his scholarly life Baldus wrote many articles on the Tapirapé, and in 1970, just before his death, he published his monumental study *Tapirapé: tribo tupí no Brasil Central.* * The appearance of that book might well have discouraged any scholar to write at any length about the Tapirapé. Baldus might have relieved me of any further obligation to my profession regarding the Tapirapé, since he cites so often my published articles, my many letters to him regarding the Tapirapé, and even our many conversations. But he prevented this by the first sentences in his book: "I wrote this book for Charles Wagley, who is tied to me by our love for the Tapirapé. I wrote it to stimulate my colleague to publish all that he knows and thinks about these Indians." So my book is also a labor of love, written to fulfill my obligation to my departed colleague and friend and to attempt to organize my own understanding of the Tapirapé culture into an integrated pattern.

Herbert Baldus, when he wrote the warm dedicatory sentences cited above, was aware that we disagreed on certain points of fact and interpretation about the Tapirapé. His actual field experience among the Tapirapé was limited to about six weeks in 1935 and an even shorter period in 1947. He was trained as an anthropologist in Germany in the 1920's and his interests were focused upon comparative ethnography, especially material culture and the historical diffusion of culture traits and custom. His book on the Tapirapé reflects his early training and interests. In it each object of Tapirapé material culture, each institution, and almost each custom or belief sets off reflections on comparative data from other South American tribes. Baldus was greatly attracted to the Tapirapé and thus was intensely interested in their history and culture. I doubt that any document with a reference to the Tapirapé is missing from the bibliography in his book. Furthermore, he hunted out the minutiae of historical references from the sixteenth century to the nineteenth which might have some clue to the origin of and the wanderings of the Tapirapé. I refer any reader wishing to look into such aspects of Tapirapé material culture and history to Baldus's book. But Baldus knew that I would write a different book. He was fully aware of the difference in our anthropological training and the difference in our anthropological interests. I know that if he were alive he would read this book avidly, and sometimes shake his head in disagreement at some of my interpretations.

---

* The many articles published by Baldus, the articles which I have published, and, in fact, a complete bibliography of all sources which provide any information on the Tapirapé appear in the Bibliography of Baldus's book. I have not attempted to reproduce that extensive bibliography here. Any student wishing to probe deeper into Tapirapé history or ethnography should consult his work.

In addition to all those people whom I have mentioned above who have been of so much help to me in my Tapirapé studies, there are many other institutions and people whose help I should acknowledge. The first field research in 1939-40 was supported by a grant from the Columbia University Council for Research in Social Sciences made to the late Professor Ralph Linton. William Lipkind, then a graduate student at Columbia University, spent about fourteen months in 1938-39 doing research among the Carajá on the Araguaia River, and the letters he wrote me in 1938 were most helpful in preparing me for local conditions.

In Brazil, my research was sponsored by the Museu Nacional of Rio de Janeiro, which also made available funds to meet the costs of assembling a collection of Tapirapé art and material culture which is now deposited in that museum. Dona Heloisa Alberto Torres, then the director of the Museu Nacional, secured innumerable facilities for my research. Antenor Leitão de Carvalho, a zoologist from the Museu Nacional, was my companion for a short time during my second expedition in 1939. In 1940, three young students of anthropology from the museum, Rubens Meanda, Nelson Teixeira, and Eduardo Galvão, joined me for a brief period in the Tapirapé village. All of my film negatives were developed at the museum, and they were filed so neatly and so well that even after thirty-five years there was no problem in selecting negatives for this volume. I am indebted to David Densmore, Sr., for making enlargements from the old negatives of my photographs for use in illustrating this book. Several people at the University of Florida helped me put this manuscript in shape for publication—Kathleen Stocks, George Vollweiler, Linda Miller, and Arlene Kelly. Charles Palmer drew the original maps and charts for me; these were then redrawn for the book by David Lindroth. Robert J. Tilley of Oxford University Press encouraged me to complete this book and in the process he made many creative suggestions. Caroline Taylor not only improved the book by her skillful editing, making her way through the maze of native terms and names, but she was also an interested and sympathetic reader. I wish to thank all those mentioned in this Preface. Finally, I wish to thank the Tapirapé Indians themselves and the many students of anthropology who for over thirty years have heard of the Tapirapé *ad nauseum* as I have drawn data from that culture to exemplify theoretical concepts in all my courses.

Small portions of this book have been published elsewhere in different form and in different contexts. In Chapter 6 I have used several
pages from my paper on Tapirapé shamanism (Wagley, 1943); in

Chapter 7 I have included portions of a character sketch of Champukwi, perhaps my closest Tapirapé friend, which was published first in the book *In the Company of Man*, edited by Joseph B. Casagrande (copyright © Harper & Row, 1960); and in Chapter 8 I have likewise used several pages which appeared first in a chapter on Brazilian Indians in *Minority Groups in the New World: Six Case Studies*, by Charles Wagley and Marvin Harris (copyright © Columbia University Press, 1958). I wish to thank the Museu Nacional of Rio de Janeiro, Harper & Row, and Columbia University Press for allowing me to use these pages in this different context.

The title of this book is taken from a custom practiced by the Tupinamba of the Brazilian coast, the probable ancestors of the Tapirapé, which was first reported in 1578. The Tapirapé traditionally shared this custom; and the mixture of sadness and pleasure evoked by seeing a visitor (an old friend or kinsman) seems appropriate and symbolic in view of the troubled, almost disastrous, epoch which the Tapirapé have weathered during the last seventy-five years.

Throughout this book I have taken considerable liberty in my orthography of the Tapirapé language. I have used a highly simplified transcription which approximates Tapirapé sounds for the English reader. Tapirapé is a highly nasalized language; rather than transcribe nasalized vowels, I have simply added "n," as in *tantan*, which might have been written *tãtã* (fire). Many Tapirapé morphemes contain a glottal stop which is often indicated by linguists with a "?". I omitted glottal stops from my transcription; thus, *name?i* ("male infant") is written *namei*. In addition to the vowels found in English, Tupí-Guaraní languages, including Tapirapé, have a high mid-rounded vowel which is generally transcripted as a "y" by Latin American linguists and sometimes as an "ï" by others. I have only vaguely approximated this sound by using the English "u." This vowel appears in such Tapirapé words as *uwu* ("land" or "earth"), which might be transcribed more precisely as *ywy* or *ïwï*. I have also used this simplified transcription in recording the kinship terms in Appendix I. Linguists interested in Tapirapé phonetics, phonemics, and syntax must await the studies of Dr. Yonne Leite of the Museu Nacional of Rio de Janeiro, who is presently doing linguistics work among the Tapirapé.

Gainesville, Fla.   C.W.
April 1977

Contents

List of Illustrations & Maps

Welcome of Tears

To the Tapirapé

My journey to the Tapirapé tribe in central Brazil in 1939 was both an intellectual and physical adventure. I was twenty-five at the time, unmarried, and had just finished writing my doctoral dissertation on the economic life of a small village of Mayan Indians in Guatemala. There were few teaching positions available for anthropologists, for it was still the end of the Great Depression; but even if a position had been offered to me I doubt that I would have given in to the temptation. I felt that I wanted a new research experience in a region of the world which was not well known anthropologically and with a problem which I felt would break new ground. Ralph Linton, one of my major advisers in graduate school at Columbia University, was then struggling with theoretical problems of acculturation. He had just completed three excellent chapters on the subject for a book which he edited, *Acculturation in Seven American Indian Tribes* (New York, 1940). "Acculturation" was the term then used to encompass the impact of continuous contact of western civilization on primitive peoples. In his writing Linton had refined the concept and analyzed it in dynamic terms. One of the interesting problems that emerged was the importance of the initial ten to fifteen years of contact between western peoples and supposedly untouched primitives. What are the aspects of western culture they first adopt or reject in this initial period? Linton found that little or nothing was known about early acculturation and that the first observations of trained anthropologists had generally taken place at least a generation or more after the acculturation process had begun. Both of us became excited over an early-contact acculturation study. Funds were found for such a study, and I set to work searching for an auspicious locale for it.

I first heard of the Tapirapé Indians in New York, and in the context of the hypothetical situation described above. Alfred Metraux, who was then Visiting Professor of Anthropology at Yale University and one of the great specialists on South American ethnology, suggested them. By chance, William Lipkind, a Columbia graduate student who was doing field work among the Carajá Indians, just to the east of Tapirapé territory, had mentioned them in his letters to Ruth Benedict. My exchange of letters with Lipkind took almost two months, but he wrote enthusiastically about the prospects for such a study. He had not visited the Tapirapé, but he had heard much about them from missionaries and from the Carajá. He wrote that there were "several" villages. The nearest one was located about a hundred miles west of the Araguaia River, inland, and north of the Tapirapé River, a tributary of the Araguaia. His local Brazilian guide, Antonio Pereira, had once visited one of their villages in the company of a missionary. They had been first contacted about fifteen years earlier, and now had sporadic contacts with Dominican missionaries. It did seem that the situation of the Tapirapé suited our research design, so I decided to spend a year or more doing research among them.

I searched the scientific journals for any information on the tribe, but they were of little help, for the few mentions of them were either second-hand or reports of information garnered from Tapirapé captives among the Carajá. Curiously, the most concrete information came from a popular book, *Brazilian Adventure*, by Peter Fleming (1933). Fleming had participated in an expedition to rescue the British explorer, Colonel Fawcet, who had disappeared some years before around the headwaters of the Xingú River. The Fleming expedition had traveled up the Tapirapé River hoping to traverse the region from the Tapirapé headwaters into the basin of the Xingú. At one point they had encountered Tapirapé Indians and met with them peacefully. He had photographs of them, probably the first ever published. The Fleming expedition tried to persuade the Tapirapé to serve as guides on the overland trek to the Xingú River headwaters, but the Indians refused. Without guides, and faced with a long march through unknown territory, Fleming's expedition turned back. But

4

Fleming's account, although rather satirical and certainly not scientific in any way, did give me an idea of what I faced in my journey to the Tapirapé. Also, mentions of the tribe in scientific journals provided some help in preparation. It was clear that the Tapirapé spoke a Tupí-Guaraní language, and there were even some speculations that they were refugees, remnants of the extinct Tupinambá who had inhabited the Brazilian coast in the sixteenth and seventeenth centuries. So I began a study of old Tupí-Guaraní grammars to learn something of the phonetics and the general grammatical structure of that language family. I also read the excellent books by Alfred Metraux on the Tupinambá, which are based upon the accounts of the early Portuguese and French chroniclers of the sixteenth and seventeenth centuries (Metraux: 1928a, 1928b).

In January of 1939 I left New York for Rio de Janeiro on the S.S. *Argentina*. It was a lovely, leisurely twelve-day trip and I had as my companion Alfred Metraux, who was en route to Buenos Aires to do further field research in the Argentinian Gran Chaco. For hours upon hours he told me of his anthropological field experience in South America. I had in my baggage some clothing and equipment purchased at Abercrombie and Fitch, New York's most famous sporting goods store, for the Brazilian interior. The rest I would buy in Rio de Janeiro. My most useful purchase in New York was several pounds of colorful porcelain beads, each about the size of a small pea, which Lipkind had warned me by mail were highly prized by the Carajá. After much searching I found them at an import firm located in a shop on the West Side of lower Manhattan. (They were made in Czechoslovakia.) Early one morning we sailed through the entrance of Rio de Janeiro's beautiful harbor, where the mountains rise abruptly from the beaches. It took my breath away. Not even the struggle with customs—both linguistically and legally—over some of the strange items in my baggage dampened my enthusiasm, for I had the premonition that I was entering a new world.

Columbia University had an informal agreement with the National Museum in Rio de Janeiro to co-sponsor ethnological studies in Brazil. I have already mentioned William Lipkind, whose research was sponsored by the Museum, but two other colleagues, Ruth Landes and Buell Quain, were also working in Brazil under the auspices of the Museum. I found that Buell Quain was in Rio de Janeiro, called back from the Trumaí tribe to renew his research permission from the Indian Protection Service. So that same afternoon I went to the Mu- 5 seum with Quain to meet Heloisa Alberto Torres, the director and our patroness in Brazil. Anxious to stimulate anthropology at the Museum, she had written letters to Franz Boas asking that young scholars be sent to Brazil. She felt a personal obligation toward and interest in those who came, and, using her great prestige and wide network of friends, she guided us through the intricate bureaucracy, which called for registration of aliens, permission to carry out a scientific expedition, and various official papers. She taught us Brazilian ethnology through the Museum's collections, pointing out books in the library which had been unavailable to us in New York. Dona Heloisa also taught us proper Brazilian manners and told us of the wonders of her country. I spent a month at the Museum—reading, listening, studying Portuguese, and planning my trip to the Tapirapé. I had a hundred practical questions, but soon learned that most urban Brazilians knew even less than I did about the great interior of their country. Except for a few rare individuals at the Museum, the reaction was that a young American who wished to spend a year or more in Mato Grosso must be slightly crazy. Why not do one's research in the libraries, or among the ethnographic collections at the Museum?

Frankly, in 1939 I was poorly prepared to undertake field research in Brazil. As a graduate student I had taken one rather badly organized course on South American ethnology—badly organized, I think, because South American ethnology had, with notable exceptions, been so poorly studied up until then. I had done previous field research among the Mayan Indians of Guatemala and had adequate training in anthropological theory and methodology as it was taught at Columbia University, but I knew practically nothing about Brazil and its history. I could speak Spanish, but knew not a word of Portuguese. In the two months before I had left New York I had learned to read the language, and optimists there assured me that I would learn to speak it quickly and easily. During my month at the National Museum I did make some progress, but it was two or three months before I could really understand it. People in small towns and the countryside were mystified when I mixed Spanish words with my poor Portuguese, and I was often equally confused by their country accent and vocabulary. Without doubt it was for this reason that I lost my baggage containing my field equipment somewhere between São Paulo and the end of the railroad in Anapolis, in Goiás state. Although I am sure that the conductor must have explained the baggage

rules to me, I did not understand that at each change of railroad lines (three were involved) a passenger must personally supervise the reloading of his baggage, dispatching it with the next company. An innocent American, I had presumed that baggage checked in at São Paulo and destined for Anapolis would be transferred automatically at each change of trains, but it was missing when I arrived in Anapolis. Only after almost three weeks of daily telegrams sent to agents along the route, with the help of a British missionary, was my equipment located and forwarded to me. Furthermore, although Lipkind had sent me a list of equipment to bring and my colleague at the National Museum had added to that list other items—such as a .22-calibre rifle, a .32 revolver, a portable pharmacy (badly selected), mosquito netting, a hammock, and a piece of canvas to protect my baggage—I was not really well equipped. I also had some useless equipment, notably a dictaphone with 200 blank discs to record music. The machine later disintegrated from rough handling on the Araguaia River, but not before I had recorded a few discs that gave some idea of Tapirapé music. In brief, I was insufficiently trained, badly informed, and poorly equipped when I left Rio de Janeiro for the Tapirapé in February of 1939.

My first stop from Rio de Janeiro en route to the Tapirapé was in São Paulo. While reading in the library at the Museu Nacional, I had run across a new book, *Ensaios de Antropologia Brasileira* (1937), by Herbert Baldus. In it I learned, to my dismay, that Baldus had carried out research in 1935 among the Tapirapé. I use the word "dismay" with good reason, for traditionally among anthropologists there has been a proprietary attitude toward the tribe or village with which they have worked. It becomes "my tribe" or "my people." I also knew that Baldus had been highly critical of another anthropologist from Columbia—Jules Henry, who had studied the Kaingang of southern Brazil. I feared that Baldus would be critical of any North American ethnologist who invaded his territory. Yet I felt that I had to visit him and to ask for his advice, if not his blessing.

He received me pleasantly, but rather formally, at his home in São Paulo. When he invited me to come and see him the next day, I began to lose my anxiety. During my second visit to his home, he encouraged me in my plan to study the Tapirapé. He reasoned that it would be an interesting experiment for two ethnologists of basically different training and different cultural backgrounds to study the same small tribe. He was of great assistance in providing names of people who might be helpful in Goiás. He asked me about my equipment and sent me off to 7 buy some obviously needful things not included on Lipkind's list. He showed me photographs of the Tapirapé and of some of their ceremonials which he had witnessed, though he did not open his archives of field notes nor tell me what I might expect to find. Thus began a long friendship which continued until his death in October of 1970.

So I left São Paulo by railroad for Anapolis. Each of the three rail lines had a different gauge; so, at each transfer, passengers, baggage, and frieght had to be moved from one train to another. The trip from São Paulo to Anapolis by train took two days—actually one night and one day, a lay-over for one night, and then a grueling final day on the wood-burning Estrada de Ferro de Goiás. I arrived in Anapolis tired, dusty, and with holes in my clothes made by the flying cinders of our mighty steam engine.

At Anapolis I found a truck to take me to Goiás Velho (the former state capital), which was then an old colonial town and the jumping-off place for the Araguaia River. There again I was delayed—this time by a serious sinus infection and lack of transportation. But with the help of the Reverend Archibald McIntyre, a Scottish missionary with many years of experience on the Araguaia River, I was able to complete my purchases—among them beans, rice, *rapadura* (brown sugar in blocks of about two pounds each), salt, and coils of black tobacco. Both the rapadura and the salt turned out to be invaluable. Among the Indians of the Araguaia River the only sweetening to be found was wild honey, and salt was a rarity sought eagerly. Finally, all my equipment was loaded on a truck and we took off for Leopoldina (now called Arauaná) on the Araguaia River. I was anxious to reach Leopoldina, for Lipkind had written to me that a commercial motorboat left there early each month for the long trip downriver to Conceição do Araguaia. Lipkind told me that we would meet at a settlement called Furo de Pedra, about four hundred miles downriver if I would travel on the April motorboat.

It was the end of the rainy season and the road was unusually bad, but the driver left Goiás Velho at sunrise. He predicted that we would arrive in Leopoldina before sundown. Everything went well until late in the afternoon; then the truck, on crossing an apparently innocent mud hole, bogged down to its axles. By the time night fell the driver, his assistant, and his passengers (we had acquired several freeloaders) were still trying to dig us out. So we spent the night sleeping on top of the baggage in the truck. At dawn we heard the toot of a whistle.

8   The sound came from Leopoldina, about eight kilometers ahead. It

was the motorboat, the *Expresso do Araguaia,* announcing its monthly departure downriver. It seemed that I would be stranded in Leopoldina for a month unless I could find some other means of transportation. I left the truck and walked ahead, accompanied by two other downhearted passengers who had hoped to travel on the boat. As we walked ahead it was soon apparent that the truck would not make it to Leopoldina this time. As we neared the town, we found the creeks still swollen, and we waded across them through water waist high. The boat had gone before we got to Leopoldina. Three days later my baggage arrived, loaded on burros and horses and some of it wet and soggy.

At that time Leopoldina was a village of perhaps a hundred Brazilian families and five families of Carajá Indians. However, it did have several general stores and a *pensão* (boardinghouse) run by a talkative young man, Sr. Tulio. He provided meals, a privy, and an open room for sleeping quarters which I shared with all his guests—male and female. He did not inspire confidence, but he was eager to be helpful. I was overly suspicious, thinking that most certainly he was trying to exploit me (though I learned later that he had been most honest and reasonable). Sr. Tulio owned a dugout canoe (called locally an ubá) which he would rent—or, reluctantly, sell. He found two young men, Brazilians from along the river, who would act as canoemen. Sr. Tulio hardly knew the men, nor could I find anyone in Leopoldina who was willing to vouch for them. But I had heard that Lipkind had made a tentative contract with Valentim Gomes, a highly respected man, to work for me as a guide and man of all services. Valentim, they said, was living at either São José (now Bandeirante), which was two days downriver by canoe, or at Santa Isabel, four days downriver. In his hands I could feel secure. So, with my two young frontiersmen, I took off. My dugout was heavily loaded, but we soon picked up a wandering Carajá Indian who would help paddle in exchange for the ride to a downstream village. We traveled in a rather leisurely fashion, making camp early each evening on islands with sandy beaches, which were just then being uncovered by the falling water of the Araguaia. We began our journey each day at dawn.

That first trip down the Araguaia River was an extraordinary experience. I did not feel secure with my canoemen, nor did I trust my own ability to give orders. I slept each night under a net, with my revolver at hand. But the river was beautiful. As we floated downstream the canoemen fished for *pacú,* a small tasty fish, and we traded tobacco 9

Valentim Gomes in 1939.

with Carajá Indians for *tucunaré*, a large trout-like fish weighing from five to ten pounds. I shot wild ducks, which were abundant along the beaches. My supplies were fresh, so with fish and game we ate well. ("Too well," said Valentim later, when he estimated the rice, beans, coffee, and rapadura we had consumed, and he accused the canoemen of selling some of the food in the Carajá villages which we had visited briefly along the river.)

As we floated near the banks, we saw flocks of parakeets; and red and blue macaws flew noisily overhead. In the early morning and late evening, swarms of water birds—giant stork-like *jaburus*, graceful white egrets, and pink flamingos—settled in the shallow water near our camp. I bathed gingerly several times each day on the white Araguaia beaches, for I was afraid of the notorious piranha (I lost that fear with experience), and at night I sat near the romantic campfire—romantic to me, for I was not yet aware that it is at the end of the day when the malaria-bearing anopheles mosquito feeds.

10   We spent the night at the ranch of Lucio da Luz, a man who lived

isolated on the Araguaia because he was wanted for murder both up-river in Goiás and downriver in Pará. But on his ranch he was law and order, for he had surrounded himself with a group of cowboys who were well armed and who served as his henchmen and bodyguards. He told me that he had ordered the execution of a man and a woman who had run off together, leaving their respective spouses. Lucio later played an important role in Tapirapé history as he expanded his ranching activities into their territory. He was hospitable, friendly, and kind to his young foreign guest. He told me of his growing herd of cattle, but complained that he could not sell them for lack of "understanding" of outside authority (the police) and the great distance to any market.

Valentim Gomes was not to be found at either São José or Santa Isabel, but according to local Brazilians he was waiting for me even further downriver, at Furo de Pedra. My canoemen threatened to quit. They had contracted to paddle me downstream as far as Santa Isabel, but they still had to return upstream to give back the canoe to Sr. Tulio. Even so, with some persuasion and an increase in wages, they continued with me. After ten days of travel we arrived in Furo de Pedra, where Valentim took charge. He paid the canoemen, dispatched them upriver (the journey was to take them twenty days), made an inventory of my equipment, and cooked a meal in the pleasant hut which Lipkind had rented. Green as I was, it was obvious even to me that I would have to depend upon Valentim to provide the necessities of life, make arrangements with local people, and do a hundred other services. Even so, it was several days before we spoke of salary or any other formalities of employment.

In 1939 Furo de Pedra was one of the largest non-Indian settlements in the middle Araguaia River region. It contained about thirty-five to forty illiterate frontier families who made a living from grazing a few cattle on the semi-flooded grasslands back from the river and from subsistence gardens. There were two miserably stocked stores which served more as trading posts, receiving hides and skins (wild pigskin; alligator, or *jacaré*; and jaguar) as well as such products as salted *pirarucu* in exchange for manufactured goods and tinned foods. Of course, their stock of *cachaça* (a raw sugarcane rum) was always plentiful, but there was a perennial shortage of cloth, agricultural implements, and other more basic items. People were so eager for salt, rapadura, tobacco, cloth, bushknives and hoes that they begged me to sell my meager supplies. I was a strange visitor and a novelty to them. *11*

They had seen few foreigners except for a Dominican priest who lived over two hundred miles downriver at Conceição do Araguaia and the Scottish missionaries who maintained a ranch at Macaúba, not many miles away, as a refuge for lepers. They had come to know "Guilherme" (William Lipkind) in the last few months. Everyone was friendly and pleasant.

By then Lipkind had given up waiting for me. He had left to visit the Javahé villages (they were a branch of the Carajá). He would return, people said, in a few weeks, a week, two weeks—time was plentiful and vague. But I was content to wait, for to my delight I found a Tapirapé Indian in Furo de Pedra. He was a youth of sixteen or seventeen. His name, I learned, was Opronunchwi, although the people of Furo de Pedra called him "José." He had spent the rainy season, October to March, with the Dominican priests at Conceição and had then made his way upriver to Furo de Pedra. There he waited for me. Lipkind had told him that a *tori* (the term used both by Carajá and Tapirapé for a non-Indian) would arrive soon to visit his people and would return with him to his village. Opronunchwi was in good health and well treated by the townspeople, who had never seen a Tapirapé before, but he was eager to return to his native village.

So I settled down to await Lipkind's return. And, equipped with a Tapirapé informant, I set to work at once. Opronunchwi had a vocabulary of about three hundred words in Portuguese, so I started the painful job of studying the Tapirapé language with him. We could communicate surprisingly well on simple subjects, and he was a willing teacher. He both misinformed and informed me. I understood clearly from Opronunchwi that there were three large Tapirapé villages, but this was not true; Opronunchwi lied because he wanted to increase my enthusiasm to visit the Tapirapé and to impress the Brazilians at Furo de Pedra as well as the Carajá. But I did learn that the Tapirapé measured the seasons by the stars: he pointed out the Pleiades (*é é chu* in Tapirapé) and said that their disappearance over the horizon in the early evenings of April and May heralds the end of the rains. The Tapirapé would then have a big festival. This proved to be sound information, and it made me even more eager to travel to his village.

William Lipkind returned to Furo de Pedra after about ten days, and, having been promised dancing and ceremonials, agreed to accompany me up the Tapirapé River to visit their village. So we loaded my baggage in his dugout canoe, which was equipped with a six-horsepower outboard motor, and in a canoe I purchased in Furo de Pedra. It was to be pulled behind Lipkind's boat. We were then five: Lipkind, Antonio Pereira (Lipkind's guide), Valentim Gomes, Opronunchwi, and myself. Antonio Pereira had once traveled up the Tapirapé River with missionaries to a point called São Domingos, where the Tapirapé were accustomed to meet with the Dominican priests each dry season. He and Opronunchwi were our guides. But the going was slow, for both boats were heavily loaded and the Tapirapé River has many meanders. We often found ourselves in lagoons or small affluents still swollen from the rainy season, having lost track of the main stream. We traveled for four days before we reached São Domingos, perhaps averaging fifty miles a day. São Domingos proved to be nothing but a shed covered by palm leaves, and it was hard to find in the thick galeria forest that lined the river.

The next day Opronunchwi removed his clothes, made a pack with the new hammock he had acquired on the Araguaia River, and set off on foot "to call the Tapirapé." Two days passed, and on the third a group of about ten Tapirapé men and women suddenly appeared from across the open savanna that lies back from the river. They were in a hurry to return, for the "Tapirapé were dancing," and they refused to carry any heavy baggage. The next day we set out. A Tapirapé Indian with a light load might easily make the trip from Tampiitawa to São Domingos in one day, but with loads (our hammocks, mosquito nets, and some small baggage), and with the torí anthropologists, the pace was slow. We spent one night camped on the savanna. The next morning we left savanna country and entered the forest, and early in the afternoon we crossed manioc plantations. Our Indian companions asked us to fire our revolvers to announce our arrival to the villagers. Then, suddenly, the forest opened up, and we were in the Tapirapé village.

I was completely bewildered. The Tapirapé were indeed in the midst of a festival. We were taken from house to house to be fed *kawi* (a liquid drink made from maize, peanuts or tapioca) and tidbits of roast peccary. Our hammocks were hung in the huge *takana*, or men's house, in the center of the village. Late in the afternoon the dancing and singing began (or, better, resumed). All of the Tapirapé were decorated with body paint, feathers, and beads. My feet were blistered from the long hike and I was exhausted, yet I felt that I must remain on my feet to take pictures and make notes. The singing and dancing continued through the night, ending only when the sun   *13* was well into the sky the next morning. At least I was told that it did, because at about 2 a.m. I stretched out in my hammock for a few moments of rest and went off to sleep, waking only at dawn. For that reason I missed a ceremonial economic exchange during the *kawió* ceremonies (see Shapiro, 1968b) which I never did witness in its full form. However, at dawn I saw the young men, covered with net hammocks and palm leaves, attacking the young women with huge phalli. It was clear what was taking place, but what it meant in Tapirapé symbolism was, of course, far beyond my comprehension.

Everyone slept through the morning, but by late afternoon Opronunchwi had persuaded a group of Tapirapé men to suspend the festivities and return to the river port to fetch my baggage. Obviously, they were motivated by his rather exaggerated story of all the presents I had brought. Lipkind and Antonio Pereira left with them at dawn. Two days later the Tapirapé men returned, each with his *pehura* (palm basket) loaded with about fifty pounds or more. It was not an orderly safari in colonial African style. Valentim had simply allowed each man to select his cargo. Along the way they seemed to have consumed at least fifty pounds of rapadura, a fifty-pound sack of salt had disappeared, and some of the men were already smoking the raw tobacco which I brought as a gift. But most of our goods and equipment had arrived intact, although some things had to be left as a reserve on a platform in the hut at Porto São Domingos.

The next two days were difficult. The Dominican priests, during their meetings with the Tapirapé, had made a general distribution of presents—cloth, bushknives, scissors, axes. The Tapirapé expected me to distribute *all* of the trade goods I had brought with me, but I was determined to give only some gifts, holding the remainder to be traded for food and Tapirapé artifacts for the museum in Rio de Janeiro. I finally parted with most of my goods, but I held on to my precious porcelain beads, which I had secreted in a small handbag. Privacy was out of the question, for Valentim and I were camped in one corner of the takana. I removed my trousers one night and went to sleep only to wake up to find them borrowed. The Tapirapé did not steal—in fact, although they often borrowed from one another, they had great respect for personal property—but at first they had a passionate desire to inspect everything about our possessions and our persons. Valentim and I took turns hovering over our belongings for fear that our cameras, rifle, medicines, and other necessities would be borrowed. So Valentim made the decision: we must have a house.

14

Using as a bribe the last of our bushknives he recruited several young men, and within two days we had a palm-thatched hut. It had no walls, but was closed in along the sides with split bamboo. It was situated just outside the circle of Tapirapé longhouses. We were not protected from the eyes of the village, but at least we were safe from inspecting fingers. Over the months that we lived with the Tapirapé, Valentim continued to improve our house. We built a platform that served as a table, and he contrived a primitive desk for me. He also made a gate-like door which we could fasten so that people would not invade our home while we were away or asleep.

In time the Tapirapé became accustomed to—even bored with—our presence. We were no longer so rich in trade goods, and they knew that we were built physically approximately as they were. I bathed publicly in the near-by brook, and soon women and children stopped coming to view the spectacle. They only wondered why I did not have a prepuce. Valentim bathed at night, for he was more modest, besides being frankly embarrassed at the outcry of astonishment which went up among the Tapirapé at the size of his genitals. The festival was over, but there was singing at night. I settled down to the difficult job of learning the Tapirapé language and inquiring about their culture. Valentim was busy cooking, washing our clothes, trading salt for food, hunting with a Tapirapé companion for meat, and doing a hundred-odd jobs.

We stayed, during this first visit, from early May until the end of September. It was marred by only two events. First, in mid-June a highly respected Tapirapé leader, Kamanaré, died of what seemed to be malaria. He had just made two lovely headdresses for me which I was going to deposit in the National Museum. He had also been my frequent visitor. On the night of his death his male relatives invaded my house. They removed the headdresses and burned them. I had the vague feeling (which later proved to be correct) that they were angry with me, suspecting that I had caused his death. At the same time, other Tapirapé seemed to be telling us to be careful. So for several nights Valentim and I took turns sleeping, each for a few hours. And during the day we stayed close to our house. I did not feel that we were in real danger, for the Tapirapé have always been very peaceful, almost timid people. But for a week or more the atmosphere was not conducive to field research, although the situation was instructive. I did brave public opinion to witness Kamanaré's burial and watch the mourners.

Then, in late July, my field work was disrupted by my own malaria. Valentim had gone with two Indian companions to the port at São Domingos to rendezvous with two Brazilians who had been contracted to bring us mail and pick up our letters. It was the first communication we had had with the outside world in almost three months. I looked forward to the mail (a service by canoe came down the Araguaia River each month), and was eager to send news to my family and friends. I remained in the village, and during the first night of Valentim's absence I came down with chills. The next day my fever was 104°F. I had some quinine and about thirty Atabrine tablets, which were rather rare at that time. That day I started the prescribed treatment with Atabrine, but I did not complete it, for by night I had lost consciousness. The rest I know only from Valentim. When he arrived two days later, I was unconscious, hot, mumbling, and sometimes raving. Urukumu, a Tapirapé *panché*, or shaman, was treating me by massage, blowing tobacco smoke over my body, and sucking. People kept saying to Valentim, "Doctor Carlo amano!" (dies!). Valentim was able to force more Atabrine down my throat and to give me liquids. I soon regained consciousness, but for almost ten days I was too weak to leave my hammock. During my recuperation, I had few visitors. The Tapirapé are not compassionate toward a visitor to their village when he is ill; they become nervous, fearing retaliation if he should die, and they fear that his disease will spread, as it well might. [That same reaction had been observed by Baldus in 1935, when his companion, Frederick Kegel, also fell ill with malaria in their village (Baldus, 1970: 450-51). On that occasion they asked Baldus and Kegel to leave. "The ill outsider is intolerable," wrote Baldus.] The Tapirapé did not ask us to leave; but for a few days, as it became clear that I was improving, people came to see me, sat by my hammock, sang for me, and told me stories. The last days of my illness were rich in data. (Incidentally, in saying "Doctor Carlo," the Tapirapé were imitating Valentim, who called me "Doctor Carlos," but there is no 's' sound in the Tapirapé language.)

My malaria did not subside so easily; I had mild attacks in August and in early September. So Valentim and I decided to return to Furo de Pedra to rest and look for new supplies. Our salt was low, our coffee exhausted, only a small can of sugar remained, my cigarettes were long gone and I satisfied my habit by smoking native tobacco in a pipe. In the company of Champukwi, who had become my good friend and best informant, we traveled downriver to Furo de Pedra. It was a memorable trip, but there I received both letters and bad news. My colleague Buell Quain, also from Columbia University, had committed suicide while in the state of Maranhão among the Kraho Indians. Heloisa Alberto Torres wrote asking me to return to Rio de Janeiro. Both William Lipkind and Ruth Landes, the other anthropologists from Columbia, had returned to New York, so I was the only representative of the Columbia group in Brazil and my presence was needed to identify Buell Quain's papers and belongings. So I started the difficult trip upriver to Leopoldina. It should have taken me twenty days, but at Santa Isabel I was fortunate enough to hitch a ride on a motor launch which had been sent down the Araguaia Rivʼr to set up a base camp for a hunting trip for Getulio Vargas, President of Brazil (he did not come because of the outbreak of World War II).[1] That ride took me all the way to Rio de Janeiro—by the motor launch to Leopoldina, by truck and car to Goiânia (the new capital of Goiás state), and then by special train from Anapolis all the way to Rio de Janeiro. On that trip I learned nothing about Indians, but much about Brazil. My companions and hosts were President Vargas's personal bodyguards from Rio Grande do Sul—a mixture of gangsters and gaúcho cowboys. I also met Acary dos Passos Oliveira, a man who loved the backlands of his country and the Indians and had been appointed by the State of Goiás to accompany the presidential expedition. Acary later became the director of the Indian Museum in Goiânia. He was as frightened as I at traveling with the "savages" of Vargas's bodyguards. They treated both Acary and me politely, but there was considerable brawling among themselves.

I did not return to the Tapirapé until early December, although I left Rio de Janeiro in early November. This time I came better equipped: I brought along a six-horsepower outboard motor. Dr. Antenor Leitão de Carvalho, a young zoologist from the National Museum, came with me to do research on the Araguaia River. Valentim was waiting in Goiás Velho with everything ready for the journey to Furo de Pedra. It was again a beautiful ride down the Araguaia River, but a swifter one. It was an easy trip from Furo de Pedra to Porto São Domingos with my outboard motor, a good dugout canoe, and the experience Valentim and I had acquired. We even had a pack train of horses to take supplies overland to the Tapirapé savanna, where

---

1. I learned of the war when I arrived at Santa Isabel. A Brazilian caboclo explained that "the Germans are fighting with the other foreigners."

we found some of the Indians camped. It was the first time most Tapirapé had ever seen horses, and they caused considerable consternation.

In Furo de Pedra, we acquired a new companion, Salvador, a short but strong *caboclo* (backwoodsman) who was better at most activities of the backlands than the Indians themselves. I say that I "acquired" Salvador, but I might as well admit that I bought him. I paid off his lifetime debt to a Brazilian trader, a matter of about $200; thus, he "belonged" to me. I forgave his debt and paid him $30 a month plus clothes, food, and other necessities. Valentim was black, and six feet tall, while Salvador looked like an Indian. Also, Valentim was a Seventh-Day Adventist, and he prayed all day on Saturday. Salvador was just a frontiersman; he thought of himself as a Catholic, but he did not know what that meant. He could walk faster and farther than most Tapirapé men. He was about thirty, and an expert and experienced hunter. I think the Tapirapé admired him more than they did either Valentim or me, who were now their old friends.[2]

So we settled in for the rainy season. Only once was Salvador able to reach Porto São Domingos to pick up and deposit mail in a cache to be relayed outside. The savannas were flooded, often waist deep, and what had been small streams could only be crossed by swimming. Food, except for manioc flour, was scarce, and I developed boils (probably a nutritional deficiency), but Salvador brought in game from time to time. It often rained for ten days on end. Everyone became irritated—the Tapirapé with one another, the Tapirapé with us, Salvador with Valentim, Valentim with Salvador, and everyone with me. I worked on my research, read Tolstoy's *War and Peace*, and thought of nothing but when I would be able to leave and return to New York. It took willpower to continue writing my field notes; and, as I read them now, I find that they are not as voluminous as those of other months.

In April, the rains diminished. In May the Tapirapé began to sing at night. Then, one morning, we heard a pistol shot. Some time later three strange Brazilians appeared. They were only youths—Eduardo Galvão, Rubens Meanda, and Nelson Teixeira. They came from the Museu Nacional, sent by Heloisa Alberto Torres. They brought letters, magazines, news of the war in Europe, and a bottle of Scotch. At first I suspected them of being spies, sent to inspect me and my work.

---

2. When I returned to the Araguaia River in 1953, my friends told me that Salvador had died from a "nose infection" in 1950.

Then I realized that they were beginning students of anthropology. They brought little in the way of trade goods, but their presence brought us all to life. The Indians announced a ceremony of initiation for a young man, our food somehow improved, and everyone seemed to relax, what with the newcomers and the sunny days. The beginning of the dry season brought whole days of cloudless skies, the mildew which had collected on our clothes and hammocks disappeared, and soon the garden crops would ripen.

We left the Tapirapé in early June. The savannas were not yet dry and it was a difficult trip to São Domingos, but about half the village accompanied us to the Tapirapé River. I have returned to the Tapirapé several times, but never again did I see them in their natural habitat as it was in 1939-40. Each time that I have returned to visit the Tapirapé, I have done so by airplane—once on a Brazilian Air Force plane, once on a commercial airline to Santa Terezinha, and once on a small plane owned and operated by the Summer Institute of Linguistics. Those trips were faster and less painful, but hardly as memorable as my first.

Though I have always been particularly interested in field methods, my research among the Tapirapé was never satisfactory to me. My previous research had been in a Mayan village in Guatemala. The Maya were an orderly people. They worked a full day in their maize fields. Few of them spoke Spanish, but I could find interpreters who would help me translating elaborate prayers and interviews into Spanish. I had regular informants whom I paid 10 cents for half a day to replace their loss of a day in the fields. The Maya helped me measure things—for instance, the consumption of food and the size and yields of their gardens. They were hardworking and rational, with a sense of formality—much like the Midwestern small-town people whom I had known from birth, yet more exotic—and protective of themselves because of the centuries of exploitation they had endured. The Maya knew about money and the value of land and hard work. In Santiago Chimaltenango (Guatemala), informants would sit for hours on end, explaining their society and their culture.

But with the Tapirapé, field research was very different indeed! At first I tried to find informants who would work with me in an orderly fashion. I wanted to record phonetically songs and stories so that I could analyze their language. I would arrange with an informant to come early to dictate to me and, incidentally, to answer questions about things I had seen or heard, but such informants would never *19* appear or they would come late in the day, and after thirty minutes they would tire of my persistent questions. A man would tell me a myth which I half understood, I would ask him to dictate it to me, and, halfway into the story, he would leave, only to return days later. A group of six to eight people liked to teach me their language. All of them would correct my pronunciation at once, and then they would launch into incomprehensible conversation among themselves. The Tapirapé were open, ribald, gregarious, and friendly, but they were never good anthropological informants. Collecting genealogies and kinship terms was a nightmare. Only a few people had the patience to sit with me alone long enough for such tasks. But collectively they loved to talk and explain.

I soon learned to hang a hammock in the takana, where I bedeviled whoever was present with questions. And I often spent most of a day in one of the longhouses, observing and asking questions. I had a kerosene lamp and candles, so late at night people would come to my little house to talk. The Tapirapé had no feeling of regular hours for sleep (they often sing all night and then sleep all afternoon), and my best hours for "interviews" were often between midnight and three in the morning. I went on hunting trips with men, and we would talk long into the night about their previous experiences and about the sex lives of the men and women back in the village. I spent days with them in their gardens; and there again, away from the village, they opened up. I knew most of the gossip of my village, just as I knew the loves and the hates. As the months went on I learned to speak Tapirapé, and I could understand what was said—after a fashion. I could ask almost any question in a rather simple way and I could understand most people when they spoke to me directly, but I was often faced with "group encounters," and then I became lost. I always had the feeling that there was a linguistic haze between the Tapirapé and me.

The Tapirapé have a keen sense of humor, and they are better linguists than I. Opronunchwi, my companion from Furo de Pedra, could imitate a Catholic mass in Latin; he did so in the takana one night, even following the physical movements of the priest. To me, it sounded like better Latin than that of some Irish priests in New York. Then Anawani, who had spent a rainy season with the Reverend Kegel, sang to me "Loch Lomond" in English with excellent diction, but without any knowledge of the meaning of the words. Valentim taught them to sing hymns in Portuguese. Several individ-

20

uals learned a pidgin Portuguese from Valentim almost as fast as I learned Tapirapé. They made fun of my attempts to speak their language. One night I overheard (and understood) someone in the takana imitating Dr. Carlo's attempts to speak Tapirapé. There were gales of laughter.

Beyond my own inabilities, the Tapirapé were not the ideal group among whom to do careful ethnological inquiry. I tried to measure the size of their gardens, but without success. It was not an easy job for one man. I took daily notes on men's economic activities, but found that a single man might do a dozen things in one day: he slept until 10 a.m., picked up his knife and axe and started toward his garden to clear underbrush; en route heard the call of a *jacu* (a black forest fowl, about the size of a chicken, which lives high in the branches of the virgin tropical forest) and spent two hours stalking it; arrived at his garden, worked for an hour, slept; returned to the village with one jacu; then spent the late afternoon weaving a basket in the takana. In short, from an ethnocentric point of view, the Tapirapé are a most casual people, with little sense of time; their life style does not lend itself to an orderly anthropological study.

Yet they are patient, and they soon learned that my curiosity about their way of life was boundless. They would come to inform me of any unusual event. I was awakened in the middle of the night to witness a birth. Two men sighted a jaguar, and with their small dogs forced it to take refuge in a tree; young boys were then dispatched to the village to call me so I could witness the kill by bow and arrow. I was even called to witness a mass rape. Of course, in a village of less than a hundred and fifty people there is little privacy, but for many months my linguistic barrier would have made me oblivious to many actions which were known to everyone else if my friends had not kept me up to date. I suspect that this was not merely good will, for it must be said that the Tapirapé are great gossips. They sometimes spread untrue, malicious rumors, especially about the sex lives of one another. Living with them day by day, I became more aware of certain realms of Tapirapé life than I could ever have learned from an informant.

Even so, there were other aspects, mainly in the realm of cognitive and ideological aspects of their culture, which I learned only in part and which continued to escape me. I spent hours translating songs only to find that they meant nothing to me; nor could anyone explain their symbolism, if any. I still do not entirely understand the basis for 21 their elaborate classification of and taboos regarding meat. And even during my later visits in 1953 and 1957, and especially in 1965, when I found several young men who had learned to speak Portuguese rather well, I got little clarification. They helped clear up some of my earlier doubts, but when I asked them for details and meanings of some of the ceremonials I had witnessed in 1939 and 1940, one of them countered: "Dr. Carlo should know better than we do. We were but small boys then. Dr. Carlo talked with Kamairaho, Urukumu, and the men who really knew." So the anthropologist with his insecure knowledge of Tapirapé culture was thought of as a tribal elder!

I must state at once that I never really carried through with the research problem on the initial stages of acculturation which I had set out to accomplish in 1939. There was nothing at fault with the research plan which Ralph Linton and I had designed, at least theoretically. But the research situation offered by the Tapirapé in 1939 and 1940 did not lend itself to the plan of study which we had envisaged.

First, the Tapirapé were not yet in continuous, first-hand contact with western society in 1939. In fact, they had had only sporadic and brief contacts with missionaries and explorers—highly selective segments of western culture. Except for a few material items, they had acquired few, if any, cultural influences from the western world. Yet their society had already been highly modified from that of aboriginal times. Foreign disease, which preceded first-hand contact with western man, had already diminished their numbers. And that depopulation, in turn, had modified their social system and their ceremonial and ritual life. In addition, the iron axes and bushknives they had acquired from sporadic encounters with outsiders had already become a necessity to them, and these had changed their gardening techniques. In 1939-40, I was actually observing a period of social and cultural change that preceded the period of continuous, first-hand contact which I had planned for in my research design.

Second, I was overwhelmed by the essential task of learning the Tapirapé language and the basic facts of Tapirapé culture. I should have known that this would be a time-consuming and intensive undertaking. Anthropologists who work with nonliterate and relatively unknown cultures are at a decided disadvantage compared to social scientists who study their own culture, carrying out research in which hypotheses are to be tested under specific conditions. Often the anthropologist must modify his hypotheses and research strategy in midstream. Just so, among the Tapirapé my original research questions

22

and strategy changed as I progressed with my research. This is not the book that I had planned to write when I first traveled to the Tapirapé in 1939.

In the course of my field work in 1939 and 1940, and over the years since then, I became interested in other problems more relevant to the data which I collected among the Tapirapé. I became interested in how that people, within the span of slightly more than a generation, adapted socially, culturally, and even physically to the new circumstances imposed upon them by the advancing Brazilian frontier. To understand this process, I had first to understand Tapirapé society and culture as it must have been in about 1900, when the people lived under aboriginal conditions, beyond the tentacles of Brazilian national society. My intent here is to describe Tapirapé society and culture as it must have been in 1900 and to chronicle their experience as they came into contact with the Brazilian frontier. Of course I cannot faithfully describe the Tapirapé society and culture as it was in 1900, before they were observed by western man. I can, however, describe them as they were in 1939-40, when they were in most ways unchanged since 1900, and by use of Tapirapé oral history I can attempt to reconstruct their society as it must have been forty years earlier. This can be a rather dubious procedure, for the unwritten memories of people are far from observed empirical fact. Therefore, whenever I do indulge in reconstruction of the past I shall indicate that I have done so; otherwise, my opinions about Tapirapé society and culture will be drawn from what I observed and learned at first hand in 1939-40 and to a lesser extent upon what Herbert Baldus observed in 1935. Likewise, in describing the process of Tapirapé social and cultural change since 1939-40, I shall depend upon the observations I made during my visits in 1953, 1957, and 1965 as well as the narratives of others, such as Valentim Gomes and the working nuns of The Little Sisters of Jesus, who have lived with the Tapirapé over a long period on a day-to-day basis. In brief, I am attempting both to describe Tapirapé society and culture and to write an analytical but not always chronological history of the tribe from 1900 to the present.

In the process, a series of broad questions relevant to the contact of small and so-called primitive societies with complex civilizations must be discussed. We are apt to picture primitive peoples such as the Tapirapé living close to their environment, exploiting their ecological niche to its maximum potential within the limits of the available technology. But we tend to forget that, just as in complex civilizations, 23 cultural, social, and psychological variables are often as crucial as environmental and technological ones in determining a society's mode of adaptation. Mechanical formulas estimating the "carrying capacity" or "man-land balance" for simple societies have too often ignored nonmaterial or cultural factors. Similarly, social and cultural variables must enter into the equation when we consider the process of change resulting from the impact of complex social systems on these less complex societies. It seems clear that in 1900 the Tapirapé technological-environmental system could have supported a population several times larger than it actually did. That it did not do so resulted from idealogical and cultural factors, not from any limitation imposed by either the natural environment or technology. Furthermore, some of the most disruptive effects of contact with the Brazilian frontier resulted from the retention of maladaptive cultural values under new ecological circumstances. For example, the Tapirapé retained a population "policy" which guaranteed zero population growth implemented by infanticide in spite of the fact that the population was declining rapidly because of new diseases. Such social and cultural factors have made Tapirapé adaptation to the new conditions much more precarious than that of other small primitive groups.

Yet the barriers to adaptation originating within the native culture are dwarfed by the massive impact of the expanding frontier of modern Brazil. Even today the Tapirapé Indians are not fully aware of the enormity of the process they face. They have no way of knowing about or coping with the political, economic, and social structure of the modern nation within which, willy-nilly, they are now embraced. They have survived the first stages of contact with the Brazilian frontier as a distinctive people with their own cultural identity, but only time will tell whether they will survive as the impact of modern Brazil becomes more intense. Their story and their predicament is only one example of the fate of hundreds of simple societies around the world which are faced with encroaching complex technological civilizations. In this book I shall document one example of the hideous process which has taken place time and time again as nation-states have expanded their area of control. Though we must remember that, from a long-term perspective, the process of more complex economic and political societies engulfing less complex societies began thousands of years ago, when the state, as a form of socio-political organization, first appeared.

24   In telling the story of the Tapirapé, however, I hope to avoid treat-

ing them and their society as a mere abstract example of a social process. Rather, I should like to give the reader a picture of them as individual human beings. I should like also to describe their society and their culture, with all of its beauty and all of its faults. To do so, I cannot be entirely as objective as an anthropologist likes to think he is. I found some individuals more attractive and interesting than others. I found some aspects of their way of life aesthetically pleasing and comfortable, and others distasteful and even cruel. Over the years, however, the Tapirapé have never been for me only objects of research, or abstractions; instead, they have been my friends.

2
Decimation & Survival

The Tapirapé Indians today inhabit only one village, situated at the mouth of the Tapirapé River where it flows into the Araguaia in the north of the state of Mato Grosso. More accurately, their village lies just north of 11° latitude and between 50° and 51° longtitude. Their location is marginal to the Amazon basin, in that the Araguaia River flows north into the Tocantins, which in turn empties into the mighty Amazon at its delta. The Tapirapé are, however, an Amazon people, since their way of life represents, in a broad sense, an adaptation to the humid tropical forest which they share with native peoples throughout the whole Amazon basin. Today they number slightly more than one hundred and thirty souls—the remnant of about 1500 Tapirapé Indians who inhabited five villages in 1900.

The territory of the Tapirapé tribe in 1900 and before extended west of the Araguaia River and north of the Tapirapé River. It was an immense area, still unexplored in 1900 and little known to Brazilians even today. As of 1900, the Tapirapé never wandered south of the Tapirapé River for fear of the Shavante (Maybury-Lewis, 1967: 3). Their expansion to the north was considered dangerous because of the various Kayapó groups who occasionally attacked them. The land to the west was believed to have been inhabited by the Ampanea, who may have been only a mythical people. And they never traveled east to the Araguaia River, for they feared the Carajá. The western fron-

tier of Brazil ended at the Araguaia River in 1900, and the Tapirapé
were unaware of the few Brazilian backwoodsmen and the scientific
expeditions which occasionally traveled along that river. In 1900 there
was no reason for the Tapirapé to wander beyond their own territory,
for it covered thousands of square miles—more than enough for their
economic needs.

The Tapirapé are clearly an intrusive people into this large region,
for they are an isolated tribe who speak a language belonging to the
Tupí-Guaraní linguistic family,[3] and are surrounded mainly by peoples who speak very different languages, usually belonging to the Gê
linguistic stock. Several hundred miles to the west, at the headwaters
of the Xingú River, there are two small tribes, the Kamaiurá and the
Awetí, who also speak Tupian languages. And several hundred miles
to the north there are small pockets of Tupí speakers, such as the
Assurini and the Parakanã, but the Tapirapé have never heard of
those people (see Map 1). Curiously, the Ampanea, whom the Tapirapé believe lived to the west of them, are thought to have spoken the
same language. Tradition has it that the Ampanea had villages like
those of the Tapirapé, that they were hard workers, and that they
planted large gardens with the same crops. But it was long ago that
a Tapirapé ever actually encountered a group of Ampanea. By 1939-40
the Tapirapé knew that they existed only from the smoke of fires on
the savanna far to the west (see Baldus, 1970: 57).

All of the small Tupí-speaking tribes in Central Brazil are probably
refugees who migrated from near the coast some time after 1500. The
main body of peoples speaking these languages were found in 1500
along the Brazilian coast, where they were known generically as the
Tupinambá. Before 1500, people speaking closely related languages
had migrated south and west into what is today Paraguay, where they
were known as Guaraní. Others had migrated west, up to the Amazon
River as far as lowland Peru, where such tribes as the Omagua and
the Cocama-Cocamilla are known to have spoken Tupí. The coastal
Tupí, although known in the literature as Tupinambá, were actually
divided into numerous tribes, among them the Caeté, the Timinino,
and the Potiguara (Metraux, 1928a, 1928b). Those coastal Tupí were
the primary concerns of the first missionaries to Brazil, and several excellent first-hand accounts of the society and culture of these now extinct people dating from the sixteenth and seventeenth centuries have

---

3. In Brazil those who speak the Tupí-Guaraní language family, which includes the
Guaraní of Paraguay, are called Tupí.

TRIBES OF CENTRAL BRAZIL

been left to us.[4] A comparison of Tapirapé culture with that of the coastal Tupinambá shows them to be closely related, in their material arts and technology as well as in their myths and religion. The Tapirapé lack, however, one important cultural complex which the early chroniclers emphasized in their descriptions of the Tupinambá—cannibalism and endemic warfare. Alfred Metraux (1927) has shown that migration from the coast was intensified by the arrival of the Portuguese in 1500. We shall never know with certainty if the Tapirapé were among the refugee groups that migrated westward from the coastal region; if they were, we shall never know their route of migration nor their experience over the last three centuries. Tapirapé tradition has it that they entered their 1900 territory from the north and east, moving always south for fear of the Kayapó and west for fear of the Carajá (Baldus, 1970: 25).

An analysis of Tapirapé culture indicates, however, that they have borrowed heavily from those two tribes. The Tapirapé have songs and masked dances which they identify as having been learned from the Kayapó and the Carajá; also, the rather elaborate system of tribal associations among the Tapirapé indicates strong influences from Gê-speaking peoples. At some time they must have lived in close relationship with both the Carajá and the Kayapó. In fact, the Tapirapé told of occasions in the distant past when they did do so. There is a story that at one time in the past a group of Tapirapé actually lived and shared a village with the Iriwehe (which is their name for the Javahé branch of the Carajá tribe).[5] And the Tapirapé spoke of male Kayapó visitors who lived in peace in a Tapirapé village for many months—perhaps as much as a year or more. But by the turn of the century the nearest Carajá village was at least a hundred miles away from any Tapirapé settlement, and the nearest Kayapó group must have lived even farther away from the northernmost Tapirapé village. In 1900 there was no competition for territory among the three peoples. Not only was there a buffer zone of uninhabited land between them, but each exploited a distinct ecological niche. The Carajá were a riverine people who made their dry-season villages on beaches, were expert

---

4. Some of the best eyewitness accounts of the coastal Tupí can be found in Soares de Souza, Hans Staden, Claude d'Abbeville, and Ives d'Evreux. Those and other early writers were used by Alfred Metraux (1928a, 1928b) and by Florestan Fernandes (1949, 1952) as the bases for their modern interpretative studies of the Tupinambá.

5. Baldus (1970: 37) quotes from an early Portuguese explorer who reported that in 1775 a Tapirapé village was located near a Javahé village on the northern point of Bananal island.

canoemen, and made a living from fishing and hunting. Their gardens were small and limited to the sparse *galeria* forests along the Araguaia River. The northern Kayapó were typically a people of the steppes or savanna, planting in *galeria* forests but ranging widely over the open country for game. And the Tapirapé were a tropical forest people, depending primarily upon their gardens for food.

Even so, the Tapirapé thought of their distant neighbors as perpetual enemies. Though they felt superior to both tribes, the Tapirapé lived in fear of the Carajá and, more particularly, the Kayapó. It was something like the fear of dangerous and warlike barbarians. "The Carajá are like dogs," they explained many times, "they sleep on mats on the ground and do not have hammocks." The Tapirapé believed that the Carajá were descendants of a large river serpent and could not be trusted. The Kayapó, whom they called Karanchahó (large Carajá), were thought to be descendants of the insignificant wood-tick, but they were more terrifying than the Carajá because, according to the Tapirapé, they lacked human sentiment and modes of behavior entirely.

The Tapirapé had good reason to fear those tribes, for they were always on the losing end of skirmishes and battles with both of them. Visitors to the Araguaia River in the late nineteenth and early twentieth centuries reported Tapirapé women and children living as captives among the Carajá and Kayapó (Baldus, 1970: 45f., 63f.). Within the memory of older Tapirapé living in 1939, there had been several clashes with Carajá who had wandered into Tapirapé territory. In 1939 my Tapirapé friends showed me a spot on the savanna near the port of São Domingos where they said eleven Carajá warriors were buried. According to the Tapirapé, the Carajá had come during the dry season one year under the guise of trading with them for arrow shafts but really to attack them. They admitted that in the battle that followed several Tapirapé had died, but insisted that the Carajá had fled, leaving behind them eleven bodies which the Tapirapé buried. However, according to several accounts recorded from the Carajá point of view, it had been an attack of reprisal against the Tapirapé in which many Tapirapé were killed and several women and children taken prisoner. The Carajá claimed that a rather large number of them had attacked a group of Tapirapé in revenge for the murder of a family of Carajá whom the Tapirapé had killed just a year previously. According to the Carajá, the battle had taken place in 1905 (Baldus, 1970: 68).

The Tapirapé were even more afraid of the Kayapó. They described how they had murdered two Kayapó men who had been living as visitors in a Tapirapé village, and they told rather vague stories of Kayapó attacks on the northern Tapirapé villages some time in the past. Perhaps these were also reprisal attacks against the Tapirapé, but the northern Kayapó are widely known for their belligerent behavior and constant warfare. They seldom needed an excuse for attacking other tribes.

No one remembered any specific occasion when the Kayapó had attacked, but there was constant fear that they might do so. During the dry season of 1939, Valentim and I were often aroused late at night or just before dawn by people who claimed to have heard noises in the forest which they identified as signals of Kayapó warriors ready for attack. They came to ask us to ready our revolver and rifle and to help defend their village. During his visit to Tampiitawa in 1935, Herbert Baldus reports the same nervous fear during the night occasioned by strange sounds from the forest (Baldus, 1970: 61-62). The Tapirapé knew that Kayapó parties wander far from their homeland each dry season, and they also knew, from stories told by their grandfathers, that the Kayapó attack late at night when there is no moonlight, or just before dawn. During my residence in Tampiitawa I took this to be fantasy, induced by stories they had heard as children, but in 1947 the Kayapó did indeed attack Tampiitawa, with dire consequences to the remaining Tapirapé. Still, I should make it clear that warfare was not a constant state of affairs among these tribes. Skirmishing and attacks were rare simply because distances were great and members of the different tribes seldom encountered one another.

Just prior to 1900, there were five Tapirapé villages within this immense territory. If we can believe Tapirapé oral history handed down over the last two or three generations, each of the villages had a population of between two and three hundred people. I estimate that number by the number of longhouses which were said to have existed in each village. Each longhouse—which was the residence of a number of families—held from thirty to forty people, sometimes even more. A village often had six to ten longhouses. The size of Tapirapé villages, and even the way they were constructed, followed the patterns that the early chroniclers described for the coastal Tupí (see Metraux, 1928a; Fernandes, 1949). Furthermore, my own rough calculations are that, given the Tapirapé ecological adjustment, their villages could not possibly have exceeded three to four hundred people. And it   31 seems to me that Tapirapé ceremonial organization, with its various balanced associations, could not have functioned fully unless a village held at least two hundred people. Thus, an estimate of at least two or three hundred people in a village under normal circumstances seems logical for several reasons. This would give the Tapirapé a total population of between 1000 and 1500 people just before 1900.

The Tapirapé remembered clearly the names of the five villages which had existed in 1900, and they could also describe their general location. In addition to Tampiitawa (*tampi,* "tapirs"; *tawa,* "village"—thus, Village of the Tapirs),[6] in which I lived and studied in 1939-40, Chichutawa (Village of the Fish) still existed, although it had been much reduced in population by 1939. The other villages, which no longer existed at that time, were Mankutawa (Village of Manku[7]), Moutawa (Village of the Mouwa Tree), and Anapatawa (Village of the Anapa Fish).[8] Each of the villages was about a day's walk from the next—or, as the Tapirapé expressed it, "one sleep" from one village to another. They formed an arc beginning some fifty kilometers north of the Tapirapé River and curving north and east toward the Araguaia River. The Tapirapé were a forest people, and the paths between villages, which were not clearly marked, led through dense forest. One may surmise also from their memories, however, that each village was never too far (thirty or forty kilometers) from an open savanna where they liked to hunt. One of the complaints about Chichutawa was that it was too far away from savanna country. Chichutawa was a six-day trip by foot to the north from Tampiitawa. All of the villages were situated in the forest, back from tributaries of the Araguaia River, just as Tampiitawa was situated some forty to fifty kilometers from the Tapirapé River. In the region occupied in 1900 by the Tapirapé, there was certainly no shortage of land (see Map 2).

In about 1910, the isolation of the Tapirapé from the outside world was broken. By that time, Anapatawa, the northernmost of the origi-

---

6. The tapir is the largest mammal of the South American tropical forest. Tampiitawa was so named because the surrounding region was the favorite habitat of tapirs. The Tapirapé did not consider tapir meat tasty; in fact, it was taboo to women and to men during certain periods of their lives.

7. Manku is said to be the name of a Carajá Indian who lived there with the Tapirapé and was finally murdered by them. Before Manku's time that village is said to have been called Kuriwatawa (Village of the Squash).

8. A sixth village, called Chanupatawa (Village of the Genipap Tree), was mentioned by two informants, but others had never heard of it. If it did exist, it was probably north of Anapatawa.

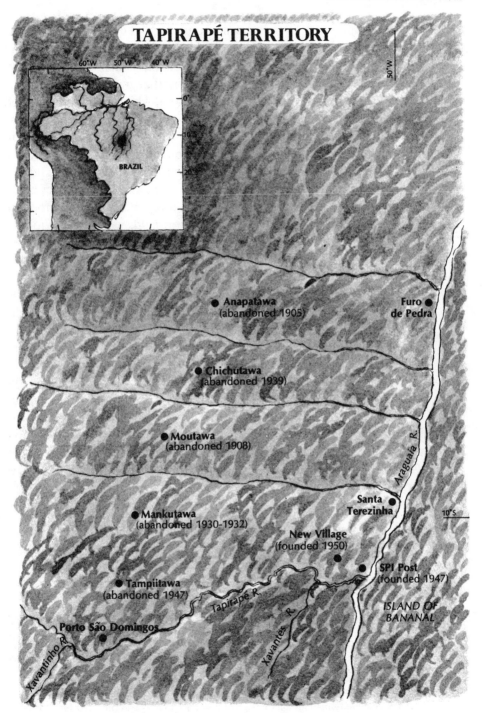

nal six villages, had already been abandoned.[9] The reason for its demise is said to have been repeated raids by the northern Kayapó, and refugees fled to join the more southern villages. Then, in about 1908, Moutawa was deserted.[10] Tradition has it that over half the population was wiped out by fever, perhaps malaria, which they had acquired from anopheles mosquitoes brought by Carajá visitors. The survivors went to live in Chichutawa, where they had many relatives. So in 1910, when the first Brazilian expedition reached Tampiitawa, the southernmost Tapirapé village, only three villages remained and the Tapirapé were already much reduced in numbers.[11] Soon afterwards, many Tapirapé died in all of the remaining villages, some from influenza, and others just from the common cold, which the Tapirapé call ó ó ('-ó' is a common augmentative suffix; thus ó ó might be translated as "Big! Big!"). In about 1930-32 Mankutawa was so reduced in population that it was abandoned; its survivors went to live in Tampiitawa, attracted by the western trade goods, such as axes and beads, which that village was receiving from the Dominican missionaries who made annual visits to São Domingos port.

The first definite record of non-Indians visiting a Tapirapé village was written in 1911. That year a group of "Cearenses" (men from the state of Ceará), led by Alfredo Olimpio de Oliveira, traveled up the Tapirapé River and walked forty or fifty kilometers across the savanna into the forest and were welcomed in Tampiitawa. They were remembered in 1939 by some Tapirapé, for they had brought considerable riches in trade goods and had stayed for a few days in the village. They were prospectors looking for stands of rubber trees, for in those days the latex of *Hevea brasiliensis* brought a fabulous price on the world market. But there were no rubber trees in Tapirapé country.

> Instead of rubber, they discovered Indian villages, the *three* villages of the Tapirapé. It was the first time that these savages saw civilized people, or, in popular terms, Christians. It was God's will that sav-

---

9. My method of reconstructing this early period is most insecure. It is based upon tradition and oral history. The information was secured in 1940, from several informants who were then in their forties. I arrived at these approximate dates in terms of the life history of Kamairaho, whose age Baldus estimated as between thirty-eight and forty in 1935. He was about forty-five years old when I knew him in 1940. This could be checked against actual dates after 1909. Kamairaho stated that Anapatawa was abandoned when he was a small boy and that he remembered refugees by name from that village.
10. Kamairaho had just "tied his penis"—taken to wearing a penis sheath—which would have made him about thirteen years old in 1908.
11. At that time Kamairaho had just "tied his hair," that is, had prepared for and undergone initiation ceremonies, which take place when a boy is about fifteen years old.

ages and Christians should meet peacefully. Alfredo became a friend of the Tapirapé and brought a group of them, consisting of an elderly woman, her granddaughter of eleven or twelve years of age, and a few men, to Conceição. During this trip, the men ran away. The girl was provided with clothes when she reached the mission" (cited in Baldus, 1970: 46. Italics mine.)

Thus reads the report of the first contact of the Tapirapé with Brazilians in a newsletter of the day published by the Dominican missionaries. In a way, Sr. Alfredo's visit was a boon to the Tapirapé. The region did not have wild rubber; otherwise there would have been a rush of Brazilian rubber gatherers into the area at once. The invasion of their homeland was postponed for more than a generation.

The very next year, in 1912, Dr. Francisco Mandacaru, who was the inspector for the newly created Indian Protection Service, led another expedition into Tapirapé territory. He brought with him an old woman and her daughter whom he had found "in slavery" in Conceição (they were probably the two removed by Alfredo), and he reported that there were between 1000 and 1500 Tapirapé. Either Sr. Alfredo or Dr. Francisco brought along a Carajá Indian called Valadar or Valadarão as a guide. He became a living legend among the Tapirapé. He returned several times, often staying in Tampiitawa for months. The Tapirapé came to fear him, but they did not kill him, for he threatened that the torí would attack if they did. Valadarão claimed to be the son of a Carajá father and a Tapirapé woman who had been stolen from her village. That may have been true, for the Tapirapé stated that he could speak their language. There is a vague story that he took several Tapirapé men and walked west toward the Xingú headwaters looking for the Ampanea, but did not find them. He had intercourse with many Tapirapé women, and the Tapirapé said he left several children among them. On one visit he brought five Carajá companions who terrified the Tapirapé. No one dared to attack him physically, but the shamans dreamed to cause his death. Valadarão is said to have become ill and fled, never to return, and the five Carajá who accompanied him are thought to have died, victims also of the shamans, in their own village. Valadarão is a villain in Tapirapé memory, but he always brought much sought after trade goods—as well as death in the form of disease.

In July of 1914, the Dominican missionaries stationed in Conceição do Araguaia visited Tampiitawa. They were guided by Valadarão, who seemed to have a monopoly on expeditions to the Tapirapé at   35 that time. Then, thirty years later, they began to make a trip each year or two in July or August, during the dry season, to a point on the Tapirapé River which they called São Domingos. There they built a large shed to serve as a camp. They would set fire to the dry savanna as a signal to the Indians, many of whom might be camped on the savanna near a small lake, hunting and fishing. The Tapirapé came to expect the Dominican visit and many trooped down to the river to visit with them for a day or so, for the padres brought trade goods as presents. They also held religious services, and it is said that not a few Tapirapé Indians were baptized, although they had no idea whatsoever of the rite's significance. The missionary bishop in Conceição do Araguaia held the reasonable theory that the Tapirapé were almost a condemned people, that the natives the padres saw might not be alive at the time of their next visit, and that therefore they should be baptized while still in their childlike innocence. The visits of the Dominican missionaries were valuable to the Tapirapé, although the padres, traveling with Brazilian canoemen and guides, must have brought infection. The padres were a source of valuable western instruments—axes, bushknives, scissors, cloth, and salt—and they did not disturb the Tapirapé's native culture, since their contact was only once each year for a few days and took place outside the Tapirapé village. Several youths did return with the Dominicans to Conceição do Araguaia to study, but only one stayed long enough to learn to speak Portuguese well, and that in the late 1940's. As a result of the Dominicans' presence, Tampiitawa became the source of western trade goods for the tribe, and for years it was the one village through which the Tapirapé maintained sporadic contact with the outside world.

Other missionaries were also attracted to the Tapirapé. Baldus reports that as early as 1923 a Baptist missionary, Benedito Propheta, encountered them camped on the savanna and spent a few days with them, but he did not actually reach their village. In 1930 Josiah Wilding of the Evangelical Union of South America, accompanied by Miss Elizabeth Steen, a North American writer, spent a few days in the village of Tampiitawa. The Tapirapé were not impressed by Wilding, but they remember Miss Steen well. It was the first proof, except for hearsay, that the strange torí actually had females. You can be sure that she was subjected to considerable inspection. Again the next year, a group of American Adventists spent one night in Tampiitawa. And in 1932 the rather unorganized English expedition described vividly by Peter Fleming met some Tapirapé at Port São

Domingos. Then, in 1934, a movie team from São Paulo camped with the Tapirapé one night on the savanna, and in 1935 a French couple, Madame Raglaire de la Falaise and her husband, arrived. They stayed two days in Tampiitawa. Every dry season the Tapirapé could expect at least one visit, and they came to depend upon them for trade goods. But none of the expeditions really had any influence upon Tapirapé culture, for they could not communicate and the visits were fleeting. The information provided by such expeditions was, in the words of Herbert Baldus, "confused, erroneous, and only fantasy" (Baldus, 1970: 47).

In 1932, Frederick S. Kegel of the Evangelical Union of South America came to the Tapirapé. Frederico, or "Pederico," as the Tapirapé called him,[12] was Scottish, and he became the most influential non-Indian in Tapirapé history until the arrival of the Little Sisters of Jesus in 1952. Frederico was loved by the Tapirapé of Tampiitawa—and sometimes just a little feared, for he became angry when men beat their wives. He came each dry season to live with them from 1932 until 1935. Each time he stayed one month or more, living in a small house just outside the village circle. It was Kegel who introduced Herbert Baldus to the Tapirapé in 1935. Kegel generally came accompanied by a Brazilian guide. He brought fewer presents than the Dominicans did, but he actually came to live with the people in their village. Baldus and Kegel lived in Tampiitawa for about two months in 1935.

In 1939-40, the Tapirapé had many stories to tell of Frederico. He went hunting with them, he danced with them, and he told them stories about Papai Grande (the Christian God in the sky). Above all, he could sing. He learned their songs and taught them new ones, and he would sit on a tree trunk and sing Tapirapé songs and hymns. The Tapirapé learned several hymns in Portuguese and even in English, which they called *pederico monika* (Federico songs). His repertoire was not limited to hymns, for in addition to "When the Roll is Called up Yonder," one Tapirapé man sang "Loch Lomond" to me in understandable English in 1939. But even Kegel was not able to modify Tapirapé culture or society. After all, he was but one man, and besides, he seems to have respected Tapirapé custom. He did leave an indelible mark in their memory as a man they loved, and he must have loved them also. Kegel was transferred to another post in north-

---

12. There is no 'f' sound in Tapirapé.

eastern Brazil in 1937 and died a few years later.[13] I myself was the next visitor to stay at any length of time with the Tapirapé.

Thus, as late as 1939, the Tapirapé had had only sporadic contact with Brazilians, or any western people. Only Kegel had spent any appreciable time in a Tapirapé village. Most of their contact with western man had taken place outside their native communities. Even so, depopulation continued,[14] and by 1939 only Tampiitawa and Chichutawa remained. Chichutawa was very small, with about 40 people, and Tampiitawa contained only 147. The casual visitors, however, "influenced" the Tapirapé much more than they knew, for they continued to bring disease. While I was in residence in Tampiitawa in December of 1939 the people of Chichutawa moved to join us, and the Tapirapé were reduced to only one village.[15]

Throughout the Americas, indigenous peoples died in great numbers from the diseases of the Old World, against which they had little or no immunity. They died easily of respiratory infections, which developed quickly into pneumonia. They also died of measles, whooping cough, smallpox, yellow fever, and, probably, new varieties of malaria brought to the New World by African slaves. Furthermore, an indigenous group such as the Tapirapé did not have to enter into direct contact with western man to acquire such diseases; they often were infected by casual contacts with other indigenous peoples who had been infected earlier. That was probably the case with the Tapirapé— they were exposed to the new diseases before entering into contact with Brazilians.

Yet despite this catastrophic loss of population, in 1939-40 the Tapirapé lived in most ways as they had in 1900. They owned—and by then needed—iron tools, but their economic life was still based upon gardening in the tropical forest, supplemented by hunting and fishing in the dry season. If anything, their slash-and-burn gardens were more productive, and easier to prepare, certainly, with steel tools than with stone axes and fire. Game was plentiful, especially on the savanna, and the Tapirapé River teemed with fish and turtles in the dry season. There were periods of shortage of meat and fish, and times when fresh garden products were lacking; but then there were months of super-

---

13. I never had the pleasure of meeting Frederick Kegel, but I feel that I knew him well.
14. Kegel reported that there were 50 to 60 deaths in Tampiitawa between 1932 and 1935, and that refugees of other villages had appeared in Tampiitawa (Baldus, 1970: 75).
15. Over 40 people arrived in 1939 from Chichutawa, but several children and one adult died soon after their arrival.

fluity when little boys would throw overripe bananas at one another in play. A few people had Brazilian cotton blankets to protect them from gnats and mosquitoes, but everyone went nude. They made their own hammocks from native cotton. A few people owned cast iron pots, but ceramic pots of their own manufacture were generally in use. Because they had no direct contact with the Brazilian frontier, the Tapirapé had not acquired a new technology or necessities, except for steel tools, to supplement their aboriginal way of life.

Still, many aspects of their social organization had already been disrupted in 1939-40 simply by the lack of people. Rules of residence were relaxed, and it was not easy for a young man to find a wife. Some of their festivals had fallen into disuse or were carried out with difficulty. Most festivals depended upon the participation of larger groups than could be mustered. The social disorganization resulting from depopulation will be discussed in a later chapter. It is enough to say here that in 1939-40 the remaining Tapirapé were not yet a dispirited and disorganized people. They were generally gay and friendly, and their culture was closer to the aboriginal state than most anthropologists have been able to experience. But it was obvious that the Tapirapé, without being aware of it, were doomed to extinction as a people and as a functioning society. That they have escaped such a fate seems a miracle to me.

From 1941 to 1947 depopulation continued, for when Baldus (1970: 77) visited Tampiitawa in 1947, he found only fifty-nine individuals. He heard that Chichutawa had again been formed several days to the north, but with a small number of people. He estimated the total Tapirapé population that year as no more than a hundred There had evidently been some movement back and forth from Tampiitawa to Chichutawa in this period. Then, in late 1947, after Baldus's visit, tragedy struck Tampiitawa. The Kayapó, evidently a group of the Gorotire-Kayapó, attacked them. As the Tapirapé told it, they struck early in the morning. Most of the Tapirapé men were away on the savanna, and others were working, clearing land for gardens. What few men were in the village tried to defend the women and children, and they claim that one man, Tanopanchowa, fought bravely and killed several Kayapó. This is most doubtful, for the Tapirapé have always been timid warriors. In any case, the Kayapó burned at least three longhouses and the takana, and carried off several women and small girls. They also looted the village of everything portable. The people of Tampiitawa fled; most of them sought refuge at a ranch 39 which Sr. Lucio da Luz had established on the Tapirapé River. Others walked all the way to the mouth of the Tapirapé River on the Araguaia River, where Valentim Gomes, because of his experience among the Tapirapé, had been hired as the agent of a new post of the Indian Protection Service (SPI)—which was appropriately named Posto Heloisa Alberto Torres. Tampiitawa was abandoned, never to be inhabited again. However, in 1965, some Tapirapé told me that there were perhaps some people still living in Chichutawa.

Later I learned of the remarkable trek of Kamairá to Chichutawa, of which little was known until 1970, when he and two others finally returned to the main group of Tapirapé, who by then were settled in New Village at the mouth of the Tapirapé River. The Tapirapé had told me that Kamairá, a strong household leader whom I had known well in 1939-40, was suspicious of the torí; and that, rather than seek the help of the torí on the ranches and at the SPI post, he had a group which set out for the old village site at Chichutawa. Nothing was heard of those Tapirapé until ·sometime around 1964, when three Tapirapé women appeared in New Village. They said that they had come from Chichutawa and that Kamairá and the others were dead, killed by the Kayapó. They had traveled for over ten days, weak with hunger, through the forest to reach New Village.

The story of those Tapirapé is remarkable enough, but it did not end with their tale. In 1970, Kamairá returned to the Tapirapé. His story appeared in the *Los Angeles Times* on August 11, 1971, under the byline of Leonard Greenwood, who tells the tale as he must have heard it from the Little Sisters of Jesus. His article seems basically accurate, and the events were verified by Shapiro when she last visited the Tapirapé in 1974. I quote Mr. Greenwood's account in full, using his orthography of Tapirapé names:

LOST 25 YEARS, TRIO REJOINS "SLAIN" KIN

SANTA TERESINHA, Mato Grosso, Brazil—The Tapirapé Indians were sleeping peacefully in their village near the Araguaia River when their old enemies, the Caiapo, swept down on them, killing and burning.

The survivors fled in two groups, the largest, of about 40 men, women and children, to a spot down river. The other group, of less than 20, traveled away from the river and were swallowed up by the forest.

Kamairá in 1939. He led a small group of refugees to Chichutawa in 1946, after the Kayapó attacked Tampiitawa.

Built New Village

That was in 1946.[16] The big group founded a new village about 20 miles south of here, growing their beans, bananas, manioc and corn. A few years later, a small group of missionary sisters, the Little Sisters of Jesus, came to open a mission post among them. The Indians grieved for their slain relatives and searched for the other survivors, but there was no word and, with the passing of the years, they forgot.

A few months ago, a Brazilian hunter tracking a jaguar in the savage country near Rio Liberdade, about 300 miles west of here, came upon a clearing in the forest with one small hut. Surprised, because

16. Actually, 1947. I am not certain whether Kamairá and his group left before the Kayapó attack or in early 1947 before Baldus's visit.

he had never heard of any Indians living in the area, the young man moved cautiously forward—and found himself facing a tall, powerful Indian warrior, bow drawn back and a four foot arrow pointing at his heart.

Joined by Others

The hunter put down his rifle and indicated that he came in peace. After a time, the Indian relaxed and called out. From the hut came an old Indian woman and an old man. They surrounded the hunter and jabbered at him. After a while, the hunter realized they were speaking a badly broken form of the Tapirapé language.

The hunter sat down with them and accepted a meal. Then he sat incredulous as he listened to the tale of horror and suffering told by the three last survivors of the Tapirapé band which fled into the forest 25 years ago.

The band had traveled many weeks after escaping the knives of the Caiapo, believing they were the only survivors. They had set up a new village deep in the forest and struggled to survive. Until their first crops ripened they lived on nuts, jungle fruits, beetles, insects and the animals and birds they could hunt. But they were hard years. There were years with very little water, years when the crops failed.

Disease Took Toll

Snakebite killed one of the valuable young warriors. Babies were born, but died of malnutrition, malaria and other sicknesses. Older members of the group died from the privations. The women grew too old to have babies, and finally there was only one young woman to keep the group alive, a beautiful young maiden.

Before she could marry, a jaguar attacked her in the forest. Other members of the group killed the animal, but it was too late. The young girl died.

By the time the young hunter arrived, there were only old Camaira and his wife, Wananai, and their son, Camoriwaro. Three days the hunter stayed with them, trying to convince them that their relatives had survived and founded a new village. Finally, they agreed to go with him and traveled to the Tapirapé village.

When the hunter led the three survivors into the village, there was a shocked silence, then cries of recognition as the tribal elders recognized the old couple. There were tears and singing and dancing and a feast the Indians still talk about.

42

Happy With Tribe

Soon after, old Camaira died. His wife is well and has settled down happily with the tribe, which in the last 25 years has grown to more than 100.

But the young Camoriwaro, so big and powerful the others in the tribe have named him "The Giant," is still suffering from profound shock, say the Little Sisters of Jesus. Carried in the womb of his mother on the night of the massacre, he was born after the small group had been wandering several months in the forest. He has never met strangers before and still spends a lot of time alone.

In the past few weeks, there have been signs of recovery. Camoriwaro still disappears into the forest when strangers approach, but sometimes he now allows the other young braves to go hunting with him. And, most encouraging of all, he has even begun to talk with a few of the village maidens.

Except for this handful of people who continued to live in Chichutawa, Tapirapé society did not exist from 1947 to 1950. The people of Tampiitawa lived in family groups scattered among the Brazilians. Sr. Lucio da Luz, who had already extended his cattle-ranching activities to the country north of the Tapirapé River, gave a few families some support with gifts of manioc flour. A few were hangers on, living near Valentim Gomes at the Indian post. Some even went to live with Brazilians at Furo de Pedra. They speak of this period as one of hunger, when both adults and children died.

In 1950, however, Valentim Gomes, with the help of the Dominican missionaries, was able to persuade the families of Tapirapé to reunite and form a village near the SPI post. Valentim was trusted by the Tapirapé since he had lived in Tampiitawa for over a year with me. Nevertheless, he had to persuade each family to move to the new village. To transport them, he bought a boat. They were deathly afraid of the Carajá, who lived near by, and of the torí, whose numbers were growing on the lower Tapirapé River and on the Araguaia. During the first year in the new locale they had to be almost totally supported while they built houses and cleared land to plant gardens. Valentim described to me how he bought manioc flour, rice, and other commodities on credit, for, as usual, funds promised by the Indian Protection Service were always six to eight months late in arriving. In any case, during that year and the next the remaining Tapirapé recon-   *43* structed their village society. In 1953, when I returned to visit them, I found fifty-one people living in five houses built in a circle around a takana. Their houses were small and built more like those of Brazilian frontiersmen than like their old longhouses, but the takana was large, and built in the traditional style. They were carrying out, as much as their reduced population would allow, their nightly song festivals, and they had performed initiation ceremonies in an attenuated form just two months before I arrived. Village life seemed little changed from 1940, except for the smaller number of people and the presence from time to time of outside visitors. The reconstruction of their society in New Village (Tawaiho) is a remarkable example of the distinctiveness and interdependence of culture and society. Individuals and families had retained Tapirapé culture as a system of rules, ideology, and abstract concepts during the period, however short, when their society was moribund. As soon as conditions permitted, Tapirapé society was recreated in terms of those abstract rules of Tapirapé culture.

In New Village, however, conditions were very different from those that had existed in Tampiitawa in 1940 and before, and Tapirapé culture had to change and to adapt to those new conditions. Most of the changes they made will be treated in the chapters that follow, but some of them must be stated here if we are to understand the recent history of the Tapirapé. By 1953 the Tapirapé were faced with almost daily contact with Brazilians and with Carajá tribesmen, the latter traditional and much feared enemies. Brazilians visited their village each day or two, and each day Tapirapé men and women visited the Indian post where they met Brazilians. Carajá Indians came frequently to New Village, and the Tapirapé had lost their fear of them to the point that two Tapirapé youths, for lack of potential Tapirapé spouses, had taken Carajá wives and lived with their in-laws in the Carajá village several kilometers away. The Tapirapé had not really lost all suspicion of the Carajá, but they had adjusted to the necessity of living in apparent harmony with them.

Also, by 1953 the Tapirapé in New Village had gained some protection against the outside world. First, there was the SPI post with Valentim Gomes in charge, and he, with limited means, provided some protection against exploitation. Valentim even forwarded to the Indian Service in Rio de Janeiro a rough map delineating a rather large area which he claimed as Tapirapé lands. Second, in 1952 the Little Sisters of Jesus came to live with the Tapirapé. They are an order of working nuns established in France by Charles de Foucauld.

The first Little Sisters to live with the Tapirapé were French, but they were gradually replaced by Brazilian recruits. The Little Sisters built their house near the village circle; they worked with axes to plant their gardens; they made manioc flour; and they lived, as closely as possible, by Tapirapé standards. One of the principles of their order is to have a knowledge of and a respect for the culture of the people with whom they live and work. They learned Tapirapé customs and they stimulated the Tapirapé to perform their traditional rituals and to continue their customs. The Little Sisters had medicines (a poor supply) which they knew how to use. And in 1954 they were joined by Padre François Jentel, a French working priest, whose theory seemed to have been that the Tapirapé would be saved from extinction by improvement of their economic condition. The physical presence of these idealistic people did more to save the Tapirapé from continued disintegration than any other single factor. They prevented exploitation by traders by simply being present at exchanges, for in 1953 the Tapirapé did not yet understand the value of money. They treated malaria, dewormed infants and children, and sometimes nursed adults suffering from respiratory infections. They treated the few cases of venereal disease which Tapirapé youths caught from the Carajá. Members of the order still live with the Tapirapé.

In 1957, when I returned for a short visit, there were only 55 people in New Village; in 1965, my wife and I counted 79; in 1966, Shapiro (1968: 14) reported "over 80"; by 1972 the Little Sisters of Jesus said that there were more than 100; and in 1976 a Brazilian government report stated that there were 136 Tapirapé. It was obvious that the population was young and growing. It may well be that in another generation the Tapirapé will have brought their population up to that of 1940.

Yet, beginning in the 1950's, a new set of factors again threatened the Tapirapé. By then the rapidly moving Brazilian frontier had reached the Araguaia River in force. The small Brazilian village of Furo de Pedra, which had been the largest center of Brazilian population within the area in 1940, diminished in importance. In compensation, a locality formerly called Morro de Areia ("Sandy Hill") grew. It is now known as Santa Terezinha. By 1965 it had a landing field with weekly service by a commercial airline (Viação Aérea São Paulo) from Goiânia to Belem and back again. Santa Terezinha became the center for land speculation. For several years it boasted a small hotel, equipped with a bathroom, running water, and beds   *45* where potential purchasers of land and sportsmen, seeking the excellent hunting and fishing of the region, might stay. The hotel disappeared when one land company, Companhia Imobiliária Vale do Araguaia, dissolved and was replaced by another, Companhia Colonizadora Tapiraguaia. That company claimed a huge tract of land on the western side of the Araguaia River which included not only the Tapirapé village and the lands where they plant their gardens, but also the little town of Santa Terezinha and its environs.

For a time there seems to have been a plan, obviously initiated by pressure from the land companies, to remove the Tapirapé from their location in New Village on the western bank of the Araguaia River to the eastern bank on Bananal Island. Bananal, a large island formed by two channels of the Araguaia River, has been formally declared an "Indian Park" by the Brazilian government despite the fact that it is occupied by privately owned ranches and numerous Brazilian squatters. Such a move would have been disastrous to the Tapirapé. Bananal is a swampy lowland, much of which is flooded in the rainy seasons, and there are only sparse forests suitable for slash-and-burn agriculture. In July of 1967, however, the now extinct SPI (replaced by FUNAI, the National Indian Foundation) secured a "donation" from landowners who were shareholders in the Tapiraguaia land company. The Tapirapé were given 9,230.32 hectares (approximately 24,000 acres) which included the site of New Village and the Indian post. At least on paper and legally, the Tapirapé became owners of the land on which they now live and a parcel on which they may plant their gardens. It is doubtful whether the area is adequate for the Tapirapé, who are still a small but expanding population, to continue their present system of slash-and-burn gardening. The National Indian Foundation is aware of that fact, and in 1975 an official of the Foundation informed me that the Foundation is attempting to secure an additional 14,000 hectares (approximately 35,000 acres) surrounding the Tapirapé reservation as a "biological reserve" on which neither the Indians nor the local frontier population would be allowed to plant gardens, but where they could hunt.

Although the Tapirapé now have a legal guarantee of a minimal area, there is some doubt whether their reservation has been adequately surveyed and its boundaries well established. There is today a FUNAI post on the site of the old SPI post, which was founded by Valentim Gomes, with an agent in charge, but he will find it hard to prevent intruders from settling on Tapirapé land. Also, the plan to establish the empty zone as a biological reserve is still unrealized and, in any case, faces real difficulties. The land is registered in large individual plots by members of the land company, and much of it is undoubtedly already occupied by Brazilian frontiersmen. The whole situation regarding land ownership along the Araguaia River and to the west of the river is in flux and legal confusion. At least for the time being, the Tapirapé have legal title to a parcel of land, and they have been saved from a forced move into a micro-environment on Bananal Island which is totally unsuitable for their traditional economy.

Paradoxically, the claims of the land company endanger the Brazilian frontiersmen perhaps even more than they do the Tapirapé. All along the Araguaia, frontiersmen, migrating mainly from northeastern Brazil, have settled with their families. The ranch owned by Sr. Lucio da Luz at Mato Verde has now become a town of more than 1500 souls. It is called Luciara and is the county seat of a huge *município* (county) of the same name. In 1965, Sr. Lucio, a former mayor of Luciara, owned thousands of cattle grazing on the savanna which extends from his headquarters to the north of the Tapirapé River. Each year, he sold over 1000 yearlings to cattle buyers who drove them to market in Goiás. Along the Tapirapé River there were over seventy families of Brazilian settlers in 1965. Some of them were cowboys who grazed cattle on shares for Sr. Lucio; others were gatherers of carnauba wax, for stands of the palm which produces this wax had been discovered in the headwaters of the Tapirapé River. All of those settlers were also subsistence agriculturalists, planting in the narrow galeria forests along the river. In the 1970's they increased in number. None of them have title to their land: legally, they are squatters, or, in Brazilian terms, *posseiros* (people who occupy the land). They, too, may be evicted by the land development company, and armed conflicts have occurred in recent years between frontiersmen and company officials.

The plight of both the Brazilian frontiersmen and the Tapirapé Indians has attracted the attention of the Church. An article in *O Estado de São Paulo* (Apr. 4, 1972) reported that the Bishop of São Felix planned to present a denunciation of the land company's activities to the National Conference of Bishops of Brazil and hoped to seek their support to influence the national government to act in favor of the Tapirapé and the frontiersmen. When Padre François Jentel came to live with the Tapirapé, he was active not only in promoting the rights of the Indians to land, but also in instructing and   47 organizing the Brazilian frontier families who attended the church at Santa Terezinha, where he preached on Sunday. However, in 1974, the padre was arrested, imprisoned, and exiled from Brazil. Ever since the sixteenth century, the Church has acted to defend the Indians. The great Padre Antonio Vieira argued vehemently in defense of the Indian in the seventeenth century, and he was expelled more than once from Brazil. But in the face of economic forces, the Church has always lost. It is doubtful that the Church in the twentieth century can successfully defend the rights of the Tapirapé and other tribes in similar circumstances.

The sad story of the Tapirapé has been repeated over and over again in Brazil, at almost every period of its history after 1500. For many tribes, the story ended with complete physical extinction. Others were reduced to a mere handful of people living as marginals in frontier society. Rocque de Barros Laraia and Roberto da Matta, in their book, *Indios e Castanheiros* (1967), have told the story of the depopulation and disorganization of the Gaviões and the Assurini tribes who lived only several hundred kilometers north of the Tapirapé. Roberto Cardoso de Oliveira, in *O Indio e o Mundo dos Brancos* (1964), analyzed a similar process among the Tukana, far away in the state of Amazonas. And Darcy Ribeiro, in various articles and books, has presented the process from a demographic, sociological, historical, and psychological point of view (Ribeiro, 1970). The story of the Tapirapé is by no means unique, except perhaps in that they are among the few tribes which have survived.

Neither the Tapirapé nor the other tribes of Brazil who have suffered extinction or severe depopulation were the victims of a gigantic conspiracy of the Brazilian nation to be rid of them, or of any conscious genocide. They were simply the victims of a process of history. By chance they were subjected to Old World diseases to which they had little or no immunity; this sped up the process of European expansion. Such introduced diseases often worked faster and were more lethal than guns. The historical process within which the Tapirapé have been enmeshed is the expansion of the metropolitan society. When the European powers moved into the Americas, that process— already ancient in the Old World—began in the New. The European nations staked out colonial boundaries, and then, little by little, the economic system and the bureaucratic powers of the state began to assert control. Brazil did not extend its control over the Araguaia River region until late in the nineteenth century. Even then that control was weak, and only now, in the last quarter of the twentieth century, is the region feeling the full impact of the expansion of the economic and bureaucratic nation-state which is modern Brazil.

In terms of this dismal setting, the story of the Tapirapé Indians takes on added significance. They are a prime example of a small tribe that has suffered rapid depopulation and dislocation from their aboriginal territory and now are endangered with the threat of being removed from the lands they occupy. Yet they have weathered such vicissitudes so far, and they manage to survive even today as a distinctive social and cultural unit. Whether they will be able to continue to expand in population, reach an adjustment with the growing population of Brazilians which surrounds them, retain their identity as a distinct people and culture, and resist the encroachment of new economic forces such as those represented by the land companies depends to a large extent upon factors beyond their control.

3
Subsistence & Ecology

The immense area inhabited by the Tapirapé in 1900 lies within the Araguaia-Tocantins River system which joins with the Amazon River near its mouth. It is situated between ten and eleven degrees south of the Equator. The region is most certainly tropical, and the flora and fauna is typically Amazonian. Most of the region is covered with tropical forest which is interspersed with *campo limpo* and *campo cerrado* savanna. There are two distinct seasons, a dry season, called "summer" by Brazilians, from April until November, and a rainy season, from November to April. The Tapirapé themselves marked those seasons by the presence of the Pleiades; their appearance on the horizon in late October or November announces the beginning of the rains, and their disappearance in April promises the coming of the dry season. During the rainy season the rivers overflow; the savannas, except for small islands, are sometimes flooded with a meter or more of water; and even the forest, which grows on somewhat higher ground, is soggy and wet. It rains sometimes for days upon end, especially in January and February, and there is hardly a day without rain from December to April. However, from late May until October it is a rare day that there is even a thundershower. There is little seasonal difference in temperature, but the high humidity of the rainy season makes the days seem cool and the hot sun of the dry season makes the heat seem much greater. The nights in the forest are cool, often downright cold.

The Tapirapé were fundamentally slash-and-burn farmers, and their villages were always located in the forest. An ideal location for a village was that of Tampiitawa in 1939-40. It was situated well within the forest, about twenty kilometers removed from the savanna, on relatively high ground which did not flood in the rainy season. Within fifty meters of the village there was a small shallow stream with clear water. Near by there was high forest suitable for gardens. Consequently, the gardens were but fifteen to thirty minutes' walk from the village itself. Not all of the area around the village was tillable, for there were large lateritic outcrops and parcels of land which were covered by low second growth where clearings for gardens had once been made but were now abandoned. The village site had been occupied for several years in 1939-40, for it seems to be the same one Baldus visited in 1935. One cannot be certain that all the Tapirapé villages in 1900 were so ideally located but the tribesmen's descriptions of the other villages indicate that they were more or less so.

Traditionally, each village moved its location every five to seven years. The slash-and-burn techniques used by the Tapirapé necessitated the annual clearing of new garden sites. In consequence, suitable high forest could only be found farther and farther from the village. As soon as people found that their gardens were located at a considerable distance from the village, they began to talk of a move. This was so in Tampiitawa in 1940, which had occupied the same location for at least seven years, although the gardens did not seem too far away. However, a move in village location was not haphazard, nor was a village moved to a completely new site. The people of Tampiitawa knew of at least five sites where their village had once been located. All five fulfilled the various criteria for a good village: the land was high enough not to be flooded in the rainy season, there was a small stream which did not dry up in the dry season, they were not too far away from the savanna, and near by was high forest suitable for gardens. To fulfill this last criterion, the forest should have lain fallow for at least twenty years or more, so they never returned to a location inhabited in more recent years.

The location of a village was important for the Tapirapé. Although they were basically a forest people, they also depended upon exploitation of the savanna and the river. Their economic activities were seasonal and required multiple environmental conditions. It could never be said that the Tapirapé were full-time workers at any economic activity. In order of importance, they were, first, farmers, then hunters, 51 then fishermen, and, finally, gatherers. The late dry season and the early rainy season, from about July through November, was the best time for garden activities. Hunting took place throughout the year, but it was especially rewarding in February and March, when high water drives wild pigs, peccaries, pacas, and other animals onto islands of high ground on the savanna and in the forest. The late dry season, from August until November, was best for fishing. Then the shallow lakes on the savanna were no longer connected by small streams to the river, and fish trapped in the lake were easily shot with bow and arrow. At that time of year also the small streams in the forest return to their channels and small minnows abound. When the Tapirapé River is at low water, schools of fish come upriver from the Araguaia to spawn, and turtles lay their eggs in the sand on the exposed beaches. Most of the wild fruits collected by the Tapirapé ripen in the dry season, so that fishing was often combined with gathering.

Those multiple and seasonal activities made for a semi-nomadic life in 1939-40 and before. That does not mean the Tapirapé did not have a permanent village, for Tampiitawa was a fixed settlement. Only occasionally, during the rains from November until May or June, would groups of men absent themselves from the village for a day or so to hunt. But in the dry season, the Tapirapé commuted from the village to the savanna. Groups of families would build temporary shelters on the savanna, where they camped while hunting, fishing, and collecting wild nuts and fruits. A favorite spot for such a camp was near a little lake called Tucunaré (named after a most sought after fish). The men would sally forth each day to fish on the Tapirapé River, to collect turtle eggs and turtles, and to hunt on the savanna. Both men and women would collect wild fruit, such as *pequi*, and *bacaba* palm nuts, which grew in the galeria forests. They often burned off the savanna so that the tender shoots of grass that sprang up would attract game. In 1940 and earlier, the savanna along the Tapirapé River teemed with game, especially the small deer, called in Brazil *campeiro*, but they were not a favorite object of the hunt for their meat was taboo to a large section of the population. But there were also wild pigs, which wandered in droves; peccaries; armadillos; wild ducks and geese near the river; and several varieties of forest fowl. Fish were, however, the main objective at that time of the year, and the Tapirapé spoke of moving to the savanna "to eat fish."

During those periods Tampiitawa was never abandoned. The gardens were near the village and there were always families in residence, the women preparing manioc flour and the men clearing new gardens to be planted at the beginning of the rains.[17] Manioc flour had to be carried down to the savanna encampment, for no Tapirapé would consider eating fish or meat without it. The job of clearing the forest for gardens might continue throughout the dry season, a man working a few days at a time; or the village men might clear gardens in a spurt, working in a communal work party called an *apachirú*.

If there is a pattern in the cycle of Tapirapé subsistence activities, there is none for daily activities. If men made a hunting expedition of two or three days' duration, or if an apachirú was organized to clear garden sites, it can be said that they spent a full day at hunting or gardening. But in 1940, when I attempted to list the individual daily activities of ten men, the tabulation soon became a hodgepodge. My records show that a man would leave early in the morning for his garden to cut the underbrush. He might work for two hours at that occupation and then decide to hunt, since he always went armed with bow and arrows. His hunting might well bring him in a circle toward the village, where he would be found in the takana at 2:00 p.m., weaving a basket. A day might produce any number of possible combinations of occupations. Likewise, expeditions from the encampment might involve shooting fish, then hunting, and then a decision to pick *caja*, a yellow plum-like wild fruit which grows on the savanna and ripens during the dry season. But if by chance in his wandering a man discovered a nest of wild bees, he would abandon all other pursuits to collect honey. With the exceptions of collective hunting parties and organized work parties for clearing gardens, daily activities were spontaneous and often determined by mood and chance. It was next to impossible to calculate the man-days expended on any economic activity.[18]

By far the most important subsistence activity and the one at which the Tapirapé men spent the most time was farming. The Tapirapé cultivated by the well-known slash-and-burn, or swidden, horticultural methods. Each year, in the dry season, a new area was cut from the forest for their gardens. First the low underbrush and small trees were cleared away and arranged into piles; then the larger trees were felled.

---

17. The Kayapó attacked Tampiitawa at that time of year in 1947.
18. Robert Carneiro calculated that Kuikuru men of the Xingú River headwaters spend "two hours a day on horticulture, and one and one-half hours fishing. Of the remaining ten or twelve waking hours of the day, the Kuikuru men spend a great deal of it dancing, wrestling, in some form of informal recreation, and in loafing" (Carneiro, 1961: 49).

In 1939 the Tapirapé camped on the savanna in the dry season.

A Tapirapé returning from the hunt with a caititú, or peccary, in 1939.

Tapirapé gardens are still a tangle of plants and brush. This was taken in 1939.

Yams (*kara*) brought from the garden in 1939.

An effort was made to cause the larger trees to fall in criss-cross pattern, and often some of the larger limbs were removed to add to piles of small trees and underbrush. Next, the trees and brush were allowed to dry until late October or early November. Finally, fire was set to the plot; the drier the underbrush and felled trees, the better the plot would burn. But if a man waited too long and heavy rains fell, his plot burned poorly, leaving unburned brush and a tangle of boughs. Following the burning, some cleaning up always took place; that is, some unburned branches and brush were piled up and set afire, and there might be some rearranging of fallen trunks to provide more open space. But a Tapirapé garden site was never clean. Rather, it was a tangle of charred, half-burned trunks. Traversing a "cleared" field was most difficult.

This arduous task of clearing a garden site could be done individually or collectively. A single man could work alone or with the help of a close relative such as a brother or a brother-in-law. If so, they exchanged labor, clearing contiguous fields together, and there was a vague border, made, perhaps, by a large trunk, which divided the fields of one from the other.[19] Or the Tapirapé cleared garden sites in an apachirú. These were organized work parties in which it was said that gardens are cleared for the "captains," that is, men who were leaders of longhouses which contained (in 1940) five to eight nuclear families. In 1935 Baldus witnessed an apachirú in which all of the men of Tampiitawa participated (Baldus, 1970: 180). Although Baldus does not say so, the work seems to have been organized and directed by the leaders of the two *Wuran* (Bird Societies), which were divided into age grades. They worked all day, directed by a Bird Society leader, clearing an enormous area which was later assigned to household leaders, who in turn allowed their followers to plant in specified areas. At the end of the day the two Bird Societies had a badly arranged relay race back to the takana in the village. During 1939-40 I witnessed an apachirú, not a large one, for only a segment of the men participated. Informants, however, continued to assure me that in the past (i.e. around 1900 and before) that was the principal method by which gardens were cleared. If so, it gave the leaders of the Tapirapé longhouses decisive control over their people, for they controlled cleared land which each could apportion to their relatives for planting. Even in 1939-40, the heads of longhouses seldom did the hard work of gar-

---

19. In 1939, Champukwi worked with Wantanamu. They left four tree trunks standing like poles to demarcate their separate areas.

den site clearing; it was done by younger men in their households. It should be said, however, that there was no concept of individual ownership of uncleared land; although the ownership of land which had been cleared for gardens was clearly recognized.

The Tapirapé planted their gardens in November and December. The principal crop was manioc, both the venomous and the nonvenomous varieties, shoots of which were planted in mounds formed with a hoe. Four or five cuttings from a stem were simply stuck into the loosened soil. The Tapirapé recognized at least twelve varieties of manioc, each of which had a distinctive name, but they made a basic distinction between those varieties which contain a high degree of prussic acid and those which can be eaten simply boiled or roasted.[20] Manioc is a relatively slow-growing plant. The tubers are large enough to be harvested in about six months, but they can be left in the ground for eighteen months before they become too fibrous for use.

As the manioc plants are slow to grow, the Tapirapé planted other, faster growing crops in the same field. The list of crops which they planted (not every garden contained all) is long. They planted a sweet squash, a variety of sweet potato, yams, peanuts, maize, brown beans, lima beans, peppers, cotton, papayas, *maxixe* (a cucumber-like vegetable), and bananas. Some of these plants, such as bananas and maxixe, were certainly acquired through contact with other Indian groups or from Brazilians. Baldus mentions one type of *kara* (yam) which was called "kara from white man," although other varieties of the same tuber were certainly aboriginal. There were seven varieties of banana recognized and planted by the Tapirapé, including a plantain (Baldus, 1970: 189-190). In addition to those, they planted tobacco—not in their gardens, but near their longhouses, where it grew without any special care—and *annatto*, or *urucu* (used for red dye), which grew wild in the forest, they transplanted near the village. Also, two types of gourds were planted near the village. The gourds they used as bowls, as containers for water, and as rattles. Certainly, the variety of crops available to the Tapirapé was unusually large.[21]

---

20. Baldus (1970: 186) states that the Tapirapé distinguish five varieties of manioc, but in 1940 I collected samples of twelve named varieties to be identified by a botanist at the Museu Nacional in Rio de Janeiro. The collection was lost in transit. There were, however, two basic terms, *mandiaga* (*Manihot utilissima*) and *waikura* (*Manihot dulcis*). See Glossary for various types.

21. Baldus (1970: 196) mentions that in 1935 the Tapirapé leader Kamairaho had planted a small area in sugarcane. It was no longer cultivated in 1939-40, though it was planted again in small patches in New Village in 1953.

While the men planted manioc, maize, and the tuberous crops, the women planted only peanuts, beans, and cotton. With the exception of beans, the crops planted by women seem to have had greater value. The Tapirapé would demand almost twice the amount of salt or rapadura for peanuts than they would for any other food. And not only did women plant and harvest cotton, but they did all the work with it, making wrist ornaments and, most important, manufacturing hammocks.

These quick-growing crops mature during the latter part of the rainy season and during the early dry season. In February, there was green corn, which was consumed on the cob and in the form of a soup (kawi). By March there were beans, pumpkins, and some tubers. In April banana trees more than one year old began to bear. The Tapirapé picked bananas green and allowed them to ripen as they hung from the rafters of their dwellings. So in late April, when the Pleiades disappeared, the time of *kaó*, or "Big Garden" began. "The Tapirapé have much to eat. They are happy and they sing kaó songs at night," explained one Tapirapé in 1940.

This was a period of abundance after a difficult period during the heavy rains in December to February. The heavy rains provided unusually good hunting conditions, but it was also difficult to move about. Not nearly enough meat came into the village to replace the garden crops. For days on end the Tapirapé were reduced to a diet of manioc—their one certain staple. Manioc was prepared and consumed in several forms. The sweet varieties can be simply boiled or roasted, but the bitter variety calls for considerable work in preparation. Men dig up the tubers, but both men and women carry the heavy load from the garden in a large basket supported under the arms and across the forehead with a tumpline. The tubers are first soaked in water, generally downstream of the village in the small stream which runs near by, for three to four days. They become soft and slightly putrified. Then the women can easily remove the skin and pass the pulp through a sieve made of woven bamboo (*taquara*) and *buriti* palm to remove the fibers. The Tapirapé seem never to have known the *tipiti*, a sleeve-like press which is commonly used in lowland South America to remove the poisonous juice from the manioc pulp. In fact, in 1939-40 they had no type of press at all. The women simply squeezed the pulp between the palms of their hands, catching the juice in a ceramic pot.[22] They then made balls of dough six to eight inches in diameter

---

22. Baldus (1970: 187) sees this lack of the tipiti as another indication that the Tapirapé migrated from the northeast, possibly from Maranhão, for Claude d'Abbeville,

and placed them on a platform, well out of reach of dogs and children, to dry out thoroughly in the sun. Once dry, the dough could then again be passed through a sieve and roasted over a small ceramic griddle to take the form of manioc flour. Less frequently, small pancakes (*beijus*) were made of the dough, but the Tapirapé made nothing like the large *beijus* ("flat cakes") of two feet in diameter, which is the basic "bread" of the Indians of the upper Xingú River (Galvão, 1967). Flour was the essential form in which manioc was consumed among the Tapirapé.

Another, simpler method of producing manioc flour used by the Tapirapé women seems better adapted to those varieties of manioc which contain less prussic acid. The skin is simply scraped off the tuber with a knife (though this was probably done earlier with a mollusk shell); the tuber is then grated by hand with an instrument made from a block of wood into which hard palm thorns from the *tucumā* palm have been driven (Baldus, 1970: 241). The women are experts at this grating process, but most of them have scars on their hands as witness to slight miscalculations.[23] Once grated, the pulp can be squeezed by hand and formed into balls for drying out in the same fashion as that which had been soaked. Again it is passed through a sieve and toasted to make flour. Manioc flour can be stored for fairly long periods, sometimes two, three, or four months, except during the very heavy rains, when it tends to become moldy. Preparation of the flour is not a task that women do every day or so. Rather, they like to have a supply stored hanging in baskets on rafters.[24]

The Tapirapé were assured of a basic food supply from their gardens, but not an adequate diet. They were fully conscious of their needs and desires. In 1939-40 salt was a great delicacy. The only form they could produce was derived from a water plant which had to be boiled for two hours and produced only a handful of salt. Children begged for the crude imported crystal salt and licked it like a lollypop. Women brought garden products and even artifacts, asking for salt in return. Game was cooked in the skin and charred to produce a salty taste.

There was a definite need for proteins, and beans from their gardens

---

writing in 1612, declares that the Tupinambá from Maranhão used their hands to squeeze the manioc. South along the coast of Brazil, the tipiti press was reported by early chroniclers.
23. In 1940 the Tapirapé were anxious to get large tins to be perforated to form graters
24. Cotton sacks were in much demand in 1939-40, and the first trousers given to the Tapirapé were used for storing manioc flour. They made excellent sacks. One only had to tie the bottom of the legs, close the fly, and tighten the waist.

lasted but a short time. There was a tremendous desire for meat and fish. It took me several months to understand what the Tapirapé meant when they said "I am hungry" when they had manioc in abundance. What they were really saying was "I am hungry for meat or fish." Herbert Baldus (1970: 232-3) tells of how well he felt eating basically Tapirapé style, but he spent only a relatively short period of time on their diet. During the rainy season of 1940, and despite reinforcement from canned vegetable oils and more meat than a normal Tapirapé was able to obtain, I was "hungry" Tapirapé-style and developed boils. For that reason the Tapirapé have a preoccupation with hunting to satisfy their needs for protein, particularly in the rainy season.

Men hunted individually or in groups. To my knowledge, the Tapirapé did not have animal traps of any kind, but they invariably took their dogs along when they went hunting. The dogs of the Tapirapé are small, short-haired, terrier-like animals, usually poorly fed and often mangy; their aid in hunting is rather dubious. However, at least once I saw dogs used to tree a jaguar.[25] In 1939-40, the Tapirapé's only weapons were the bow and arrow and clubs formed of a heavy hardwood. There were lances, but they were never used for hunting. Instead, they seemed to be a symbol carried by dance leaders. The Tapirapé were expert with the bow; from the time a boy was five years of age he practiced with a miniature bow and arrow, hunting lizards in the village. The Tapirapé were agile and indefatigable in running through the forest, laced with lianas and sometimes thorny bushes, after peccaries or wild pigs, which they would finish off with clubs. They also had a sharp eye for forest fowls such as jacu and *mutum*. Hunting in the forest was not as productive as on the savanna, and certainly more difficult.[26] In the rainy season, the range for hunting was limited by swollen streams, and few Tapirapé knew how to swim at all at that time.

In the rainy season men often left the village in the morning for a

---

25. Dogs may not have been indigenous; they may have been received from other Indian groups before contact with Brazilians. They were a real menace to strangers. For several months neither Valentim nor I could walk through the village without a club. The owners were not offended at all when one of us had to use a club on his dog.

26. It was dangerous for me to hunt in the forest with the Tapirapé. The sight or noise of wild pigs or a peccary would set the hunters running through the forest at a pace impossible for me to follow. I would soon be left far behind and generally lost. The only thing to do was to sit on a log, fire my gun in the air, and wait to be rescued. Furthermore, while I could shoot a gun with average marksmanship, I could seldom spot a fowl until it flew. The Tapirapé in 1939-40 could see the birds but they could not sight with a rifle. It was the case of a blind man with a gun led by a man with sight but no gun! Only Salvador could really be of help to the Tapirapé in forest hunting.

one-day hunt alone or sometimes with one companion. Not all men were adept or energetic enough to hunt by themselves. Several men went hunting three or five times in a week (a "week" is my own unit of time). Ipawaní, for example, was known as a hunter. He was proud of his little dog, which he said tracked animals for him. He loved to hunt and talked about the chase whenever possible. In January of 1940, he made many one-day excursions alone. He always seemed to return with something. On three one-day excursions, he returned one day with a small monkey and two jacus; two coatis and two jacus, on the second day; and one peccary on the third day. Other hunters who went out alone fared less well. Champukwi, for example, left one morning at 6:00 a.m. and returned at about 6:00 p.m. with three coatis, which are not choice game animals. He also left another day at 6:00 a.m. and returned at 3:00 p.m. empty-handed.

Perhaps ten men in the village would go hunting alone on various occasions during the rainy season. When such men returned to the village with meat there was always a problem. When Champukwi returned to the village with three coatis, his sister, Mariampunwunga, came with other women to welcome him. Their husbands had not hunted that day. She stood by as he took out the entrails, obviously hoping for a gift. Then she said directly, "Your sister's son will eat entrails." Champukwi said "Yes." She gathered the entrails together and boiled them for her whole family. It killed the monotony of manioc flour. Some individual hunters would sneak into the village with game to avoid begging relatives.

The most productive hunting expeditions of the rainy season were group hunts organized by the Bird Societies. Several took place between December 1939 and May 1940. The best way to describe them is to use one example which the author followed throughout. On February 10, Kamairá, leader of one of the Bird Societies, announced that there would be a collective hunt. For two days the women made manioc flour despite the rains and lack of sun. On February 13, most men left for the savanna. Only the older men who were shamans and important household leaders remained behind. At about 11:00 a.m., the hunters arrived at the edge of the savanna. It was already partially flooded. They quickly constructed lean-tos with palm fronds because it was already raining. All of the men set off in small groups in search of game. Only two or three deer were killed that day. They were barbecued at once and everyone ate well except for a few men with infant children (to whom deer were taboo).

The next morning the group left early, wading through water to   61 "high areas" where wild pigs might take refuge. About 11:00 a.m. they discovered a band of pigs. They shot several with arrows, but the wounded pigs fled. Fortunately, the pigs were "angry"; they turned and attacked the hunters, who quickly climbed into the branches of low-growing trees. The dogs acted as bait and the pigs returned to attack several times. So, the Tapirapé shot them as they passed below their perches and then descended to club the wounded pigs. About twenty were killed. One dog was so badly gored that it was simply brained with a club. The pigs were carried back to camp where fires were started and they were butchered. That afternoon the men ate livers, entrails, and other small pieces while the pigs were roasting.

The next morning at dawn the meat was packed in baskets wrapped in wild banana leaves to be carried back to Tampiitawa. By late afternoon the men arrived in Kananchipa's garden, about 500 yards from the village. There they made camp. As soon as it was dark, they began to shout, giving the characteristic cries of each Bird Society. Then, suddenly, two pairs of masked dancers appeared from the forest clad in buriti palm skirts, with palm masks covering their heads. They were the *anchunga ampukáya* (crying spirits), and they danced from household to household in the village. Two tufts of hair from the wild pigs crowned their masks, and on their ankles they wore rattles made of pig hoofs making a sound like "pigs running." Soon the dancers entered the takana and all was silent.

At dawn the men entered the village with their loads of meat, which were taken directly to the takana. There the meat was divided into six piles, one for each Bird Society age group.[27] The meat was not divided equally, for two of the groups were composed of small boys. The largest amount of meat was allotted to the groups composed of middle-aged and prestigious older men. Each group guarded its portion through the day.[28] At about 4:00 p.m. all of the men gathered in the takana, with each age group of each Bird Society around its portion of the hunt. The feast began. Women came to the door of the takana to bring them manioc flour, and each man, as he received the flour, gave her a piece of pork. Wives served manioc flour to, and received meat from, their husbands. Small boys were served by, and gave small pieces of meat to, their mothers. As the men finished eating their fill, the remaining meat was then divided to be taken to the resi-

---

27. There are two sets of Bird Societies and each set is divided into three age grades.
28. Three men were accused of stealing; they took pieces of meat to their hungry wives before the men's feast and the general distribution of the remaining meat.

Tapirapé men wrestling in 1940.

dences for their families—again, the older men receiving the largest portion.

At dusk, after the feast, the dancing area in front of the takana was swept. The two Bird Societies stood facing one another inside the takana. Two men from one Society took burning sticks from the fire and rushed at their opposites as if to harm them. Two men from the opposite Society retaliated. No harm was done on either side; this was a challenge and an acceptance to a wrestling contest. The two groups reformed outside on the dancing area. A pair of opponents stood face to face, arms linked and with a firm grip in each other's hair. Each tried to throw his opponent to the ground with a quick trip of the legs and the sudden use of the arms and shoulders.[29] Men of either Bird

---

29. The Tapirapé are not so adept at this sport as the Carajá. Even so, they threw Valentim to the ground several times, though his short hair gave his opponent little to

Society challenged individuals of the other Society. A challenge was made, at first, by simply pointing a finger and, if accepted, a match began. At one time that afternoon two wrestling matches were taking place simultaneously. But after a time several challenges were refused. The challenger then set fire to dry *bacaba* palm leaves and rushed the man who had refused. The reluctant opponent was forced to grab his challenger in order to push aside the firebrand which was directed at his face. In that way the challenge was accepted and a wrestling match followed. There were no insulting remarks, nor did either side count their victories. A few men quietly stole away and their absence was noted with laughter. Suddenly the leader of each Bird Society gave out the characteristic cry of his Society. The contest was over and the two groups intermingled, grasping each others' hands. Such contests relieve tension; men select opponents whom they know or simply suspect to have had intercourse with their wives while they were away from the village on the hunting expedition.

Several group hunting expeditions occurred during the rainy season of 1939-40. Some were not as successful as the one described above. In two group hunts, only one of the two Bird Societies participated while the other remained in the village. Yet the hunters shared their game with the Society that stayed home. In another group hunt only a portion of each Society participated. There was some grumbling about the "lazy" men who stayed at home, but again the meat was distributed, although hardly equally. The Bird Societies, although fundamentally ceremonial in their functions, were important production groups in farming and, more important, in providing meat during the rainy season. Even by 1939-40, the Tapirapé complained that they did not function as well as they had in the past because of their reduced membership.

The Tapirapé also collected palm nuts, which supply some of their need for fats. Bacaba palm nuts were collected in the late dry season while the Tapirapé were camped on the savanna. They also collected *tucumã* nuts during the early rains, and in the wet season they collected a species of palm nuts called *uriwá* in Tapirapé. Both men and women collected palm nuts. The women crushed them in a wooden mortar,[30] then squeezed out the oil from the pulp by hand and stored

---

hold on to. Both Valentim and I gave up experimenting with the sport after taking several rough falls administered by much smaller men.

30. Baldus reports that manioc is crushed with mortar and pestle, but I never saw this done. Only mature maize, peanuts, and palm nuts are so crushed.

it in gourd containers sealed with beeswax. *Tucumã* nuts must be boiled to separate out the fat. Curiously, however, little of this palm oil entered their diet. Instead, most of it was used for personal decoration. It was smeared lightly over the body mixed with annatto or used thickly on the hair to make it gleam. At one time it was so highly valued that it was the payment demanded by shamans for cures or by the specialists who performed the scarification operation on women's faces. Seldom was palm oil consumed; only when people felt starved for fat did they add some palm oil to dry manioc flour.

Other than meat, fish was the main source of protein for the Tapirapé. Fish were available in considerable quantity only in the dry season and mainly during the period when the people were encamped on the savanna. But as the waters receded in the small streams in the forest in April and May, conical fish traps made of woven buriti palm fiber were placed in small streams to catch minnows. These were roasted or boiled and consumed like sardines—that is, bones, head, and all. This was a time of year when any source of protein was very scarce and these minuscule fish were eagerly sought.

One man would make several conical traps, placing them in several small streams not too far away from the village. The catch from a trap varied from day to day and sometimes, even though one could see the small fish in the stream, a trap seemed to yield no fish at all. If that happened the spirit (*anchunga*) of the trap was considered to be ill. An anchunga could become ill in several ways. Men who placed traps in the streams could not eat pumpkins, nor could a menstruating woman eat fish caught by the trap. Likewise, if an electric eel entered the trap, the spirit could become ill and it would not "call" fish. When this happened, the trap would be removed from the water and rubbed with the leaves of an unidentified herb called *amumaia*. Then it would be anointed with palm oil mixed with annatto dye, and, finally, tobacco smoke would be blown over the apparatus in the same way that a shaman treated human illness. If the cure was carried out correctly, I was told, the spirit of the fish trap would get well, and within a few days it would again begin to "call" fish. And, because the trap had a spirit, it could also be dangerous. Men were discouraged from manufacturing such a trap within the sight of a small child. The spirit of the trap could call the soul (also called anchunga) of the child and the child would die. Tapirapé gossips told me that they believed this was the reason why Champukwi's first son died. Champukwi had been very careless indeed: he had allowed the crawling in-   65 fant to touch the fish trap he was making. It seems significant to me that an apparatus which in fact supplies the Tapirapé with such a small part of their total food supply was imbued with such sensitive supernatural attributes. The supernatural importance attributed to fish traps must be related to the fact that they do supply an essential element in their diet at a crucial time of the year. At the end of a long rainy season during which meat was only available sporadically, the small minnows boiled as a soup or simply toasted over the fire were a welcome break in a dull diet.

As the water receded more, the Tapirapé sometimes used the shredded roots of the *timbó* vine to poison the water of pools which were drying up. Timbó kills some small fish, but it simply stuns larger fish, which then may be speared by arrow. Most fishing, however, was done by men who shot fish in the clear water of a lagoon or the Tapirapé River. Hooks seemed to be totally lacking in aboriginal times, as were nets. In 1939-40, the Tapirapé were not interested at all in the hooks and line which we had brought as trade goods. Fishing, except for occasional poisoning of pools with timbó, was an individual economic activity, limited to the dry season and never organized by the men's Societies. Baldus (1970: 175ff.) emphasized fishing among the Tapirapé because he was in residence at the time of year when fish were available. But throughout the year, the great preoccupation of the Tapirapé was meat, which they got from hunting.

Despite their hunger for meat, the Tapirapé imposed barriers upon themselves in satisfying that hunger. In 1939-40 and earlier, there were elaborate taboos on its consumption. The flesh of many animals was limited to classes of people according to sex, age, and condition of life. For example, the small savanna deer could only be eaten by adult males. It could not be eaten by women, children of either sex, or men who were the fathers of infants. Few types of meat, notably wild pork and peccary, could be eaten by people of both sexes and all ages. Some meats were not eaten at all. Adult males whose children had been weaned suffered least from food taboos, and women past the age of menopause could eat any meat allowed to adult men. Fathers of infants were subject to the same taboos as women and children. What they ate influenced the health of the child, and the death or illness of an infant was often attributed to the fact that the father had broken food taboos. No satisfactory ideological or religious justification could be elicited for these taboos. Informants explained, for example, that the savanna deer had a strong anchunga, but they could not explain

66

how this extended to other animals, nor why women and children were more vulnerable to the deer anchunga than adult males were. Other informants said that certain meats, such as the mutum and wild goose, carry *eangwurup* (epilepsy), to which children and women were thought to be especially susceptible (see Chapter 6). Before women could eat those meats, a shaman had to extract eangwurup by blowing tobacco smoke over the meat. It was explained that the electric eel was taboo for women and children because it caused chills. However, there was no consistent ideological explanation offered that explained the whole system of meat taboos. Nor can I offer a consistent ecologically adaptive theory for the Tapirapé system of such taboos. In view of their hunger for meat, the whole taboo complex seems decidedly dysfunctional. It is a striking case where, for reasons of culture, man has not been able to make full use of his total environment. The taboo complex cannot be fully explained as a system of conservation of animal resources, although it must have had that result to some extent. Nor can it be explained as the guarantee of protein to those of certain ages who needed it most. Rather it seemed to limit the protein possibilities for most people.

It should be said, however, that such taboos had one functional advantage. They tended to promote exchange between relatives and friends within the village. A man who was the father of an infant and thus prohibited to eat armadillo, for example, would kill such an animal if he encountered it, even though it was also taboo to his wife and daughters. He would bring it to the village as a gift to a brother-in-law, a sister's son, or a special friend (*anchiwawa*) who did not have an infant child and perhaps had growing sons (boys can eat armadillo). He would not expect immediate payment of any kind, but in time he would expect his relative or friend to remember his gift. Thus, if the recipient had chanced to kill a peccary, he would have reciprocated with a choice piece of meat. In consequence, the limitation on diet resulted in cementing social ties. Unless it was an animal which all Tapirapé found repugnant, such as the sloth, there was always someone anxious for the meat.

Those taboos did not mean that the men hunted selectively. When I was living with the Tapirapé, men with small children killed a jacu, which they could not eat. They proudly presented it to us as a gift, asking salt in return. We often had dried and salted venison, and there were always a few people who came to beg for it. Yet men who accompanied us to the savanna on hunting trips would go to their 67 hammocks hungry because only deer meat was available. Women refused to eat venison while encamped on the savanna when other meat or fish was lacking. And later, we shall see that such food taboos have been slow to change, making it difficult for the Tapirapé to adapt to modern frontier conditions.

The only way to adequately present these elaborate taboos is to do so in the form of a list. It is derived from Baldus (1970: 209-25). He compiled this list from the information he collected in 1935 and from my field notes as of 1939-40.[31] The basic distinction seems to have been between meat that may be eaten by all segments of the population and those that were taboo to women, to children, and to fathers of infants. There were others that were dangerous for children, but they could be treated by a shaman to remove the danger. In addition, there were meats avoided entirely by all Tapirapé, although eaten by other native peoples. Only two types of fish, the gigantic pirarucú and the large *pirarara*, were taboo. All other fish were eaten by everyone. Following this dichotomy, animals were divided as shown in Tables 1 and 2.

In addition, the Tapirapé abstained from eating snakes, the sloth, the opossum, the freshwater dolphin, and the largest of all American rodents, the *capivara*.[32] Baldus listed a series of insects which were illustrated in the book by von Ihering, referred to earlier (Baldus, 1970: 222-25); none of them were considered edible, but informants told of eating the larva of two insects, one called *kawa* (wasp) and another *uwurantana* (that which lives in the wood). Neither could be identified by their scientific names.

New sources of meat, which were acquired from the Europeans, were integrated into this system of dietary rules. By 1939-40, the Tapirapé owned some chickens, which missionaries had given them. The chicken was called *wuran champokaiya* (the bird which cries). They could be eaten by adult males, but, like the mutum, chicken meat was considered dangerous for females and children unless treated by a shaman. At one time before 1939-40, the Tapirapé had several domestic pigs which the missionary Frederick Kegel brought to them.

---

31. Baldus used the textbook of Rudolpho von Ihering, *Da Vida dos nossos animais do Brasil* (São Leopoldo: Rotermund e Co., 1934), which has pictures next to each animal described. My early notes were more pragmatic. Valentim taught me the Brazilian names of animals, and I witnessed most of the meat taboos as people refused to eat the meat of the animal in question.

32. Baldus (1970: 211) states that adult men could eat capivara meat, but the Tapirapé told me that "the meat smells."

TABLE 1

Meats which could be eaten by all people

English	Portuguese	Scientific Nomenclature
Wild pig	*queixada*	*Dicotyles albirostris*
Peccary	*caititu*	*Dicotyles tayassu*
Paca	*paca*	*Coelogenys paca* (also, *Caniculus paca*)
Agouti	*cotia*	*Dasyprocta*, sp.
Anteater	*tamanduá-bandeira*	*Myrmecophaga jubata*
Tortoise	*jabuti*	*Testudo tabulata*
Coati	*quati*	*Nasua narica*
Cebus monkey	*macaco-prego*	*Cebus*, sp.
Turtles:[a]		
Large river turtle	*tartaruga*	*Podocmemis expansa*
Small freshwater turtle	*tracajá*	*Podocnemis unifilio*

[a] The eggs of turtles could be consumed as well. However, they were considered dangerous to children.

They were eaten by all people, just as were wild pig. In 1939-40 most Tapirapé had never seen cattle, but they knew of them from the descriptions given by the young men who had visited mission stations on the Araguaia River. Dried beef was offered them by visitors at the river port, but beef was identified with venison, and was, therefore, taboo to females, to children, and to men with infants. There was considerable discussion about some canned sausages, which no one would eat until we assured them that they were pork.

Despite the taboos on meat and despite their periodic hunger for proteins, the Tapirapé in 1939-40 had an adequate diet and often even a surplus of food. There were no indications of kwashiorkor or other serious vitamin deficiencies. Most people, especially children, probably had intestinal worms. The people were lean, but no one was emaciated. Theirs was not a subsistence system that guaranteed any 69

TABLE 2

Meats prohibited to women, children and fathers of infants

English	Portuguese	Scientific Nomenclature
Savanna deer	*veado-campeiro*	*Dorcelaphus bezoarcticus*
Forest deer	*veado-mateiro*	*Mazama americana*
Large savanna deer	*sussuapara*	*Dorcelaphus dichotomus*
Armadillo	*tatu*	*Euphractus sexinctus*
Howler monkey	*guariba*	*Alouatta,* sp.
Tapir	*anta*	*Tapirus americanus*
Small anteater	*tamanduá-mirim*	*Tamandua tetradactylus*
Electric eel	*peixe elétrico; puraquê*	*Electrophorus electricus*
Jaguar	*onça*	*Felis onca*
Wildcat	*Gato do mato; maracajá*	*Felis,* sp.
Jacu (fowl)	*Jacu*	*Penelope,* sp.
Mutum (fowl)	*mutum*	*Crax,* sp.
Ynambu (fowl); also Tinamou	*Inhambu*	*Crypturus,* sp. (can be eaten by women if the meat is treated by shaman)
Wild duck	*marreco-caboclo*	*Dendrocygna discolor*
Wild goose	*pato do mato; marrecão*	*Alopochen jabata* (can be eaten by women and children if the meat is treated by shaman)
Macaw	*arara*	*Ara,* sp.[a]
Alligator	*jacaré*	*Caiman,* sp.
Pirarucu (fish)	*pirarucu; piraucu*	*Arapaima,* sp.
Pirarara (large fish)	*pirarara*[b]	*Phractocephalus hemiliopterus*
Frog	*rã*	Rana L.

[a] The macaw was not killed for food, but mainly for feathers. Its meat is very tough, so that it has to be boiled for hours before it is tender enough to chew.

[b] The pirarucu and pirarara are the only fish on which there were any dietary restrictions.

large or long-term surplus, but everyone had access to food. In fact, people were amazingly free in allowing others to harvest manioc from their gardens. Some men and women were known as hard workers and others were called lazy, but the men who were hard workers did not have a standard of living very much better than the lazy ones. They did, however, have more stable marriages, for women hung on to good providers. It was not difficult to correlate Anawani's inability to keep a wife with his well-earned reputation for laziness. So, without a wife, he depended upon female relatives for female services. His hammock was dirty and falling apart. He did not eat as well as most men. His sexual life was limited to quick, furtive encounters with married women. The sexual division of labor among the Tapirapé was sharp and clear; women held the power of withholding certain services from men, and men without wives had a somewhat lower standard of living. Yet such distinctions were minor compared with those of most societies. To the outside observer, it might seem that there were no rich nor poor among the Tapirapé.

However, I soon learned that there are differences in wealth. Gardens (not land) were the property of the nuclear family. The longhouse, though built by the men, was considered the collective property of the women who lived there. But all articles of personal use were individually owned. Hammocks, baskets, clubs, bows and arrows, cooking utensils, ornaments, and, in fact, practically every object which was individually made was privately owned. This was also true of trade goods acquired from Brazilians, such as bushknives, axes, hoes, mirrors, and beads. Likewise, "personal objects" were extended to cover pets such as hawks, macaws, dogs, and chickens, again acquired from Brazilians. Children had the same rights over their property as adults did; a basket made by a father or a mother's brother as a present for a child could not be given away or exhanged without the permission of that child.

Since the village was not large, almost every adult could identify an object and its owner. A woman brought peanuts for exchange and an onlooker remarked: "Isn't that the basket belonging to Wanatu?" (the small son of Urukumu). Valentim Gomes borrowed an axe to cut firewood; as he returned to the village, a man said, "that axe belongs to Kamairaho." Especially highly valued personal property in 1939-40 were the porcelain beads, which were strung on native cotton and rated according to size and color. Beads about one-eighth of an inch in diameter were best, and red was the favorite color. Owners of 71 beads did not wear them every day. Rather, they were stored away in a basket and hung on a rafter near their hammocks. The Tapirapé could identify beads by their source. There were beads "brought by Baldus," "by Kegel," "by the Dominicans," and so on. Almost equally valuable were the long tail feathers of the red macaw. These were stored carefully in a long bamboo tube. Other macaw feathers were also highly valued, such as the tail feathers of the blue macaw and wing feathers of both the red and the blue macaw. Some people owned macaws taken from nests and clipped their wings before they could fly. These "pets" were fed, and each year or so plucked for their feathers. Only when there was an important ceremonial would such valuable feathers be used to construct a headdress. They might not be worn by the owner, but everyone would know that they belonged to Kamairá, Wantanamu, or some other important man. Once the festival ended, the headdress would be dismantled and the feathers would be carefully stored away by the owner.

This highly personalized system of individually owned objects had some interesting and even comical consequences. First, there could hardly be any theft, although people borrowed the personal property of others rather freely.[33] Most people found it hard to deny their kinsmen and friends the use of objects, although beads, macaw feathers, and hammocks were seldom borrowed easily.[34] To deny another the use of an object made the owner "stingy" (*ankantaum*)—a harsh criticism among the Tapirapé. The comical consequence had to do with gifts. People made gifts both to kinsmen and friends on various occasions and especially, as we shall see, at the kawió ceremonies in the beginning of the dry season. They were, however, public transfers of personal property which everyone knew about. But men would frequently make gifts of beads to women in return for sexual favors while their husbands were away on a hunting trip. The adulteress might hide her beads for a short time, but she soon was tempted to wear them. Immediately the husband would know of her indiscretion and with whom, and the adulteror's spouse recognized her husband's beads as well. So, generally, two family quarrels ensued—one in which a man

---

33. Valentim had some trouble in distinguishing between theft and borrowing. When one of our pans would disappear he would call it theft, but then he would be told that Maripawungo, a woman in a near-by house, was merely using it to boil some sweet manioc.
34. People would, however, stretch out or sit in another's hammock without permission during the day. The only way to prevent this was to roll up the hammock and tie it in a ball against the wall of the house. I found it convenient to have two hammocks, one for visitors during the day and another carefully stored away to sleep in at night.

might beat his wife and another in which a wife stopped cooking for a day or so.

It soon became apparent that certain individuals were "richer" than others. Important household leaders such as Kamairá, Kamairaho, Wantanamu, Panteri, and Urukumu accumulated by gift and exchange more axes, bushknives, baskets, macaw feathers, and beads than others. Kamairaho owned at least three kilos of beads, three "pet" red macaws, several axes, and other objects. Opronunchwi spent several months with missionaries, and when he returned he was relatively wealthy in beads and trade goods.[35] But he soon had little left because he had to make gifts to important elder relatives and friends. Shamans, particularly, accumulated property because payment for a cure was always made in personal objects. The shaman often knew exactly what the patient or the family owned, thus he could name his price. Other special services, such as performing the scarification on a young woman's face, called for payment in personal property. In 1939-40 Urukumu was the only specialist in the operation, and he asked for and received a bushknife and ten arrows for performing the bloody task. It should be noted that there was no interchange between the subsistence system and the prestige system. One never gave food for arrows, baskets, or beads; nor did one ever exchange food (even meat) for personal objects.

There were, however, several mechanisms of redistribution in Tapirapé society which guaranteed that no man could accumulate so much in the prestige system that he was far richer than all others. The first was hardly a redistribution, but rather a reduction in private property. At the death of a Tapirapé his or her personal objects were buried with the body. The second was minor in its results, but effective. An offense against a person, even an accidental one, had to be righted by a gift. For example, once, when I was wearing boots, I accidentally stepped on the foot of a small girl. She cried for some time; later that day the parents came to demand a pair of scissors. On another occasion Kamairaho's dog bit a young boy, and his parents let it be known that they wanted a small string of beads. Both offended parties were paid what they demanded. A third mechanism of redistribution involved the establishment of formalized friendship (*anchiwawa*). Such a friendship was always formed between individuals of the same sex. They could be distant kinsmen, but the new relationship drew them

---

35. He also had the first crack at my wealth, since I had found him on the Araguaia River and had depended upon him as a guide to lead us to the Tapirapé village.

even closer. Yet the tie involved respect and formality.[36] According to Shapiro (1968: 12), the relationship was established by an intermediary, which is a function of the ritual avoidance of friends-to-be. Although Shapiro's description is based upon an informant's memory of the past (the institution was no longer functional in 1967), it seems worthwhile to quote it here since I am attempting to describe Tapirapé economic life as it must have been circa 1900.

> I was told that *anchiwawa* give one another their most valuable possessions: hammocks, macaws, clay cooking vessels, rifles, etc. Such friends also give food to one another and the initial setting up of the relationship involves a presentation of *kawi* . . . , but the most important transactions connected with formalized friendship seem to involve items of personal property other than food. One man told me that he once gave his "friend" his best hunting dog; the "friend" in turn gave him a machete. All communication between the two took place via their wives, who could receive the gifts destined for their respective husbands. Sometimes parents may initiate *anchiwawa* relationships on the part of their children and, in such cases, the parents carry on exchanges until the children are old enough to do so themselves.
>
> Since the *anchiwawa* relationship is not supposed to be set up between close relatives, it creates a tie between individuals who would not be likely to exchange goods in the course of normal, everyday interaction. Ceremonial friendship thus acts to widen the sphere of distribution or redistribution of items of personal property, constituting an additional pair of statuses defined in terms of mutual prestations. (Shapiro, 1968: 12-13).[37]

However, a man could have several formalized friends, sometimes six or more. I was told that such friends could be in the same village, but that at the time when several Tapirapé villages existed they were more often individuals from other villages. There were exchanges of gifts when the relationship was first formed and exchanges when the individuals visited the village of his or her "friend." Of course, such

---

36. Shapiro (1968) states that it involved avoidance. She writes, "were 'friends' to be coming towards one another on a path, for example, the two would have to turn away in order to avoid the encounter." My notes and memory of 1939-40 do not bear out this extreme avoidance, but I am in basic agreement with her description of the friendship relationship patterns. In 1939-40, I was called anchiwawa by several men, but I do not remember any avoidance patterns in our daily relationships. However, calling me anchiwawa may well have been just another way of attempting to separate me from my trade goods.

37. I have taken the liberty of simplifying her transcription of Tapirapé terms.

friends tended to be of approximately the same prestige level and might have owned about the same amount of personal property at any one time. Therefore, exchanges between "friends" tended to distribute personal property, but the relationship did not siphon off property from the hands of those who were rich in personal goods to those who had less. That was the function of still another institution of redistribution—the ceremonial redistribution at the time of the kawió ceremonial at the beginning of the dry season each year.

The kawió was the culmination of the season of dancing and singing called kaó. It took place when the garden products were ripe and there was considerable food in the village. I shall describe the details of the ceremony later. It is enough to say at this time that two adolescent girls and their families sponsored the ceremony and the girls and their female relatives prepared the kawi. The ingredients were crushed in the mortar and then boiled with water. Women took the liquid into their mouths, spitting it back into the ceramic vessel. If this process were repeated several times and the kawi allowed to age for a few days, it would ferment, producing an alcoholic drink. But the Tapirapé did not allow their kawi to become alcoholic; instead, it was consumed on the same day. Baldus found it particularly appetizing (Baldus, 1970: 198).

There is a "bad" kawi, however, which was produced upon that occasion. Judith Shapiro stated that it is made of maize (Shapiro, 1968: 11), but in 1939-40 I was told that it was made of a variety of bitter manioc (i.e. one which contained a relatively high degree of prussic acid). This bad kawi was the same which the assassins of shamans had to drink to purge their bodies of dangerous spirits (see Chapter 6). Shapiro (1968: 11), who witnessed the kawió ceremony in 1966, calls it a "nauseating beverage"; in 1939-40, people who drank it were literally nauseated—they often vomited violently.

At dawn on the last day of the kawió ceremony, a bowl of bad kawi was carried from house to house throughout the village. Everyone was invited to drink. *Capitães*, men and women of prestige and of considerable personal property, refrained from drinking;[38] they simply washed out their mouths, spitting the fluid on the ground. In doing

---

38. The word *capitão* ("captain") or *capitães* (plural: captains) a Portuguese word, was used by the Tapirapé as early as 1935 (Baldus, 1970: 340) and in 1939-40 for men of prestige who were household heads, shamans, and Bird Society leaders. I could not elicit a Tapirapé term for chieftain. The most common Tupí term for "chief," *murubixawa*, was not known to them; yet there was a definite distinction between those who were *capitão* and descendants of *capitães* and other people.

so, however, they obligated themselves to make gifts to anyone who actually drank the kawi immediately afterward. If several people drank kawi just after an individual had refused it, then all who did so might claim gifts. It was considered humiliating to drink it, but in compensation the drinker received gifts. On this occasion a man of prestige and wealth could be forced to part with a large amount of his personal possessions. Even children of prestigious parents were expected to refuse, and the parents were expected to give gifts to those who drank kawi after the child. Fortunately, the author, exhausted from walking from the river, was asleep when this ceremonial took place in 1939. Shapiro, who witnessed it in 1966, was forewarned by my notes (Shapiro, 1968: 18) and wisely refrained from participation.

Informants told me of valuables they had given away in 1939-40—beads, ceramic vessels, macaws, axes, bushknives, bows and arrows, and feathers. Judith Shapiro described the demands made in 1966. Although at that time personal objects included more Brazilian trade goods, she states that some of the young bachelors who had considerable personal property made it a point to be absent, and one man (a capitão) with considerable "wealth" refused to take the part of a man of prestige (Shapiro, 1969: 19). The Tapirapé told her that the ceremony had degenerated; the Tapirapé were ankantaum (stingy). And yet Shapiro has this to say about the kawió ceremony:

> I was told that just about anything could be asked for, though no one would demand another's only hammock or other such indispensable items. The headman, who had expressed concern over not having anything good to give, brightened when he remembered his fine large canoe which he had obtained from his Carajá co-parent-in-law. Among the items which changed hands during the kawió which I witnessed in 1966 were cooking pans of clay and aluminum, machetes, bullets, an axe, spun cotton, beads, and some red dye of the type used in ceremonies. The headman kept his canoe that year, but upon returning the following year, I learned that he had just lost in that season's kawió a heavy woolen blanket which had been given to him by a tourist in return for some particularly well-made artifacts. (Shapiro, 1968: 11-12.)[39]

In the past, the Tapirapé had had a smaller variety of personal objects, but many more of them had changed hands at the kawió ceremony.

---

39. She also (1968: 18) tells of a "less fortunate European visitor who attended the kawió of the previous year, left behind a good part of his clothes, a blanket, a heavy sleeping bag and a number of other valuables."

This ceremony functioned more than any other institution of redistribution to prevent the accumulation of personal property in the hands of a few. It was based upon the principle that it was more prestigious to give than to receive; but then again, there were mechanisms of prestige that channeled personal property back into the hands of those who gave.

After 1950, when the remaining Tapirapé were relocated at the mouth of the Tapirapé River, their ecological adjustment was strongly modified. Many of their economic institutions were retained, as indicated by Shapiro's description of the kawió ceremony in 1966. The men's Bird Societies continued to exist, and from time to time they functioned as productive units in hunting, but for the most part they became almost entirely ceremonial, acting as groups for festivals. The clearing of gardens, which already in 1939-40 had become more of an individual undertaking than a cooperative venture, became even more individualized. Judith Shapiro (1968: 15) notes that "the clearing of gardens was begun by men working alone on their respective plots, but was completed by communal labor" (an apachirú). But in 1967, communal clearing of garden sites did not take place at all. Sometimes, however, the village did undertake a cooperative activity. Shapiro (1968: 14) speaks of the expeditions to fish with timbó vine poison in lakes and slow-running streams, which "may involve the whole village." But she also remarks that such expeditions may involve only a single family or two men aided by women and children. Because of their small population and the resulting disorganization of their productive units, the Tapirapé were more individually oriented in their economic activities in 1965 than they had been in 1940.

The Tapirapé are still fundamentally slash-and-burn horticulturalists. They continue to plant the same crops as they did in the past, although now dry rice, which they have come to appreciate as a food, is an important crop. By 1965 there were no adequate sites anywhere in the near vicinity of New Village for gardens. The nearest high forest suitable for gardens in their terms was as far as ten to fifteen kilometers distant from the village—which meant an hour and a half to two hours' walk. Much of the land near the village is savanna which is annually flooded, low brush, or secondary growth. Each year the Tapirapé have to travel farther from their village to find suitable forest to clear for gardens. By 1965 several families had built open sheds in their gardens where they camp while they plant, harvest their crops, and clear new areas for gardens during the coming year. 77

Women prepare manoic flour at the garden site rather than in the village to avoid carrying the heavy tubers from garden to village. This means that families often spend considerable periods away from the village camped in their gardens.

Padre François, the missionary priest, attempted to partially solve the problem of the long walk and of transporting produce to the village. He purchased a tractor which pulled a large four-wheeled cart. At his direction the Tapirapé cleared a path wide enough for the tractor and the cart to reach a point within a short distance of the garden area. And Ipawungí (also known by his Brazilian name as Cantidio), who was one of the village leaders, learned to drive the tractor. The padre frequently allowed groups of families to use the tractor for transportation, especially when there were heavy loads of produce ready to be taken to the village. But gasoline was very expensive at the Araguaia River (it arrived by riverboat in 150-gallon drums), and neither the padre nor the Tapirapé would afford to use the tractor very often. I am unaware of what happened to the tractor after Padre François was arrested and exiled from Brazil in 1974. Almost certainly it is no longer in use. I am told that in 1975 at least one Tapirapé man had purchased a bicycle to shorten the trip from his garden to his permanent dwelling in New Village.

Without doubt, the shortage of suitable agricultural land within a reasonable distance from their village may ultimately prove to be the major impediment of Tapirapé adaptation to their new circumstances. It might seem that a reservation of slightly more than 9000 hectares would provide enough land for just over 100 people. But much of this land is not suitable for tropical forest slash-and-burn farming. In the years to come that portion of the area which is covered by high forest will have been cleared and planted at least during one growing season. Following their indigenous system of agriculture, the Tapirapé seek to clear a new garden site from high forest. They are fully aware that a garden site planted two years in succession loses much of its fertility as measured by production. They are also aware that planting in secondary growth which has been fallow for only a few years is about half as productive as gardens planted in high forest. Under indigenous conditions, they moved the location of their permanent village each six or seven years as suitable garden sites became too distant. In the past the Tapirapé rarely made use of forest land that had not lain fallow for twenty years or more.

78

New Village has been located at the same site for well over twenty years. If the Tapirapé continue to occupy this same location, they will have to search even farther away for high forests, and there is a limit to the distance in which they can expand. Soon they will move into territory beyond the as yet unmarked boundaries of their reservation into territory now being exploited by Brazilian backwoodsmen; or they will be forced to spend more time living next to their gardens. They would not like to live isolated near their gardens, for they are by tradition a village people whose way of life places a high value on living in a nucleated settlement. Soon the Tapirapé will be forced to make use of secondary growth of only a few years' standing for their gardens. Their agricultural production will thus suffer more and more as the years go by. They may be forced to follow the pattern of the rural Brazilians in the vicinity—combining agriculture and the grazing of a few cattle on the savanna. In 1965 the Indian post already had a few head of cattle which were said "to belong to the Indians," but the Tapirapé still consider cattle strange beasts and they have little knowledge of cattle raising.

And in that year, garden produce was not as plentiful as it had been in the past. There was even a shortage of manioc flour late in the rainy season, and some Tapirapé had to buy flour from Brazilian frontiersmen. Yet there was still a rather free and easy distribution of food. A group going off together to harvest food might all harvest from the garden of one, though each gathered his or her own supply. Women who prepared a large pot of kawi frequently gave portions to kin, especially those called "mothers," "aunts," and "sisters" (Shapiro, 1968: 3). Men who returned from hunting or fishing generally distributed portions to kinsmen and friends as in the past.

Food taboos still functioned in 1965, but in an attenuated form. In 1953 and 1957 women would not eat beef since it was equated with deer, much to the consternation of the administrator of the Indian post, who occasionally killed a steer to distribute to the Tapirapé. By 1965, most people ate beef except one or two older women. At that time, two male informants gave me a list of meat taboos. They did not agree with one another nor did they agree with those which were listed in 1939-40. Both informants listed fewer meats as taboo to females and men with small children. Both the pirarucu and the pirarara which which were taboo in 1940, and prohibited to females, were being eaten by all sectors of the population. Wild ducks and   79 geese were no longer dangerous to children. Yet men who were the fathers of small children continued to bring jacu and other wild fowl as gifts to us because they could not be consumed by their families.

Since 1939-40, however, the Tapirapé have experienced a drastic shift in ecology which has improved their access to food supply, particularly proteins. It must be remembered that in 1939-40 the Tapirapé lived far from the river. They were "foot Indians" and most of them could not swim. They ate fish only for a short period in the dry season. By 1953, to my surprise, I found Tapirapé boys and girls who lived in New Village swimming for hours in the Araguaia River. Some men were by then excellent canoemen. Most people could swim well, though the older people, of whom there were but few, could not. As late as 1965 the Tapirapé did not know how to build dugout canoes, but they owned canoes which they had purchased from their Carajá neighbors. Men fished as they had in the past, along the banks of the rivers and lakes with bow and arrow, but now they also fished with hook and line. Where hunting had once provided them with most of their protein needs, now fishing is more important. In much less than a generation they have changed from "foot Indians" to "canoe Indians" (Wagley, 1955).

The Brazilian frontier population along the Araguaia River has grown progressively from 1950 to the present. Not only has the permanent population of frontiersmen increased enormously, but the Araguaia River has attracted commercial traders and even tourist expeditions. Numerous motorboats navigate up and down the Araguaia River carrying trade goods to exchange for animal hides and forest and river products such as dried and salted pirarucu. There is even an elegant, air-conditioned tourist boat that brings Brazilian and foreign tourists on a "Brazilian safari."[40] Every day or two a trading boat stops in the Tapirapé port just inside the Tapirapé River from the Araguaia. The Tapirapé have pelts to trade, and *regatoes* ("ambulatory traders") make their port a regular stop. Furthermore, in distant airports and curio shops Indian artifacts have become readily saleable items, so the traders seek Carajá dolls, decorated Tapirapé bows and arrows, and, particularly, Tapirapé masks made of wood which they call *cara grande* ("big faces") and the Tapirapé call upé. There are even traders who collect for European, Canadian, and American museums. The Tapirapé now have not only the forest products such as

---

80   40. In 1966, Judith Shapiro met John dos Passos in the Tapirapé village.

pelts available (they carefully skin the wild pigs), they also produce Indian artifacts for sale.

The Tapirapé had no basis in their aboriginal culture for commercial exchange. Formerly, exchange was in the form of gifts to kinsmen or friends or by demands at the kawió ceremony. Generally, food was not equated with personal property and they little understood how to buy or sell foods. Yet when I visited New Village in 1953 several men had Brazilian currency. They understood that it was valuable, like macaw feathers, but no one knew the value of the different bills of Brazilian paper currency. Even an illiterate frontiersman can count and can recognize the different denominations of currency, but the Tapirapé language only has numerals up to five—ten is two hands, twenty is two hands and two feet, and more than that is simply *wetepe* (like the hairs on your head). The Brazilian paper currency circulating at the time was in 50's, 100's, 500's, and 1000's, since there was the usual formidable Brazilian inflation in progress. But I doubt that the Tapirapé were cheated too often, for the Little Sisters of Jesus were present at most exchanges which involved money.

When I returned in 1957, several men had become adept at recognizing the value of money. Three bright young men, although illiterate, showed me their wealth (no more than the equivalent of $10 to $15 each) and correctly counted it; but three somewhat older men, including Opronunchwi, who had spent considerable time with Brazilians, had no idea of the value of the bills they kept in their baskets. But by 1965, most Tapirapé were quite aware of the value of money (again, except for the older people). They estimated what a mask would bring from a trader and they knew the price in money of manioc flour. By this time food and privately owned objects had been integrated into the same economic system. My wife and I paid "rent" to a Tapirapé family for the house we lived in. The daughter of a village headman (Cantidio) washed clothes for us and did other household chores for wages, although in both cases there was an element of a favor involved. But definitely, the Tapirapé had become a part of the monetary economy of the Brazilian nation.

It has been a short and abrupt road from an isolated tribal economic system into the modern world. By 1965, the Tapirapé had many more objects of material culture. Most men owned .22-calibre rifles. People owned and generally wore clothes. They also owned cast iron pots and aluminum pans. The variety of material objects had multiplied several times over. And yet their concept of individual private property   81 remained, for it was strangely consistent with the modern capitalistic world. As late as 1967, Judith Shapiro (1968: 15) listed, as an example of the individualization of property, the ownership of chickens in two households. In one there were seven chickens: two were the property of the household head; another two belonged to his wife; and each child (aged one, three, and five) owned one. In another household, the division was: son (2 years), 1 rooster; son (8 years), 1 rooster; daughter (13 years), 3 roosters and 1 hen; son (17 years), 1 rooster; son-in-law (*c.* 25 years), 2 roosters, and the adult woman, 1 rooster.

The Tapirapé still borrow other's personal belongings with great ease. In 1965 my wife was surprised when they borrowed her comb and hairbrush. One village leader, Cantidio, would walk into my house, take my shotgun from its case, ask for shells, and then walk off to his garden. If he did not return the gun that night I would go to his house the next day to retrieve it. Neighboring Brazilian frontiersmen have difficulty understanding the habits which the Tapirapé have retained from the past.

The Tapirapé can cope with the frontier Brazilian society, which they face every day, but they are hardly adjusted to it. They can cope with the new economic system perhaps because the Little Sisters are present. The Sisters give them support indirectly, not by intervening in relations between the Tapirapé and the western world, but by just being present. They also discuss with the Tapirapé their economic plans, which, after all, are the Little Sisters' as well, since they must live like the Tapirapé. In one sense, the Tapirapé are today an ethnic group of over one hundred and thirty people. They have a functioning social system, strong cultural identity, and some protection given them by the nuns and FUNAI. In contrast, the caboclo is an illiterate Brazilian without any special protection. In some ways the Tapirapé can confront the encroaching outside world of the frontier better than the unorganized backwoodsman can. But neither the Tapirapé Indians nor the poor caboclo can deal with or even understand the motives of the giant land companies that claim their land and would displace them. Both are being swallowed by an economic system which neither can comprehend.

Social Organization ⁴

I n 1900 the Tapirapé were a socio-cultural system made up of five villages. They formed a "people" rather than a politically organized "tribe." There was no tribal organization—no chieftain, no council, nor any other political organization which might have made possible any decision or action on a tribal basis. The five Tapirapé villages formed a people in the sense that they shared a common language, common institutions, and common cultural patterns distinct from other groups such as the Carajá and Kayapó. They were also united by the fact that the Tapirapé villages formed an endogamous unit. Although most people married in their own village, marriage was possible between individuals of different villages, so the villages were linked together by kinship ties. This allowed inter-village migration of individuals and families which further increased such ties between villages. Since each village was divided into the same Feast Groups (*Tantanopao*) and men's Bird Societies (Wuran), there were organized groups which were found in each of the five villages. So, in addition to a common language, a shared culture, and inter-village kinship networks, the various Tapirapé villages contained formal named associations which tied the villages into a single, inter-village socio-cultural system.

The relations between the Tapirapé villages were always essentially peaceful. They were situated at a considerable distance apart from each other, so they did not compete for land or other resources. The only antagonism between villages ever remembered was that commonly held by Tampiitawa toward Moutawa, which was said to have been dominated for a time by a Carajá "Big Man." My informants also mentioned peculiarities of speech among the people of Moutawa. They spoke of differences in minutiae of cultural behavior, the aggressiveness of the people, and their bad manners (i.e. lack of respect for expected behavior in a given situation). Yet when Moutawa broke up as a village, the refugees were readily accepted in Tampiitawa.

Village affiliation and identity must once have been relatively strong, because people retained the memory of the natal villages of their parents and grandparents long after those villages had ceased to exist. It must be remembered that by 1939-40 Tampiitawa was a refugee village containing people who were born in other villages and people whose recent ancestors were natives of other villages. Individuals did not boast about their village of origin, but almost any adult Tapirapé could assign others to the village from which their family came. There was a certain pride shown by those who could claim that their fathers and grandfathers were born in Tampiitawa. Kamairaho, for one, often told me: "I am Tampiitawa. My father and grandfather were Tampiitawa." He would list the names of various people and assign each to their family's village of origin—somewhat like a person of a Bostonian family who was born in New York. He explained that Wantanamu, another village leader whom Kamairaho did not particularly like, was from Moutawa. This fact, it seems, explained Wantanamu's abrasive behavior and obvious dislike for torí visitors. During 1940, after refugees from Chichutawa had joined Tampiitawa, the rather timid behavior of some people was explained to me on the basis that "they have never seen torí before. People of Chichutawa have always been frightened of torí." Of course, many young people were of mixed village origin. Ipawungí (a man about twenty-five years old) was one such: his father came from Chichutawa, but his mother was from Tampiitawa. By 1965 practically no one living in New Village could be labeled as a native of any particular village; everyone had recent ancestors from different villages, but almost everyone had been born in Tampiitawa. Yet the memory of the native village of their parents and grandparents was not entirely forgotten. Despite their assigning of people to various villages, neither in 1939-40 nor later in New Village was there any factionalism deriving from such village identity. Far more basic than village affiliation was being a Tapirapé.

When there were several villages, visits from one village to another did take place from time to time, but they were not frequent because of the distance from one to the other. Families from one village sometimes visited other villages. Both men and women would find kinsmen and the men would have anchiwawa. Men who came alone on a visit were always housed in the takana and they could always find female relatives to provide them with food. Young men sometimes visited other villages seeking a wife, especially when girls of the appropriate age and kinship were not available in their home village. The existence of several villages also provided a much needed escape valve for pent-up frustrations and irritations. Living as they did in small villages, people became bored, irritated with one another, and often were suspicious that a shaman was practicing sorcery against them. When that irritation became unbearable, then an individual, a nuclear family, or even an extended family would migrate to another village, either for a visit or with the intention of living there permanently. The importance of this escape valve was brought home to me in 1940, when only one village remained. Time after time, Tapirapé men, even families, would come to me announcing that when I left they would go with me to live with torí, because the "people of Tampiitawa are no good." As depopulation took place, the remaining Tapirapé felt caught in a limited world from which there was no escape.

Each Tapirapé village conformed to a culturally determined, physical plan (see Map 3). The village was always built in a clearing in the forest near lands suitable for gardens and near a small stream that furnished water for drinking, bathing, and soaking manioc. The central structure of the village was the enormous takana. The takana which Baldus saw in Tampiitawa in 1935 was over 30 meters long and almost 7.5 meters wide (1970: 141). It had the form of a large, elongated, over-turned bowl. It was made of a framework of wooden poles and bamboo lashed together with strips of bark from the *embira* tree and covered with palm fronds and the leaves of the wild banana. There were four doors. The takana which existed in 1939-40 in Tampiitawa was slightly smaller but almost identical to that described by Baldus. I will discuss the use of the takana later. For the moment it is enough to say that it was the central structure of any Tapirapé village, and the meeting place of the men's Bird Societies.

85

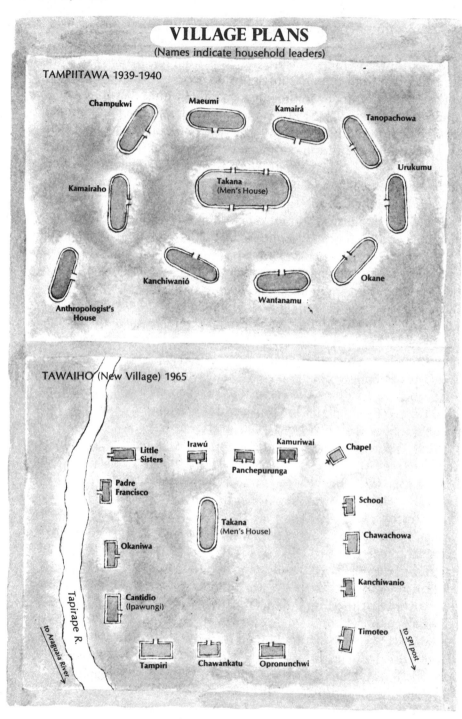

VILLAGE PLANS

(Names indicate household leaders)

TAMPIITAWA 1939-1940

- Champukwi
- Maeumi
- Kamairá
- Tanopachowa
- Urukumu
- Kamairaho
- Takana (Men's House)
- Kanchiwanió
- Wantanamu
- Okane
- Anthropologist's House

TAWAIHO (New Village) 1965

- Little Sisters
- Irawú
- Kamuriwaí
- Chapel
- Panchepurunga
- Padre Francisco
- School
- Takana (Men's House)
- Chawachowa
- Okaniwa
- Kanchiwanio
- Cantidio (Ipawungi)
- Timoteo
- Tampiri
- Chawankatu
- Opronunchwi

Tapirape R.

to Araguaia River

to SPI post

Around the takana were the family dwellings, the longhouses, placed in a circle. In 1935, when Baldus (1970: 141) visited Tampiitawa, there were eight family dwellings in the village circle. In 1939-40, there were nine. They were constructed essentially like the takana, yet were always smaller and with only one door. These houses were not dwellings for a single nuclear family, but rather multifamily longhouses containing from three to eight nuclear families. They were, therefore, never of the same size—one or two were 20 meters long and 5 meters wide, but others were smaller. The area within the circle of houses, which we might call the plaza, was kept clean of vegetation and often the ground was swept. In 1935, Baldus reported that a few tree trunks had been left in the plaza—they served as a place to sit and were also often used for firewood. In 1939-40 the plaza was clean of tree trunks, but some grass had been allowed to grow in front of the less well-kept longhouses. There seems not to have been any specific directional orientation of the takana or the longhouses. The village plan of 1935 (Baldus, 1970: 141) and that of 1939-40 did not conform to any north-south or east-west orientation. Nor did informants speak of any traditional orientation of family dwellings or of the takana.

The interior of a traditional Tapirapé longhouse seemed at first to be utter chaos: hammocks crisscrossed, and cooking pots and other personal belongings hung on the walls and were suspended from rafters. Children, adults, dogs, and chickens seemed to mill about. The house had no partitions. However, that apparent chaos took on some order as one observed more closely. Each nuclear family had its own area in the longhouse. Their hammocks were hung in such a manner that they formed a triangular or square area, in the center of which was the family hearth. There they cooked separately from other nuclear families of the same large household. Each hearth was formed by several stones on the floor, and within each a fire was kept going continuously. A man and wife often shared the same hammock. Sometimes each spouse had a separate one, but more often they shared their hammock, along with an infant or small child. Children of three or four and older generally had their own hammocks. Around their hammocks, hanging from walls and from the roof in baskets, gourds, bamboo containers, and sacks, were the personal belongings of the family. Cords made of embira fiber were stretched between rafters near the roof like a clothesline, and on them ears of dried corn and green bananas were hung. Along the walls the men's bows and arrows were 87 hung on pegs, and occasionally there was a club hanging by its handle.

The floor of the Tapirapé house was built up slightly above the surrounding ground and there was a trench to carry off rainwater from around the house. The floor was made of beaten gray clay. At intervals there were mounds in the house floor. They marked the graves of recently deceased occupants, for until the 1950's the Tapirapé buried their dead in the floor of their longhouse, just underneath the area where they had slept.

In 1935, and in 1939-40, Tapirapé households were plagued with cockroaches, not the large tropical waterbugs, but the ubiquitous urban species, which plagues city dwellings all over the world and which the Tapirapé called *anawe*. How they reached the village no one knows. Perhaps they came as eggs in some traveler's knapsack, or perhaps some wandering Indian visiting some distant community returned with a few. In any case, this plague seems to have been unknown in the Brazilian settlements and in the Carajá Indian villages of the Araguaia River, and it was limited to Tampiitawa. They descended at night from the roof to the floor, consuming anything edible in their path—including the oil on my boots, camera cases, the shellac on book covers, and wax candles (which might be consumed in one night). The anawe made sleeping in a Tapirapé house uncomfortable, to say the least. They would crawl down one's hammock strings and attack any open sore until it was infected, causing the infection to spread. After the first nights in Tampiitawa, I always slept in a mosquito net, not so much to escape mosquitoes but as protection against the anawe. At morning's light they would return to the thatched roofs, to return in droves only in the dark.

The Tapirapé moved the site of their villages and built new houses each five to seven years not only in order to seek new garden areas, but also because the number of graves in the house floors were many and the anawe were unbearably numerous. Of course, the people carried with them eggs in their gourds, hammocks, and other belongings, and in a short time the anawe plagued them again. When I returned in 1953 to New Village, the anawe had miraculously disappeared, and Baldus does not mention them in his 1947 report. The DDT which Valentim Gomes introduced among the Tapirapé—and the burning of the longhouses and takana by Kayapó attackers in 1947—must have freed the Tapirapé of that terrible plague.

88   Although I could reproduce the scene from my field notebooks and

from memory, I cannot improve upon Herbert Baldus's graphic description of a night he spent in a Tapirapé longhouse:

Chickens which roost at night on top of the house stir without stopping, and from all sides comes the constant noise of the uncountable cockroaches. Hens, even fryers and chicks, accustomed since they were small, have become "night birds" spending the whole night eating cockroaches to the light of the house fires. The movement of the hammocks makes the rafters creak. The smoke from the fire is not enough to protect the nude body from mosquitoes. For this reason, the Tapirapé stretched out in their hammocks swing themselves constantly using an arm or leg to pull on a rope or now and again giving a push from the floor with a leg. They swing until they go to sleep. Now and again, a dog wakes up and lazily walks about the house looking for some gastronomical possibilities. But the large pots of *kauí* [kawi] are well closed and other food is suspended well beyond their reach. It opens its mouth, yawns, then urinates on a house upright and returns to its place near the fire. Now and again a flame illuminates the house and everyone and everything stirs and makes a noise. Despite the noise the people are not upset, for they soon cease to converse. In general, two or three hours after sunset no one talks except those who, about midnight, enter the house after dancing or feel cold while sleeping in the men's house. These talk in a loud voice, awakening others, and conversation becomes animated for a while. I spent a long time stretched in my hammock without being able to sleep. It was not possible, because of the smoke and lack of space in the house, to hang my mosquito net. Thus, I pulled my woolen blanket over my head and when I was almost suffocated and covered with sweat, I delivered myself again to the mosquitoes and the smoke. This I repeated an unknown number of times. The cockroaches which visited me now provoked no reaction from me. Several times, my shirt, which I used as a pillow, fell onto the grave which was separated from me by a meter and a half of air and earth, since the body lies as an inhabitant of the house. After having rescued it, and shaken out the dust, I tried not to think of the human saliva, the dog piss and the chicken excrement it might contain and I placed it back underneath my head. During these movements, I had to take care to prevent my revolver and flashlight, which were in my hammock as a defense of Tampiitawa against a possible night raid of the Kayapó, from falling to the floor. All of a sudden, a roar reached my ears. The noise came from my neighbors, the two *pajés* [panchés] Kamairaho and Urukumu, who are often consulted at night. Violent belches and other noises relating to vomiting are part of the therapy they use. My hammock was hung not far from the house door and each 15 minutes or so a pair of dancers appeared, singing and beating time with resounding stamps of the feet. Also, the other inhabitants were not able to sleep through the night. After midnight it becomes cold.[41] So an Indian takes a burning piece of firewood from the fire near his side and places it under his hammock. A young boy sleeps curved in a hammock which is too small for him. He does not have a mother to make him another, larger one. His long lip plug of bone from the Emu sticks up in the air. All of a sudden the boy groans in his sleep; the mosquitoes and the cold have disturbed him, and he gets up full of sleep to squat near the fire which is now almost dead and blows on it to bring flame. Finished, he sits again in his hammock rubbing one foot against the other to rid himself of the gray dust from the floor, and he lies back, swings himself, and sighs: 'Ai! Mosquitoes!!' As the pale morning light penetrates the door, everyone awakens. First the women get up, blowing up the fires and placing their pots over them. They look for their cotton and spindle and sit next to their husbands, who remain stretched in their hammocks; they spin cord for a while. Then they look for some bananas for a morning meal and stir their pots. Then the men get up, and so, little by little, all of the household becomes alive." (Baldus 1970: 149; translation mine.)

On the other hand, here is a daytime scene of a Tapirapé household, taken from my notebooks. One afternoon in 1940, while I was pretending to doze in a borrowed hammock inside a Tapirapé longhouse, I took notes on the activities of one family over a period of about two hours. Only six people were then at home; the other families were away harvesting manioc tubers to make flour. The family consisted of Ikoriwantori; his wife, Tankaí; and their three children— a daughter about 18 months old, a boy about 5 years old, and a girl about 8 years old. In addition, Tankaí's mother, who was about forty-five, was present. It was a hot and sleepy afternoon. I quote from my field notes, taken as the scene unrolled:

The mother lies in a large hammock with her baby daughter in her arms. Ikoriwantori sits on a bench near by weaving a basket. The small boy lies in another hammock with his older sister. The boy leans out of the hammock drinking kawi from a pot just underneath him with a shell used as a spoon. Mother gets up and asks the father

---

41. The nights in the dry season are uncomfortably "cold," with quick temperature drops due to the condensation in the forest.

to take the baby. He stops working on his basket and lies down in the hammock with the baby, which seems to fall asleep at once. The mother goes to work cleaning a *jabuti* (land tortoise), taking the meat out of the shell and cutting it into pieces. The older woman comes to ask for the liver, which she is given. She moves across the house to her area and fans the fire near her hammock. Then, she takes a small basket of manioc flour from the wall and lies down. She then slowly roasts the jabuti liver over the fire and eats as she rests in her hammock. She asks her young granddaughter to bring her a knife to cut the liver into smaller pieces.

There are two dogs and three small puppies asleep on the floor near Ikoriwantori's hammock. Chickens wander in and out of the house. Hanging on the wall near his hammock are five gourds, a bow and five arrows, a bushknife, a hunting knife, and a tin can (which I have given him). Two baskets and three cloth sacks hang from the rafters above his hammock.

One of the dogs wanders near the older woman who is eating. She hits the dog with the blade of her knife and it yelps. The small boy says that he is going to sleep but his sister starts teasing him by pulling his toes. He laughs. The older woman asks the girl to come fetch the knife for her mother; instead of returning the knife to her mother, the girl hands it to her brother to play with. The father finally comes to take the knife. The baby is asleep alone in the hammock but the small boy soon begins to make animal cries (imitating the sound of masked dancers) and the baby wakes up. The sister stretches out again with her brother in the hammock but now she hits him to make him shut up. He kicks her and they begin to wrestle in the hammock; neither is angry but the father tells them to stop. The mother squats before the fire where she is boiling jabuti meat for the evening meal. From time to time, she fans the fire with a fan made of palm fronds. Then, she goes to work on wrist-string ornaments for the baby, holding her ball of string with her toes. She stops work to throw a stick at one of the dogs which approaches her pot.

The small boy seems to suddenly remember the observer. He comes across the house and without a word climbs into the hammock with him. He wants to play and writing is not easy now.

The mother goes to fetch the baby and she hands her husband a small basket of manioc flour. Without rising from the hammock, he begins to eat, plucking jabuti meat out of the boiling pot with his fingers and dropping it into the manioc flour before he eats. Two dogs gather around him but he hits them with the flat of his hand. Soon, he gets up to get more manioc flour from one of the sacks hanging from the rafters. The small boy asks for a piece of meat and the

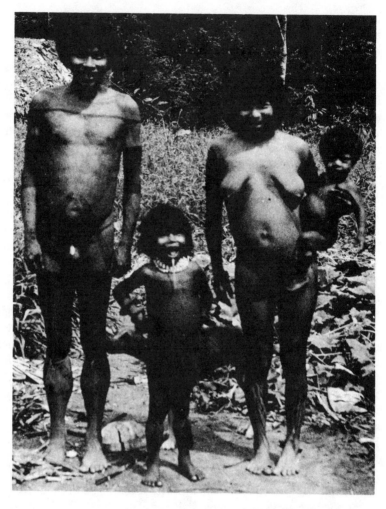

A Tapirapé family in 1939.

father gives him a piece and a handful of manioc flour. The boy begins to play again with the cooking knife. The older woman complains that the boy will hurt himself but no one pays attention. After Ikoriwantori has finished eating, he asks his son for the knife to cut tobacco for his pipe (a short tubular pipe carved out of wood). He holds his pipe between his toes while he cuts tobacco. The mother continues to work on the string ornaments; evidently neither she nor her daughter are hungry as yet. The father blows smoke over his body to relieve fatigue (he worked clearing the garden this morning). Then, he begins to work again on his basket. The small boy becomes bored with the observer who is quiet and does not want to play. He wanders out of the house perhaps to find a playmate. The older woman complains to the observer that she has fever and insists that he go fetch her some medicine [aspirin]. The noise of voices of those returning from the gardens can be heard, so everyone including the observer goes to the door to see people file into the village with their loads of manioc tubers. It is rare that one finds so few people in a household. The tempo of life is slow and relaxed, but there is always movement and always conversation.

In 1939-40, the Tapirapé were able to describe for me the composition of a household as it should have been around 1900, when their population was larger. Of course, this may have been an abstract model in their minds—an "ideal pattern" which they aspired to but which may never have existed in reality. Neither my own observations of 1939-40 nor those which Baldus collected a few years earlier indicate that households actually conformed to this ideal model. In fact, Baldus doubts (1970: 309) that the ideal pattern ever existed. Nevertheless, the Tapirapé described clearly for me how a multi-family household ought to be composed, and there are many indications in my notes that they do try to achieve this model.

Ideally, a Tapirapé household consisted of a group of related females of two to three generations, their spouses, and their children. The Tapirapé were strictly monogamous. Neither Baldus's data nor my own provide any indication of plural spouses. My Tapirapé informants insisted that this had always been true. In anthropological terms, the household consisted of a matrilocal extended family. Residence after marriage was matri- or uxori-local; that is, the husband came to reside with his wife's kin. The women of such a household were thus daughters, sisters, cousins (equated with sisters), mothers, and maternal aunts (equated with mothers). The men living in the household were often not close kinsmen, but they stood in the relationship of son-in-law to the elder males and females and in the relationship of brother-in-law to men of their own generation. Although the core of a household was formed by a group of matrilineally related females, the household head was a male. He was generally a man of forty years of age or more and married to an older female. He stood out as a leader for other reasons, too, for he was also a shaman, a famous singer and leader of a Bird Society, or had other leadership characteristics.

Ideally, the related females of a household cooperated daily in wom- 93 en's tasks, such as carrying drinking water and firewood, harvesting women's crops, carrying heavy loads of manioc tubers from the gardens, and especially preparing manioc flour—an arduous and time-consuming task. And, equally ideally, there was a strong feeling of solidarity among those females.

The men of the household were "outsiders," related to one another affinally as fathers-in-law, sons-in-law, or brothers-in-law. But there was a pattern of etiquette according to which a son-in-law should "avoid" both his father-in-law and mother-in-law. He should not look at them directly and should never address them directly. He should speak to them through others: for example, he might say to his wife within the hearing of her mother, "Perhaps your mother would crochet wrist ornaments for our son." And the mother would reply via her daughter. Actually, that rule of etiquette was hard to carry out, especially under the crowded conditions of the Tapirapé longhouse, which afforded little or no privacy. People readily admit that in-law avoidance was more often honored in the breach.[42]

Brothers-in-law, therefore, were supposed to have solidarity among themselves. In fact, that relationship was one of the strongest and most respectful in Tapirapé society. Brothers-in-law should make gifts to one another, offering each other meat from the hunt or arrows which one has made. Brothers-in-law should not joke in front of one another; that is, they should not tell ribald stories nor boast of their sexual conquests. Often, when a man was relating a tidbit of village gossip to me and others, another man would abruptly take his leave. "It is his brother-in-law speaking" would be the explanation. And brothers-in-law should cooperate in work. Although economic cooperation, when it occurs in Tapirapé society, is generally organized by the Bird Societies, there are occasions, such as building a house or repairing the roof or walls of the residence, when affinally related males work together.

This ideal model of a Tapirapé household may never have existed in fact, for it is well known that people do not act as they think they ought to act, and real societies do not conform to their abstract models of society. Herbert Baldus states that after "analyzing the eight households which in 1935 surrounded the takana I must repeat that

---

42. However, a young Carajá traveling with me said that he was not eager to end our trip and return home. He was only recently married and he told me that he suffered intense embarrassment when confronted by his in-laws. His young wife brought him his meals to a lonely spot down the beach so that he could eat out of sight of her parents. Only when he became the father of a child would he feel more at ease in front of them.

my data does not allow me to speak of the existence of matrilocality or patrilocality among the Tapirapé despite the repeated statements by Wagley as to matrilocality in that tribe" (1970: 309-10). Neither in 1935 nor in 1946 could Baldus find evidence of the matrilocal extended family as described above (see Baldus, 1970: 154-55).[43] In 1939, when I first visited the Tapirapé, only four out of seven households even approximated the model described to me as the ideal. Those four households were led by important men—Kamairaho, Wantanamu, Kamairá, and Urukumu. Also, theirs were the largest households, containing 25, 20, 19 and 18 people out of a total of 147. A strong and prestigious man was able to maintain his hold over his wife's sisters and "daughters," thus building his household as far as possible in the image of the ideal model. Other households combined a variety of kin—such as (1) two brothers and their wives and children, a married daughter of one of the brothers and her husband; (2) a man and wife, their married daughter, husband, and children, and their married son, wife, and child; and (3) a man, his wife and children, two young men whom he called "sister's son," their wives, and children. These "irregular" households tended to contain smaller numbers of people than those of important household leaders. They also seemed more fluid in membership. During my residence in 1939-40, several couples from these smaller houses changed their residence, moving in with other relatives.

There were several extenuating circumstances which accounted for this deviation from the rule of matrilocality even in 1935 and in 1939-40. By that time the Tapirapé had already suffered severe depopulation, not so much from direct contact with the outside world as from indirectly acquired diseases. All but two villages had disappeared, and one of those remaining was reduced to a handful of people. There were simply not enough people to realize the ideal model, yet the ideal way that a household should be composed and the way the people of a household ought to behave toward one another was clear in their minds.

Another extenuating circumstance derives from the nature of the Tapirapé kinship system and kinship terminology. As among so many societies of the world, the Tapirapé kinship system and terminology

---

43. **Baldus's** carefully annotated data concerning household composition is rather confusing. Approximately the same individuals were present in 1935 and in 1939-40, but they were slightly differently distributed by household. Baldus often attributed actual biological relationships to individuals who were in fact sociological kin (Baldus, 1970: 154). His demographic data, however, is precise and firm.

differed strikingly from our own and was highly classificatory. Their system has been labeled "bifurcate generational." It resembled the Iroquois system of kinship terminology, in that maternal aunts (mother's sisters) tended to be classified with the mother and paternal uncles (father's brothers) tended to be classified with the father. Also, and again like the Iroquois system, brother's children from a male point of view were classified with one's own children, and females equated the children of those whom they called sister with their own children. There were distinct terms for mother's brother (maternal uncle) and for father's sister (paternal aunt). Likewise, a male used distinct terms for his sister's son and daughter, and a female used distinct terms for brother's son and daughters. However, the classification of kin on one's own generation Tapirapé nomenclature departed from the Iroquois system, or "bifurcate merging" terminology. All those to whom a person could trace kinship were called siblings; thus the terms for brother and sister were the same as those for all male and female cousins. However, women had distinct terms for "older sister" (and older female cousins) and for "younger sister" (and younger female cousins), but they used only one term for all brothers (and male cousins) irrespective of whether they were older or younger. Likewise, men had terms for "older brothers" and "younger brothers," but only one term for all sisters. This generational grouping of siblings and all cousins is characteristic of the Hawaiian kinship system.[44] Finally, there were but two terms used by both males and females for any relative two generations above ego (the person speaking), namely *cheramuya* ("grandfather") and *chanuya* ("grandmother").[45] And for grandchildren there was but one term which a man used (*cheremamino*) and another term which a woman used (*cheremianiro*)— each word being used for both male and female children.

In addition, there were often multiple terms for some relatives, one descriptive or referential (i.e. one used when describing or referring to a relative) and another vocative (i.e. one used in speaking directly to that relative). For example, a person referred to his mother as cheu, but used the term ampí when addressing her; he referred to his father as cherowa, but addressed him as cheropu. The Tapirapé language also has a suffix ('-tehé') which, added to a kinship term, means distant

---

44. It may amuse the non-anthropological reader to learn that our own system of kinship terminology is labeled "Eskimo type" by anthropologists.

45. The first phoneme ('che') used in kinship terms represents the first person possessive —"my."

kin; thus, cherowa ("my father") can become cherowa-tehé ("my distant father," or "classificatory brother of my father").[46] Furthermore, there was a common use of the diminutive suffixes in both referential and vocative kinship terms. Thus, men called their mother's sister cheu uraní (cheu, "my mother"; uraní, "little," or "diminutive") while women called their father's brother cheropuí (cheropu, "my father"; -í, "little," or "diminutive"; literally, "little father").

A complete list of such terms may be found in Appendix I. However, the important point to emphasize here is the enormous possibility to extend one's kinship network which this system provides. With it all the people of the community might, if they wish, call everyone else by a kinship term. And more often than not an individual might call another by more than one term, if genealogies were carefully analyzed.

The Tapirapé, however, had short genealogical memories. In recording genealogies of individuals no one could remember the personal names of relatives further back than their grandparents, and even then it was difficult to be certain whether the individual referred to was a biological grandparent or a classificatory one. Generally, a simple method was used to decide what kinship term to use for another individual. In 1939-40, after I had lived with the Tapirapé for a time, Kamairaho, the important household leader, decided arbitrarily to call me cheriwura ("younger brother"). Thus he became my older brother (cherikeura). In turn, those people whom he called "brother," "sister," "son," "daughter," "sister's son," "grandson," and "granddaughter" became the same for me. In this manner I became established in a widespread kinship network. As in the case for any individ-

---

46. On this point, my notes taken in 1939-40 differ from Judith Shapiro's observations of 1966 (Shapiro, 1968a: 10-11). Shapiro translates tehé in the opposite way, namely to mean "close." She writes:

> "Degree of relationship is distinguished by means of a suffix, -tehé or -te which is added to sibling-cousin terms and to terms for relatives on other generational levels as well. This suffix is used only in reference. It can best be translated as meaning "close" and is used in other contexts as an intensifier; for example, one may suffix to a verb for "walk" or "hike" to indicate that one had walked "walked hard" (rapidly and for a long distance). It is difficult to establish the exact meaning of -tehé in kinship usage since the influence of neo-Brazilian kin categories was evident in many informant responses. My own impression is that "closeness" is meant in a strictly genealogical sense."

I cannot resolve this difference, for I always felt most insecure in my understanding of the Tapirapé language. However, it is clear that the suffix '-tehé' (whether genealogically "close" or "distant") was used in reference to kin to distinguish siblings of the same mother and cousins of the first degree from other kinsmen.

ual Tapirapé, I found that I had a choice of terms for many people. For example, Champukwi might have been recognized by me as "younger brother," but he was married to a woman I might call "sister"; so we called each other "brother-in-law," which gave him somewhat stronger rights over any favors I might extend. Later, when Champukwi's son was born, I became the child's "mother's brother," an even stronger tie. There were, however, people in the community whom it was convenient to ignore as kinsmen. Anawani, who was known to be both lazy and ugly, was most often referred to simply by his personal name; but people generally made a point of calling Kamairá, who was strong, hard-working, and generally admired, by a kin term. While a member of the community, I tried to use personal names when referring to or speaking to my fellow villagers, because, with a hoard of salt and other trade goods, I was vulnerable to the demands of so many relatives.

One can see at once how this system of recognizing kin might influence the composition of a household. Given the fact of depopulation by 1935 and 1939-40, people had few "real" sisters and brothers. It was common for adults to adopt male and female orphans and to give them kinship status. Thus, Kamairaho, who was probably sterile,[47] had many "children" and among them many "daughters." It was not difficult for him to organize a household in which most women could call each other "sister" and whom he could call "daughter" ("wife's sister's daughter"). It was not biological kinship which drew these people together into a longhouse, but Kamairaho's prestige as a leader. Thus, by 1935 and 1939-40, when the Tapirapé were most intensively studied, neither matrilineages nor a true matrilocal extended family did in fact exist. Yet, with the model of the matrilocal household in their minds, they were able to create households that were analogous to the abstract cultural concept.

It must be further stressed that important roles of expected behavior were attached to kinship status. A mother's brother was to be especially protective of his sister's son. One would have a warm but joking relation with a "grandfather" or "grandmother." When the carcasses of wild pigs were divided after a hunt, a man would send the entrails (a choice bit) to his elder brother; a shank to his sister, for

---

47. This judgment is based upon the fact that none of the women for whom he had exclusive sexual rights from 1935 to 1940 became pregnant. Yet one of these women, abandoned by Kamairaho, soon conceived after cohabiting with other men.

"my sister's son to eat"; a leg-bone to his "grandmother," so that "she will not go hungry." And, more important, it was a group of men who considered themselves "brothers" who would unite to execute an evil shaman in revenge for the death of a relative; just as important, a man with a growing reputation as a shaman depended upon a strong group of siblings and sister's sons to protect him against the danger of the inevitable criticism and suspicion resulting from his reputed shamanistic powers. The actual fulfillment of these roles *vis-à-vis* one another was generally highly attenuated when the kinship relationship was distant.

Anthropologists have long been interested in the influence of a changing ecology, residence patterns, and property rights on systems of kinship nomenclature and kinship determined behavior. The Tapirapé would seem to be an excellent society for the reexamination of many hypotheses and theories. During more than a half-century they have been subject to rapid social changes and many vicissitudes—severe depopulation, attacks by alien tribes, a change from a forest to a riverine habitat, and an always intensified influence of Brazilian frontier society. During forty years, the Tapirapé have been subject to periodic observations by professional anthropologists. It has been postulated that at one time, long before the ethnographic record begins, the Tapirapé may have had a consistent Iroquois-type system of kinship nomenclature; that is, a system which has distinct terms for cross cousins (mother's brother's children and father's sister's children) and for parallel cousins (father's brother's children and mother's sister's children). If this were so, it is possible that sometime in the past the Tapirapé may have had the preferential marriage rule for marriage with a cross cousin which has been reported for other Tupí-speaking groups (McDonald, 1965; Arnaud, 1963; Shapiro, 1968a). That change, if it did take place, is based upon evidence from other Tupian groups and not upon specific ethnographic data on Tapirapé society. Such a system, however, would seem logical if the Tapirapé did indeed once have truly functioning matrilocal extended families and matrilineages. It would provide the exchange of men, who were the most important providers to the domestic group, between matrilocal extended families, rather than the exchange of women—as so many anthropologists have viewed preferred or prescribed cross cousin marriage (see Levi-Strauss, 1969: 63ff, and others). Yet this fundamental change in the kin terms and the loss of a preferred marriage rule must remain in the realm of conjecture.

On the other hand, some changes have occurred in kinship nomenclature and usage since 1935. These were studied by Judith Shapiro during her visits in 1966 and 1967 (1968a). Her data indicates a strong tendency (which I believe began before 1939-40) for the kinship terms on the generation level of one's parents to shift from a bifurcate merging system to a bifurcate collateral one. Thus, a male most often calls his mother's sister not ampí ("mother"), but cheu uraní ("my mother's little sister") and he calls his father's brother not *cheropu* ("father"), but *cherowuraní* ("my father's little brother"). Women call their father's brother *cheropuí* ("little father") and their mother's sister either ampí or *cheu uraní* ("my mother's sister"). In the generation below ego, the bifurcate merging terminology remains unchanged, but Shapiro reports a strong trend to use personal names or age status terms, such as *chekonomi* ("my little boy"), rather than kin terms. She notes that the terms used by women have suffered less change than those used by men. These changes in kinship terminology in at least the first ascending generation indicate emphasis on a lineal principle, that is, the terms for "mother" and "father" are to be used only for specific parents in one's line of descent. This change, along with the decline of the matrilocal extended family, "is connected with the emergence of the nuclear family as the most stable kin unit" (Shapiro, 1968a: 22) in Tapirapé society.

The change from a multi-family to a nuclear family household has been noted by all visitors to the Tapirapé since 1939-40. Households have become progressively smaller in size. The traditional longhouse inhabited by five, six, or even seven nuclear families no longer exists. When I first visited New Village at the mouth of the Araguaia River in 1953, I noticed that residence units were smaller and that some Tapirapé had built their house with adobe or wattle and daub (*taipa*) walls, in imitation of those of the Brazilian frontiersmen. When I returned in 1957 and 1965 that trend had intensified; and it was also noted by Shapiro in 1966 and 1967 (Shapiro, 1968a). By 1965, several houses were occupied by only one nuclear family (man, wife, and children). Others held but two nuclear families; one or two held as many as three. In 1965 only one household appeared at all like the old longhouse dwelling I had known in 1939-40, and it contained a hodgepodge of refugees. This trend toward nuclear family residential units has modified certain work habits. People tended to undertake certain tasks individually rather than with kinsmen. The clearing of garden sites which was often done by communal work parties in 1939-40 was now almost entirely an individual task.[48] In 1965, housebuilding was a man's own problem, not something undertaken by a group of brothers-in-law. Women cooperated less with sisters in making manioc flour. Seldom, if ever, did men go on a group hunt. The Tapirapé nuclear family had become more isolated and economically independent, similar to our own.

Kinship is not the only principle or category which organized Tapirapé society. In a sense, two sets of associations cross-cut kinship groups and constituted important social units with important functions. The first were the men's Bird Societies, called, generically, Wuran, which have been referred to earlier. The second set of associations, which we may call Feast Groups, were called, generically, Tantanopao (tantan, "fire"; opao, "to eat around"). Each man belonged to a Bird Society, generally that of his father. Everyone—men, women, and children—belonged to a Feast Group. Membership in Feast Groups followed parallel descent; a woman most often belonged to that of her mother and a man to that of his father.

Of the two sets of associations, the Bird Societies had the most important economic and ceremonial functions. The takana, which dominated and was the central edifice of the Tapirapé villages, was the home of these societies. It was also a general clubhouse for men, being limited to their use only. During the day a few men generally lounged there in hammocks, away from the noise of their family dwellings. And there men often gossiped while weaving baskets or manufacturing arrows. Or they might just nap in their hammocks. The takana was also a guest house for men from other villages and for male aliens. I was told that the Kayapó warriors who spent several months in Tampiitawa many years ago slept in the takana. Male torí visitors to Tampiitawa were immediately shown into the takana, where they would be sheltered. The Tapirapé men never spent the night sleeping in the takana unless they were quarreling with their wives, and they normally returned to the family dwelling to take their meals. For a short period, adolescent boys were expected to sleep in the takana, as I shall explain later, but normally it provided only a gathering place for adult males.[49]

---

48. Shapiro reports a communal work party which took place in 1966 (1968b: 15, n. 2) but she states: "This group activity, which involved the felling of large trees, seems to have been performed on my behalf, the Tapirapé being extremely obliging to ethnographers."

49. The takana was always an excellent place for the male anthropologist to gather information, and I spent considerable time there during my residence with the Tapirapé.

A Tapirapé man weaving a basket of buriti palm fiber in the takana in 1940.

More formally, the takana housed and was the center of the activities of the Bird Societies. There were six Bird Societies divided into unnamed ceremonial moieties—three in each moiety. Furthermore, the three societies in each moiety formed age grades. Thus, there were pairs of Bird Societies—a pair of young boys' societies, a pair of mature males' societies, and a pair of older men's societies. Although the moieties were unnamed, the name of each society clearly indicated the

TABLE 3

Bird societies		
White Birds		Parrots
Wuranchinga	(youths; 10-16 years)	Wurankura
Wuranchingió	(mature men; 16-35 years)	Ananchá
Wuranchingó	(older men; 35-55 years)	Tanawe

---

moiety to which it belonged. One set of Bird Societies carried the names of various parrots and the other the names of white aquatic birds. For convenience, I shall refer to the ceremonial moiety divisions of Bird Societies as "White Birds" and "Parrots." The names of the societies and the approximate age of their constituents are given in Table 3.

The exact species of the birds from which the Bird Societies took their names always escaped me, but it was clear that one set referred to aquatic white birds and the other set to parrots of various sizes. Wuranchinga is composed of two morphemes: wuran, "bird"; chinga, "white." Wuranchingió contains the identical morphemes but is qualified by the suffixes -i ("diminutive") and -ó ("augmentative"), which taken together seem to mean, roughly, "middle size." Wuranchingó means, literally, "large white bird." When I pushed for positive identification I was always told: "like the small egret" (Wuranchinga), "like a larger egret" (Wuranchingió), and "like the tall jaburu stork" (Wuranchingó). Likewise, Wurankura was described "like the parakeet," Ananchá "like the talking parrot," and Tanawe "like the macaw." The names of the societies do not correspond with the names used in day-to-day usage for these birds. I cannot say whether the names for the Bird Societies are mythological. In 1939-40 and during my other visits, despite my inquiries, I heard only one myth which accounted for the origin of the Bird Societies and perhaps for their names.

According to the Tapirapé, long ago, in the time of their ancestors, a culture hero named Anchopeterí encountered in his travels a large number of birds gathered together on a large flat rock. They were assembled into six groups, like the Bird Societies into which men are divided today. In one group were the macaws, a large bird called cham- 103 poó, and the large hawks which Anchopeterí called tanawe. There was another group, calledananchá, which included the wild goose, ducks, the vulture, and smaller parrots. And a third included the turtle dove and the parakeets, which Anchopeterí called wurankura. Likewise, he saw the large jaburu stork, tall cranes, the rhea (South American ostrich), and other large birds in a group which he called wuranchingó; another group included the small parrot, two types of hawks which the Tapirapé call champií and tamungó, and others, which he called wuranchingió; and, finally, several small birds, including the small white water birds, which were wuranchinga.[50] Anchopeterí gave those names to the Bird Societies. He heard the birds sing and brought back songs for the Tapirapé men to sing. Anchopeterí saw the birds wrestle and fight by throwing arrows tipped with beeswax at one another. Anchopeterí himself fought with the wild goose and then with the larger jaburu stork, but he escaped to teach the Tapirapé men the songs and the ceremonials he had witnessed.

I have mentioned the fact that membership in a men's society is by patrilineal descent: what this means is that the son enters the unnamed ceremonial moiety to which his father belonged. In 1939-40 Champukwi belonged to Ananchá of the Parrot moiety. His father had been Tanawe and Champukwi had earlier been a Wurankura. Likewise, Awantikantu, a man of about thirty-three years of age, was a member of Wuranchingió because his father had been Wuranchingó. As a youth Awantikantu had been a Wuranchinga. Tampirí, who was a village leader in 1965, was Wuranchingó. When I first knew him in 1939-40, he was Wuranchinga and when I returned in 1957, he was Wuranchingió. At any one time, the largest number of Tapirapé males were either Wuranchingió or Ananchá—that is, members of one of the two mature males' societies. In 1939-40 there were only 5 men who claimed to be Tanawe and only 3 who considered themselves Wuranchingó (members of the older males' societies). Some 15 men identified themselves as Ananchá and 16 as Wuranchingió (mature males) and 9 youths belonged to Wurankura and 10 to Wuranchinga (youth's societies). Life expectancy in 1939-40 (and probably even before) hardly exceeded thirty-five years of age, and there was a shortage of men who would have belonged to the two older age societies.

---

50. Informants insisted that all birds were assembled when Anchopeterí encountered them; but only "our grandfathers" could tell the names of all the birds there and how they were subdivided.

By 1939-40 both the rule of patrilineally inherited membership in a society and strict age groupings of the various societies had been partially disrupted by depopulation. There were a few men who told me that although their fathers had been of the Parrot moiety they had joined the White Bird moiety as youths because of personal preference. And, at least one man, Anawani, of the Parrot society, who was approximately twenty-eight years old, told me that he was Tanawe and was so identified by others. He was known to be lazy and without any skills; thus he had been "promoted," so to speak, to the older society of his moiety despite his age. The Tapirapé found my curiosity about Anawani's membership in Tanawe amusing. Anawani "acts like an old man," they explained. There seems to have been a conscious effort to balance the numerical strength of the societies by 1939-40 so that each might function properly. This was done by sometimes ignoring the patrilineal rule of society membership and, at least in one case, by arbitrarily assigning a younger man to an older men's society.

I am uncertain just when men entered the youngest societies and when they moved into the next older society. When a boy in his early adolescence was described by the age status term as churangí (youth) rather than konomí (boy), he was expected to sleep for a period of several months in the takana.[51] At that time he became active in a youth's age society. This does not coincide with the colorful coming-of-age ceremony at which a youth "ties his hair"—that is, assumes a man's hairdress with a short pigtail bound with cotton string—and after which he may marry. This initiation ceremony (described later) takes place several years after a youth has been frequenting the takana. Some Tapirapé men stated that one becomes a Wuranchingió or Ananchá when one becomes the father of a child. However, my listing of members of these two societies indicated that there were several members of each who were not as yet fathers. Informants explained that when one's son becomes Wuranchingió or Ananchá then one should become Wuranchingó or Tanawe, but among the few members of these older societies of 1939-40, only two had "sons" (i.e. their own son or a brother's son) in the mature males' societies. Again, it seems that movement from one age society into the next took place in a rather arbitrary fashion, perhaps as a result of depopulation. In any case, there are no rites of passage which mark the progression of a male through the various age societies of the men's moieties. My approxi-

---

51. These age status terms and the behavior associated with them are explained in Chapter 5.

mate estimate of the ages of the members of each society in 1939-40 clearly indicates that each society was composed of men within a certain age range with but two or three exceptions. Once again there seems to have been numerical balance in the societies maintained by rather arbitrary means.

Finally, there comes a time in life when old men (marikeura) relinquish membership in Bird Societies. "When they are old and thin and when they have no teeth but must crush their food between two stones, they sit in a house near their relatives. They do not come to the takana anymore." There were no men in 1939-40 who had reached this stage of life, and even in the remote past they must have been rare.

I have said that the takana belongs to the Bird Societies. In fact, the area inside the takana was divided, at least theoretically, among the six societies and this division of the takana reflects clearly the dual division of the societies.[52] One half of the men's house belonged to the White Bird societies and the other half belonged to the Parrot societies. Furthermore, the central portions under the vaulted roof belonged to the two societies of older men, Tanawe and Wuranchingó. The next two sections of the interior space belonged to the two mature men's societies, Ananchá and Wuranchingió. And finally, at the two ends of the men's house, where the roof is low, were the areas assigned to the societies made up of youths, Wurankura and Wuranchinga. The takana had four doors. The two doors on the White Bird side were to be used by its three constituent societies and the two doors on the Parrot side by its three. Each of the two Bird Societies was thought to be responsible for the construction and the repair of their respective portions of the men's house.

In fact, however, when the takana was rebuilt, which it was every year during the rainy season, all of the men in a village seemed to cooperate in the task of repairing the frame and re-roofing, irrespective of either moiety division or age society. There was frequent mild, sometimes joking, recrimination by the men of one society to another regarding the disrepair and unkept condition of their respective areas of the takana. Likewise, all men seemed to make use of any portion of the takana in their daily use of the house without respect to the moiety and age society division. Nor did men take the rule of using the

---

52. Baldus (1970: 320f.) disagrees with me in my interpretation of the Bird Societies organized in unnamed moieties with age-graded societies. He believes them to be a tripartite organization. Shapiro, on the other hand, reaffirms my opinion (1968a: 26).

doors assigned to their moiety division seriously, but used the handiest door to enter and leave. They were amused when I began to use only the doors assigned to the Parrot societies, for I considered myself Ananchá since my "older brother" (Kamairaho) was Tanawe. The division of the men's house by Bird Societies seemed to be important only during ceremonials.

Each of the men's moieties seems to have had a leader who was generally of one of the two mature men's Bird Societies. This did not seem to be a formal office which was either inherited or to which a man was formally elected. Rather, the leader must be, first, a man with a good voice, for he led the singing of his moiety side and he should also be an energetic hunter, for he assumed leadership in the group hunting parties. In 1939-40, Kamairá (the same man who led a group of dissenters to Chichutawa and long isolation from their fellow tribesmen) was the leader of Wuranchingió and Kamanaré was the leader of Ananchá. When Kamanaré died in 1939, Tanopanchowa seemed to assume the leadership of Ananchá. I could not elicit a clear-cut native term for this position, although there must have been a descriptive term in the past. Instead, such a man was referred to as "capitão monika" ("singing captain") and sometimes by a term which translated as "walking captain." As we shall see, even in 1939-40 the question of leadership among the Tapirapé was rather vague, and it remained unresolved by both Baldus and myself.[53]

As I have said, the takana had important ceremonial functions. During different periods throughout the year, a large variety of spirits, or anchunga, came to reside in the takana. There were in Tapirapé ideology a very great variety of anchunga. Most of these were spirits of aquatic and terrestrial animals. Others were spirits of specific enemies (Kayapó and Carajá) whom the Tapirapé had killed in the past in armed skirmishes. These enemy anchunga, each known by a personal name, were owned by specific Tapirapé who had acquired them through inheritance from a male line. The anchunga of fauna were said to be owned by the Wuran groups. The anchunga of the electric eel, the rhea, and the jacamim (a forest fowl) were said to belong to Tanawe. Likewise, the tortoise spirit, the howling monkey spirit, and

---

53. Baldus reports these leaders of the Wuran societies and records the term anta-uwa (1970: 323). Both Baldus (ibid.: 323) and Shapiro (1968a: 20) state that each men's group had a pair of leaders. My notes indicate that there may have been a pair of leaders who led songs and dances, but I have the names of only one leader for each society.

ABOVE: The interior of the takana in 1939-40.
OPPOSITE, ABOVE: Each year the *Wuran* (Bird Societies) repair the takana. This was taken in 1940.
OPPOSITE, BELOW: By 1965 the takana had become a veritable factory where the Tapirapé manufactured masks and artifacts for sale.

the large kururu toad spirit belonged to Wuranchingó. Ananchá owned the mutum spirit, the owl spirit, and many others, and Wuranchingió owned the spirits of the peccary and wild pig. It is amusing that the youth's Bird Societies were considered the owners of the mosquito spirit (Wurankura) and the spirit of cichó, a small minnow (Wuranchinga). Ownership of a specific spirit, however, simply meant that the members of a specific Bird Society were, in a sense, the hosts of that spirit during the time which it spent living in the takana, and they were supposed to construct the masks which represented that spirit.

While a specific anchunga (or set of anchunga, for more than one came to live at the same time) occupied the takana, many of them were represented by a pair of masked dancers—symbolic, no doubt, of the dual organization of the Bird Societies. The costume of the male dancers representing an anchunga followed a general pattern. It con-

sisted of a skirt, a cape, and a head covering made of buriti fiber. The costume covered the whole body of the male dancer—only his feet and hands could be seen. Each specific costume-mask had some distinguishing features. The wild pig spirit mask, for example, could be distinguished by tufts of pig bristle stuck into the headdress and by rattles made of pig hoofs which the dancer wore around his ankles. Other anchunga had feathered decorations on their headdress. Thus, irancha anchunga (the spirit of a fish), which is among those spirits which resided in the takana in the dry season, can be recognized by the tuft of tail feathers of the red macaw on the headdress and the ceremonial bow, highly decorated with red feathers, which each dancer carried.

The masks of upé, representing the spirits of enemies killed in battle, were the most elaborate. Like the others, the costume consisted of a buriti skirt and cape. The mask itself took the form of a giant face. The basis for this was a half-moon shaped face carved from the umbaúba tree (*Cecropia palmata*). Holes were bored into the wood to provide the eyes and the mouth. It was covered with beeswax on which the face was designed with red and yellow breast feathers from the macaw. Mother of pearl stuck into the beeswax formed circles around the eyes and teeth for the mouth. Then, above the face, there was a headdress of two layers of tail feathers—first, the black feathers from the hawk, and then a veritable diadem of the tail feathers of the red macaw. This is the most elaborate festival garment and headdress fabricated by the Tapirapé, and the appearance of the upé anchunga at the beginning of the dry season was a spectacular event. (See Baldus, 1970: 245-46). Such upé masks, which have come to be known along the Araguaia River by the Portuguese name of Cara Grande ("Big Face"), have been eagerly sought by collectors for museums in recent years.[54]

As among so many lowland South American tribes, the men kept it secret from the women that they disguised themselves with costumes and masks and actually impersonated the dancing and singing anchunga. However, unlike other South American tribes, the Tapirapé did not claim that in mythological times this secret was known only to women and unknown to men, that it was used to exploit the men, and that men discovered the women's secret and consequently wrested

---

54. In 1965, such masks were being constructed in large numbers to be sold to collectors of Indian "artifacts." Since their masks represent Kayapó and Carajá enemies, the Tapirapé in 1965 merely whispered their names, for fear of offending the Carajá, who lived near by and who came to witness the dances of the upé. These masks are also called, collectively, *tawa* by the Tapirapé.

it away from them by force (see Murphy and Murphy, 1974: 88-89, for a full transcription of this myth as told in almost "classical" form by the Mundurucu Indians of the Tapajós River in central Brazil). Furthermore, the Tapirapé men had neither trumpets nor the bull roarer, as do other groups who have the men's secret societies. Such groups usually try to impress upon the women that the voice of these instruments represents the voice of the dangerous spirits. Nonetheless, the Tapirapé prohibited women from entering the takana, where they would see the accoutrements of the costumes and masks. And during my various periods of residence with the Tapirapé I never saw a woman step beyond the portals of the takana. Kamairaho, however, told me of women who had looked inside the takana while the men were making anchunga masks. "Their husbands beat them and pulled their hair," he said. The only overt attempt to frighten women occurred during the festivals at the beginning of the dry season called kawió. At that time the anchunga jacakonya, represented by young men wearing buriti skirts and capes with hammocks draped over their heads, attacked younger women with huge penes made of palm fiber. The young women retreated back into the safety of the family dwellings crying shrilly and giving the appearance of being badly frightened.

In fact, the Tapirapé women knew the men's secret, but there was an unstated rule of etiquette that the two sexes did not discuss it. The masked dances were really more performances than a sacred rite to impress or frighten the women. In 1939-40, when I witnessed a variety of masked dancers representing numerous anchunga spirits dance in pairs in the village plaza, the women carried out their roles dancing in a circle around anchunga figures and providing kawi to the spirit dancers when they approached the door of the family dwellings. On the other hand, the women certainly did not stand in awe of the masked dancers. As we stood watching the dancers there were older women who "guessed" in a low voice as to the identity of the men. "That is Champukwi [or another man], I know his voice and his feet," they would whisper to me shyly holding their hands before their mouths. Women also knew what went on and what was stored in the takana. As the dry season progressed and the nights became rather chilly, the men lounging in the takana made use of handfuls of palm fronds torn from the walls to feed their fires. Gradually, the side walls all but disappeared, so any female could look inside. She had a full view of the anchunga masks hanging from the rafters and could see the men lounging and chatting inside. A woman would often come to   *111* the takana's door to call her husband for an early evening meal. When the side walls were dismantled, she could easily see if her husband, son, or brother were inside. In reality, the takana held no mysteries at all for Tapirapé women.[55]

The men's Bird Societies were more than ceremonial organizations. They had fundamental economic functions. During the dry season they sometimes were the basis of organization for communal work parties to clear garden sites. On such occasions, it was generally not the individual Bird Societies which comprised the work party, but all of the able-bodied men. But during the work, members of each moiety would be urged to work by their group leader. They would sing out animal cries characteristic of their own society as they worked. In a sense, the Parrots and the White Birds competed during the apachirú work parties. And afterward, the Bird Societies traditionally danced and raced against one another (Baldus, 1937: 110; 1970: 324). In addition, the Bird Societies organized group hunts, particularly in the rainy season when meat was most scarce. On such hunts, sometimes one moiety (i.e. the Parrots) would remain in the village while the other moiety hunted. Sometimes all Bird Societies participated in a group hunt. But however the hunt was organized, the meat brought back was arranged in six piles, representing the six Bird Societies within the takana, and the men held a communal feast before the rest was finally distributed to the women and children.

Because the men's societies were so fundamental to Tapirapé social organization I was not surprised to find a takana in the center of New Village when I returned for the last time in 1965. In fact, my arrival seemed awkward to me. Since I was accompanied by my wife, I could not be taken directly to the takana, where my baggage normally would have been deposited and where I might hang my hammock to rest

---

55. A Carajá Indian who accompanied me to the Tapirapé New Village in 1953 was horrified at the Tapirapé's conduct. The neighboring Carajá share the men's house and the masked dancers complex with the Tapirapé. In fact, some of the costume masks of the Carajá are identical with those of the Tapirapé and they are symbols of similar spirits. But the Carajá men's secret is strictly kept. Their men's house is set apart at the back of their residences. No woman may walk by the door of the men's house, and she must take a different path than the men when walking from one end of the village to another. A Carajá woman who by chance or out of sheer curiosity learns the secret of the men is subjected to mass rape. From that time, she becomes a "free woman"— similar to a prostitute in our society. She seldom has a steady mate. She offers her sexual services to the young men in return for gifts and sometimes she is taken into the men's house to serve the bachelors sexually. "Now I know why the Tapirapé women are completely nude and without shame," said my Carajá companion. (The Carajá women wear a bark cloth skirt to cover their genitals.) And, when the Tapirapé men heard of this Carajá custom, they exclaimed, "Like dogs!"

after my journey. Instead, my good Tapirapé friends found a family residence for this purpose, for women still did not enter the takana. When I visited the takana the next day, I found it somewhat smaller than those I remembered from times past, and the floor seemed unusually unswept and filled with debris. There were no costumes for masked dancers hanging from the rafters as in the old days. The men assured me, however, that the Bird Societies continued to function. They easily identified themselves with one of the societies or the other. During my visit, upé masks did dance one day in the village plaza. The men told me that when the dry season was under way they planned to make anchunga costumes and to dance, but I left before this took place. In 1966 Judith Shapiro witnessed an apachirú organized by the Bird Societies. It was followed by a communal meal which was then followed by dancing and a race. I quote from her account, which indicates the strength of the Bird Societies despite the vicissitudes which Tapirapé society has suffered in the last half-century:

The communal meals which I witnessed at the conclusion of each day's work were similar to that described by Baldus [i.e. in 1935]. The women carried pots of food to a clearing just outside the village and awaited the return of the men. The food was set down according to the group affiliation of the women's husbands: there was a place of Ananchá and Wurankura, another for Wuranchingió and Wuranchinga, and a third for Tanawe. [Earlier she explains that in 1966 Wuranchingó had no members. Ibid.: 26.] As the men arrived, each went to the place where the food for his group had been set down and began eating out of the pots placed there. The women sat on the side with their children. The men, especially the younger ones, were not as strict about eating only their group's food as they apparently had been at the time of Baldus' visit. As the meal progressed, I saw men going from their own group over to another especially if their wives had been remiss in preparing a sufficient amount or variety of foods.

At the conclusion of the meal, the women preceded the men back to the village, carrying empty pots and accompanied by the children. The men followed and upon entering the village went to the takana whereas the women had gone to their respective homes. The men organized themselves for dancing, each with his partner, the two embracing one another around the waist, which is the usual dance position. They wore no special ornaments but many did carry weapons in their free hand, as described by Baldus. The men danced out of the takana and over to one of the houses in the village circle, from

which point the races were run taking place in the manner described
by Baldus. (Shapiro, 1968a: 27-28.)[56]

This communal work party and the following activities observed by
Shapiro in 1966 seems more traditional than anything I witnessed in
1939-40. In the same article, she suggests that the Tapirapé leaders
might have been "anxious to show that the Tapirapé still knew how
one ought to behave," but the very fact that they knew how to and
did hold an apachirú and related ceremonies attests to the fact that
the Bird Societies continue to be important in Tapirapé social organization.

In fact, in 1965 I found that the takana had acquired a new function. Men had always used it as a place where they could weave baskets, make arrows, or work on costumes and masks away from the
distractions of women and children, but in 1965 I learned that the
takana had become a veritable "factory" of Tapirapé artifacts for sale.
Each afternoon three or four men could be found there, hacking away
at pieces of wood with bushknives to provide the base for the grotesque and colorful upé masks. Others were making small wooden
benches and some were weaving baskets. Such objects were being manufactured for sale to Brazilian traders who came by boat periodically
during the dry season, and who resold such objects to tourist shops in
the large cities; to collectors of Indian "art"; and even to museums in
Europe, Canada, and the United States. The objects being fabricated
for sale followed traditional models as far as was possible, but there
was a serious shortage of raw materials. In 1965 the Tapirapé did not
own captive red macaws from which they had traditionally plucked
feathers to make ornaments. In fact, both the red macaw and the
blue macaw had become scarce along the Araguaia River, due, undoubtedly, to the new demand for their feathers. So the tail feathers
of the hawk were sometimes used to form the diadem of the large upé
mask. And sometimes colored cloth, rather than breast feathers from
the macaw and hawk, was used to form the face of the upé mask. I
even saw black paint purchased from a store, rather than genipap
juice, used to color some objects, and red store paint used rather than
native annatto. Some of the men working on upé masks (which were
much in demand by the traders) felt called upon to explain that these
were not real upé masks, for the torí who bought them did not know

56. I have changed Dr. Shapiro's orthography of Tapirapé words to conform to the
114 rather simplified orthography used throughout this book.

what they meant. They complained that the Carajá had criticized them for selling "sacred" objects, but any possible guilt which they may have felt was easily overcome by this new source of income.

I have said earlier that each Tapirapé village was also divided into Feast Groups, or "Eating Groups," as Baldus called them (1970: 330ff). These associations were made up of both women and men; ideally, membership was inherited by parallel descent, that is, a man belonged to the association of his father and a woman belonged to that of her mother. In 1939-40 this rule of affiliation was not strictly followed; people seemed to associate themselves with the Feast Group of their own choice. It must be emphasized that these associations had no connection with the regulation of marriage. In fact, it was even considered preferable that a man and wife belong to the same Feast Group. Thus, often a woman moved to her husband's Feast Group or a husband to his wife's. I cannot say whether the rule of affiliation was more strongly enforced sometime in the past. The main function of the Feast Groups seems to have been always the distribution and consumption of food. Each Feast Group had an appointed spot in the village plaza which was its "fireplace" and meetingplace. From time to time, especially in the dry season, the Feast Groups met for common meals, something like a picnic. They sometimes met en masse at the same time, each at its plaza section—or now and again only one Feast Group would meet.

Baldus attended one Tantanopao on July 3 of 1935, during which six of the Feast Groups met simultaneously for a group meal. He wrote:

At sundown, six fires were kindled in the plaza near which pots and pans full of food were set. I saw the whole population of Tampiitawa bring bananas, peanuts, manioc flour, cooked fish, fish soup with manioc flour and pepper, various species of yams, kauí [kawí] soup made of peanuts, and other edibles. I saw also that people of the same dwelling separated to join one of the six different groups in the plaza. . . . Before the groups sat down in their respective places, there was a general distribution of presents. Each person offered beads and other objects of esteem to others whom they liked and admired. Those who received the most presents were the chiefs [household leaders] who the day before had offered kauí [kawi] soup to the whole village. When finally, they accommodated themselves squatting around the pots next to the tatáupaua [tantanopao] ("place of the fire"), the group was so compact that there remained almost no empty space. Everyone had something of everything—men, women, and children together. . . . Everyone was very cheerful. Within a quarter of an hour nothing remained of the food. The people began to leave and to separate (returning to their dwellings). (1970: 330-31; translation mine.)

Again on July 15 of that same year, Baldus attended another Tantanopao feast. This time only one of the Feast Groups held a communal meal. It met to eat wild pork which one of them killed the day before. The women of the *Awaikú* Feast Group had cooked the pork barbecue style and cut it up into small pieces. After distributing pieces to kinsmen, the meat, along with manioc flour, was placed in pots on a palm leaf mat at the Awaikú station in the plaza. An announcement was made that all Awaikú were invited, and at sundown they met to consume the meat and manioc flour. Baldus remarks that members of other groups did not attend, but that some of them were given pieces of meat which they moved away from the group to eat (1970: 331). In 1939 I attended one such Feast Group meal held by five groups simultaneously. A variety of food was brought from the family dwellings. It was suggested to me that I should bring salt and rapadura from my house to the *Chankanepera* fire, which I did. The feast was rapid and again there were no ceremonials nor singing following the meal. Both Baldus and I were told that Feast Groups often meet in the late dry season, when men are most apt to discover and collect wild honey. Other than these group meals, which stimulated a measure of hunting and collecting during the dry season, I know of no other function of the Feast Groups.

Perhaps sometime in the past the groups had other, more important activities. They were present in all Tapirapé villages and provided a mechanism of group association common to all villages which transected residence and kinship groups. The origin of these Feast Groups is established in mythology. In 1939-40, I recorded the names of eight Tantanopao groups: *Ampirampé* ("those of the first people"), *Maniutawera* ("those of the manioc people"), *Awaikú* ("those of the sweet manioc people"), *Tawaupera* ("those of the village people"), *Chankanepera* ("those of the alligator people"), *Chanetawa* ("our village people"), *Pananiwana* ("those of the river people"), and *Kawano* ("those of the wasp people").[57] These names indicate places where

---

57. My translations of the meaning of these terms are glossed and perhaps not strictly correct. Baldus lists seven Tantanopao societies; he omits Chanetawa but lists Kawanoí rather than Kawano (1970: 331). Shapiro lists nine societies; in addition to Kawano, she also lists Kawanoí (1968b: 4).

the mythical ancestors emerged from the earth. Ampirampé (the first people) emerged first and then pulled Maniutawera and Awaikú from the ground. Even in 1939-40 I was unable to get a coherent story of the order and the events of the emergence of the ancestors of the other societies. However, the adventures of Chankanepera, the ancestor of the society which carries his name, was well remembered. This is one version of Chankanepera's story:

After Chankanepera emerged from the earth, his wife left and went to live with a people who lived far away. Chankanepera set off to find her. He walked very far and the first night he met a large snake which caught him up in its coils. The snake (a constrictor) tried to have anal intercourse with Chankanepera sticking its tail in his anus. A large hawk seeing Chankanepera's situation swooped down and saved him. All of the next day, Chankanepera walked and that night he met a large kururu toad which was larger than a man. The toad told him that he must walk until he crossed a large river. The next day, Chankanepera reached the river and there he met a small alligator. Chankanepera asked how he could cross the river and the alligator said: "Wait here, I will bring my father." In a short time, a very large alligator appeared and told Chankanepera to sit on his back, and the alligator ferried him across the river. On the other side, Chankanepera was swallowed by the maguari [a large fish-eating water bird] but when the maguari put its neck down to catch more fish, Chankanepera escaped. He traveled on and one night he found a nest of wild bees and ate honey; another day he found an anajá tree and filled his backpack with wild fruit to eat; and still another day he met some armadillos who had a peanut plantation. The peanuts were full of worms but he watched the doves eat the worms and selected those which were clean. Finally, he met a band of monkeys and he told them that he sought his wife. The monkeys set off in front of him saying "this way, this way, this way"—and they finally led him to the village where he found his wife.

My informants told me that some of the Tantanopao groups owed their names to Chankanepera's travels, but it was not clear at all to me how they figured in the tale.

Shapiro states that in 1966 the Tantanopao "groups continue[d] to function, though no doubt to a more limited extent than in the past" (1968b: 5). Even in 1939-40 they seemed to have a very limited importance in Tapirapé social life, meeting as they did only periodically and then only to consume surplus food. This same function of distribution of food beyond the nuclear family and beyond the household unit was also well served by other institutions—namely, the   *117* widespread kin network and the men's Bird Societies. Despite their persistence in Tapirapé culture, I fail to see that Tantanopao groups were ever basic social units in Tapirapé society.

Up to this point we have described subgroups of Tapirapé society— the village, the household, the kinship network, the men's Bird Societies, and the Feast Groups. I have mentioned in passing that each household had an older man who acted as the household leader and that the men's Bird Societies had leaders who directed their singing and led them on group hunts. The problem of leadership in Tapirapé society is, however, moot. As I wrote earlier, there was no chieftain or tribal council able to make decisions affecting the tribe as a whole. On the other hand, Baldus (1970: 334ff) states definitely that there was a village chief, Kamairaho. Baldus writes: "I never doubted in 1935 that Kamairaho was the principal chief of Tampiitawa." Frederick Kegel, the missionary, had told him that it was Kamairaho who had selected the site for the village and who, before it was built, had ordered the men to clear a large garden for him near the village. Baldus noted that Kamairaho's dwelling was the largest in the village; he found that his informants were hesitant to talk about other villagers in front of Kamairaho. He was impressed with the respect with which Kamairaho was treated by almost all of the people of Tampiitawa. My interpretation of Tapirapé social structure, on the other hand, is that it was acephalous. There was no village chieftain or leader, in my opinion; instead there were several leaders, who in no way formed an organized village council, but who achieved prestige and authority through a combination of roles.

In 1939-40, five men stood out as leaders in Tampiitawa. These were Kamairaho, Urukumu, Wantanamu, Kamairá, and Kamanaré. They had arrived at their positions of prestige and leadership by different routes. All five were recognized as household heads; in fact, the family dwellings in the village circle were commonly referred to by their names—"the house of Kamairaho," for example.[58] In 1939-40 most of the women of their households might call each other by kinship terms such as "sister" or "daughter," although the actual relationship was usually classificatory rather than close genealogically. The men of their households were affinals (sons-in-law or brothers-in-law), although many of them were also classified as consanguineal kin, such as "sister's son." These men were almost invariably younger than the

---

58. There were nine separate households in 1939-40, but four of them seemed almost adjuncts to other households and did not have leaders of recognized prestige.

household headman; thus household leadership generally came to a man in his mature years, when he was between thirty and forty-five years old. Over their lifetimes they had been able to attract to themselves a network of kinsmen, mainly through their own or their wife's maternal line.

There were no forms of obeisance or special terms of address for these household headmen, yet they were treated with considerable respect. They seemed to have always the choice location within the longhouse, where they and their wives (and children, if any) hung their hammocks and had their fireplaces. That location was near the only door, where there was some light, and, on very hot days, just a semblance of a breeze. Furthermore, when any headman visited the takana or another family dwelling, someone always appeared with a low stool for him to sit upon. When a headman would come to visit me in my house, people would make room for him on the long narrow bench which we had provided for visitors. The headmen seldom did any heavy work in clearing gardens, although two of them, Kamairá and Kamanaré, who were younger than the others, did work with their followers in clearing a garden site. The older men explained that the younger men of their kinship network, and sometimes the Bird Societies in communal work parties, cleared gardens for them. Although I did not learn of any rule by which gifts in food should be given to household headmen, their wives seemed always to have relatively well-stocked larders. I suspect that garden products flowed to them as prestigious kinsmen. All of these men were well off in personal objects such as beads, red macaw feathers, baskets, and even extra hammocks. All of them were referred to by the Portuguese word "capitão" (captain) and on the occasion of the kawió ceremony they refused to swallow the bad kawi and thus were obliged to give away personal belongings to those of their followers who did swallow it. Such men were therefore known as generous—or, to put it another way, they were not ankantaum.

Three of the household headmen were panchés, or shamans—Kamairaho, Wantanamu, and Urukumu. As will be described later, the shaman was a central figure in Tapirapé society; people depended upon him for health and protection against dangerous supernaturals. All three of these men performed shaministic cures, and I saw them participate in the annual challenge of the Thunder ceremony. Shamans received gifts for cures and this was one source of wealth for all three, although among them Urukumu was by far the most famous, *119* performing more cures than the others. He also acted as the surgeon-operator who undertook the scarification of women's faces. For this operation he also received gifts. Yet Urukumu did not seem noticeably wealthier in personal objects than either Kamairaho or Wantanamu. In fact, both their households were larger in number than that of Urukumu, who, it must be said, was also feared because of his supernatural powers. It was noticeable that none of these three men actually took part in the dancing and singing at the various ceremonials. They remained rather aloof, attending as spectators. But people could be heard to say about some of the dancers, "he wears Urukumu's beads"; or, the tail feathers which made up a headdress "belong to Wantanamu."

Both Kamairá and Kamanaré were younger than the three important shamans. Each was a leader of his Bird Society. Kamanaré was the singing and "walking" (i.e. hunting) leader of Ananchá. He was known for his knowledge of songs and was an excellent hunter. The baskets he wove were considered the most beautiful of any made by Tapirapé men. He was generally called upon to make ceremonial headdresses and the masks for the anchunga figures. He died during the dry season of 1939 while I was in residence in Tampiitawa and his position was filled by his "younger brother" Tanopanchowa, who was also respected for his singing and hunting. Kamairé, the leader of Wuranchingió, was a famous hunter, and many stories were told of his feats. He was also known for the beauty of his voice—an attribute much admired among the Tapirapé. He was rather tall for a Tapirapé male (about 5′ 9″) and very strong. He was said to have been an ardent lover in his youth, but in 1939-40 he seemed well satisfied with his young wife, who was well kept and a hard worker. He was a silent man and seldom took part in the frequent joking in the takana, but now and again he would break out in sudden rage. People stood somewhat in awe of Kamairá; he was a "killer." Several years before my arrival he had assassinated a shaman—the father of Kantuowa, who was the wife of Kamairaho. Of all the Tapirapé men I knew, Kamairá was the most impressive: he had a quiet dignity and a rather aloof demeanor which demanded respect. Yet at garden clearing work parties he worked harder than others. Events which took place after 1947 show the confidence which many Tapirapé had in Kamairá as a leader, for it was he who led a group of his followers to Chichutawa and isolation in the forest for over twenty years.

120   Of the five household headmen, only Kamairaho laid claim to any

inherited status. He claimed that his was a "big name." It had been the name of his father and grandfather before and they had been "captains." Kamairaho claimed that, as the son of a "captain," he had been raised as a "beautiful child" (anchirikakantu). Such children, according to various Tapirapé informants, were given special treatment during their early years. A straw mat was provided for them so that they would never crawl on the dirt floors. They were said to have been fed especially well. As they learned to walk, they did not have to go to the stream to bathe—water for that purpose was carried in gourds to the house. From the time they were babies they wore special decorations—strings of beads, feather ornaments in their hair and ears. Their bodies were carefully painted with elaborate designs with black genipap dye, and they always had wrist and ankle ornaments crocheted from native cotton. I never saw a "beautiful child" among the Tapirapé, although I did see one among the neighboring Carajá, who share this custom with the Tapirapé. Kamairaho said that he was treating his stepdaughter as a "beautiful child." If so, it was in a fashion highly attenuated from that described of the past, although she was visibly better decorated than most children. In any case, this special treatment as a child as described by Kamairaho seems hardly aimed at training a strong and decisive leader.[59]

Never did I see the household headmen sit as a group to consider a question concerning the community as a whole. In no way could they be called a "village council." In fact, the people of each household seemed instead to form a faction within the village. People tended to come to my house as visitors in household groups. When people from one household would leave, a group from another would replace them. There were definite antagonisms between household heads, but they were never aired in public. Kamairaho had not been

---

59. Kamairaho described the treatment of an anchirikakantu in some detail, but he was the only informant who gave emphasis to such a privileged status. According to Kamairaho, both boys and girls might be accorded this status. It tended to be inherited, in that a father who had been a "beautiful child" generally was anxious to give his eldest son this status and a woman who had been given this special status as a child was apt to make her first daughter a "beautiful child." Formerly, each Bird Society moiety had one anchirikakantu; thus, there was one for Wuranchinga and one for Wurankura, according to Kamairaho. These two boys were central figures in the kaó ceremonies at the beginning of the dry season. If his description was true (and Kamairaho was usually a good informant on the past), the practice had fallen into decline by 1939-40. However, I did witness one boy who was highly decorated and wore a large headdress at the head of a line of dancers at the kaó festivals in 1939. He was the son of Urukumu, the powerful shaman. Those who had been "beautiful children" were "captains" when they grew older. They never drank the bad kawi at the kawió ceremonies (see Chapter 3).

friendly at all with Kamairá since Kamairá had killed his wife's father. Kamairaho and his wife would always leave a gathering when Kamairá arrived. Kamairaho and Wantanamu also had their differences. I cannot remember an occasion when both of them came to visit my house at the same time. It was said that the two differed on their policy toward the torí. Kamairaho liked to have torí visitors to the village because they brought trade goods, but Wantanamu disliked them. He was always very distant to both Valentim and me and he was offended when we gave presents to Kamairaho and Kamairá. He was said to have disliked the missionary Frederick Kegel, whom most Tapirapé had liked so much. Members of one household often spread rumors about the people in another—for example, when my Swiss pocketknife disappeared Champukwi said that he was certain that someone from Wantanamu's house had taken it. Those antagonisms were never severe, except in instances where a shaman was suspected of sorcery; yet Tampiitawa was not a village with solid unity and an *esprit de corps.*

Since the people of a Tapirapé village had neither a village chief nor a village council, it is hard to understand how they ever reached a group decision. On the lower level of household units, and on the level of the men's Bird Societies, which intersect households, there were leaders who were able to urge their kinsmen or fellow Bird Society members to act as a group. The dilemma involved in village decisions presented itself during the last two months of my residence in Tampiitawa in 1939-40. Kamairaho had spoken to me many times about the ceremony that would be held at the end of the rainy season for the coming of age of his sister's son. Late in April of 1940, I announced that I would soon have to leave for my house, which was far away. Kamairaho came to me to say that I must delay my leaving so as to attend the ceremonies in which the whole village would participate. Nothing happened during the whole month of April; in fact, many Tapirapé had moved out of Tampiitawa to their near-by gardens. In early May I began to prepare to travel. It became known that I had given away my axe to a Tapirapé friend because I would not need it in my village. Kamairaho came to reassure me that the ceremony would start any day—perhaps tomorrow or certainly the day after tomorrow, if it did not rain. I became interested, for I did want to see the ceremony and to take photographs. So I waited. Then friends from other household groups came to explain that few wanted to cooperate with Kamairaho to organize the ceremony. "The Tapirapé have too little food," they said. "First we must go on a hunt so that there will be meat." It soon became apparent that Kamairaho was getting little cooperation from the others. The plaza needed sweeping, manioc flour had to be prepared, beads had to be restrung, the takana needed cleaning, the giant headdress which the young man wore in the ceremony had to be made, and many other tasks needed to be done for the ceremony to take place. Finally, however, in late May, the initiation ceremony did take place. Kamairaho and his kinsmen had prepared the headdress and other ornaments. It was, for me, a spectacular festival. But critics noted that not all of the men of the village were dancing, the food gave out, and the village plaza was dirty. Kamairaho had evidently put his prestige on the line by trying to undertake a major ceremony without full village cooperation. Such occasions involved long drawn-out testing of public opinion and agreement by the various household heads.

That was a bad year to carry out a major ceremony, for the people of Tampiitawa were faced with another major decision. During April and May of 1940 almost everyone seemed to agree that the time had come to move the village of Tampiitawa. The floors of most homes contained several graves. Near-by tillable land was becoming scarce. The cockroaches, as I can attest, were becoming unbearable. Several men went off on a scouting expedition to two old village sites and told me that it was time to start clearing gardens at one of these sites, if the village were to move. But where should they move, and when? None of the household heads would make the decision. Kamairaho and his householders moved about a half-mile to the west to live in gardens in temporary huts. Wantanamu and his household group took up temporary residence in gardens in the other direction. I accompanied Kamairá and the male followers from his household on a hunt. For a time in May, Tampiitawa was inhabited by only about half its people. (This was, of course, one of Kamairaho's problems in organizing the coming of age ceremony.) I left in June before any decision was made, but I learned later that the village was moved. How the decision was finally reached I shall never know.

It should be apparent that Tapirapé social organization was not a well-oiled mechanism attuned to village action. On the village level it was egalitarian to an extreme—even to the point of frustration for those who had to live in it. There was only one occasion when violence or coercion took place. This was the execution of a supposedly dangerous shaman. Such an execution was generally the act of one man or a

123

group of kinsmen whose anger and sorrow had been built up for several years over the deaths of relatives. But then the killer had to be cleansed before he could again take part in normal social affairs. The execution left factionalism, even hatred, which could break out again in later years. Given its multi-unit nature, however, the Tapirapé village could not easily fission. That is, extended family groups could not easily move off and establish a village of their own. For the Tapirapé, a village had to have sufficient people to support various kinship groups, to provide membership in the various men's Bird Societies, and to have members for the various Feast Groups. Without these units present in a village, economic activities and ceremonial life would not function. According to my older Tapirapé informants, an ideal Tapirapé village would have séven or eight longhouse dwellings, a takana with all of the Bird Societies, and members of all the Feast Groups. Thus any Tapirapé village would have to have at least two hundred people according to my own estimate.

By 1965 Tapirapé society had become no more authoritarian, nor any better organized to reach village decisions. Yet there had been changes. It had always been the policy of the Brazilian Indian Protection Service (SPI) to recognize and nominate a village chief (capitão) through which the service could issue orders and, it was hoped, secure the cooperation of villagers. In many tribes throughout Brazil where there had never been a village chieftain or headman, the SPI created "captains." In 1965, when I was living in New Village, the missionary nuns of the Little Sisters of Jesus seemed to recognize one man, Tampirí (also known as Marcos in Portuguese), as the village chief. Another man, Ipawungí (known also as Cantidio), was also known as a "captain." Since households had by then separated into nuclear family dwellings, neither man could be called a household headman, though both were active middle-aged men and Marcos (Tampirí) was the leader of his Bird Society, which still functioned on a modified basis.

I could not see that either exercised much authority. They tended to lean on the Little Sisters of Jesus and upon Padre François Jentel, the missionary priest who also resided in the village. But the missionaries firmly believed that they were there to help the Tapirapé do what the Indians themselves wanted to do and not to make decisions for them; thus the old question persisted as to who would make village decisions. Without strong village leadership, it is difficult for the Tapiripé today to confront the many problems which contact with the

124

outside world has brought them, such as the encroaching Brazilian backwoodsmen and, above all, the problem of the huge corporations which would dispossess them of their land. The Tapirapé's position was summed up by a Tapirapé "chief" who attended the First Assembly of Indigenous Chiefs, called together by a Catholic missionary group at Diamantina in the state of Mato Grosso on April 17, 1974:

We come from the Tapirapé post at the invitation of the Bororo tribe. Here all of us who are Indians come together. We would like to tell you something about the way we live. The ranches are surrounding us. The CODEARA, the Tapiraguaia [land companies] are taking away all of our land. Why did the whites want to pacify us? Afterwards what is going to happen to us in the middle of whites working for the whites who want to take away our land? Is it meant that the Indian should have nothing and to put an end to the Indians? The whites arrived and decided that the Indian could find another place to live. Where shall we go? The Indian lives in the place which he knows. If he moves to another place on the river bank, in the hills, in the lowlands, this is not good.

There was a padre who lived there with us [Padre Francisco Jentel]. He was a poor man. He was young between twenty to twenty-five years of age when he arrived. He stayed with us. We carried things for him and he also carried loads at the same time. He could not speak Portuguese; he was a foreigner and did not understand anything. Each time a Brazilian came, he spoke all mixed up. Then, he studied Portuguese and in five years he spoke well. Everyone liked him. The Tapiraguaia Company wants to take all of our land. It wants to give us a small piece of bush land [cerrado] which is not worth anything. Where we plant is good forest. The whites say, "Look, the Indian is not equal to us. Let's take away their land because they do not have guns nor machine guns, nor bombs, nor money. All they have are bows and arrows and clubs. Only these are for the Indian to use." Because of this they took away Padre Francisco. The police arrived while the men were away and there were only women in the village. The women were afraid of the police and they took the padre away. We feel until today his absence because he was poor as we are. We are homesick [saudade] for him. (Txibae Ewororo, 1976: 42.) [60]

---

60. This speech is not translated literally from the broken and child-like Portuguese which was recorded. Instead, I have followed ideas as they would have been expressed had the Tapirapé been speaking in his native tongue.

In Padre François Jentel the Tapirapé had found a leader who helped them make decisions and was able to articulate their needs in regard to their new situation. They recognize the need for leadership. Now that the padre has been exiled from Brazil, it is hoped that the FUNAI will appoint an Indian agent for the Tapirapé who will work in their favor. Such an agent could not, however, count upon help from any native Tapirapé social organization unless the unexpected should occur and a strong native leader emerges from those Tapirapé who are acquiring some western education.

Man Comes Naked into This World 5

The Tapirapé Indians come naked into this world just as we do, but they lived naked all their lives. And just as the people of the western world developed a sense of shame, a set of styles, and an etiquette about the clothes they wear, the Tapirapé had an etiquette for nudity and a style for decorating their bodies. Tapirapé women wore nothing that could be called clothes or any article to hide a part of the body. Men wore no clothes—unless the palm-fiber cone about half an inch thick with which they tied the prepuce can be called clothes. The only portion of the body for which men felt any shame was the head or glans of the penis. But by stretching the prepuce and tying it with the palm fiber band, that small portion of the body could be covered from view. Men took considerable caution not to be seen without their *chirankonya-chiwawa* (penis band). To be seen without it was analogous to a North American being seen on Main Street without his pants. Men squatted to urinate. When they washed the head of their penis while bathing, or when their penis band had been misplaced for some reason, they covered themselves with their hands like a shy maiden on a September morn.

Likewise, women had a sense of body shame. They learned to squat with knees tightly held together so as not to show the lips of the vulva. Furthermore, no well-behaved Tapirapé woman would sit with her legs apart or propped up in any fashion for the same reason. To be-

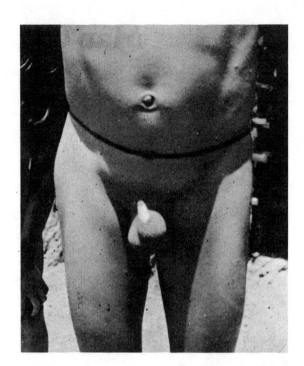

A close-up of the penis band (*chirankonya-chiwawa*) worn by all Tapirapé men in 1939.

have in this manner would have been tantamount to welcoming sexual advances. There was no special feeling about female breasts except that they might be attractive parts of the human body—like the nose, for example. Necessary bodily functions such as excretion were done in private. There were no privies, but men and women were careful to move at some distance from the village into the bush to deposit feces. It was in perfectly good manners to ask of a person leaving the village: "*angkuruk?*" which means, literally, "You go to urinate?" Copulation normally took place privately either deep in the forest, in the garden, or sometimes late at night in a family dwelling when the couple was protected by darkness.

The Tapirapé had, however, definite aesthetic concepts involving the human body. They found body hair disgusting. Fortunately, they are not a hairy people, thus removal of that hair was not a major operation for them. Males and females from their early years plucked the pubic hair and any hair that might grow in their armpits. They also pulled out the eyebrows and, generally, the eyelashes. This was done with tweezers made of two clam shells or of bamboo. Ashes were rubbed into the body hair to make the tweezers more secure. It was a

128

common sight to see a woman plucking her husband's pubic hair (or vice versa). It was a cozy domestic scene.

There were many ways of decorating the body. The simplest was to rub the entire body after a bath with an oil (either a fish oil, or more commonly, a palm oil) with which red annatto (called urucu in Portuguese and uruku in Tapirapé) had been mixed. It gave their normally brown skin an attractive reddish tone, but it also gave them an acrid smell, and the red dye rubbed off easily on almost anything they touched.[61] More complex were the different ways of "painting" the body. There were many distinct styles for each age and sex group. Most styles had names, some of which had significance, such as *chawana*, which means jaguar, and others, such as *kwanchiana*, which refers only to the geometric pattern itself. Essentially, all body painting is done with two elements. One is the juice of the fruit of the genipap tree, which was chewed and spat into a gourd. When this liquid is applied to the body it becomes black. Genipap dye is durable, for it cannot be washed off even with soap for two weeks or more.[62] The other is annatto dye, which, as I have said, is less durable.

During their lives most of the Tapirapé wore a variety of body paint designs. Relatives started painting the bodies of infants after they were but a few days old. Little girls were most often painted with the kwanchiana design. Little boys were painted in various designs—most often with a design said to resemble the scales of a fish. Adult males liked to come from the garden and, after a bath, be painted by their wives. First their feet and calves were painted bright red with annatto and then the rest of the body was decorated with a series of line designs made with black genipap. Generally the face was not painted at all. Rather, the design stopped at about the shoulder or collarbone. Sometimes the design was solid black, resembling a cutaway jacket, and was called wurankane (kingfisher) or just horizontal black lines called upuhawáwa (some kind of fish). Adult women had their bodies painted less often. On important days all young people wore body designs, just as westerners dress up for special occasions. There were children who were more often painted than others because they had doting parents, but others seemed to be neglected. There were also some adults who gave undue attention to their decorations and others

---

61. At special festivals, the Tapirapé coated their hair with a thick red urucu paste.
62. Judith Shapiro, who had been called away suddenly from field research among the Tapirapé, appeared in New York with her face blacked with genipap dye in kwanchiana style, much to her chagrin.

Kamanaré, the household leader who died during the dry season of 1939. On this occasion he was painted with a body design called wanakané, a diving water bird of the family Coumbidas.

Tapirapé men, unless they are quite old, paint their bodies with genipap dye. This body design is called Cha-achawa, the piaba fish (Carácides).

who were rather careless. Few Tapirapé men and women over about thirty years of age painted their bodies except on very special occasions, but even in 1965 I saw Panchepurunga, a man well into his forties, having his feet and calves painted with annatto and the rest of his body painted with genipap in the kingfisher style.

The Tapirapé also decorated their bodies with anklets, calf bands, single-string waist bands, and wrist ornaments made of cotton string. These string ornaments are permanent; that is, they are fabricated directly on the body and are worn until they are old and must be cut 130 off. The work was done by women by a crochet technique, using a

ABOVE: Tapirapé women. One is crocheting a wrist ornament while the other combs her hair with a native comb.

LEFT: A small girl (*kotantani*) in 1940. She is wearing crocheted anklets and necklaces of enameled beads with two jaguar teeth, and her body is painted in a geometric design.

bone needle. Anklets were worn mainly by small girls, but some boys also wore them. Almost all males had a narrow band woven around the calf of each leg just below the knee, with a short tassel hanging down in front. The waist string worn by men is just that, and it can hardly be called an ornament. Wrist bands were frequently worn by girls and boys and by most young men. They consisted of a narrow band around the wrist with a disc-like projection which is sometimes six inches in diameter. The string ornaments were coated thickly with annatto dye and stood out bright red against the body. To be seen wearing new anklets or wrist bands increased one's self-esteem—it showed that the person had a female relative who cared enough to make the ornaments.

The lower lip of the Tapirapé males was perforated at birth with a sharp monkey bone; then the hole was tied through with a string so it would not close. For the rest of his life a man wore a lip plug of one kind or another, depending on his age. As a small boy he wore a slender lip ornament made of a wild pig or emu bone; then, as an adolescent, a smaller one made of mother of pearl, and, finally, as an adult, a plain, small, round plug, which simply closed the hole in his lip. Once in his life a boy would wear the invaluable lip plug made of milky quartz at his coming of age festival. Only one of these ceremonial lip plugs existed in 1939-40 (it still exists today), and it was guarded by one of the household leaders. Some Tapirapé men, but not all, had their earlobes perforated in order that they might wear feather ornaments. The Tapirapé have never seen (except in photographs) the enormous lip plugs used by some Indians of the upper Xingú region. They talked with some awe of the large earrings which the Kayapó Indians wear.

In 1939-40 the most sought-after ornaments of all were European beads. They valued only porcelain beads of a type manufactured in Czechoslovakia. In size the beads had to be just a little smaller than a pea. The favorite color was bright red, but other colors were acceptable. On my first visit to the Tapirapé in 1939 I brought a few strings of imitation pearls, but these they crushed between their teeth and handed back to me in disgust. Fortunately, William Lipkind had warned me to buy the proper kind of beads in New York and I was not empty-handed. The Czechoslovakian beads were worn as necklaces, but seldom on a day-to-day basis. On special festival days a person might wear strand upon strand of bead necklaces, sometimes weighing as much as a kilogram or more. But by 1965 the great value

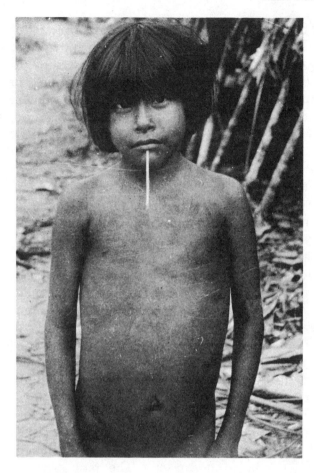

A small boy (*konomí*) wearing a long bone lip plug.

placed on beads had passed. Men and women wanted other things, even though many still had a treasure trove of beads squirreled away. I cannot guess what kind of indigenous ornaments imported beads replaced—perhaps necklaces made of colored forest seeds or nuts—but for several generations imported porcelain beads were the most valued objects in Tapirapé culture.

Haircutting and styling changed with age; and as I shall discuss later, that style was a diagnostic feature of age group, especially for males.

The Tapirapé were perfectly aware of the process of human conception, although they held a rather different view of it than we do. They realized fully that conception results from human sexual intercourse, and that the semen of the male had to enter the female's womb to set   *133* off the process. But for the Tapirapé it did not end there; one act of copulation was not considered sufficient for conception. Intercourse had to continue. A male had to provide more and more semen "to build the flesh of the child." They laughed at me when I ventured to say that a single copulation was enough and that in my land women sometimes found themselves pregnant after one sex act. In any case, intercourse had to continue during pregnancy, but it did not need to be with the same male. All men, however, who had intercourse with a woman during her pregnancy were considered the genitors, not merely the sociological fathers of the child. It thus often happened that a child had two or three or more genitors. One was publicly known as the mother's mate at the time, so he was called cheropu (father). The others were known by gossip. It was widely believed that Champukwi had helped sire several small children I knew in 1939-40. Several young men told me that they might call Kamairaho "father," for their mothers were known to have copulated with him while bearing them in the womb. And several men, in confidence, pointed out children whom they believed to be their offspring. Matters could, however, become too complex. When it was known that a woman had had intercourse with several men (four or five or more), then the child had "too many fathers." This could endanger the child's health and well-being, for in such cases the child, live or dead, more often than not was buried at once with the afterbirth.

Not even repeated intercourse was enough to bring a child into this world, according to traditional Tapirapé thought. In the anchunga world there are a finite number of human souls. The spirit of a child comes to enter a woman at the call of a shaman (panché), who, in his dream travels, calls the spirit to the woman. "How else can you explain that some women 'eat' and 'eat' [the word for eating is the same as that for sexual intercourse] and have but one child or none at all?" is the way one Tapirapé tried to explain it to me. So the shaman could be blamed for barrenness, and he could be responsible also for too many children. But sometimes the spirit of the child itself made the decision to whom it would be born. A Tapirapé explained: "The panché brings the [spirit of the] child. He takes the child to a house. The [unborn] baby says: 'No! She is not good enough to be my mother.' The panché then takes [the spirit of] the child to another house." Thus older women, couples beyond middle age, women with old husbands, and even just ugly people seldom had children. When a woman wanted children she might take honey to a shaman, or she might ask him to treat her by blowing smoke over her head and body. Then he would dream and bring a child to her. The shaman was given a jacamim fowl by one woman and he dreamed of jacamim when he found a spirit which became her child. I was told that certain animals and fish had spirits of children which the shaman could steal and bring to a woman. If the shaman took a spirit from the monkey, the child would be born as a male and would grow up to be a skilled adulterer, according to several Tapirapé informants. Thunder (who lives in the sky) also had "child spirits," and many children were stolen from that supernatural.

The Tapirapé seemed always to desire and cherish children, but until about 1954 they had a clear and precise rule limiting their number. It was an ironclad rule that no woman should have more than three living children. Furthermore, no more than two could be of the same sex. A woman could raise two boys and one girl, or two girls and one boy. A fourth child, or a third child if it were of the wrong sex, was buried immediately after its birth. During my residence in 1939-40 I witnessed the interment of two unwanted newly born children. No woman in Tampiitawa had more living children than prescribed by the rules. To my knowledge there were no religious beliefs which imposed or validated these limitations on family size. Instead, Tapirapé men gave me a most logical and materialistic explanation: "We do not want to see hunger in their eyes." They pointed out to me the difficulty of providing food, especially meat, for more than three children.[63] Furthermore, men were motivated to respect those rules, without doubt, by the imposition of food taboos on the fathers of infants; and both men and women were motivated to respect the rule by the prohibition of sexual relations between the couple until the child was at least one year old, could crawl, and could take foods other than its mother's milk.

The full significance of this "policy" of zero population growth in relation to the rapid depopulation should be stressed. Given these limitations on family size, and even given the rather stable conditions which must have existed before 1900, the Tapirapé population could hardly expand. Three living children per woman would have been just enough to replace the population from one generation to the next. There were undoubtedly always women who did not reproduce at all;

---

63. These rules of limitation on family size have been confirmed by other anthropologists who have done research among the Tapirapé, especially Baldus (1970: 279). They were also confirmed by the Little Sisters of Jesus, who ended the practice in 1954.

in 1939-40 there were two women between the ages of twenty and thirty years of age, both of whom suffered from epilepsy, who were active sexually but had no children. Other women had only one or two children. Furthermore, mortality among small children and adults was undoubtedly relatively high even before 1900, when the indigenous way of life was undisturbed.

Shortly after 1900, Tapirapé society began to feel the influence of the Brazilian frontier. They acquired diseases, unknown to them before, indirectly from other tribes, then directly from Brazilians. Mortality increased rapidly, often as the result of epidemics of measles, smallpox, mumps, and, above all, the common cold. But their population "policy" remained unchanged and their very delicately balanced ecological adaptation was thrown out of kilter. This was the overwhelming reason for the decimation of the Tapirapé people from about 1900 to 1954.

In about 1954, infanticide came to an end through the direct intervention of the Little Sisters of Jesus. The Brazilian social anthropologist Roberto Cardoso de Oliveira, who accompanied me to the New Village of the Tapirapé in 1957, when there were but fifty-four Indians in the village, tells how this change took place:

> The missionaries having verified the reality of the existence of this practice which was incomprehensible to them, decided to destroy it by any means without confronting tribal culture. Finally they hit upon the following tactic which had magnificent results. When they saw that one woman· was pregnant but already had three children, they began to watch her closely. On the eve of the child's birth, when she began to feel birth pains, they proposed to "buy" the child from her for a good price (i.e. valuable gifts). In fact, they did "buy" the infant, but soon afterwards the mother came asking for its return. The missionaries agreed and made gifts to the mother and the father (in the name of the child). In this way they broke a taboo which was efficient in its time when a population of a thousand people existed with some difficulty in this region with their traditional technological equipment. Now that taboo, that same taboo, that same technique of controlling the birthrate, had turned against the group which more than ever before needed an increment in population. (Cardoso de Oliveira, 1959: 10. Translation mine.) [64]

---

64. The Little Sisters had been forewarned by reading an article of mine and discussing the problem during my visit in 1953. During our visit to the Tapirapé in 1965, the Little Sisters told my wife, Cecilia Roxo Wagley, another version of the incident. According to the Little Sisters, they were present when the child was born. They asked

From that date until now, with only medical aid from the Little Sisters, the Tapirapé population has increased slowly from internal growth until today (1976) there are 136 Tapirapé. It should be noted at once, however, that the result, i.e. more children per couple, reinforces to some degree the anxiety expressed by fathers in 1939-40. In 1965 the wives of three men had more than three living children: Imanawungo's wife had seven and Cantidio's wife had five. Imanawungo, whom I had known well in 1939-40, complained bitterly that sometimes his family went hungry. He was a hard worker and a good hunter, but he was also a man who held to traditional values. He abstained from eating meats tabooed to fathers of young children. He equated beef with venison; thus beef was prohibited to the women of his family and to him while the children were infants. He experimented with beef and was nauseated by it. He was anxious to earn money with which he could buy fish from the Carajá and even begged for a mutum (which anyone can eat) when one was killed by a villager. He frankly complained, "I have too many children."

A woman whose child had been so disposed of at birth seemed to deny that a child had ever been born. In 1940, I observed the wife of Kanchiwanio who was pregnant and already the mother of two small girls. One morning I heard her cry from labor pains. By noon she had given birth to a female child, but her husband had already dug a rather deep hole inside the house. The umbilical cord was not cut and the child was buried alive with the afterbirth almost immediately. There was no sign of grief, and by late afternoon Kanchiwanio and his wife visited me at my home. There was no mention at all by anyone of a child having been born.

On another occasion Chawaniuma's wife, Mikantú, who already had two boys and a girl, gave birth to a fourth child outside the village near old garden sites. She fell down in the brush and gave birth quickly. Almost immediately she stood up and walked back to her house to lie in the hammock. A group of women (and the author) gathered around the child, who seemed to be a healthy boy. There was considerable discussion, most of which I did not understand, but I was able to express my opinion that the child should be kept. "Perhaps a

---

the mother if they could keep the child as their own, since they had no children. They took the child to their house, but after one day became horrified to find that they had no way to feed the infant. They returned to the mother the next day and asked her if she would nurse the child for them. The mother agreed, and after a few days of nursing the child asked them if she could keep it.

A newborn child being washed in the stream in 1940. It was Mikantú's fourth child, and was not allowed to live.

family would keep the child," I remember saying. I seemed to win out at least for the moment, for the umbilical cord was cut and tied with a cotton string. An older woman bathed the child in the near-by stream and smeared its whole body with red annatto and palm oil. As a group we took the child to Mikantú, who seemed pleased. Chawani-uma protested mildly that his wife had done the right thing. She had run into the brush to rid herself of the child, and it was hard to feed too many children. I did not visit the family for several days for I felt that I had intruded enough upon their personal affairs. But several

138

days later Chawaniuma came to visit me and told me shyly that the infant had died. It had died, he said, because he himself had eaten a forest fowl which is taboo to fathers of infants. But my friend and informant Champukwi said that everyone knew Chawaniuma had buried the child at night. "He does not want more children. He does not want to stop eating venison. His wife did not want to nurse another child," Champukwi said to me.

There were other reasons for infanticide besides the rule on the number and the sex of children allowed to one woman. I was told in 1939-40 that a couple should never eat twin bananas, for if they did the mother might well die in childbirth or she might have twins, one or both of whom would be interred.[65] In the last days before a child was born a father should shun hard labor and he should respect the taboos on meats which he must follow until the child is weaned. His behavior was crucial to the health of the fetus and to the safety of the mother at childbirth. The child born with several fathers (i.e. men who had copulated with the mother during pregnancy) was highly vulnerable before birth, as it was during early infancy. Such casual lovers hardly bothered to respect the taboos. A hard labor and the death of a small infant was generally charged to "too many fathers." I was told that when it was known that a child was the result of intercourse with several men it was sometimes buried at birth. I am not sure whether there have been any cases of infanticide for those reasons since the Little Sisters persuaded the Tapirapé to break their rule on family size. I would rather doubt that infanticide has disappeared entirely, though the Little Sisters still keep careful watch over pregnant women.

A normal birth took place in the family longhouse. The mother was surrounded by female relatives—her mother, other mothers, and sisters. Men were not excluded from the scene, but only one or two were present at a birth I observed. To my knowledge, there were no midwives among the Tapirapé, at least there were no women who were specialists at attending births. Almost every older woman knew how to position a woman in labor. She was placed in a string hammock with her legs stretched over the sides. A slit about two feet long was cut in the bottom of the hammock, exposing her vulva and allowing attendants to observe as the infant emerged. Women held wood poles placed upright on each side of the hammock which provided support for the

---

65. Baldus misunderstood. He stated that a couple ate twin bananas hoping to have twins which were wanted (1970: 278).

woman in labor should she wish to "push" with her legs. To the attendant, the birth scene which I witnessed seemed excessively drawn out. Several people expressed worry that the mother might die, so a shaman was called. He smoked on his tubular pipe, blew smoke over the woman, and lightly massaged her body. He sang for a time, calling his spirit associate, but he did not go through a complete curing session, nor did he achieve a trance state as he might have in another situation.

Finally, the child was born, to everyone's relief. An older woman cut and tied the umbilical cord about three inches from the child's stomach. Two women brought water from the stream, and taking the water in their mouths to warm it they spurted water over the child to wash it and then rubbed its entire body with red annatto mixed with palm oil. On the day of the birth neither the father nor the mother should drink water. If there was any kawi in the house, I was told that it should be thrown away. The father of the child should go immediately to his hammock to rest and should continue to do so for several days.[66] There were some postnatal food taboos for both the father and mother. On the day after the birth, until the "natal skin" (i.e. the rough scale added to the dried annatto paste) falls off, they could eat only manioc flour, freshly made kawi, roasted sweet manioc, and some yams. Neither should do any heavy work at all. The husband sometimes rubbed red annatto on his hair, announcing the birth of the child.

At the one birth which I witnessed throughout the whole process, some of the women attending the mother asked the father for presents. Four women, although they were relatives, each asked for a strand of beads about five inches long. Another woman asked for a new bushknife which I had just given the father (Champukwi) a few days before. The shaman who came briefly to assist the birth did not ask for a gift, but, according to Champukwi, he could have asked for a whole string of beads or a bushknife. Champukwi said that requests for gifts on this occasion could be refused, but it was bad manners to ask for too much. He was rather depressed over his sudden loss of wealth. He said that it was hard to believe that his own wife's sister would claim anything, but she did. When this woman, Tanui, came

---

66. This almost worldwide custom, called the "couvade," is poorly observed by the Tapirapé men, though it does provide the basis for a joke. Whenever a man seems to be just idly resting in his hammock, a passing companion may ask him in jest, "Has your wife just had a baby?"

to ask for beads, Champukwi rather harshly refused, and she left, insulted.

On the other hand, Champukwi was pleased that he did not have to make gifts to have his new son's lower lip and ears pierced. This was done on the day after the child was born by Areowa, Urukumu's wife, whom he called "sister." Usually he might be expected to give the woman who performed this operation a string of beads. Areowa quickly perforated the child's lower lip with a bone needle and inserted in the holes a thin piece of wood and then made small balls of beeswax to hold the temporary ear plugs in place.

A day or two after the child began to feed at the breast, it was customary also to give it small amounts of honey. Honey was smeared on the finger and shoved into the infant's mouth. Little by little the Tapirapé added a thin soup, made generally of sweet manioc, to the infant's diet. The mother took the liquid in her own mouth and carefully spat it into the mouth of the child. Infants who died during their first year were buried in the longhouse floor just as adults were. The burial was not as elaborate as that of an adult, and mourning was neither intense nor prolonged. In the two cases I observed only the mother and father cried for a day or two at sundown, which is the appropriate hour for mourning.

The birth of the child set off a new way of life for a couple. For a time after a child was born, people called the parents "father of a boy" (*konomiowa*), "father of a girl" (*kutantanowa*), "mother of a boy" (*konomiu*), or "mother of a girl" (*kutantan-u*), rather than by either their personal names or a kinship term. This seems to have been a way of reminding the new parents of their obligations. They were expected to refrain from sexual intercourse with one another at least until "the child crawls" or until "the child is weaned." The time at which they ended their abstinence was vague, for a child is allowed to crawl at 6 to 8 months, but infants are often not fully weaned until they are over 2 years of age. During this period the mother ought to abstain entirely from sex. A man also ought to abstain from sexual relations entirely, but if he would not, at least he should leave the mother of his child alone. He, therefore, generally sought other sexual outlets, and husbands watched men who were fathers of infants rather closely, for they were apt to seduce other men's wives. However, promiscuity on the part of a new father was thought to cause illness to the infant. Even so, few fathers of infants were without occasional sex partners. A father of a small infant also had to respect the dietary rules   *141* which were imposed upon him. He must not eat venison and other meats which were now taboo to him. When a child was thin and weak, when it cried too much, or when it suffered from intestinal disorders, public opinion blamed the father. People searched in their memories for an occasion when they saw the father break a dietary rule. But two men, Champukwi and Awanticantu, bragged to me that the rules did not apply to them. They claimed to have fornicated often and eaten what they pleased and that their infant children remained strong and healthy. They were, of course, roundly criticized by others for their behavior.

Tapirapé individuals acquired several different names during the course of their lives. I have never fully understood this system of acquiring names and changing names during a lifetime, despite the serious efforts of several people to explain that which seemed obvious to them. I know that males changed their names at least three times, sometimes four or five, in a lifetime. Females changed names at least twice. It seems to me that Tapirapé culture had something like a "bank of names." Some of these names were being used at one time by living individuals and some remained, as it were, in the bank to be used at any time.[67] In genealogies the same names reappeared almost every generation, and some names did not appear in one generation, but reappeared in the next. I know that as they grew older Tapirapé were ashamed of the names by which they had been known as small girls and boys. When I returned in 1953 and in 1957, I called people, then adults, by the names by which I had known them as children. This threw everyone into gales of laughter except the person concerned. It was then explained to me that the person had a new name. I learned that some childhood names were descriptive, such as Chiwi (a small rat that runs in the forest), Kaí (monkey), Konomichinga (white boy), Uwuta (the wind), and Waiwí (old woman), to cite but a few examples.

No one was able to explain clearly to me exactly at what point a person changed his or her childhood name and exactly why she or he had a right to a particular new name. Some people insisted that a boy lost his childhood name when he began to wear the penis band and

---

67. It would seem that names are seldom added to this bank. However, two names were added—"Doktor" (honoring Herbert Baldus) and Carlo (Carlos, after me). But it remains to be seen whether those new names will remain in the "bank." Both boys called by those names died, and I know of no one in the present generation who has adopted them.

took an adult name. Girls were said to take an adult name on the occasion of their first menstruation. Champukwi told me that he took that name when he "tied his hair," that is, passed through the ritual of becoming a man. He said he might some day take the name Kamairaho, for his grandfather was called Kamairaho, but that name was at the time already in use by the well-known household head. Kamairaho himself told me that his father, his grandfather, and his great-grandfather had been known by that name. In 1953, after Champukwi had died, I met another man named Champukwi; he explained that my deceased friend had been his mother's brother. Between 1939 and his death in battle with the Kayapó in 1947, Tanopanchowa changed his name to Kamanaré, the name of his older brother who had died in 1939.

Between 1953 and 1965, when I again worked with genealogies and made a village census, several of my adult friends had taken new names. After my field research in 1939-40 I became aware of the fact that among the Gê-speaking tribes such as the Sherente, Akwe-Shavante, and the more distant Eastern Timbira names are inherited, and that along with names come certain rights and inherited roles (Nimuendajú, 1946: 77-79; Maybury-Lewis, 1967: 232-36). In later visits to the Tapirapé, therefore, I kept looking for a structure or a series of rules of descent to explain why Tapirapé assumed specific names and at what point in their lives they did so. I learned that names were changed with changes in age status, but my field notes do not show this always to be true, for an adult would often change his name to that of a deceased kinsman.[68]

But in 1965, when I again visited the Tapirapé, most people had added still another name to their repertoire, for most were also known by a typical Brazilian name as well as by their Tapirapé names. Men were Cantidio, Raimundo, Antonio, and João; women were Clara, Cecilia, and, of course, Maria. The Brazilian backwoodsmen with whom they were often associated found it hard to remember and repeat the strange names in the Tupí tongue. The Indians continued to use their Tapirapé names among themselves.

The Tapirapé divided the life cycle into a series of cognitive periods, which differed somewhat for the two sexes. Those age periods are

---

68. Baldus reports that Kamairaho had three names before he assumed that one at the time he got married. "Kamairaho" had been the name of his father and of his grandfather in the paternal line (1970: 281). One day Kamairaho listed for me fourteen names which he claimed he might call himself. None was the name of a living person.

TABLE 4[a]
Tapirapé age periods

	MALES		FEMALES
nameí	male infant	tantaní	female infant
konomí	small boy	kotantaní	small girl
churangí	young adolescent boy	kuchamoko	adolescent girl
awauahu	young boy about to undergo initiation (i.e. to tie his hair)	—	—
awachewete	man	kuchan	woman
—	—	kuchanwete	somewhat older woman
marikeura	old man	waiwí	old woman

[a] Although some of these terms already contain the diminutive 'í,' that diminutive may be added to yield somewhat different meanings, e.g. *kotantaní-i* designates a girl eight or nine years of age.

given in Table 4. For each of those segments of the life of men and women there were ideal expected behavior patterns indicating how a person ought to behave and how a person ought to be treated by others.

Infants seem to have been treated about the same regardless of sex. Mothers and mother's sisters made wrist and ankle ornaments for babies even though they had to be cut off within a matter of months because the babies grew so fast. The mother carried the baby astride her hip supported in a cotton sling. She nursed the child at any time or place whenever it began to cry. The female relatives of the mother (i.e. women of her household) often carried an infant. Fathers were seen rather frequently carrying infants in their arms, especially late in the afternoon when they had returned from the garden or hunting. There were a series of songs, analogous to lullabies, called "grandmother songs" which women sang to babies. One of them had (in a rather rough translation) these simple lines: "My little grandchild, I wrap your feces in a leaf that grows near the village." Another roughly translates: "My little grandchild, I saw you come out of an armadillo hole." Infants were given considerable attention and care.

144   When boys and girls were able to walk they became *konomí* and

kotantaní. Boys then wore a long thin lip plug made of monkey bone.[69] Both boys and girls wore ankle and wrist ornaments when they had female relatives willing to fabricate them. Girls more often than boys were painted with elaborate geometric designs with genipap dye. Both were given considerable liberty to play. They moved easily about the village, subject to little or no repression. Boys spent hours shooting at lizards with miniature bows armed with bamboo splints as arrows. They sometimes played house and included little girls as wives. Adults roared with laughter when the children imitated quarrels between husband and wife. And I saw boys and girls imitating copulation without being reprimanded by adults. They even imitated the male masked dancers. On one occasion two small boys dressed in small versions of the "crying bird spirit" masks danced about the village asking the residents for food. This was found amusing, and not at all sacrilegious. Young boys and some young girls joined in dancing in public festivals, taking a place at the end of the line. They were decorated with white feathers glued to their bodies and they wore anklets and wrist ornaments. Their bodies were generally painted elaborately. On one occasion, the kaó ceremony, one small boy (konomí) was selected as a somewhat central figure. He danced first in the line of dancers who arranged themselves in pairs one behind the other. The small boy wore a headdress of red macaw feathers. I have already said that both konomí and kotantaní were considered to hold personal property. Every child was supposed to have its own sleeping hammock, but in 1939-40 some did not and were forced to share a hammock with their parents.

But not all children behaved pleasantly at all times. I have seen children of both sexes (aged three to six years) exhibit temper tantrums. One day a small boy named Chiwí fell to the ground screaming because his father refused to give him a small tin box. The father did nothing, ignoring the child until he finally calmed and stopped crying. On another occasion, the daughter of Ananchowa (aged about three years) stood screaming in mid-plaza because the mother refused to give her some food. The mother stood peacefully to one side conversing with another woman. She stopped talking only long enough to ask the child, "Is not your nose running?" All the women laughed, and in time the child ceased to cry. Often, Tapirapé parents seemed to give in to a child when it was crossed, apparently to avoid

---

69. Baldus states that it was made of the leg bone of the emu or rhea (1970: 149).

ABOVE: Kamairaho fabricating the headdress for the kaó dances in 1939.

RIGHT: Wanapio, son of Panterí, decorated for the kawió dances in 1940.

LEFT: A small boy decorated for the 1939 kawió ceremony. He is wearing crocheted wrist ornaments, white bird down is glued to his legs, and he is playing with an unfinished anchunga mask.

BELOW: Ewaí, the small son of Urukumu, dancing at the head of the men's line during the kaó ceremony at the beginning of the dry season of 1939.

A pre-adolescent youth (*churangí*) in 1939. His hair has been cut, he has been painted black with genipap dye, and he has assumed the penis band.

Two youths of *churangí* age in 1965. Only one has had his hair cut in the traditional style; the other looks like a Brazilian.

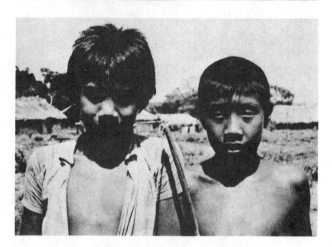

such scenes. I seldom saw a Tapirapé parent use corporal punishment, except in extreme irritation. More than once I saw a Tapirapé father shoot an older son, a mischievous, slightly older konomí (about nine to ten years old), with a blunt arrow tipped with beeswax. On one occasion a father who was irritated with his son took aim from about 148 twenty yards away without rising from his hammock; he hit the boy on the thigh. The boy cried and it raised a lump. The whole affair was highly amusing to the whole village, and villagers teased the small boy because of his "wound." On another occasion I saw a mother, angry with her son of about ten years because he refused to run an errand for her, pull his hair and hit him on the back with her fist. He cried but others found it amusing.

When a boy became churangí (young adolescent), his behavior was likened to that of a monkey. His body ornaments were changed. He now had to wear the penis band tied around his prepuce. Mothers and older sisters sometimes cried when a boy first assumed the penis band, for an infant had been taken from them. On the day that he tied his prepuce he moved from the family dwelling to the takana, hanging his hammock on the side of the building belonging to his moiety of the Bird Societies. During his first night of residence there his mother brought water in a pot to the door of the takana for him to bathe and his father brought him a bow and arrow tipped with beeswax, with which he had to kill two birds for his father to eat. The next morning the men rubbed red annatto paste into his hair. Until the red annatto paste wore off, the men called him each morning to bathe. Then, when the red dye had disappeared, his hair was cropped short and a portion of his scalp was shaven, giving him an appearance not unlike that of the capuchin monkey; in fact, people often made an analogy between that monkey (kaí) and boys of this age status. At the time that his hair was cut his whole body was painted black with genipap dye. He then replaced the thin bone lip plug of the small boy with a short lip plug made of mother of pearl.

Boys of this age status were expected to live apart from the women in the takana for several months, perhaps a year or more. In 1939-40 not all stayed for so long, and all of them returned to their mother's residence for meals after a few days. This was considered the age for training and learning. For a time, the boy could not eat manioc in any form, but was given maize flour instead. He could not eat peanuts or bananas; it was feared that if he did his teeth would fall out. His meat was supposed to be cooked in a pot and not roasted. He was taught to sleep with his legs closed and with his testicles cupped in his hands; by doing so he would never have large testicles and a baggy scrotum, which was considered ugly. He was instructed by his father not to scratch his head or body with his nails, but to use a body scratcher made of bamboo. The Tapirapé did not teach such boys the arts of war; rather, they stressed the art of escape. Churangí were   149 often greased with palm oil so "they would be slick" and unable to slip through the fingers of the Carajá or Kayapó if they should attack. In the middle of the night, adult males would suddenly douse a boy of churangí age with water. Then, they would lift him, groggy with sleep, from his hammock by his armpits. This was done, I was told, to stretch the boy so that he would grow tall and agile in order to run from the enemy.

During the time that a boy lived in the takana, he was supposed to learn the male manual arts—how to weave baskets, how to make a bow and straight arrows, how to fabricate the spirit masks that the men wore in different ceremonies, and other handicrafts. However, I never witnessed any express attempt on the part of an older man to teach a young boy such pursuits. On the other hand, the takana was the place where adult men generally worked, and a boy had ample chance to watch them at it. In addition, boys were supposed to learn songs of the Bird Societies and of the various masked dancers during this period. Again, I cannot remember that they were consciously taught such songs, but it was in the takana where older men sang, often not for ceremonial reasons, but just for their own pleasure. Older men found boys of this age rather amusing in their attempts to carry out adult activities. Wearing the penis band could be rather· painful until the prepuce stretched. Adult men laughed when such boys tended to finger their sexual organs repeatedly, and especially when the irritation caused an erection.[70]

At this same age girls lived with their mothers. They were more frequently decorated with body paint than older women, but they were expected to carry out the work activities of adult women—to help with infants, to carry water, to tend the fire, and to cook. When their first menstruation took place, they ceased being referred to as kotantaní and became kuchamoko. By that time some girls were already married, although it is doubtful that they ever had sexual relations with their "husbands," who had moved into the family dwelling as sons-in-law. There was no ceremony, to my knowledge, which marked a girl's first menstruation or the assumption of her new age status. The village, however, was informed, for she was given a bath, decorated with body paint, and wore several necklaces of beads for several days.

---

70. The Tapirapé claimed that they had never heard of masturbation. Opronunchwi, who had slept in a school dormitory during the months he spent in Conceição do Araguaia with the Dominican priests, told me that he learned of masturbation from the Brazilian boys. "Neither the Tapirapé nor the Carajá boys did it," he told me.

She was not isolated in a special hut or in a portion of the house as girls so often were in other lowland South American societies.[71]

When a boy was older, when he was clearly physically mature, he was no longer a churangí, but an *awauahu* (young man). There were no ceremonies which marked this change of age status; it seemed to be a matter decided between a young man and his older male relatives who would sponsor his initiation rites one or two years later. This period of a young man's life was ambiguous. On the one hand, he was a physically mature male. He no longer painted his whole body black with genipap dye, he removed the mother of pearl lip plug of the churangí, and he allowed his hair to grow long. He could go hunting, he was able to do the heavy work of clearing a garden, and he could perform any adult male pursuit if he wanted to do so. But, on the other hand, he was still tied to his mother's household, where he ate his meals, and he was still under the control of his father. He could not marry until he had gone through the initiation rites. He did not have full adult responsibilities. Young men in this stage of life tended to go hunting or just loaf away the day in the takana. There were no secrets of the takana which were closed to him, but then such young men were rather ignored because they did not as yet take full part in the adult male roles. Awauahu were expected to be chaste, but their sexual urges were, of course, strong. Village gossips related their successful—and unsuccessful—attempts to seduce young girls and even older women. Older men often ordered them about as if they were small boys and they sometimes refused. Champukwi remembered that he insulted his mother's brother, Kamairá, who asked him to go fetch his bushknife. When a young man of this age status was known to be having sexual relations, or when he seemed to be getting too imperious in his behavior, then his father or mother's brother scratched

<hr />

71. Baldus witnessed the decoration of a girl at her first menstruation: "In the morning of June 27 of 1935, Mariampinió, a young Tapirapé girl of twelve to fourteen years of age who had for two years lived with a man, was decorated in a very special way. This was done by Taipá, a widow of mature years, who lived in the same house with her. On this day the first menstruation of Mariampinió had ended. Taipá covered her ankle ornaments with a red annatto paste. Some annatto paste was rubbed into her hair which was pushed back from her forehead so that it seemed to form a close fitting cap. While all this was done, Mariampinió sat on the ground rather apathetically. When the decoration was finished, she reclined in her hammock maintaining the same apathetic appearance. That night, the annatto was removed from her hair and she participated with the older women in the dance of maize kawi, maintaining all the time a serious and apparently tired air about her. During the next rainy season in the time of tall corn, she will receive her tattoos which are characteristic of adult women." (1970: 290, translation mine.) My observation indicated that the tattoo markings, which are scarifications and not true tattoos, are acquired several years later.

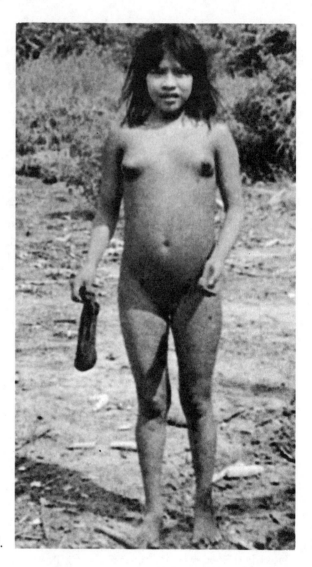

An adolescent girl
(*kochamoko*) in 1940.
She was already married.

him over his thighs and arms with the teeth of the agouti until the
blood flowed freely. Champukwi remembered that he was scratched
several times by Kamairá, who had raised him. This bloodletting was
thought to make the young man stronger as well as to punish him.
Older men showed such scars with considerable pride.

As the young man's hair grew longer, reaching well down below his
152   shoulders, he was considered old enough for his coming of age cere-

mony.[72] This was an occasion to which all youths looked forward and which all older men remembered with nostalgia. The coming of age ceremony was not celebrated every year, for the Tapirapé liked to have two, three, or more youths of the proper age for the ceremonial. With several kin groups cooperating, the occasion became an elaborate affair. In this way there was more food for the festival and everyone was personally involved in collecting the feathers and beads to decorate their young kinsman. So some youths had to wait a year or so until there were others ready to celebrate the ceremony.

At the end of the rainy season in 1940, Kamairaho announced that he would hold a coming of age ceremony for his sister's son, Kanchinapio. This was the occasion I described earlier, in which there was considerable indecision and delay of the rites. Kamairaho lacked support from other households because Kanchinapio was the only youth that year who was ready for the ceremony. But finally, in late May, it began. Throughout the night before the ceremonial, the men of the White Bird Society (Wuranchingió) sang kaó songs in the takana in honor of the initiate, who was a member of Wurankura, the opposite Parrot moiety. If Kanchinapio had been Wuranchinga (youngest society of the White Bird moiety), Ananchá would have sung kaó songs in his honor.

On the morning of the ceremonial the men of the village gathered in the takana and began to dance and sing songs called monikahuya. On this occasion, they danced in the plaza before the takana in single file, moving in a circle, each carrying an arrow in his hand. Monikahuya songs have a quick rhythm, and the pace of the dance was rather fast. Each man had at least touched up his body paint or had been decorated especially for the occasion. The women brought kawi and other food to the door of the takana as gifts or donations to the festivities. Early in that morning, Kamairaho, the sponsor of the ceremony, brought to the takana the paraphernalia and equipment to decorate the young initiate. Preparing the youth for the ceremonial was a slow and painstaking task, but it seemed to be a work of love. The initiate already had new chipampu (wrist ornaments). To these ornaments were tied strands of red string about three feet long. His chest and arms were covered with soft white bird down, glued to his body with a sticky sap. His long hair was oiled and combed and then bound with

72. The ceremonial is called in Tapirapé anchin-kungitanchin, which can be translated rather loosely as "to tie one's hair and wear the large headdress."

At his coming of age ceremony the initiate's hair is bound with cotton cord to suport the large headdress. This was in 1940.

cotton cord into a long pigtail. His pigtail held a wooden block which weighed well over one pound, and in turn this block supported the enormous headdress made of the tail feathers of the red macaw framed by yellow and blue feathers from other forest birds. Also attached to the headdress, and trailing down his back, the initiate carried a mantle of red cotton string. He was then decked with many necklaces of beads; this was an opportunity for his sponsor (and perhaps

Kanchanapió, fully decorated for his coming of age ceremony in 1940.

other relatives) to display their wealth. I estimated that the apparatus which the initiate wore must have weighed about twenty pounds.

There are other small details of the decoration of the initiate. His body was decorated with black genipap dye in an elaborate geometric design. On his feet and legs as high as his calf were ornaments that were bright red with annatto paste. He also wore ear pendants made of parrot feathers shaped like flowers. His mouth was painted with red annatto paste at the corners to make it seem wider. But most im- *155* portant, he then was given the very valuable labret, or lip plug, about eight inches long and made of white quartz, to wear in his lip.[73]

When the decoration was completed the initiate was a "very beautiful" (anchikantu) young man, but he was also a very uncomfortable one. He emerged from the takana and began to dance with the men in a line which formed a large circle. His eyes were downcast, almost as if he were embarrassed. In fact, there seemed to be a sentiment that he was being subjected to a test of endurance. He was expected to dance all through the day, even in the blazing sun of the afternoon, and throughout the night until the morning of the next day. He rested in the shade of the men's house briefly, and even as the men took naps during the night he danced alone. He was given sips of water and a gourd of kawi to sustain him. Finally, about noon the next day, he removed the heavy ornaments and was allowed to sleep. Toward the end of the twenty-four-hour period he was dragging himself along rather than truly dancing.

There is a Tapirapé myth which explains this ceremony as a symbol of a trial and a victory. It tells of a distant ancestor, Chawanamú, who was captured by an enemy people called the Wanchina. He was eaten by these people, but he had a son, Mankanchi, who escaped. Mankanchi was tied by the arms and legs, and was burdened with a headdress. He was expected to dance before he was killed and eaten. But he worked himself loose from his bindings and, freeing himself of the headdress, he ran into the forest where he hid in a hollow log. The next day the Wanchina found only his ankle ornaments, wrist ornaments, and the headdress. They knew then that he had escaped. Mankanchi was the age of the initiates (awauahu) and the many decorations worn by the initiates symbolize the bonds of the young Mankanchi. Thus the coming of age ceremony represented a trial of endurance and a passage to adulthood, and at the same time it was a high point in a man's life. Champukwi remembered his rites of tying

---

73. In 1940 there was but one of these lip plugs left. By common understanding, it was considered "tribal property" and kept by Kamairaho. The Tapirapé said that once they had owned several but each belonged to an important man and they were buried with the owners when they died. Some of them were traded to the Carajá, they say, in return for only a bushknife or a few strands of beads. The Tapirapé did not remember ever seeing these ceremonial labrets made but they claimed that their ancestors knew how to make them. There were no deposits of milky quartz in the region, but Kamairá said that it could be found far to the north where the old village of Chichutawa had been located. The one used in the initiation I have described was broken somewhat later, but it was flown to Rio de Janeiro to be cemented together. As far as I know, the Tapirapé still guard carefully this valued lip plug, for without it they could not "tie the hair" of the young men.

his hair with some nostalgia. He laughed and said, "I was handsome. I shall never again be so beautiful." And, afterward, "A man marries and works hard. One has children and then becomes old." In fact, from this time on men discard decorations progressively as they grow older. At middle age and later, they decorate their bodies hardly at all.

Following the coming of age rites a youth became awachewete, a mature man. He now looked actively for a spouse. I was told that in the past a young man sought a wife in his own village, but if there were none available of the right age, or to his taste, he would visit other Tapirapé villages. By 1939-40 it was not easy for a man of eighteen to twenty years old to find a wife of about his own age or a little younger. Ideally, about a year after he has tied his hair a young man should find a wife and go to live in her mother's household, taking up his role as a son-in-law. There was no marriage ceremony, nor a bride price. When a young man reached an understanding with a young woman he would carry a load of firewood across the village plaza and deposit it at her family dwelling. This was a public announcement of his union with the girl. He then moved his hammock next to hers and became an economic participant in her household. First marriages between young men and young women were proverbially brittle—almost trial marriages. The young couple often broke up after only a few months. This, in part, resulted from the shortage of, and competition for, women of marriageable age. Young couples quarreled mainly over marital fidelity. Young women were said to be rather promiscuous and easily seduced. Irate husbands would take their personal belongings and move back to their maternal household, and the next day another man would take his place. During my residence in Tampiitawa one young woman had four husbands and another had three. But as soon as a woman became pregnant her marriage became more stable and the union might last for several years.

In 1939 one or two young men were forced to marry much older women. For example, Opronunchwi, who was about twenty years old, lived with a woman of about fifty for almost a year. And several mature men took small girls as young as six and seven years of age as their "brides." They justified such unions by calling it "raising your own wife." I was told that it was an old practice which had taken place even before there was a shortage of women, and that a wife raised from childhood by a husband would be a very compatible mate. I rather doubt such justifications for taking a child bride; it seems to have been a case of making the best of a bad situation. In fact, mature 157 husbands did not have sexual access to their child brides and none of them was willing to wait for six to seven years until the girl was old enough for sexual intercourse. These men, however, became members of a household for a time. Their wives' mothers cooked and carried drinking water for them, and they worked alongside their brothers-in-law to support the household. But they had to find sexual satisfaction surreptitiously. This was not difficult in a Tapirapé village, but it did make life complicated—there were quarrels with husbands and the trials of hiding an affair. So a man wanted a wife who was also an active sexual partner. In time, most men left their child wives and formed unions with older women.[74]

There is no typical pattern of Tapirapé marital relations. Some marriages were calm; others were stormy and full of drama. One observation stands out in my mind and in my field notes. Though Tapirapé couples showed affection, kissing seems to have been unknown. When I described it to them, it struck them as a strange form of showing physical attraction, used only by the torí, and, in a way, disgusting. It was common, instead, to see a married couple walking across the village plaza with the man's arm draped over his wife's shoulder. A couple might stand close to each other during a conversation with the man's arms over his wife's shoulders and she holding him around the hips. During a conversation a woman might casually lean against her husband. When resting in a hammock, a couple might lie embraced. People were never self-conscious about these public signs of affection and there were no comments about them from others.

Sometimes such physical contact progressed beyond the line of mere affection. I remember vividly sitting in a hammock not more than four feet away from Kamairá and his young wife. It was a hot

---

74. By 1966 the shortage of women had forced three young Tapirapé men to take Carajá wives, something unheard of in the past. Shapiro has this to say about the phenomenon: "This demographic imbalance which is causing Tapirapé men either to look for Carajá wives or remain single for a longer period of time, is a major factor in speeding up the rate of Tapirapé acculturation. Tapirapé who marry Carajá women usually become commercial fishermen along with their in-laws [both tribes are matrilocal or uxorilocal]. Young single men whose bachelorhood is prolonged due to a lack of available women in their own village spend much of their time fishing and tend to associate with the Carajá. Not yet married, they do not as yet have a cleared garden. Even if young men eventually marry Tapirapé women, this period of their lives during which they have found commercial relations with Carajá and neo-Brazilians has served to introduce them to a mode of life different from the agricultural round of traditional Tapirapé society" (1968a: 26).

158

and sultry afternoon, and they were stretched out in their hammock, arms intertwined and her buttocks thrust into his groin. We were carrying on a casual and rather lackadaisical conversation. Gradually their affection turned into sex play. Kamairá's hand moved slowly down over her loins. She wiggled slowly, pressing against him. His fingers found her vagina and penetrated. He swung their hammock gently. This continued for almost half an hour. He had an erection. But our conversation never stopped. Finally, they rose from the hammock, Kamairá carefully keeping his back to me. They excused themselves, saying "angkuruk" ("we go to urinate"), and walked out of the village to complete their sex act.

The Tapirapé were rather experimental in sexual expression. At least they did not limit themselves to the "missionary position." Sexual intercourse generally took place on the ground, in the privacy of the forest, or late at night protected by darkness in the dwelling. The latter was considered very unsatisfactory, for a hammock is unstable and does not allow ample movement. And the couple must maintain silence inside the dwelling. During intercourse women, I was told, often uttered exclamations. I never, of course, witnessed copulation under normal circumstances. I did, however, witness copulation during a group rape of a young woman who was being punished in this way for refusing to work alongside her female relatives. The circumstances will be described later, but on this occasion I was able to observe several different positions during intercourse. The techniques used by various men differed as the girl became more cooperative. One man lay over the female, face to face, allowing all of his weight to rest upon her. Another squatted on his haunches facing the woman and lifting her buttocks off the ground to meet his penis. Still another supported himself on his knees and elbows with his weight off the woman while she wrapped her legs about his waist. Under more normal circumstances, I was told that Tapirapé women sometimes took the superior position, mounting the male who lay on his back. This was done particularly when the male had some difficulty in achieving full erection. Champukwi assured me that Tapirapé women sometimes performed fellatio on their husbands, but he professed not to know what cunnilingus was and doubted that this took place even among the torí. I will never know whether or not this was true or if it was a case of male chauvinism on Champukwi's part. Likewise, I will never know whether Tapirapé women ever reached orgasm. I rather   159 think they did, but I could find no word for female climax in the Tapirapé language, and Champukwi, my most intimate friend, professed not to know what it meant when I tried to explain it to him.

People told me of males in the past who had allowed themselves to be used in anal intercourse by other men. They were treated as favorites by the men, who took them along on hunting trips. There were no men alive in 1939-40 with such a reputation. Kamairaho gave me the names of five men whom he had known during his lifetime or about whom his father had told him "had holes." Some of these men were married to women, he said, but at night in the takana they allowed other men to "eat them" (have anal intercourse). His father told him of one man who took a woman's name and did women's work. "He made manioc flour, he cooked, he carried water, and he knew how to make cotton string ornaments and hammocks. He painted his body with genipap like a woman. His husband was a Bird Society song leader." Kamairaho never saw this transvestite, but said that he remembers that older men had said that the "man-woman" had died because she was pregnant. "Her stomach was swollen but there was no womb to allow the child to be born." None of my informants had ever heard of a woman who had taken the male role or who preferred sex with another female.

Homosexuality continued to form a part of male sexual joking in 1939-40. Since I did not then have a wife and since Valentim performed female tasks such as carrying water and cooking, we were sometimes the butt of such jokes.

Pederasty also appears in Tapirapé mythology. In one story told of Tortoise, who is a trickster, and of Jaguar, who sought to catch Tortoise, they agreed to have anal intercourse. Jaguar agreed to let Tortoise penetrate him first because Tortoise is so small. Jaguar did not know that the Tortoise has a very long phallus. Tortoise penetrated Jaguar in the anus and Jaguar ran off through the forest howling with pain. This same theme recurs in the stories told to me regarding the dream-experiences of Waré, a great shaman who lived long ago.

Sometimes Tapirapé marital life could be rather stormy. I have already mentioned that men sometimes beat their wives, but Tapirapé husbands also often felt somewhat downtrodden and put upon when their wives stopped cooking and carrying drinking water for them. Baldus, in a short article, caught the timidity of the Tapirapé men
160   faced by their wives in the following description:

Generally the couples live well together, and there are not many divorces. But sometimes a Don Juan appears and has his adventures. And there are also women who take the initiative for an escapade. Maeuma was an assiduous, hard-working, ugly man married to a beautiful and lazy woman. One day he beat her with a club because she had not prepared food for him. Moreover, she had had intercourse with Kamairá during Maeuma's absence. Then, the adulteress left her husband in order to live together with the widowed Kamairá, a strong, good-natured man. For a few days Maeuma was angry at him and kept out of his way. He sat down in the men's house and composed a satirical song about the adulterous couple which he sang loudly innumerable times. Then he was reconciled to Kamairá and remained without boiled food while the woman continued living with the strong, good-natured man.

The following dialogue with Kamairaho, the most important leader, gives an idea of the difference between wished and real behavior.

K.: "Are white men's women quarrelsome?"

B.: (anxious to know the background of this question) [75] "No."

K.: "All Tapirapé women quarrel" (he means: with their husbands).

B.: "Do the men quarrel also?"

K.: "Men's quarrel is small, the women quarrel big."

B.: "Man flees with his feather ornaments and hammock when his wife is quarreling."

K.: smiles and confirms it. . . . (I observed too often that an angry woman threatens to throw in the fire the most valuable possessions of her husband.)

B.: "Your wife is quarrelsome also?"

K.: (lying) "No. But Wantanamu's wife quarrels big, and Tanopantshoa's wife quarrels." (These two leaders are his political rivals.) K. continues: "When woman is angry, she moves to another house. Mangambi's wife moved to another house."

B.: "Maeuma and Mangambi have beaten their wives."

K.: (lying) "They haven't beaten them." He adds: "Many women beat their husbands." (I never observed this.)

B.: "Are the men afraid of their wives?"

K.: "Men are afraid."

B.: "Are the women afraid of their husbands?"

K.: "Women have no fear. All Tapirapé women quarrel big."

B.: "All?"

---

75. Statements within parentheses are Baldus's observations.

K.: All."

B.: "Your wife also?"

K.: "My wife doesn't quarrel." After a while he asked: "Does your wife quarrel when you will make a great journey?"

B.: "No. And yours?"

K.: "Mine? Oh no!"

(Baldus, n.d. 604-5.)

Adultery was, in fact, very common within a Tapirapé village. The only women who were free of charges of adultery were the wives of men of considerable prestige, such as the household heads and shamans. Gossips told me that Kantuowa, the wife of Kamairaho, had many men before she married Kamairaho, but that now other men were afraid to approach her. They also told me that Kamanaré, who had died during the dry season of 1939, had been having sexual relations with Urukumu's wife and that they suspected Urukumu, a powerful shaman, of having perhaps caused Kamanaré's death. Except for the wives of these important men almost all other women were suspected of adulterous affairs by the men. Men, therefore, kept rather careful watch over their wives. They often accompanied their wives to the forest when they went there for bowel movements and to the gardens even when other women went there to harvest peanuts or cotton, which chores are women's work. But when men were forced to absent themselves from the village on hunting expeditions, some of them felt that certainly their wives had been unfaithful. Sometimes they had proof, for it was customary for an adulterer to offer a woman a gift such as a string of beads. Such gifts were hard to hide and presented material evidence of unfaithfulness.[76] Few marriages were actually broken up over a real or suspected adulterous affair; men might beat their wives with a stick or with broad side of a bushknife and a woman might stop cooking or carrying water for a day in retaliation, but then the couple resumed their normal life.

Women, too, could be jealous. Some younger men had reputations as Don Juans, as Baldus called them. One of these was my good friend Champukwi. He was very careful to deny extramarital affairs before

---

76. Women could sometimes know if a man had had sexual intercourse by his eating habits. A man who has sexual relations was not supposed to eat the next morning until the sun was high in the sky (mid-day). Some men did eat the morning after adulterous sexual relations and became ill. Others lied to their wives, stating that they were not hungry. Likewise, men believed that a woman who had made kawi should refrain from intercourse that day. If she did not, the kawi would be filled with semen and a man who eats it would develop a paunch.

anyone in the village. However, when the two of us were alone on a hunting trip, he listed fifteen women with whom he had had sexual relations and named four of them as his current mistresses. He asked me not to speak of his affairs in the village because "his wife's brothers might hear."[77] His wife, Ipareowa, however, had heard of his affairs. She tried to beat him, but he ran laughing from their house. Champukwi complained that she nagged at him, and one day he stuck his two forefingers into her mouth, stretching her cheeks until they obviously hurt. She cried, and for two days Champukwi came to our house begging Valentim for food and water, for Ipareowa had stopped cooking or carrying water for him. He slept for two nights in the takana, where he took his hammock and personal belongings for fear that she would destroy them.

After a young woman became a young wife, and, ideally, before she had a child (i.e. sixteen to eighteen years of age), she was faced with a most painful ordeal. She was expected to subject herself to facial scarification. This traditionally consisted of a quarter-moon design on each cheek and a half-moon design under the chin. It is a lifetime decoration and the Tapirapé believed that only women who carried that design on their face were truly beautiful. The design was drawn in charcoal and then cut into the face with crisscross lacerations using the sharp incisor teeth of the agouti or paca. The lacerations were about one-eighth of an inch deep and into these wounds genipap juice was rubbed so that it would become permanently black. This was a most painful ordeal and Tapirapé women were frightened of it. They put it off from year to year. It is understandable, then, that when I returned in 1953 the practice was already in decline. By 1957 only a few older women sported the facial designs. One woman had a half moon design only on one cheek. I was told that she began the operation but gave up because of the pain and never had it completed. In 1965 only two older women had facial designs. They were women I had known in 1939, when the practice was almost obligatory. One of these women was among those who had gone to live in Chichutawa in 1946 and who wandered through the forest with the small band led by Kamairá, only to reappear in New Village in the early 1960's. If my memory serves, however, I think both women had gone through the scarification operation in Tampiitawa before 1939.

---

77. Whenever there was a marital quarrel, even a loud one with wifebeating and cries, the wife's brothers preferred not to know anything at all about it. However, if a woman was constantly ill-treated they could demand that the husband move out of the house.

A young Tapirapé woman (*kuchan*) in 1940 with scarifications on her face. The red macaws were kept for their feathers.

Urukumu operating on Taniwaya's face in 1939.

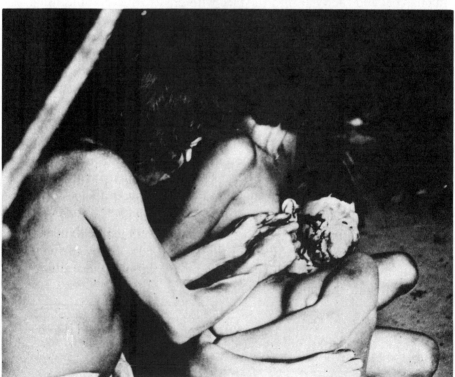

Taniwaya as she looked the day after the scarification operation.

Taniwaya's brother allows Urukumu to scratch him deeply in order to show that men can also bear pain.

In 1940 I had the rather dubious opportunity to witness the operation performed on a beautiful girl called Taniwaya. She was almost twenty years old at the time. She had been married for several years to an able young man, and theirs seemed to be a most stable union. The couple did not have children. The time selected for the operation was late in March or early April, the time of the "new corn." In 1940 only two men, Urukumu, who also was a shaman, and Kamairá, were said to know how to perform the operation, which was called *kuchan achahut* (literally, "woman cut"). Kamairá did not like to perform the operation and generally refused to do so. The burden fell most often upon Urukumu. This operation took place just inside the door of Urukumu's residence, where there was sufficient light. The woman lay on her side with her head held between Urukumu's knees. Her older sister sat near by to be of assistance. First, Urukumu sketched the outlines of the design on the woman's face with charcoal; then, using a knife made of the incisor of an agouti or a paca (both are rodents), he cut, following the outlines on one side of her face. Urukumu used three knives, which from time to time were sharpened at the edge of a stone. Once he had cut the outlines of the design on one cheek, he began to make horizontal and then vertical cuts until that part of the cheek was a bloody crisscross—almost slashed into a pulp. He then poured genipap mixed with water into the wound. Then leaves of the kaona (literally: ka, "plant"; ona, "black;" an unidentified herb) were plastered over the wound. The operation was slow, and from time to time a female assistant brought water in a gourd to wash away the blood so Urukumu could see to follow his design. When he finished one cheek, he began the other and then proceeded to the half moon on the chin. The patient whimpered but did not struggle. From time to time she groaned, "ankai! ankai!" ("it hurts!"). The operation lasted from 9 a.m. until 4 p.m. That night Taniwaya slept in a hammock in Urukumu's house, and late into the night she could be heard moaning lowly. Her husband stuffed his tobacco pipe with cotton leaves and blew the smoke over her face. This was thought to relieve the pain somewhat. I saw no compresses applied at all.

The next day Taniwaya appeared in the village plaza; her whole face was swollen horridly. She returned after a bath and spent most of that day and the next reclining in her hammock. I was told that for several days she could eat only kawi, so painful were her face and jaw. The swelling continued for more than a week; then her wounds formed scabs which she was not supposed to scratch with her fingernails. After about a month the dried scabs began to fall off and the black design similar to a tattoo design was left on her face for the rest of her life.

Tapirapé women have always been genuinely afraid of this operation. Stories were told to me of a young woman who died of it, without doubt from secondary infections.[78] On the day after he operated on Taniwaya, Urukumu began to work on the face of Tampaputunga, a woman of at least twenty-eight to thirty years of age and the only mature woman in the village at that time (1940) without facial designs. (She was the widow of Kamanaré but now married to Ikoriwantori.) After he had merely sketched in the design with charcoal on one cheek she struggled free and ran off to hide in the bush. She stayed hidden all day and returned home only in the dark of the night. All day people made jokes about her and laughed at how fast she had run. Her husband, Ikoriwantori, did not go to search for her, and he made no comment. People said that he could have shown his disgust for her by publicly announcing that she was available to all men for a group rape. If she had been without a husband, she would have been automatically available for a raping party. Kamairaho told me of five women who had been raped because they ran away from the scarification operation. He said that sometimes the men raped a woman despite her husband's wishes. Now that she had desisted before finishing the operation, Tampaputunga would have to wait for another year if she wished to continue it, for Urukumu refused to take up the operation again that year on a frightened and unwilling patient. Some women have been known to go through life with only one cheek decorated, such as the woman I saw in New Village in 1965. To be in such a condition in 1939-40 meant that her prestige was low, that she was not fully respected by her husband, and that she was ridiculed by other women. At that time if a woman without facial scars did not have a husband, she would only attract a man of low prestige. However, by 1965 no Tapirapé woman even planned to undergo the operation. They made exclamations of horror when they viewed photographs of Taniwaya's operation of 1940. I rather think they were mystified as to why their mothers and grandmothers before them had subjected themselves to such pain.

---

78. There is a night bird whose cry sounds like "kuchan iunga! Wu! Wu!" The Tapirapé said that it was the anchunga of a young woman who had died from the operation.

After a woman had been scarified, and on the same day, it was traditional for a man, either her husband or brother, to stand publicly and to allow himself to be scratched deeply over his arms and legs with the teeth of the dogfish. The operator was the same man who had performed the operation on the woman. In 1940 it was Taniwaya's brother who undertook this obligation and Urukumu who did the scratching. The cut ran deeply from shoulder to elbow and from thigh to kneecap. Blood flowed freely and the victim should not have uttered a sound (and did not) during the process. As Kamairaho commented: "Men must show that they too can stand pain."

The operator was paid for his services, but there was no fixed price and it was considered to be a gift. In the case of Taniwaya, her husband presented Urukumu with a bushknife and ten arrows. A generous woman, however, would spin the cotton and fabricate a hammock for the man who performed the operation upon her. Likewise, the operator received gifts for scratching the man who publicly endured pain for his wife or sister. After the operation the young woman was no longer described as kuchan (young woman) but was now a kuchanwete (fully mature woman).

Few Tapirapé could expect to reach old age. To be old was to be over forty-five or fifty years of age, but people spoke of individuals who were probably senile. The treatment of old people (i.e. men known as marikeura and women known as waiwí) is best described as "toleration." They were neither highly respected nor sought after. Such people never wore body paint or decorations. They were fed and they had a hammock, although it might be ragged and torn. They were allowed to sit in the sun or shade, whichever was more comfortable. Old women were relieved of all food taboos. The only relatively old Tapirapé I knew in 1939 was an almost blind woman who seemed to be just waiting for death. She was Tanipa, a woman of about sixty. She lived with her daughter and her son-in-law but often she moved her hammock to sleep and eat in the near-by household where her married grandson lived. When she died in 1940, mourning was brief.

When a Tapirapé dies his anchunga leaves the body. Anchunga may be translated as soul, shadow, the image as revealed in a mirror or a pool of water, or spirit. Anchunga or iunga ('i' is third person plural possessive, thus their spirit) is used to mean not only spirits of the human dead, but also the spirits of living things of the water and of the forest as well as of other supernatural beings that inhabit the

168   forest. Iungwera seems to mean a "place of spirits," or other world,

but there does not seem to be a special other world for ordinary men. The Tapirapé told me that there is a "world below the earth" which no Tapirapé had ever seen and which the shamans did not know "even in their dreams." They had heard about it only from their grandfathers. In that world conditions are ideal. There are no mosquitoes, no one is ill, and there are no plagues. There people have children, dogs, chickens, and pets. They do not have bushknives, for there is no need to plant gardens. "No one knows what, where, and how they eat." Other Tapirapé told me of a place in the sky where some Tapirapé go after death. There are large gardens and lots of tobacco there. It had been seen by shamans in dreams. But this concept of an afterworld in the sky seems rather suspect to me, for the missionary "Frederico," whom they loved, was, it seems, always talking about Heaven. The Tapirapé were certain, however, that there is a village of deceased shamans far to the west called Maratawa or panché iungwera (place of the souls of the shamans). Most Tapirapé seem to believe that the ordinary man's soul or spirit leads a somewhat errant existence—sometimes coming near the fires of the living in their villages, sometimes just lingering in the forest.[79]

During my residence with the Tapirapé in 1939-40 I was present at the death of several individuals. Not much attention was given to the death of an infant under one year old; only the mother cried for one night. The death of the elderly woman seemed rather to be expected. She was thin and wasted, and she lay in a coma for several days before she died. People spoke of her as dead long before she finally succumbed. At the death of a young man there was considerable mourning and a ceremony was suspended that had just begun. The death of Kamanaré, however, brought forth the full enactments of the rites of burial, of mourning, and of all the characteristic behavior on such an occasion. Kamanaré had been a man in full bloom of male maturity, about thirty-five years old, strong, handsome, and considered to have a fine voice. He had been the song leader and hunting leader of the Ananchá Bird Society. Just before his death he had become a household leader. He therefore had a large network of kin and followers. He had been much admired by most people. His death was a shock to most people in Tampiitawa. He fell ill one day and re-

---

79. Baldus reports four levels of the Tapirapé universe—an underworld, the earth which we inhabit, a world above called "sieve" (urupema), a world above that is called "near the wild banana plants," which only the shamans can see (1970: 357). The Tapirapé world view is described in more detail in Chapter 6).

mained in his hammock with a high fever. There was much talk about his condition. I suspected malaria and meekly suggested large amounts of water and some quinine, but no one paid any attention to my advice. Several people simply predicted early death. Then, in the early morning hours of June 26, 1939, loud screams issued from his house and his wife kept shouting "amano! amano!" ("he is dead!"). I went to see him; his lips were cracked and dry and he was barely breathing. His two brothers were holding on to the strings of his hammock and moaning. They danced slowly, beating one foot strongly into the earth. People began to gather in the house as the news spread. By ten o'clock the next morning his sister and brother felt his head and arm. He was cold.

The body, still in the hammock, was moved slightly to one side to accommodate the large number of visitors. His wife lay prostrate with grief in another hammock alongside the body. By noon, eight men were stomping out the dance of mourning. The wailing was stylized; it had a rhythm, and it rose and fell almost as if it were a mournful song. I asked if the sounds they made were "songs of death." "No" they answered, "this is crying." The large room was filled with dust from the rhythmic stomping of feet and the constant coming and going of people.

That afternoon Kamanaré's younger brother, Tanopanchowa, prepared the body for burial. Kamanaré's hair was molded by a mixture of beeswax and red annatto dye until it took the appearance of a bonnet. The face was painted black with genipap. Then white bird down was stuck to the chest. The body lay stretched in the hammock. The grave was dug directly under the hammock. It was sufficiently deep so the hammock could be suspended in the grave without touching the earth. Three strong bamboo boughs were cut. They would act as crossbars, supporting the body in the hammock and the earth to be piled on top. Then, as people mourned, the personal belongings of Kamanaré were accumulated to be placed in the grave. I saw five bushknives, a bow, about fifteen arrows, a pair of scissors, a hunting knife, two small pocketknives, a shirt which I had given him, and some cotton cloth. Then Kamanaré's beads were removed from the gourd in which they had been stored. He had owned about four feet of beads, strung on one long string. There was some conversation. I could not make out if his relatives wanted to keep some beads, but the long strand was broken and the beads were thrown into the grave. At sunset the noise of the dancing became louder. The grave was closed by placing three woven mats of palm leaves over the crossbars. Women began to throw handfuls of earth over the mats. Soon it was filled to the level of the house floor, but they continued until a mound about two feet high marked the grave. Then water was poured over the mound to settle the dust. The mourning group danced through the household door in a group and on to the plaza. The men of the group danced into the takana and out again and, joined again by the women, they danced back to Kamanaré's house.[80]

Kamanaré's wife, his mother, and his sister (actual sister) had their hair cut that evening. It was cut close to the head, about a half-inch from the skull. Tanopanchowa, his younger brother, had his hair cut as short as that of the women. Other men who were relatives or friends cut back their hair "in sorrow." The peculiar stomping type of dance of the men accompanied by a stylized "cry" and the low wailing of the women continued until after midnight. Then the village was quiet.

It was early the next morning that a group of Kamanaré's male relatives appeared at my house, about a hundred feet away. Their faces were serious, and certainly not friendly. Without saying a word, they entered and removed from the walls and from the rafters a ceremonial bow, two baskets, a headdress made of macaw feathers, and a decorated lance, all of which Kamanaré had made for me. (I had been planning to take them to the Brazilian National Museum.) Valentim wanted to protest, but I could see that the atmosphere was tense and cautioned him to be quiet. The group took the articles just a few feet away and burned them. It was explained to me later that it was dangerous to preserve anything belonging to, or recently made by, the deceased. Keeping macaw feathers which had belonged to him would attract his anchunga to my house.

Furthermore, people told me that Kamanaré's relatives were in a rather dangerous state of mind that day. They were iwuterahu (the one word means both "angry" and "sad"). The Tapirapé recognize that people die from the blow on the head by a heavy war club, from being shot through with arrows, from the shot of a rifle, or sometimes by accident, such as being crushed by a falling tree. But death from illness is almost always interpreted as being the result of magic or

---

80. Baldus was told that shamans who were executed because of suspected sorcery were not buried in the house, but near the village in the forest where their relatives could go to mourn them (1970: 302). I have no information on this subject.

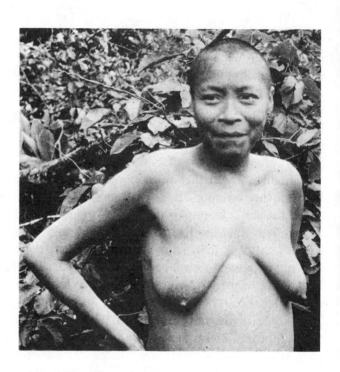

In 1939, after Kamanaré's
death, his sister, Tanui,
cut her hair.

sorcery. As soon as anyone dies, especially a man as prominent as
Kamanaré, suspicion turns on strong shamans who are known to be
able to cure and, at the same time, kill through sorcery. So for a day
or so Kamanaré's male relatives were in an ugly mood. Valentim and
I stayed close to our house to avoid them. The shaman Urukumu was
not seen about for several days, and when he next came to visit me he
asked if it would not be possible for him to go away with me when I
returned to my homeland. He was obviously afraid.

For at least two or three weeks after Kamanaré died, each evening
at sundown the sound of a low ritual wailing issued from his house
and from several other houses where he had female kinsmen. It lasted
only a few minutes each day, but it is at that sad time of day that
women come to think of the departed. Occasionally at sundown, without warning, a woman will sit in her hammock and wail for a few
minutes for a departed child, son, or husband who died—sometimes a
year or more earlier. Five days after Kamanaré's death a group of his
relatives gathered around the door of his residence. Then, chanting,
they danced around the village plaza and down a path that led to the
172   forest. They returned silently. Champukwi explained that although

the anchunga leaves the body when death takes place, the spirit likes to remain around the living. Kamanaré's relatives had led his anchunga out of the village. There were no special annual ceremonies to honor the dead. Nor were there any taboos on the use of the deceased's name. When I returned in 1953, I found that Tanopanchowa, the younger brother who had taken Kamanaré's death so hard, had assumed that name to honor his brother.

Kamanaré's widow mourned every day at sundown for almost one month; then her daily wailings were heard no more. Now said Okané, one of the young men, "she will have intercourse every day with different men." A widow passed through a period of sexual license before she married again. Tanpanputunga, Kamanaré's widow, seemed to take advantage of this widow's right. In fact, she was rather blatant in her behavior. She stood in the village plaza talking to several young men with her arms around one of them and resting her head on his shoulder. Gossips gave me a list of ten men with whom she had intercourse. Kamairaho was angry with his sister's son, Kanchinapió, who was about sixteen years old and who had not as yet tied his hair, because he was known to have accompanied the widow to the forest several times. Within a month or so, Tanpanputunga had taken a new husband—a young man, Ikoriwantori, who left his child wife to live with her.

By 1965, when we visited the New Village, the Tapirapé had abandoned the custom of burying their dead within their houses. There was a small cemetery just outside the village. It was explained that just a few years before a Dutch woman scientist, a visitor to the Tapirapé, had died, the victim of a snake bite. The little cemetery was established for her burial, and a few days later her husband died of a heart attack and was interred by her side. The missionary, Father Francisco, used the example of the burial of the two Europeans in a cemetery to persuade the Indians to change their old custom. There was never any smell within the Tapirapé house from the putrefaction of the body, nor any way that I know of for the body to have caused contagion to the house inmates. Yet the practice offended Brazilians and Europeans. However, the shift in burial from the house floor to a near-by cemetery was a necessary adaptation to new conditions. Now that the Tapirapé would no longer be able to move their village (and houses) periodically, it was almost a necessity for them to give up their traditional practice of burying their dead inside their houses. *173*

6 A Spirit for Every Season

The Tapirapé view of the supernatural world, and their relationship to it, was not well organized. That world was made up of a multitude of aquatic and terrestrial animal spirits, sky and forest spirits, and spirits of the dead. These spirits, most of which were considered alien and dangerous to man, were controlled and manipulated by the shamans, or panché. The Tapirapé had no true religious rituals, if one means by that term the manipulation of sacred objects and prayers to influence supernatural beings. Likewise, they had no priests who, through their knowledge of ecclesiastical rituals and prayers, influenced and controlled animistic beings and forces. Rather, Tapirapé shamans had certain personal characteristics which allowed them to associate directly with the supernatural. And, with the passage of time and experience, they were able to translate the supernatural to the layman. The Tapirapé also had a series of festivals or ceremonials throughout the year in which masked men impersonated animistic beings and during which their shamans exhibited their powers. Compared to other tribal groups—the Zuni of the southwestern United States, for example—the Tapirapé religious and ceremonial system was inconsistent; it nonetheless provided a relatively coherent view of man's relationship to both the natural and the supernatural world.[81]

---

81. It is, of course, more than probable that Tapirapé religious thought and its re-

Central to an understanding of Tapirapé religion is a knowledge of their ancestral culture heroes and the activities of Tapirapé shamans. In a sense, the culture heroes, who made the world as man knows it, and the living shamans were closely related. In fact, the ancestral heroes of the remote past were shamans. Sometimes they were described in exactly these terms—as great panchés.[82] Both the legendary heroes and the contemporary panchés continued to live after death in Maratawa, the Village of Shamans. Knowledge of horizons beyond their direct experience—of far-off places and people, of the heavens, of the origins of people and things—came to the Tapirapé only through experiences of their legendary heroes and their shamans. Myths described the origin of fire and cultivated plants, and the genesis of social institutions, in terms of the adventures and travels of ancestral heroes who were very great shamans.[83] Contemporary shamans traveled widely in their dreams and in trance; they whisked off to faraway places—to the Araguaia River, to the villages of the Kayapó, to the heavens, to the home of Thunder—in their "canoes" (gourds such as those used by the Tapirapé for eating utensils) or in flight, transfigured into birds. Since the Tapirapé had a wealth of vicarious experience to draw upon, they seldom tried to explain directly those realms of distant places, of supernatural beings of other times, or of the astral bodies. Instead, the Tapirapé resorted to the travels and exploits of a shaman "who had been there" to explain the world beyond their own experience.

When Champukwi traveled with me to the Araguaia River for the first time in 1939, he identified a large rock formation at the mouth of the Tapirapé River as the place where Panterí, a contemporary shaman, had seen the giant red macaws from which the supernaturals

lated ceremonial organization was more coherent before 1939-40 and prior to severe depopulation. Furthermore, one more fluent in the Tapirapé language than I was in 1939-40 would have understood Tapirapé religion, particularly in its more abstract concepts, better than I did.

82. My description of shamanistic activity is based upon field data from 1939-40. There are no longer strong shamans. For purposes of ease of exposition, I have pluralized panché by suffixing the English plural allomorph '-s'. This is incorrect Tapirapé; the proper Tapirapé term is panché-iawera ("the panché collectively").

83. They share such legendary heroes with the coastal Tupí of Brazil and with other lowland South American tribes. Alfred Metraux (1928b: 7) wrote: "Pour les Tupinambá, comme pour la plupart des tribus sudaméricaines, certaines personnages doués d'une puissance supérieure à celle du commun des magiciens on été les artisans du monde tel qu'il se présentait à leur yeux, mais ils n'ont été souvent moins les créatures que les transformateurs. Je veux dire par là que, même s'ils ont creé le ciel, les astres, et la terre leur œuvre est toujours partielle et incomplète, ne s'achevant que postérieurement à la suite d'incidents divers."

pluck tail feathers. Similarly, Opronunchwi told me that when he traveled down the Araguaia River with the Dominican priests he recognized the rapids near Santa Maria do Araguaia as those created by Kaowaho, a legendary ancestor. Tradition has it that Kaowaho created those rapids to commemorate the spot where he had eaten many fish.

The Tapirapé considered the present time to be the third creation. Twice before, people were destroyed: once by flood and once by universal fire. Before those catastrophes, the people were pre-Tapirapé and called *Karajuntuwera*. Those ancient people lacked the many refinements which were later brought to the Tapirapé by their own ancestral heroes. They ate several varieties of wild seeds, but lacked manioc, maize, and all of the modern garden plants. They also were without bow and arrow. I am not certain whether the Karajuntuwera lived before or after the flood, but when the great deluge came one man and one woman climbed a palm tree which grew as rapidly as the water rose, carrying them above the flood. After they had been there for some time, the man began to spear fish and snakes which swarmed in the water, using the long palm leaves as spears. As he killed a fish or a snake, the waters gradually diminished and finally returned to the riverbeds. From the primordial snakes of the flood, the Tapirapé told me, had descended the people of the Carajá tribe. "They [the snakes] had circles under their eyes" (the tribal facial marking of the Carajá). Four ancestors seem to have escaped the universal fire. Those people were birds—two male jacu, one female parakeet, and one female mutum. These four escaped underground, and, I presume, the rest of the Karajuntuwera were destroyed. From the union of these two couples came ampa-awa, men and women as we know them today.

The legendary ancestral heroes came to live with the Tapirapé during this period after the fire and flood. In what sequence they lived as men among the Tapirapé is not clear, but they lived a long time ago. All of them were transformers of life on earth rather than creators; that is, they did not create man, garden products, and fire, but they modified man's life, transferred ownership of natural phenomena, or brought plants with them. I know little about some of these ancestral heroes; their names were mentioned only in passing and I never was able to collect a full legend concerning their passage on earth. Such is the case of Kaowaho, to whom Opronunchwi attributed the rapids of the Araguaia River.[84] The myths about other ancestral heroes, such as Apuwenonu, Petura, Imanawungó, Anchopeteri, and the twins Tomatochiri and Mukwuraura, were better known and I was able to record fairly coherent accounts of their exploits.

Among the legendary heroes, Petura was important. He brought many gifts to mankind and otherwise transformed the world by trickery. For example, Petura stole fire from the King Vulture and brought it to mankind. Before that time, men were cold and could not cook. To gain fire, Petura laid down and acted as if he were dead. Maggots came to cover his body and the King Vulture came to feast on these maggots. First he brought "red fire," then "yellow fire," then "black fire"; when King Vulture was bloated with maggots, Petura picked up "red fire" and ran. King Vulture shouted, "Bring it back and we shall eat maize," but Petura replied, "No. From now on you will eat carrion." In consequence, vultures do not eat maize today.

Petura also stole day or dawn from the owls. Before then the world was dark all the time and men were afraid to go to their gardens because jaguars would attack them. Petura set off to the house of the owl; it was very far and Petura slept many times en route. When he arrived, the owl showed him a place to hang his hammock. The next day, he watched the owl take "morning" out of a sack. Then the owl invited Petura to go with him to the garden, but Petura excused himself, claiming that his feet were sore from the trip. That night Petura stole the sack containing daylight and ran. Now the owls do not have daylight and can only see when it is dark.

Petura had other adventures of lesser importance. He stole genipap from the monkey and the Tapirapé began to use it for black dye. From the anteater he learned how to manufacture a war club. Since the anteater was making the club in order to kill Petura, he punished the anteater by sticking the club into his anus (thus the anteater has a long tail) and thrusting a wooden stick up his nostrils (thus the anteater has a long, curved proboscis). Petura also met the land tortoise and asked: "Where is your house?" When the tortoise answered: "I have no house," Petura tore bark off a tree and made the tortoise a "house" (i.e. its shell). Now the tortoise travels slowly, carrying its house, and it can be caught easily by the Tapirapé. And Petura met the rhea, who was clearing a large garden from the forest. This gar-

---

84. Kaowaho seems to have been the ancestor of one of the Feast societies (see Chapter 4).

den is now savanna country, where the rhea lives. Petura helped the rhea to clear the forest. He worked faster than the rhea, although the rhea used a bushknife and a steel axe. The rhea offered to trade tools and Petura gave him a clay knife and axe in exchange for the steel tools, which Petura consequently gave to the Tapirapé.[85]

Petura left the Tapirapé, but he still lives today. Some people told me that he lives in Maratawa with the other great shamans, but others said that he lives in the sky.[86] Wherever he lives, he never died; he lives and re-lives his life cycle as the cycle of seasons. In the early rains of October to December, Petura is a small boy (konomí). During the heavy rains of January to March, he is an adolescent youth (churangí). He is a mature man (awachewete) as the rains diminish in April and May, and as the year draws to its close, Petura becomes a marikeura (old man). But as the year begins anew with the refreshing rains of October, he begins a new life cycle. This symbolizes the agricultural year. The Tapirapé planted when Petura is young (October-November) and they harvested most of their crops when he is a mature man (May and June).

Another legendary culture hero was Apuwenonu, who came down from the sky to live with the Tapirapé. He took a Tapirapé wife, by whom he had a son called Imanawungó. He brought with him manioc, maize, peanuts, yams, cotton, and all the other plants which the Tapirapé cultivate in gardens today. The Tapirapé did not know how to plant them, so Apuwenonu called the birds, such as the white egret, the wild goose, parakeets, and many others, to help in the garden. Apuwenonu's wife taught Tapirapé to work with cotton—to make hammocks and to fabricate wrist and ankle ornaments. When Apuwenonu became old he left the Tapirapé, taking his son Imanawungó with him. Both became stars, and the Tapirapé were able to point out Apuwenonu and his son for me.[87] Apuwenonu's wife, Anuntero, was carried away by water and some people said she became a freshwater dolphin.

It was chiefly through their ancestral culture heroes and the shamans who live today (i.e. 1939-40) that the Tapirapé knew of the sun, the moon, and other heavenly bodies. As the sun is male, so the moon

---

85. I have no idea what the original version of this legend may have been before metal tools were known among the Tapirapé.

86. I suspect this information may be due to the efforts of the missionary Frederick Kegel, who explained to the Tapirapé that Jesus Christ and God live in the sky.

87. It seemed to me that Apuwenonu was Venus and Imanawungó might have been Vega, but I had poor celestial charts with me in 1939-40.

is female. In the legend, both were thought of as people and given human names. The sun was called Ancheriko and the moon Tamparawa. The moon was sister to the sun and she married Anchopeteri, a legendary ancestor of the Tapirapé. From him the Tapirapé learned that the sun is an old man without hair on his head. He travels through the heavens wearing a large headdress of red macaw feathers, and since red macaw feathers are "hot," the headdress gives off heat. Each night, after limping through his daily orbit (for the sky was described as "rough," and the sun was believed to have thorns in his feet), he returns underground to the east to his house at Maratawa. There he eats very little and in a short time sets out again. The sun, I was told, slapped his sister (the moon) full in the face because of her adulterous behavior. His hand was wet with genipap, thus the marks on the face of the moon.[88]

·Anchopeteri could not have intercourse at first with his moon wife. She had a piranha fish in her vagina which would have bitten off his penis. So he bathed her vagina with the fish poison which the Tapirapé use to kill fish in pools and streams. He was still afraid, so Anchopeteri asked a monkey to have intercourse with her. Only afterwards, when he knew that the piranha fish was dead, did Anchopeteri have sexual relations with his wife.

Anchopeteri brought tobacco and firewood to the Tapirapé. He taught them how to wrestle and to sing many songs. It was Anchopeteri who once encountered the birds (and other animals as well) dancing and singing in the forest; it was that scene, I was told by two older Tapirapé men, which gave rise to the men's Bird Societies (see Chapter 4). It is not clear to me whether the Tapirapé believed that Anchopeteri lives in the sky or in Maratawa since he died.

Then the Tapirapé told of the twins Tomatochiri and Mukwura-ura, the sons of Mukwura. According to this legend, an ancestral hero left to live far to the northeast, perhaps in Maratawa.[89] He left his wife, who was pregnant, behind. She soon bore a son also called Mukwura. The wife decided to search for her husband and took her

---

88. In another version of this myth, the sun and the moon have incestuous relations and Anchopeteri marries their daughter, not the moon herself. Because the sun and the moon once committed incest, they are always far apart in the sky. The sun is in the heavens when the moon is underground returning home to the east, and when the sun arrives in Maratawa, the moon is in the sky.

89. In the two versions of this legend which I recorded I do not have the name of this ancestral hero. However, it is a well-known story told by various Tupian groups in which the culture hero is generally called Maíra (Metraux, 1928b; Wagley and Galvão, 1949: 137ff.).

son to travel with her. Mukwura, who was an evil son, gave his mother bad directions. One night, Mukwura copulated with his own mother and she consequently became pregnant with twins. Two sons were born, Tomatochiri and Mukwura-ura, just before the mother was killed by the *anchunga-aiuma* (water spirits without eyes who dance around a pot of boiling water). These anchunga invited the twins' mother to dance and during the dance they pushed the woman into the boiling water. The twins miraculously grew to manhood almost overnight. They revenged their mother by killing the evil anchunga. Then, following the directions of a giant jacu, they found their way to their "father's" house (actually their "grandfather," but in the myth he is called "father"). There the father gave Tomatochiri the bow and arrow which he brought back to the Tapirapé. The "father" gave Mukwura-ura, who became the ancestor of the Brazilians, guns.[90] Both were handsome men, but Tomatochiri (the Tapirapé) had "light" skin and Mukwura-ura (the Brazilian) was dark (i.e. ipion, "blue or black").

The exploits of the ancestral culture heroes explained much of the world as the Tapirapé knew it, but it was from their shamans that the Tapirapé knew of the world of the spirits. As stated in Chapter 5, these spirits were known by the generic term anchunga,[91] which can refer to the souls of human beings, to spirits of animals, or to spirits of the sky and the forest. The ordinary Tapirapé without any shamanistic qualifications might sometimes encounter anchunga of deceased human beings. Such "ghosts" sometimes traveled about at night, and especially during the rainy season they were attracted to the warm dwellings of the living because they themselves were "cold." When a ghost encounters a living person, it was said, it may throw a dust-like substance over that person, causing him or her to fall to the ground senseless. Several Tapirapé saw ghosts during my stay with them in 1939-40. One woman saw a ghost bathing in the small brook when she went to fetch water after sundown. A man who remained alone in his garden to sleep saw the ghost of a person who died over ten years before. "He was white," he said, "and his eyes had fallen out. He still

---

90. In the early seventeenth century Claude d'Abbeville recorded that the Tupinambás stated that their ancestor had selected "a wooden sword" and the European ancestor had taken the metal sword (n.d.: 251-52).

91. These are the anhanga or aygnan of the Portuguese and French chroniclers who wrote in the sixteenth and seventeenth centuries about the now extinct Tupinambá of the Brazilian coast.

had annatto in his hair."[92] Such ghosts which have been dead for many years "have no flesh. They have only bone," I was told. Accordingly, people were afraid to venture beyond the village plaza, or even beyond the light of a fire, at night. After an indeterminate period such errant spirits became incorporated into animals and birds. I was told that such ghosts become toads, deer, frogs, or doves.

Shamans, however, were not afraid of ghosts of the dead, nor of the spirits of the animal world, nor even of the demonic spirits of the forest. In their dreams and in trance induced by tobacco, shamans encountered ghosts and other anchunga. The iunga (soul) may free itself from the été (body) and move freely during dreams and trance in space and time. Obviously, anyone may dream, but too much dreaming could be evidence of potential shamanistic power. Laymen who dreamed often were afraid, for they did not belong in this supernatural world. Champukwi, who was not a shaman, indicated this anxiety when he told me of his dreams. When he saw dangerous anchunga in his dreams, he had no recourse but to run. "I am not a shaman," he said. "I was afraid and I ran. They would have killed me." Only shamans had the supernatural power to move freely in the dream-world of ghosts and demons. To a shaman, ghosts were his friends, and the power of a shaman grew in proportion as he fraternized with, or defeated in combat, the demonic spirits of the forest. After a dream visit, breeds of such demonic spirits could become his familiar helpers, obedient to his call for aid. Or the shaman could defeat dangerous anchunga. Turning himself into a bird or launching himself through the air in his "canoe," he could travel to villages of ghosts, to the houses of demonic spirits, or to such temporal places as Brazilian, Kayapó, or Carajá villages. Then, too, time was no obstacle; in sleep or in trance of a few minutes' duration the shaman could experience three or four days of adventure.

The Tapirapé told me of one great shaman, called Waré, who had lived sometime in the distant past. He was not, they insisted, an ancestral culture hero such as those described above. He did not transform the physical world, but he did transform the spirit world. Waré killed many dangerous anchunga. Champukwi, trying to explain the activities of Waré to me, said: "He killed all the anchunga there (pointing to the south), but he did not kill all of them there (point-

---

92. See Chapter 5 for a description of the preparation of the body for burial. 181

ing to the north)." Today Waré lives in Maratawa, and "Panterí has seen him there." Nonetheless, the legends concerning Waré place him in the role of a trickster who fought the dangerous demonic spirits of the forest, making the spirit world safer for the Tapirapé.

In his dream travels, Waré encountered many anchunga. Once he encountered the anchunga which were called "those whose anus has a geometric design."[93] Waré made a hunting blind (a small hut made of palm fronds) where he knew the dangerous spirit came to drink water. When the spirit arrived, Waré confronted him. The spirit addressed Waré as "friend" (tuhawa) and suggested that they have anal intercourse. Waré had intercourse with the demon but when he finished he leaped off the anchunga's back and ran. Waré caught a deer and substituted the deer for himself. The anchunga penetrated the deer in the anus, but during intercourse the demon discovered that it was not Waré and that Waré had escaped. The demon chased Waré, but Waré climbed a large tree and hid in a macaw's nest. The demon saw him and said: "Come down for I will eat you."[94] Then the anchunga climbed the tree, but as he came near Waré three white macaws came, and they flapped their wings at the demon until he fell to the ground and was killed.

Waré killed all of the mamupi ank anchunga—the spirits who killed the Tapirapé and drank their blood. Waré searched for their village and when in it they invited him to drink kawi and "called him friend." He refused to drink the soup because he knew that it was made of blood. He saw the spirit women making red annatto paste; one woman offered to rub annatto in his hair and on his feet because he was very tired. Waré refused; he smelled the annatto and recognized it as blood. Then he took his club and killed men, women, and children.

Waré met another dangerous spirit in the forest who looked like a man and also pretended to be his "friend." They hunted together and came upon a coati which was hiding in a hole high in a tree. Waré climbed the tree and killed the coati; but when he reached the ground, the anchunga hit Waré with his club. The spirit tied up Waré and the coati in his carrying basket and set off for home. The load was very heavy and the anchunga sat down to rest. When he did so, Waré escaped, placing rocks in the basket in his place, and taking the coati

---

93. *Ei kwana pu pé kwanchiana mae*, in Tapirapé. *Kwanchiana* is the name given to the geometric design used as body decoration and also incised upon gourds.

94. The word for "eat" and for "have sexual intercourse" is the same.

with him. Waré returned home and gave the coati to his mother-in-law to roast. But when the anchunga arrived home, his son found the rocks rather than a coati and Waré. So the anchunga went to Waré's village and found the mother-in-law burning hair from the coati before cooking it. The anchunga killed her, thrusting a lance up her anus until the point emerged from her mouth. At first, Waré did not know she was dead. "She stood upright and she looked as if she were laughing." Then, when he realized that she had been murdered, he became very angry. He ran to the village of the anchunga and killed men, women, and children.

Among his other exploits, Waré killed the anchunga who had penes "as large as the trunk of a tree." Every day they went to a pool of water and washed their genitals, saying over and over again: "Kuchi! Kuchi! I want a woman. I want a man." Waré made a powder of red pepper and poured it in the pool. When the anchunga washed their genitals, the pepper began to burn them. They cried and ran, and subsequently died. Another demonic forest spirit found Waré gathering fruit of the anajá tree.[95] (It was the "grandfather" of the anajá tree and the fruit were enormous.) "Come have intercourse with me, my friend," said the anchunga. "No!" responded Waré, "have intercourse with your wife." The demon began to climb the tree but Waré dropped a giant anajá fruit on the anchunga and it killed him.

Waré lived many years ago, but the Tapirapé shamans who lived more recently also were said to have had bloodcurdling experiences in their dream travels. The dream experiences of shamans in 1939-40 were in a similar pattern with those of the ancestral culture heroes and with the legendary exploits of Waré. Frequently, however, the shaman did not kill the anchunga, but enlisted them as "his friends" and eventual aids. Ikananchowi, a powerful shaman who died a few years before my visit in 1939-40, had such a dream experience.

In his dream, Ikananchowi walked to the shores of a large lake deep in the jungle. There he heard dogs barking and ran in the direction from which the noise came until he met several forest spirits of the breed called *munpi anká*. They were tearing a bat out of a tree for food. They talked with Ikananchowi and invited him to return with them to their village, which was situated on the lake. In this village he saw parakeets and many *socó* (*Butorides*, sp.) birds which they kept as pets. The anchunga had several pots of kawi and invited Ikanan-

---

95. The anajá bears a fruit much appreciated by the Tapirapé.

chowi to eat with them. He refused, for he saw that their kawi was made from human blood. Ikananchowi watched one spirit drink of the kawi and saw him vomit blood immediately afterwards; the shaman also saw a spirit drink from another pot and immediately spurt blood from its anus. He saw the spirits vomit up their entrails and throw them on the ground, but he soon saw that this was only a trick; they would not die for they had more intestines. After his visit, the munpí anká called Ikananchowi "father" and he called them his "sons"; he visited them in his dreams frequently and he had munpí anká near him always. When Ikananchowi danced and sang in the annual shamanistic ceremony against Thunder (to be described below), he painted his chest and chin red with annatto, representing the kawi of blood which drools from the mouths of the munpí anká after they vomit, and he called those spirits to his aid in his songs. Other shamans who lived in 1939-40 had familiar spirits but none had such dangerous ones as the munpí anká of Ikananchowi; thus, "people were very much afraid of Ikananchowi, for these anchunga are very dangerous," said one Tapirapé.

In another dream adventure of Ikananchowi, the shaman met the forest spirits called *oreya*. These have long hair wound in a mass on top of their heads and they carry one arrow for the bows with which they kill men. The oreya were about to shoot the shaman, but when he shouted: "No, I am a shaman," they did not harm him. Instead, they gave him food and helped him return through the deep forest to the village. Another shaman had *anchunga anú awa* as his familiars. These forest demons have protruding eyes and sharp pointed chins. They kill Tapirapé by grabbing them from behind as they walk unsuspectingly through the forest, clapping their hands over the victim's mouth and driving their pointed chins into the back of his neck. A man caught by one of these anchunga dies gurgling and staring, unable to speak; thus, although found alive, he may never explain what happened to him. A shaman with such dangerous familiars as these protected the laity by keeping these spirits under control.

One powerful shaman could have several demonic familiars, and his responsibility and prestige grew with their numbers and strength. Panterí, perhaps the most powerful shaman living in 1939-40, had several breeds of familiars garnered from his dreams. He was, of course, accustomed to visiting the villages of ghosts in his nightly dreams. He had visited the *anapí anchunga*, beings with huge penes with which they killed people by sodomy and copulation. Panterí traveled once in his dreams over a high mountain ridge to the north of the Tapirapé country, where he visited with the ghosts of the hostile Kayapó. These enemy ghosts too became his familiars and he said that they would warn him if and when the living Kayapó planned to attack the Tapirapé. Again, in one of his dreams, Panterí traveled two days through a thick forest through which no paths led. Suddenly he found himself at the mouth of the Tapirapé River where it runs into the Araguaia. Inside a near-by hill he visited *anachowa*, a giant red parrot from which supernatural beings and the souls of dead shamans pluck their everlasting supply of red feathers for decoration.[96]

Panterí also visited the forest demons called *peropí awa*, who have the power to send fevers to the Tapirapé. About this visit to their "house" he related the following: "I saw many pets. They have parakeets, parrots, many pets. . . . I had not seen them before. I saw there a paca. The paca was cold; it was shivering. The paca had fever chills; I knew that the Tapirapé would all have fever. I told many people that this would occur but there was nothing I could do about it." During his many dream travels Panterí also visited Maratawa, the home of heroic ancestors and deceased shamans, and he had looked down upon many Brazilian settlements on the Araguaia River.

There were certain of the shamans who were said to make frequent trips to the sky in their "canoes" and who counted powerful celestial phenomena among their powers. The Milky Way was spoken of as the "Road of the Panché." Once, when comparing his powers with those of another shaman, one shaman told me that he dreamed only on earth level and thus was not so powerful as the other, who frequently traveled in the sky. Another shaman claimed that he visited the Pleiades and *kopia chawana*, the "Jaguar of the Skies." It was thought that many terrestrial jaguars, sent by the Jaguar of the Skies, would haunt the confines of the village when a shaman died. I was told, too, that when the powerful shaman Wantanamu died the "sun was large and red with the blood of the shaman"; he was "hot" and "angry" because a shaman had died.

The Tapirapé told of great battles between strong shamans, each supported by his own retinue of powers. During my stay with the Tapirapé there were rumors of a possible combat between Urukumu and Panterí, the two strongest shamans. Many people believed that it

---

96. Ancestor heroes, Thunder as a supernatural, and souls of dead shamans were always being described as having a plentiful supply of red feathers—something that every living Tapirapé envied.

would be caused by the death of a warm personal friend of Panterí through the suspected sorcery by Urukumu. One man even described how he thought the combat would take place. "Panterí will smoke much tobacco and then he will go to his hammock to sleep. In his dream, he will go in his canoe to the top of a high mountain. From there he will look about until he sees the soul of Urukumu. From there Panterí will throw his *ankungitána*;[97] it will wrap itself around the soul of Urukumu, carrying him off into the sky." Now the various familiar powers of both shamans would hasten to their aid. It was at this point that the narrator, visualizing the possible battle of powers, listed the powers that would come to the aid of each shaman. A shaman whose soul had thus been captured by another fell prey to chills and fevers and soon died, with his last breath whispering in song that he was leaving the earth and possibly even telling gaspingly the name of the shaman who caused his death. Both shamans involved in the rumored combat denied knowledge of it or any intention to wage it.

As might be expected, the same methods said to be used by shamans against one another might also be used against a layman. Shamans were believed to steal souls that were wandering in dream journeys. The shaman could send his ankungitána to strike the soul of his victim over the head or to tie it up and carry it off. The one whose soul was thus either incapacitated or imprisoned would soon die. A shaman could call upon his familiar demonic spirits of the forest to deal with a chosen victim or could in his dream shoot a victim's spirit with small arrows which caused at times death and at other times only boils. Still another method of attack was for the shaman to throw fishbones (*ipira kunya*) or gnawing worms (*uuáka* or *áwai*) at his victim's body, causing illness and death. The treatment of illness consisted of removing from the victim's body these malignant arrows, fishbones, and worms.[98]

As I have said before, all Tapirapé who died of disease were generally thought to die by sorcery, and at each death suspicion turned to-

---

97. The ankungitána is a ceremonial headdress made of three or four long tail feathers of a parrot and worn by the Tapirapé down the back tied to the short "pigtail" headdress.

98. In illness and other misfortune, sorcery was always suspected by the Tapirapé and, accordingly, a shaman was always believed to be responsible. Sorcery, however, was considered an action performed by shamans in dreams or trance. Thus, sorcery was never consciously practiced. As far as the writer knows, there were no incantations or mechanical devices for the deliberate inducing of sympathetic black magic.

ward a shaman.[99] At the death of a child or woman of low status, suspicion would arise and soon die down; however, when the deceased was a man of high status, his brothers, sons, or sister's sons became violent in their grief and murdered the shaman toward whom suspicion pointed. Sometimes, after a long series of deaths, suspicion was fixed upon one famous and strong shaman and the Tapirapé decided informally that he must be killed. Most often, revenge murder occurred within the first few days after a death, when the relatives were "sad" and "angry."[100] If the first depression of mourning wore off without violence to the shaman, the anger toward him passed and he was out of danger—at least temporarily. Thus, after a man of rather high status had died, both Urukumu and Wantanamu, panchés of sufficient power to be suspected of causing his death, were not seen about the village. Wantanamu left for the savanna, ostensibly on a fishing trip, and he stayed away until the brothers of the deceased had calmed down again.

In 1939-40, there were eight living men who had assassinated panchés, which attests to the frequency of revenge killing of shamans. Within the memory of one informant, Kamairá, who was approximately thirty-five years old at that time, ten shamans had been killed.[101] During his youth he himself had killed a shaman named Panchewáni because he believed him responsible for his younger brother's death. Going to the shaman's house the second night after the death, Kamairá found the shaman asleep and killed him with several arrows through the abdomen. According to various informants, the epidemic of deaths that had been occurring then came to a halt, proving Panchewáni's guilt. In another case, a panché assassin hid in the forest and shot the suspected shaman as he passed on his way to his garden. Still another shaman was clubbed to death as he sat with his family in the village plaza. Two of the living assassins had murdered women shamans by clubbing them to death. Kuchananché (i.e. kuchan,

---

99. Informants readily admitted that people may be infected by others, as in the case of the common cold which they recognize as a disease from whites, but it is believed that a person who has a cold slowly gets well if no sorcery is working against him. Death is caused only by sorcery.

100. A Tapirapé used the word iwuterahú to describe the condition of anger and sadness.

101. Within the span of Kamairá's life the tremendous depopulation of the Tapirapé from imported diseases had taken place. It represents an abnormal period with more than the usual number of deaths, and, perhaps therefore, an unusual number of assassinated shamans.

"woman"; panché, "shaman") generally died by violence because, according to informants, they were dangerous. "They dream more than men shamans and they kill many Tapirapé in dreams," said one man. Ironically, all three of the more powerful shamans living in 1939-40 had themselves murdered shamans during their youth, and at least two of them were currently in danger because they were considered powerful enough to be suspected of "evil dreaming."

Informants could not remember any occasion when a shaman thus murdered was avenged immediately by his relatives. Yet informants did say that a shaman with several adult brothers (that is, true siblings) strong enough to avenge him was generally not murdered. A powerful shaman made an effort to have a strong family group about him for protection. Informants could not remember that murdered shamans had ever been avenged by their familiar spirits, although one man made the point that shamans were murdered only by persons under the influence of great anger or grief, for people normally were afraid of the familiars of shamans.

Special rites were observed by anyone who had murdered a shaman. These rites were performed to protect him and the rest of the tribe against possible danger. On the day following the murder, the assassin had to retire to his hammock, eat a white clay (uwu chinga), and drink a brew made by boiling a man's leg ornaments in water. He had to drink the brew until he vomited in order to cleanse his body "of the blood of the shaman." The assassin had to paint his entire body black with genipap and rub red annatto paint in his hair. Furthermore, he had to scratch his chest, arms, thighs, and back with dogfish (in Portuguese, *Peixe-cachorro*) or agouti teeth—just as he was scratched as a young boy to make him a strong adult. Then, each year at the annual ceremony during the harvest (in May and June), all assassins had to drink kawió[102] until they vomited, again cleansing themselves of the shaman's blood for the period until the next harvest.

Just one year after I left the village of Tampiitawa, I received a letter from Valentim Gomes, who had returned there on a short visit. He told me of the execution of Urukumu, the strong shaman whom I have mentioned several times above. His suspected shamanist combat with Panterí had not caused his death. But Valentim reported that, in 1940-41, fifteen males and fourteen females had died in an epidemic of influenza. Among those who had died was the household

---

102. See Chapter 5.

leader and strong shaman, Wantanamu, and a highly respected younger man, Champukwi, who had been my close friend. Urukumu, as I have already indicated, had often feared for his life, and, in a sense, foresaw his own death. He was killed by Irawú, a younger brother of Wantanamu who lived in Urukumu's household in the status of a "son-in-law." One could have predicted that Urukumu would be assassinated shortly. His reputation as a shaman had grown far too great for his own safety. Irawú, in his anger and grief over Wantanamu's death, had clubbed Urukumu as he lay asleep in his hammock.[103]

As usual, Urukumu was not revenged immediately, but his execution was not forgotten. On his death Urukumu left a young son of about six years of age. When I returned in 1953, this boy, Chawachowa, was a young man, and, for lack of available girls of his own age among the Tapirapé, he had married a Carajá girl. By 1953, Irawú had become a man of prestige and he had changed his name to Wantanamu, the name of the shaman and household leader whose death had incited him to kill Urukumu in 1941. By 1953, this new Wantanamu had the reputation of being a strong panché. The Tapirapé villagers were already somewhat frightened of him. In fact, his reputation for aggression had extended beyond the Indians themselves. Valentim Gomes, the Indian officer at Posto Heloisa Alberto Torres and my old companion, complained that Wantanamu was hard to handle. He had killed two cows that belonged to the SPI post. The local Brazilians spoke of Wantanamu as a *caboclo de coragem* (a courageous Indian), and some referred to him as "the chief of the Tapirapé." Wantanamu owned a rifle and always walked about armed. It would seem that his own reputation both as a shaman and as an overly aggressive leader had now grown strong enough for him to fear for his own life. In 1965, when we returned again to New Village, I heard of the end of Wantanamu's career—and perhaps of shamanism among the Tapirapé.

In 1963 Chawachowa, the son of Urukumu, had killed Wantanamu, thus avenging his father's assassination twenty-two years earlier. The Tapirapé said that Wantanamu had become an irritable man. That year an epidemic of measles had hit the village and several people had died. Wantanamu, the only living shaman of considerable reputation, was, of course, suspected of sorcery. Chawachowa, although he then lived among the Carajá, returned one day to shoot Wantanamu

---

103. It was also reported that Panterí was executed about 1943, but I was unable to gather any details of the event.

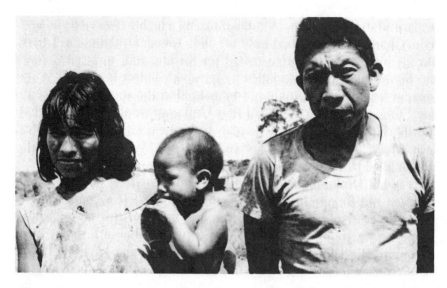

Chawachowa with his Carajá wife and their son in 1965. After twenty-two years Chawachowa killed Wantanamu (Irawú), the last powerful Tapirapé shaman, thus avenging the murder of his own father, Urukumu.

through the back of his head with a .44-calibre rifle. But by then times had changed, and the Tapirapé were within the reach of Brazilian law. The Indian officer (Valentim Gomes had been transferred to another SPI post) thought it necessary to turn Chawachowa over to the Brazilian police, and he was charged with murder. Chawachowa was taken upriver to the city of Goiás (the old capital of the state) where he was jailed. Justice is slow in those small towns, so Chawachowa languished in jail for about three months, spending his time cleaning up the cells and, according to him, being treated exceedingly well by the townspeople, who gave him food, clothes, and "many presents." When his case was finally brought before a local judge, Chawachowa was able to explain that he had killed the man who had killed his father. This was easily understood by the Brazilian judge, who acquitted him at once and ordered that he be returned home by Air Force plane. The Tapirapé, in 1965, said that Wantanamu was the last Tapirapé shaman. If so, the Tapirapé have now lost perhaps the most important figures of their traditional culture, for the shamans had performed the roles and duties crucial in their relationship to both the supernatural and the natural world.

Treatment of the sick was the shaman's most common duty, and the use of tobacco was always a necessary prelude and accompaniment to this. Unless the illness was serious enough to warrant immediate treatment, shamans always cured in the late evening. A shaman came to his patient, squatted near the patient's hammock and lit his pipe. When a patient had a fever or had fallen unconscious from the sight of a ghost, the principal method of treatment was massage. The shaman blew smoke over his own hands, spat into them, and massaged the patient slowly and firmly, always toward the extremities of the body. He showed that he was removing a foreign substance by a quick movement of his hands as he reached the end of an arm or leg.

A frequent method of curing, however, was by extraction of a malignant object[104] by sucking. The shaman squatted alongside the hammock of his patient and began to "eat smoke"; that is, he swallowed large gulps of tobacco smoke from his pipe. He forced the smoke with great intakes of breath deep into his stomach; soon he became intoxicated and nauseated; he vomited violently and smoke spewed from his mouth. He groaned and cleared his throat in the manner of a person gagging with nausea but unable to vomit. By sucking back what he vomited he accumulated saliva in his mouth.[105] In the midst of this process he stopped several times to suck on the body of his patient and finally, with one awful heave, vomited all the accumulated saliva on the ground. He then searched in this mess for the intrusive object that had been causing the illness. Never once did I see a shaman show the intrusive object to observers. During one treatment, a Tapirapé panché usually repeated this process of "eating smoke," sucking and vomiting several times. Sometimes, when a man of prestige was ill, two or even three shamans would cure side by side in this manner and the noise of violent vomiting resounded throughout the village.

Among the Tapirapé, tobacco was a sacred plant necessary for curing and for all shamanistic activities, but it was not the exclusive property of shamans. While it was found widely near any Tapirapé village and near their gardens, it was not strictly a cultivated plant. People knew where a patch of tobacco was growing and went there to pick it. Occasionally they transplanted tobacco nearer to their houses or to their gardens, but for the most part the patches seeded themselves. When an individual discovered a new patch of tobacco, he hastily built a low fence around it to inform others that it

---

104. Such as a fishbone, worm, or arrow which had been injected into the body by sorcery.
105. It hardly needs be said that a panché did not eat before curing in this manner. They prefer to cure on an empty stomach.

belonged to him. This native tobacco was smoked by laymen in short tubular pipes made of wood or clay and by shamans in long tubular clay pipes, sometimes 30 centimeters long.

Tobacco was smoked for pleasure, but its principal uses among the Tapirapé were as a stimulant and as a medicine. Each night after a long day's work, or while traveling or hunting, Tapirapé men blew smoke over their legs, arms, and backs, and sometimes men could be seen fumigating their tired wives or companions. They accompanied the fumigation of their bodies with massage, rubbing their arms and legs toward the extremities. Tiredness and soreness were considered extraneous substances acquired during the day through exercise and it was believed that they could be fumigated and massaged from the body.

One other method of curing was observed. During an epidemic of fever, Panterí made a collective cure to drive fever out of the village and to protect the people of the village from it. Two men were dispatched to collect wild honey; this was then mixed with water, making a weak honey mixture. Panterí, after first smoking for a time, went from house to house taking the honey mixture in his mouth and spraying it over the house and its occupants. He carefully sprayed and massaged the patients who had fever and removed the foreign substance from their bodies. For several hours he worked, spraying both the inside and the outside of their houses, including the central ceremonial house of the men. It was explained that the honey alone did not have a therapeutic effect against fever, but sprayed from the mouth of the panché it drove away fevers.

Shamans also protected the Tapirapé against ghosts. As described earlier, people who saw ghosts fainted from fright or from a white substance which the ghost sprayed over their bodies. Shamans were called to blow smoke over them and to massage this substance from their bodies. During one funeral dance, the shaman Panterí "saw many ghosts" in the environs of the village, recognizing some as long-dead relatives of the deceased. By blowing tobacco smoke about and by going among the ghosts with a large mirror he drove the ghosts away before they did any harm.

Shamans were necessary in several other life situations other than illness. For instance, shamans were thought to control the pregnancy of women. As I have said, the Tapirapé knew that pregnancy is related to sexual intercourse. However, they thought that conception takes place only when a shaman "brings a child to a woman." Several species of birds, fish, and insects as well as a number of natural phenomena, especially Thunder, had children; that is, they were thought to control "spirits of children."[106] Shamans stole, or, more simply, took the spirits of children from these sources and brought them to a woman while she slept. Parents who wished children brought presents to a panché to "make him dream and bring a child to them." Some Tapirapé parents could identify the source of their children and the shaman who brought them. One father explained that he had taken honey to the panché Urukumu to make him dream and that Urukumu had consequently traveled to the house of Thunder from which he had brought back a child. Another gave a fish to a shaman; in return, the shaman brought back a child from the small fish called *piau*. Another man gave honey to a panché who brought back a child from the horsefly.

The Tapirapé laid all good—and, likewise, all evil—at the door of the shaman. Consequently, a phenomenon such as barrenness was considered the fault of the shaman. A barren woman or a man without children by his wife must have "quarreled much with the panché." For example, it was clear to Kamairaho that his failure to have children by the three wives with whom he had lived during his lifetime was due to a shaman. "They do not want me to have a child," he explained.

The safety of Tapirapé men depended upon the power of their shamans during the period from October to November when some swam while they fished and shot turtles;[107] for in this region of Brazil the rivers were infested with alligators, sting rays, and piranha. The Tapirapé also believed that large snakes lurked in deep pools of the rivers, ready to wrap themselves around men and to pull them beneath the water. During the year men would not swim in deep water unless it was absolutely necessary and they fished only in shallow, clear rapids. If they had to swim to catch turtles, a shaman guaranteed their safety. A powerful shaman would travel to the river in his dream, tie the jaws of the alligators with wires, strike the piranha across their teeth so they could not bite, and tie up the large snakes into knots with their own tails.

---

106. Thunder, night, monkeys, wild pigs, *jacu* (*Penelope*, sp.), *jacamim* birds (*Psóphidia*, sp.), and fish called *tucunaré* (*Cichlas ocellaris*), *pacú* (*Mylinae*, sp.), piranha (*Serrasalmo*), and *jeraqui* (*Prochilodus*, sp.) were listed as sources of "spirits of children."
107. In 1939-40 only a few Tapirapé men knew how to swim.

Abundance of game was also the responsibility of the shaman. Some powerful shamans had the ability to control the movements and the increase of the bands of pigs. These shamans visited in their dreams the "home of wild pigs" near the Tapirapé River on a hill called by them Towaiyawá (i.e. ringed tail of the coati). There the shamans had sexual intercourse with female pigs, causing a large increase in the bands. Those pigs that ran fastest and were the hardest to kill were the "children of the panché." The shaman's control over the movement of bands of pigs came through his control over the anchunga called *ampukáya* (crying spirits). Wild pigs were thought to be pets of these spirits and to follow them about. Shamans who were powerful enough captured these spirits and took them, followed by their pets, to an appointed place where Tapirapé men waited to kill the pigs. None of the living shamans were believed to be capable of these controls over the wild pigs and several people blamed their lack of success at hunting and the apparent scarcity of pigs on the declining power of their shamans.

The dream journeys of the shamans also gave them the power of prophecy, as was indicated by Panterí's vision of the fever which he had when in the village of the peropí awa. Such dream experiences were not limited to the demonic world, but sometimes occurred in earthly regions. A shaman may have visited Carajá villages or Brazilian settlements along the Araguaia River, for example, where he sometimes learned facts of great interest or importance to his fellow tribesmen. When Panterí visited the Brazilian settlements along the Araguaia River for the first time, he said that he recognized some of the faces; he had been to these settlements many times in his dreams. When I returned to the Tapirapé village after three months' absence in late 1939, one shaman claimed to have prophesied my arrival to the day. He had traveled in his dreams, he said, to the Araguaia River and had seen my canoe moving up the Tapirapé River. Another, in the same way, foresaw the arrival of a young Tapirapé who was returning from several weeks on the Araguaia. Frequently, shamans learned in their dreams where large bands of wild pigs could be found and advised the Tapirapé how to approach the band.[108]

The cleansing of food could be accomplished if the shaman tasted it and blew smoke over it. Several times each year these rites were per-

---

108. Many such prophecies were found wanting, and several times I heard people speak of a shaman's prophecy as a "lie." Often, prophecies were only made known to people after events had proved them true.

formed over the first fruits of the harvest to ensure their wholesomeness before the people tasted the crop. In January the first ears of the new maize were picked and presented to a strong shaman who then gave them to his wife to cook. At sundown of the day on which this was done the shaman walked to the central plaza followed by his wife who carried the cooked maize and placed it in a pile before him, ready for the ceremonies that followed. In 1939 Panterí was the shaman who initiated this ceremony; he was joined by five other proven shamans. The people of the village gathered about the shamans, who sat in a circle facing the maize. One by one, the shamans took deep draughts from their burning pipes and blew the smoke over the maize. Then, one by one again, each pinched off a few grains from an ear and ate them. When the last shaman had tasted the new maize, the ceremony was ended. The youngsters of the village then fell upon the pile of maize; the crop had been tasted by the shamans and found free from danger for the people. The next day maize was eaten in all houses. A similar ceremony was performed in August or September with the first wild honey of the season, and again about January or February when new corn was ground to make kawi. I did not hear of such "tasting of the fruits" by shamans for other garden crops, and informants were unable to remember any occasion at which shamans had found new maize or honey too dangerous for consumption by the people. Also, each year during the first months of the rainy season when the new crop of maize was threatened by the first heavy rains and electrical storms, Tapirapé shamans had to "fight" against Thunder and his supernatural minions in order to protect the gardens and even the people themselves from their violence.[109]

The Tapirapé depended on their shamans to control the dangerous spirit world, to remove danger from first fruits, to predict the future, to bring spirits of children to their prospective parents, and to cure the ill. In all life situations where chance or the unpredictable figured, the Tapirapé depended markedly upon their shamans. Thus the greatest prestige which Tapirapé culture offered accrued to its shamans.[110] That prestige was reflected in the concepts of a separate afterlife for shamans and in the identification of ancestral culture heroes as shamans. Petura, the introducer of such phenomena as fire and daylight, and Waré, who killed so many dangerous anchunga, were frequently

---

109. This spectacular ceremony will be described later.
110. The unusual importance of the shaman to the Tapirapé was well put by one of my informants: "Without our panché, all we Tapirapé would die."

referred to as "great shamans." While a Tapirapé layman was thought to become a disembodied soul at death, the afterlife of a shaman was only a continuation of his present life, but under ideal circumstances. His soul went to Maratawa, the home of the culture heroes.[111] This home of the privileged dead lies far to the northwest, "where the earth ends and the water begins" and where the sun returns to sleep after his travels across the sky. In Maratawa shamans have an inexhaustible supply of tobacco, many red parrot feathers, much manioc, kawi, bananas, meat, and all the other necessities and luxuries of life. Frequently, a shaman was buried with a filled tobacco pipe in his mouth so that he might smoke to drive out fatigue on the trip to Maratawa; and sometimes food was buried with the body so he could eat, for the journey to Maratawa is long.

Aside from these nonmaterial considerations, there was one very real factor which ensured societal respect for the Tapirapé shaman. Shamans were in general the wealthiest men among the Tapirapé. Although they would at times receive meat or honey for their cures or as presents for bringing the spirits of children to parents, payments to them were usually in personal objects, which were the mark of "wealth." The beads and hardware which I gave as presents to the Tapirapé soon passed into the hands of shamans as payments for cures.

Payments to the shamans for curing the ill depended upon the seriousness of the illness and upon what the patient or his family had to offer. Frequently, a shaman named his fee when his cure was successful, asking for specific objects for he knew full well what each family owned. For example, for the treatment of his sister's son and of his daughter, who were both sick at once, Kamairaho, a shaman himself, called three shamans and paid each the price that he asked. He paid Panterí with a bushknife and two strings of beads; and to Urukumu he gave an axe, a pocketknife, a pair of scissors, and five tail feathers of a red parrot; but he gave only four strings of beads to Kamairaí, who was considered a shaman of less power than the other two. Another young man with few possessions gave five arrows to a shaman

---

111. If a shaman met death by murder, his trip to Maratawa is delayed. He goes temporarily to another "home of shamans" in the west until his wounds are healed; only then does he go to Maratawa. If his skull has been crushed by a club, a new cranium of metal is made for him at this temporary residence. A "metal" cranium is obviously an introduced concept, yet informants were not able to explain of what material the new cranium might have been made before metal was known among the Tapirapé.

who successfully treated his wife. Still another paid with the breast feathers from his parrot and four strings of beads. When Chawani-uma killed a paca, the meat of which was highly prized by the Ta-pirapé, he gave some to his companion of the hunt and divided the rest between two shamans who had treated his small daughter successfully. Neither shaman had to ask for any specific gift or payment, but often a shaman would demand specific gifts. People often complained to others about the high price they had to pay a shaman, but generally they paid what was asked. "Stinginess" was a severe accusation among these people, and to complain mildly about what highly valued gifts they made to a shaman was one way of announcing one's generosity. However, it must be remembered that during the annual harvest ceremonies, shamans (and other men of prestige) had to give gifts to all those who drank kawió. At that time, then, there was a siphoning off of wealth from the shamans back into the hands of their patients. But during the next year fees and gifts channeled it back into their hands.

At the time of my first field research among the Tapirapé in 1939-40, there were six men recognized as full-fledged shamans who were called upon to treat the sick and to perform various ceremonials. Pan-terí and Urukumu were the two clearly outstanding ones; they assumed leadership in shamanistic ceremonies and were the ones most frequently called for cure. Besides these six recognized shamans, there were four young men who were working to develop shamanistic powers and gain recognition as shamans.

Within the memory of persons living in 1939-40, there had been three female shamans, but there were more, either practicing as recognized shamans or working as novices, at that time. The female shamans were remembered as having been especially malevolent. They were supposed to dream more than the men and work much harm to the people. People who remembered them explained that when they had sung in the annual ceremony of calling and fighting Thunder they had sung the usual male shamans' parts. The female panchés had smoked and fallen into trances as the male shamans did. Nothing possible to men shamans appeared to be beyond the power of the women. None of them was described as masculine in behavior; on the contrary, they were described as "good wives," and one of them was remembered as small and particularly attractive.

Certain people, regardless of sex, were early recognized as future shamans because of their natural inclination to dream. Several infor- *197* mants, for example, told me that one young boy, an orphan and therefore badly cared for, would certainly make a powerful shaman. This boy turned and talked in his sleep and had been known to cry during a nightmare. He remembered few of his dreams but spoke of seeing the spirit of his mother; he also described an evil spirit which he met during a dream. One of the then living powerful shamans also had had a predilection for dreaming as a youngster. As children such individuals were nervous and sensitive, yet no distinct personality traits were observed among adult shamans. Shamans were frequently emaciated and thin, which is attributable perhaps to their constant use of tobacco and the resulting nausea. One shaman, then dead, was described by informants as interested only in the supernatural world and easily irritated by family and friends.

Persons who lacked the predilection for dreaming but had aspirations to shaminism could solicit dreams. Each year during the late dry season all young men who aspired to shamanism, even those who had shown potentialities during boyhood, gathered each evening in the central plaza of the village to seek dreams. A novice sat upon the ground near a panché, his mentor, and swallowed smoke from his mentor's pipe until violent vomiting occurred. When the novices were too ill to hold the pipe, the shaman held it for them, forcing them to continue "eating smoke." Generally the neophytes fell backwards in a trance and ill from the smoke; during this state they might dream. In any case, when they regained their senses the pipe was again placed in their mouth until they fell backwards, ill and unconscious once more. The process might be repeated several times over a period of two or three hours. Later, when the novice retired to his hammock for the night, he might expect a dream.

Such sessions occurred frequently during the few weeks before the Thunder ceremony and several novices attended all sessions. During this period the novice had to refrain from bathing and so became grimy. He could not eat those animals which "walk at night," such as the land tortoise and the monkey, because he had to be friendly with all creatures he might meet in his nocturnal dream travels. He could eat manioc flour, yams, pepper and such bland meats as jacu, coati, peccary, mutum, and chicken; of other foods he could eat sparingly or not at all. The novices were "tired" and "thin"; many did not continue after the first few nights because they were "lazy" or because they were "afraid." Champukwi, who was my good informant, did not continue because he did not like the dirt, the nausea from the tobacco, the lack of food, and the sexual continence.

Other novices, more successful and more persistent, did dream. At first they reported seeing smoky forms of ghosts and sometimes forest demons; they as yet did "not know how to walk with such spirits." Usually, the first season or two during which a young man sought dreams, he might expect only mild dreams. After several seasons the novice might see dangerous forest demons in his unconscious state and he might talk with ghosts. Traditionally, young Tapirapé shamans become wild and uncontrollable when they had their first dangerous dreams. They were reported sometimes to stand up suddenly from their induced trance state and run wildly through the village, sometimes killing chickens, dogs, and parrots, or breaking pottery. Although no novices "ran" in this way during the 1940 training period, an informant described the state of a young shaman who had "run" several years before. "He jumped up. He shouted and ran through the village. He carried a club in his hand (usually weapons were placed well out of reach). He killed two chickens and broke through the side of a house. He killed his brother's dog. All the women and children ran from the village, afraid. Finally, Maeuma grabbed him, but he was strong and he hit Maeuma with a club and blood ran down Maeuma's face. Many came and held him and Urukumu (his mentor) blew smoke over him," thus bringing him back to his senses. He had seen a dangerous spirit and was "afraid," informants told me. This reaction was common among those who had potentialities toward shamanism.

The mere fact that a young shaman had several dangerous dreams did not make him a shaman of proven ability and power. To prove himself, he had to take part in the "fight against the beings of Thunder," and by the side of his mentor he had to perform cures. If successful, he would be called now and then by people for cures. With a reputation of several cures, and with continuous dreaming during which he had supernatural encounters, he built his reputation as a shaman over a period of many years. Panterí and Urukumu were about fifty years old when I visited them; informants gave no indication that their power was expected to decline with age.

With this background concerning the traditional role of the shaman in Tapirapé culture, we can appreciate the drama of the annual ceremonies during which Tapirapé shamans fought the powers of   *199*

Thunder. These ceremonies were held each year in January, and in reality they were shamanistic exhibitions aimed at impressing the laymen. Furthermore, they gave the shamans an opportunity to display their powers. The avowed purpose of the ceremonies, however, was to protect the Tapirapé from the dangers of thunder and lightning.

In common with many Tupí peoples, the Tapirapé considered Thunder a powerful supernatural. He was called Kanawana. Kanawana lives in his house in the sky surrounded by his various supernumeraries. He has with him the souls of the deceased Tapirapé shamans (panché-iúnwera); messengers called awampewa, who carry news to the panché-iúnwera; and, finally, *topu*.[112] Topu were described as small anthropomorphic beings about the size of a man's hand. Their bodies are covered with downy white hair, and they wear European beads, little headdresses of parrot feathers, and lip plugs. They travel with great swiftness through the air in small "canoes" (which, like the "canoes" of the shamans, were vessels made of a gourd), and they carry with them red feathers and beads to use as arrows to shoot at Tapirapé. Sometimes topu were referred to as "pets" of Thunder, and sometimes as his children; but in any case they were many and did his bidding.

In approximately late December and January, when there are heavy thundershowers, lightning, and strong winds, the Tapirapé believed that Thunder was angry. The noise of the storm was considered the rumbling of his topu's canoes and the lightning was explained as the topu's speeding arrows. Once, when a strong wind ripped off part of the roof of a dwelling, Tapirapé men were frightened because they knew that panché-iúnwera had caused the wind. At that time each year shamans "called" Thunder and matched their powers against him. In frenzied intoxication from gulping tobacco smoke, constant singing and dancing, they fell into trances during which they traveled to the house of Thunder. Shamans and a few courageous laymen who take part in the ceremony, were struck down by topu arrows and fell writhing upon the ground. Violent behavior was the keynote of these ceremonies against Thunder and his beings.

In January 1940 this ceremony was announced without warning by

---

112. Topu is obviously the Tapirapé equivalent of Tupã, the word recorded as used by the Tupinambá and other coastal Tupí. Among the coastal Tupí, Tupã was the supernatural being who caused thunder and lightning. Tupã was so important that the early Catholic missionaries used the word for "God," (see Metraux, 1928b: 52-56). Note, however, that among the Tapirapé topu were merely creatures of Thunder.

Panterí. Very early one morning, before dawn, Panterí woke up, lit his pipe and swallowed tobacco smoke as if he were performing a cure. Then he began to sing, accompanied by his wife who sang counterpoint in a higher key. His song challenged Kanawana (Thunder) to come to the village; he announced that he would see topu and panchéiúnwera the next day. He also sang that "many Tapirapé would die."[113] By daybreak he had finished his song and all those who had heard him sing had gone back to sleep again. The village now knew that Panterí had announced the ceremonies. By noon that day, Urukumu took up the songs; he swallowed smoke, vomited and sang. He also was accompanied by his wife. After an hour or more, Urukumu retired into his hammock and the singing was continued first by one and then by another shaman or novice to shamanism. The singing continued until sunset.

Then the shamans and novices came one by one to the dance ground in front of the ceremonial house and repeated the performances of swallowing smoke until intoxicated. In turn, each of them stood up with his wife (the two facing each other and about five feet apart) and sang together. By nightfall the cycle of singing in the plaza ended. Thunder had been called and all his creatures would appear in the village the next day.

For the three following days the ceremonies continued, and sunset always marked a distinct change in the activities. There seemed to be two distinct ceremonial phases: one for the daylight hours and the other for the twilight.

Early in the morning of the second day of the ceremonies, preparations were made for daytime activities. In each of the nine dwellings a door was broken through each side wall at the point nearest to the neighboring house. Paths were then swept between the houses, leading from one of these new doors to another and so forming a circular path about the village and passing through each house. The inhabitants of the largest of the dwellings ("A" on Map 4), which was to the southwest, moved their belongings back against the wall, cleared the house floor of their cooking hearths, and took down their hammocks. This house was to be the central point of the ceremonies during the next three days.

About midday, Panterí began again to sing and to gulp smoke from his pipe. After he had become ill and intoxicated, he came with his

---

113. To "die" in this ceremony is to fall into a trance from the effect of topu's arrows. During this trance the soul leaves the body and travels to the house of Thunder.

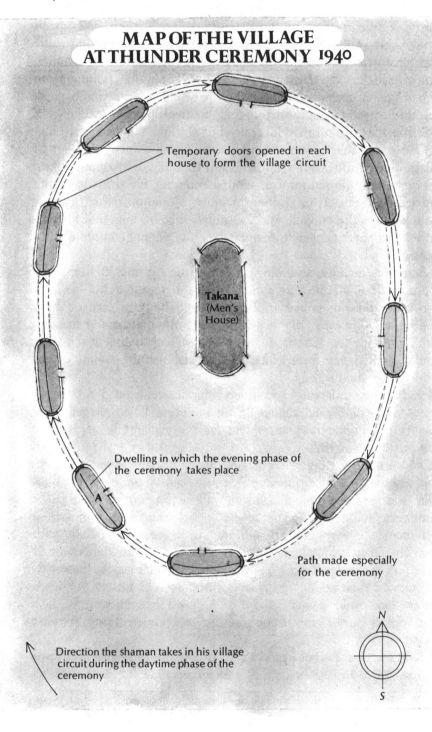

MAP OF THE VILLAGE AT THUNDER CEREMONY 1940

Temporary doors opened in each house to form the village circuit

Takana (Men's House)

Dwelling in which the evening phase of the ceremony takes place

A

Path made especially for the ceremony

Direction the shaman takes in his village circuit during the daytime phase of the ceremony

N

S

wife out of one of the new side doors of his house, "eating smoke" as he came. From this door the couple moved in clockwise direction along the circular path until they came to the center of the next house. There they stopped, faced each other and sang. Panterí punctuated his song with deep draughts from his pipe and vomiting. At each house they repeated this performance. When they reached their own house again, Panterí took up two ceremonial rattles decorated with parrot feathers and the couple continued on a second round through the village houses. After making the circuit four times, they stopped in their own house, where Panterí retired into his hammock. The rattles were left in the southwestern house on his last circuit.

Urukumu and his wife then made four similar trips about the new circular path. After he had finished, a young shaman took up the ceremony, but he was not able to complete even one round without help. After singing in several houses, he began to stagger as he walked and he stumbled blindly into house posts. He was noticeably in a state of trance. Young men led him from house to house. Suddenly he shrieked, his body stiffened, and he fell to the ground. His muscles quivered for a few moments and then his body became rigid. He had lost his battle. He had seen topu and had been shot by their arrows, for he did not have the strength of Panterí and Urukumu. Several young men immediately raised him up on their shoulders and carried him through the remaining houses of the circuit, depositing him finally in the southwestern house. One of the powerful shamans was then called, and he massaged and blew smoke over the prostrate shaman's body until life again appeared in it.

Throughout the remainder of the afternoon, aspirants to shamanism and several laymen took up the ceremony of calling Thunder by traveling the ceremonial circuit of the village. At one time there were three men moving with their wives over this circular route. Some never reached a trance state because "they did not know how to eat smoke" or because "topu did not hear their songs." Several novices "saw topu" and were struck down as the young shaman had been earlier that day. One novice, staggering blindly and vomiting violently, tried to break away from the young men who were partially supporting him. When they caught him, he fell immediately to the ground. Finally, toward sundown, Panterí took up his song again. He still was "stronger than topu" and was able to perform his song without falling into trance.

At sundown, men began to gather in the southwestern house, which   203

The powerful shaman Urukumu is struck down by topú during the Thunder ceremony in 1940.

Urukumu's body becomes rigid, and he is carried around the circle of houses.

had been cleared of personal belongings. Some twenty men came to take part in this ceremonial phase. The bulk of the villagers was gathered inside the house. Spectators crowded close against the walls of the house and those standing outside looked through the doors and holes in the walls. The two powerful shamans, Urukumu and Panterí, stood in the middle of the house facing each other. They lit their long pipes and began to swallow smoke. At the back of the room were two young men with the ceremonial rattles which the shamans had used earlier. These young men were in particular danger, for their rattles attracted the special attention of Thunder's creatures. In front of them, Ikoriwantori, a young man noted for his singing, stood on a bench and began to sing the songs of Thunder. The young men with the rattles played accompaniment for his songs. A young boy sat behind them and beat time to the song with a hollow trunk of bamboo. Now and again, young men standing against the walls took up a chorus with the solo singer. The shamans kept going to the young men with the rattles, offering them smoke to swallow from their pipes until they were unsteady on their feet. At times they were able to stay on their feet only when they were held up. They then began walking back and forth to the front of the house, shaking the rattles towards the roof threateningly, challenging topu and panché-iúnwera to come.

Shamans now offered their pipes to their novices and to laymen. The two shamans soon began walking back and forth the length of the house, first alone and then each taking a novice with them. One by one, men joined the shamans as they moved up and down the house. By now almost all the men seemed thoroughly intoxicated (though the only stimulant was tobacco) and the atmosphere grew tense. All the participants spewed out smoke until it fairly engulfed them as they moved vomiting and reeling about. Everyone took up a grunting chant of "Hew! Hew!" Some carried mirrors and red parrot feathers as weapons against the topu. The two powerful shamans carried bushknives and at each end of the house they stopped and motioned threateningly toward the roof, defying topu and panché-iúnwera to come. During all this time the singing continued with its accompaniment of rattles and the hollow bamboo tube, except for intervals when some participant collapsed.

Suddenly Panterí stopped his marching back and forth, retired a few steps and pointed to the corner of the house. It was explained to me that he had seen panché-iúnwera. He rushed to the far end of the house and pointed again; he saw a topu. He moved backward in   205

During the Thunder ceremonies young men accompanied the shamans as they moved from house to house. At any moment a shaman might fall in a trance, defeated by the beings of Thunder.

A young shaman, already in a trance, challenges Thunder.

An aspirant to shamanism sings to Thunder while wearing the dangerous headdress. This man later became a powerful shaman and assumed the name Wantanamu.

The headdress of red macaw feathers infuriates Thunder, and a young shaman is struck down.

fright; then appeared to threaten, point, run in fright, and finally retreat, completely confused by numerous enemies.

One young shaman broke away from the group and ran through the circle of the houses like a hunted animal, dodging about and staring with glazed eyes. He fell to the ground, rolling on his side and groaning. His body twitched and then became rigid. His wife, who had been standing among the spectators, rushed to his aid and dragged him out of the path of the group. She propped him up in a sitting position against her legs. Several others fell in this manner, struck down by the beings of Thunder, and were dragged to the sidelines where someone blew smoke over them and massaged them. With this treatment they soon regained consciousness, yet they remained reclined upon the ground because they were "weak from the fright."

Finally, as it grew dark outside, Panterí, still leading those men who had not been struck down, pointed directly over his head. Urukumu looked where Panterí had pointed, put his hands over the back of his neck and ran quickly from side to side, dodging. "There are many panché-iúnwera and many topu in the house," one of the spectators told me. At this point all the men who were participating in the ceremony fell suddenly to the ground; only Panterí and Urukumu were strong enough to stand before the forces of Thunder. The wives of the fallen men came to their aid and other men fumigated and massaged them. One by one they came "to life." It was explained that "we die and tobacco brings back life. Without tobacco Thunder would kill us." All men who had participated in the ceremony now returned to their own houses by way of the circuit path, stopping for a moment in each house to perform again the ceremonial singing. Two young boys brought this phase of the ceremony to an end by picking up the ceremonial rattles which had fallen to the ground and running with them around the whole circuit of the village.

The third and fourth days of the ceremony followed closely the pattern of this day, but there were some important variations. On the last two days a new danger was added, accounting for even more violent seizures. During these days each man making the ceremonial circuit wore an elaborate headdress, the *ankungitána*. This headdress is made of the red tail feathers of the macaw; it infuriates Thunder and attracts his creatures to the wearer.[114] Without exception, all who wore

---

114. Red parrot feathers are "hot like fire" say the Tapirapé; the sun is hot because he wears a large headdress of red feathers. This heat always attracts the supernatural. The Tapirapé told me that an attack of malaria I had was caused by my having left a headdress of red parrot feathers hanging openly in my house.

the headdress, even Panterí and Urukumu, fell unconscious before the forces of Thunder, and genuine fear was shown by those who wore it.

Before a man could put the headdress on, a shaman waved it slowly before his eyes. The shaman then placed the headdress on the man's head, blowing smoke through the feathers to take out some of the terrific "heat." When Urukumu wore the ankungitána, he began to weave and stumble even before he left the first house of the circle. He then had to be led and supported by two young men. Before he had completed one circle of the village, he was seized in a trance that seemed even more violent than those of the younger men. His body was rigid, and he was carried through the remaining circle of the houses to the southwestern house, where he was treated by Panterí. Panterí, likewise, was defeated and fell when he wore the headdress. During his trance he sang snatches of a song and when he regained consciousness he said he had traveled to the house of Thunder. Later, Panterí related to me his experiences during his trance. His story, freely translated, was this: "I ate much smoke and then smoked again. I sang; I saw one large sun. It came toward me and disappeared. I saw many small suns. They approached and left. I saw Thunder. It was small and came in a small canoe. It was Thunder's child (a topu). It wore a small headdress of red parrot feathers. It had a small lip plug. I reached to pull out the lip plug (thus he would have vanquished the topu) but it left the house. Then all was dark (he had not defeated the topu and it had consequently shot him with an arrow). I saw many suns. I traveled, singing as I walked. I walked three days and I climbed a large mountain on the other side of the Araguaia. There it is that the sun comes up. I saw Thunder; he is big and his body is covered with white hair. He had many feathers of the red parrot. I saw many topu and many souls of shamans near him. I did not talk but returned fast." He added that later if he had touched Thunder's rattle he would have had to stay in the other world; he would have died.

A few novices, and now and again a rare layman, wore the headdress and people marveled at their courage. Most Tapirapé men, however, did not have the courage to wear it. The headdress added danger and violence also to the sundown phases of the ceremony on the third and fourth days. At the height of the excitement, when it was apparent that both powerful shamans had sighted creatures of Thunder, Panterí grabbed the headdress which was hanging from a rafter and waved it in the air, threatening and challenging these enemies. He fell immediately, stricken by a panché-iúnwera. Urukumu picked up the head- 209 dress. He too fell unconscious, and all the participants with him. The two young boys, as before, ran through the circle of houses at the end of the day's ceremony, but this time they carried both the rattles and the headdress. The participants, on regaining consciousness, returned singing to their houses.

On the fourth and last day of the ceremony, an additional ceremony followed the usual evening performance. As the ceremony ended, the two strong shamans walked out of the house to the dance ground, taking the rattles and the headdress. There they and several others re-enacted, but with less violence, the ceremony just completed in the house. Following this performance, all the men of the village gathered, facing north "toward the house of Thunder," and Panterí walked across the plaza away from the group toward the north, shaking the rattles over his head. Returning to the group, he touched several men on the head with the rattles, much as a priest performs a blessing with a crucifix. He repeated this performance until finally all men who had taken part in the ceremony had received this "blessing." Women, and later the children, came forward to be touched by the rattles as well. Thus they were freed of danger from Thunder. After this, I was told, Thunder goes far away to his house until the next year.

That evening men sang the songs of the *anchunga aiwiró*, the spirits that come to live in the dance house after Thunder has gone. Late that same evening the men danced single file over the circuit, starting from the large house where the principal ceremonies had been held. As thy danced, they sang that Thunder had gone and all was safe once again.[115]

During the four-day period of the combat against Thunder and his creatures sexual intercourse had been taboo, but on the night after Thunder left "all Tapirapé would have intercourse with their wives and many women would become pregnant." Traditionally, women were freer with their favors for a few days after this ceremony. People, however, sometimes broke the taboo and so brought trouble on themselves and their tribe. Panterí reported: "I was weak when I returned from Thunder's house. Many mosquitoes drank my blood on the road. This was because Tapirapé men were with their wives. I dreamed that night and saw many Tapirapé having intercourse and knew that

---

115. During this serpent dance, one might steal maize which was hanging from rafters in the houses through which they passed. Youngsters did steal some, and women ran after them trying to get it back. There was much gaiety and laughter.

Tapirapé would be bitten by many mosquitoes when they called Thunder."

In 1965, when I returned to visit the Tapirapé, I was informed that the ceremonial of the fight against Thunder had not been held for many years—not at least since the attack of the Kayapó in 1947. It is quite possible that the ceremonial I have described above, as it took place in January of 1940, was the last one that occurred. When I asked about Kanawana in 1965, both Tampirí and Ipawungí told me that there were no real panchés left. People looking at the 1940 photographs of the ceremonial did not compare it with others that took place later and the Little Sisters of Jesus, who have lived continuously with the Tapirapé since 1953, do not remember seeing it. In fact, when trying to clarify some points about the ceremonial with Tapirapé friends in 1965, I was put off by the statement: "You should know better than we do. You knew powerful panchés like Urukumu and Panterí. You talked with them and saw them fight Thunder. We were only children at the time and we do not remember it well." They also explained that Opronunchwi and Chaneó are only "little shamans." They can treat children and minor ailments, but they cannot cure the sickness of grown people.

One night in 1965, I heard Opronunchwi vomiting in a near-by house. My wife and I went to see him cure. He was blowing smoke over a child said to be ill with fever. He used massage. But his shamanistic performance was a poor imitation of those I had seen many years before and only a few people gathered about to witness his cure. The next day, Opronunchwi came to visit. He claimed that he was not really a panché; he did not have important dreams. My wife was much amused when he begged her during his visit to give him an injection of penicillin. He himself was ill with chills and fever—only an "injection" would relieve him, he insisted. Although Chaneó and Opronunchwi were, in 1965, more or less respected elderly men, they did not have the prestige of younger men such at Tampirí and Ipawungí, who were then the recognized village leaders. The latter had gathered their prestige from another route—by recognition as hard workers and by the accumulation of western objects which provided them a standard of living somewhat better than that of most Tapirapé. Ipawungí, for example, owned a .22-calibre rifle, he had plenty of shells, he owned two canoes, he had a house near the river with adobe walls, and he was so trusted by Father François that he often drove the missionary tractor. By 1965 there were ways of gaining prestige less hazardous than shamanism, and life had become more secular. When people became ill they sought medicine from the Little Sisters of Jesus. They realized that their children had been cured not by interaction with the supernatural, but by "torí medicine."

Yet the Tapirapé felt vulnerable without their shamans. They had not fully replaced their sacred view of the world with a profane one. Several of my Tapirapé friends complained that they were subject to *feitiço* (sorcery, in Portuguese) made by the Carajá shamans, whom they knew to exist. Several men in the village put much faith in Sabino Velho, an old Carajá Indian who lived upriver some thirty or forty kilometers. They went to consult him when someone in their family was ill and did not seem to improve as the result of medicine dispensed by the Little Sisters. Sabino Velho divined for them, telling which of the many Carajá shamans might have caused the illness. He also "treated" against feitiço, but no one was able to describe just what his methods were. He once "cured" Ipawungí, who had been suffering from some kind of a skin disease. He demanded in payment an "old carbine" (.44-calibre rifle) and twenty shells. Likewise, the other current leader, Tampirí, went to Sabino Velho when his daughter was very ill. His fees were again, it seemed to me, rather exorbitant. He charged Tampirí one pair of pants, several strings of beads, and one-half of the produce of Tampirí's garden due for harvest several months later. When the garden was ripe, Sabino Velho came with a canoe to fill it with manioc, beans, squash, and other vegetables. Sabino Velho seems to prey upon the traditional fear the Tapirapé have of the Carajá. He told Ipawungí that "when I die, the Tapirapé will be in great danger. They will die again as they did before."

After the shamans had performed their ceremony of fighting Thunder, the heavy rains came. This was a period of little activity in the Tapirapé village. People stayed rather close to their homes fighting gnats and mosquitoes. Men spent much of their time in the takana gossiping, weaving baskets, or just lounging. The monotony of the rain was broken by men going on individual hunts or on group hunting expeditions organized by the Bird Societies. When these collective hunts took place, there was also a short song festival. Although the kaó festival properly begins at the end of the rains, men sometimes sang and danced during the rainy season in kaó style. The singing and dancing began inside the takana. This consists of a pair of men, both from one Bird Society, dancing bent forward as a pair with their arms over each other's shoulders. They sang songs belonging to their society, beating out the rhythm by stomping one foot. Soon they were joined by another pair from the other society who sang and danced facing them. Slowly other pairs joined in, and the music took more the form of choral singing. Hearing the men sing, the women gathered in front of the takana. Soon the men issued forth in pairs, continuing to dance and sing. Then, as the pairs of men advanced and retreated from one another, the women sang in two groups behind the men. A kaó style song and dance often lasted throughout the night unless it was raining too hard or people suddenly lost interest for one reason or another. Typically, such a songfest continued in strength with a goodly number of singers and dancers until about midnight. Then some abandoned the festival to sleep until just before dawn. Finally, they joined again, singing strongly until the sun rose. Many times kaó singers invaded my house just at dawn to invite me to join—or just to wake me up, like a group of partygoers who had spent the night carousing.

These kaó sings are not ceremonials at all; they are recreational. The songs the Tapirapé sing are generally old (they seem less influenced by borrowing from other tribes), but some can be new. Champukwi, who was known as a good singer, explained to me how a new song comes about. A man is walking alone, perhaps on the way to his garden. He sings old songs, but then he experiments with new words and changes the tune. If he likes what he has produced, he will sing it softly at night to his friends in the takana. If they like what he produced, they will sing it loudly at the next kaó sing. Thus, new songs never present profound innovations. There are some new words, a different accent to the music, and perhaps a slightly different rhythm. In 1974, Judith Shapiro, returning from a short visit to the Tapirapé, brought to me a new song which she had recorded. It seemed to me to follow the kaó style. In it there were references to Doctor Carlo who had lived with the Tapirapé and then had gone far away beyond the "big waters." No one knows if this song will become a permanent part of the Tapirapé repertoire. In 1939-40, kaó songs were sung irregularly at night in the men's house from late January until late April. Some people told me that songfests were the rotating and alternate responsibility of the two older age groups of the Bird Societies—that is, Wuranchingó, Tanawe, Wuranchingió, and Ananchá—and they claimed that the irregularity of the songfests was due to the lassitude of those societies. Other people did not substantiate this claim, but simply criticized the village as a whole. "The Tapirapé are lazy this year," they said when many nights went by without singing.

It should be emphasized that the central focus of all Tapirapé cere- 213 monies was vocal music. One cannot exaggerate the role of singing in Tapirapé life. Men were judged by and granted prestige on the basis of their voices. It should be remembered that each Bird Society had men known for their ability to sing and to act as singing leaders. The men generally sang in chorus, with their singing leader introducing the song and the group joining in. Often, women, standing behind the men, sang just a line behind the men and almost in counterpoint, a few notes higher on the scale.

On some occasions, some men sang long, rather monotonous songs in solo, interrupted now and again by a low male chorus. These were songs referring to stories of ancestors who lived long ago. One of these long songs was called "Chawanamu." In 1939-40, it was said that only one man, Maeuma, knew all of the Chawanamu cycle. I heard him sing it several times; it was slow with little variation of tune, broken by the sounds imitating animals which Chawanamu met in his travels. After long hours of trying to get the exact words in phonetic transcription, I was forced to the conclusion that the song did not tell the story. One had to first know the story and then the words relating to incidents of the ancestor's travels took on some meaning. In other words, it was not an epic song poem. It did not relate the whole story of how Chawanamu traveled, met dangerous enemies, was captured and escaped, had a son, was captured again and finally eaten by his captors. Or how one day his captors ate his leg, the next day his other leg, then his arms, then his chest, and so on until he was entirely consumed. I also made an effort to find the meaning of the songs which men and women sang in chorus, only to find that they often referred to events of the past or mythology which in themselves had no meaning without a knowledge of the mythological context. One well-known song had these words:

The little birds sang, hé, hé
The large birds sang, hé, hé
All the birds sang, hé, hé

It referred to the singing of the birds which Petura witnessed and to the origin of the men's Bird Societies.

Earlier I related how the Tapirapé learned hymns from the missionary Frederick Kegel. Evidently, they were remarkably receptive to songs from other cultures. Even to my inexpert ear the Tapirapé sang songs which I was certain they had borrowed from the Carajá Indians of the Araguaia River; even the words were in Carajá and thus untranslatable by the Tapirapé. In 1965, when I paid a quick visit to the Gorotire (Kayapó) living several hundred miles to the north (one of the Kayapó hordes which had attacked the Tapirapé), I heard them sing songs which I had heard among the Tapirapé. In 1957, when I visited the Tapirapé with Roberto Cardoso de Oliveira and my nephew George Whyte, the youths entertained us at night by singing in Tapirapé, in English (hymns), in French ("Frère Jacques"), and in Portuguese. Music is a central focus of their culture.[116]

Later in the rainy season and throughout the dry season came the period of the year *par excellence*, when the takana became the residence of anchunga. When anchunga resided in the takana, each was represented by a pair of male masked dancers. There were a multitude of these anchunga in the Tapirapé cosmology, and they "resided" at different periods of the year in the takana. They seem to represent a variety of things in the natural and the supernatural world. There are those, for example, which represent wild pigs and seem to be the protectors of wild pigs. They were referred to by several names: anchunga ampukaiya, anchunga tampanchi, and simply anchunga tachaho (wild pig spirits). They came to the takana from their home far away on "the hill"—an actual hill which can be seen in the distance from the flat savanna lands near the Tapirapé River. The panché in his dreams went to their home, visited with them, and brought them to reside for a time in the takana. They were represented by a pair of buriti costumes and masks in which men danced while uttering the grunting noises of wild pigs. And, characteristically, the dancers wore rattles tied to their ankles made of the hoofs of wild pigs which they had killed. Anchunga tachaho in one of its variations generally came to the takana in celebration of a hunt in which wild pigs were killed and there was meat to eat.

Other anchunga masks represented other animals. *Iriwe-anchunga* is said to represent the electric eel which was eaten by the Tapirapé but was hardly an important element in their diet. It does not seem that Iriwe-anchunga protected (or "owned" the electric eel. Instead, a myth explains why this spirit visited the takana. Long ago, it seems, a spirit (or ancestor) called Chureni killed all of the Tapirapé who resided in a faraway village. Then, Chureni was, I judge, the ancestral

---

116. The reader must be warned about my description of music. I like music, but I have no technical training whatsoever in it. Furthermore, I cannot carry a tune. I may not be tone deaf, but the results are about the same. I was a bitter disappointment to my Tapirapé friends for my total lack of any singing ability.

spirit of the electric eel. In any case, later Chureni came to a Tapirapé village bringing his wife and son. The Tapirapé women killed his wife, giving her body to the men, who buried it in the takana. Then the Tapirapé killed his son, cutting off his head and burying the body in the takana also. Chureni left very "sad" and "angry" and now when he comes to visit the takana in the form of Iriwe-anchunga he is always sad and angry. Despite the single character which appears in the myth, Iriwe-anchunga is symbolized by a pair of masks and costumes. His stay in the takana was not a pleasant visit and the women were supposed to be especially frightened. But it must be said that none of the masked costumes were grotesque or frightening to look at, and they were not intended to inspire fear.

As the rainy season ended, the real season of masked dancing and of visits of a variety of anchunga began. It must be remembered that the beginning of the dry season was marked by the harvest ceremonies which were the culmination of the kaó sings, the dancing and singing at kawió when there was an exchange of personal property, and the coming of age ceremony for young men. All of these occasions have been described in different contexts in this book. On such occasions the singing and dancing, especially the dancing, were characterized by distinct styles. On one occasion, the women danced with the men. As the men stood about in the plaza, a woman would approach one, selecting him as her partner and the pair would join the circle of the dancing group. They danced with their arms over their neighbor's shoulders in a curious step which consisted in kicking their feet straight in front in unison. The dancers formed a large circle which slowly closed and then opened as the pairs retreated from the center. It seemed to be pure entertainment, although each man was expected to give a gift of some kind to the woman who had selected him as dancing partner. On the occasion of the coming of age ceremony men danced in a single file, but in a circle. And, at the culmination of the harvest, men danced in place in a long single line and the women (generally the wives of the dancing men) danced directly behind them.

In the dry season, the anchunga spirits which came to reside in the takana represented aquatic and terrestrial animals. During 1939-40, only two pairs of such anchunga were represented—*irancha*, which clearly was the spirit of fish, and *jakuí*, which was the spirit of the jacu. Each of these anchunga was represented by a pair of masks and costumes. The masks themselves were tall, conical, basket-like contraptions which left only small slits through which the dancers could see and guide themselves. The jakuí mask was set off from the irancha by two red macaw feathers tied to the tip of the cone. Each costume had a jacket or waistcoat that covered the dancer's arms and breast and there was a skirt that covered the dancer well below the knees. These masks were, or seemed to be, twice as tall as the ordinary man. Pairs of men, ideally one from each Bird Society, danced and "sang" irregularly throughout the summer months. (I put "sang" in quotation marks here because most of the sounds these men uttered were shrill cries said to be characteristic of that particular anchunga.) As a pair of anchunga emerged from the takana they danced in a particular swaying motion along a definite route. Sometimes girls and young women danced around as if offering homage to them. But they moved from the takana to the door of each longhouse until they had danced the whole village circle. At each longhouse they danced and uttered their characteristic cries until a young woman emerged through the longhouse door to offer them kawi (soup made from maize and manioc). Covered by their buriti masks, the dancers, of course, could not actually drink the kawi, but it was clear that they begged—or perhaps demanded—the offering. Then they wove their way back to the takana and the other pair of anchunga emerged to make their village round. It was usually in the cool of the late afternoon or in the early evening when the anchunga danced.

The Tapirapé promised that other anchunga would come during the summer of 1939-40, but only these two actually appeared. They had promised that iranchahó (a larger irancha-fish spirit) would come; and they described iranwuré (another spirit of wild pigs), moro (a fish), and akmukó, a spirit which is the special "pet" of the Carajá tribe. But then, when they did not appear, one man told me, very pragmatically, "we have no more buriti [to make costumes] and we have no more feathers [to decorate the masks]". I had to be satisfied with irancha and jakuí. But they told me of numerous other anchunga that occasionally came to the takana which I did not see. There was anchunga awanaí, who was said to be friendly to the Tapirapé, but was mischievous. This spirit usually came in the rainy season for two or three days and visited gardens, stealing ears of maize. Then there were the anchunga aiwo, spirits which the Tapirapé say they stole from the Kayapó men who once visited their village. The Tapirapé bragged that they ran after the retreating Kayapó (an unlikely story) and rescued their spirits, who were thin and maltreated. They took   *217*

Masked dancers representing the *anchunga* spirits which visit the takana in the dry season.

Young girls dancing around the *anchunga* masked dancers.

A young girl "feeding" kawi soup to the *anchunga* spirits.

them back to the takana where they were fattened on manioc and maize soup. My notebooks are filled with names of other anchunga, none of which I saw and for most of which I do not even have a good description. It is clear to me that the number of anchunga which perhaps sometimes visited the takana was great. If they all did come, there would be a veritable series of them all through the year. It was also clear that the Tapirapé were remarkably receptive to other peoples' supernaturals. As I said, they themselves spoke of "stealing" anchunga from the Kayapó, and their irancha and jakuí masks were identical to masks I saw among the Carajá. It must be said that the Carajá are noted for their masked dancers, whom they call *Arawana*, 219 and who dance constantly during the dry season. Furthermore, it must be stressed that none of the Tapirapé anchunga which "visited" the takana was considered malevolent—except perhaps for the anchunga of the jakaconya (Guariba monkey), which attacked the young girls with their enormous phalli, and even then the situation seemed more salacious than frightening.

When I returned in 1965, the Tapirapé assured me that they had not forgotten their festivals and ceremonies. The Little Sisters of Jesus respected their customs and, as is their practice, they urged the Indians to organize their song festivals, masked dances, and ceremonials marking rites of passage. The Little Sisters believe, quite rightly, that such festivals and ceremonies secure the Tapirapé an identity as a people. In fact, they had not discontinued their ceremonial life. In 1964 they had celebrated the coming of age ceremony of a youth. In the late rainy season (March through April), they sang kaó several nights in the men's house. And then one afternoon, the great masks called upé tawa, representing the spirits of dead enemies, emerged from the men's house and danced about the village (it was, however, somewhat out of season). They promised that if we would stay through the dry season that pairs of irancha, iranwuré, and other anchunga would live in the takana and dance through the village. Then, in 1966, Shapiro witnessed the gift exchange at kawió and she saw an apachiró. And almost every year I have received letters from the Little Sisters of Jesus, urging me to come visit them. The Tapirapé, they tell me, have two or three youths ready to tie their hair and I would be most welcome at the ceremonies. And in 1976 I received a taped message from Cantidio (also known as Ipawungí) to come visit New Village during the dry season of 1977, when there would be many anchunga dancers.

So the Tapirapé resettled in New Village have continued their ceremonial life to the best of their ability. Of course, they have been able to do so only in an altered form. They have fewer people and they have new ecological conditions, settled as they are on the Araguaia River with their gardens so far away. And then it must be remembered that the yearly cycle of festivals and ceremonials always had a most tenuous schedule. At the death of any person (except, perhaps, an infant) a festival was subject to postponement or cancellation. Even in the old days it was seldom that a whole yearly cycle of festivals and ceremonials was ever realized. Thus, nowadays, as in the past, the festivals and ceremonials are easily postponed for another year.

It is to be expected that the Tapirapé today, with almost daily relations with Brazilian frontiersmen, would adopt some Brazilian customs, especially in view of Tapirapé receptivity to foreign music. So, in 1965, some Tapirapé had begun to organize Saturday night Brazilian *festinhas* (little parties). These are dancing parties in western style during which men and women dance in pairs to the music of a *cavaquinho* (a small stringed instrument similar to a ukulele), a tambourine, and a flute. One Tapirapé had learned to play a bamboo flute quite well. Both the men and the women were at least adequate in dancing Brazilian style. Brazilian backwoodsmen and their wives attended, and sometimes there were a few Carajá guests. Almost always Tapirapé men danced with Tapirapé women, but now and again there were mixed couples shuffling about the room. Such dances took place not in the takana, although it would offer an excellent site for a festinha, but in a house just at the edge of the village. It was a strange sight to see Tapirapé dancing Brazilian style, but the whole scene was not out of keeping with that frontier environment, where two Indian tribes live side by side with simple Brazilian frontiersmen. Yet the Little Sisters and the resident Indian officer did not encourage these festinhas. In fact, they did their best to discourage them. For the visiting Brazilian backwoodsmen brought cachaça (raw sugarcane rum) to these dances, as was their custom, and they also came armed with machetes and sharp, dagger-like knives. They encouraged the Indians to drink, a habit which they had never acquired. Often such festinhas broke up in fights, generally over a woman. An Indian, misunderstanding the situation, tried to seduce a Brazilian's wife, or a Tapirapé woman removed her blouse because it was hot, thus seeming to invite a sexual approach from the Brazilian men. Plans for festinhas worried the Little Sisters of Jesus, who urged the Indian officer to prohibit them.

7
Four Tapirapé Friends

In this chapter I have tried to recapture some of the human and personal element in my anthropological research among the Tapirapé. Anthropological research is never an entirely detached and objective process, however many anthropologists might like to think it is. It involves something of the "art of human relations," in which emotions, subjective attitudes and reactions, and, undoubtedly, subconscious motivations participate. It is a profoundly human endeavor. Faced over long periods with individuals of a culture other than his own, the anthropologist in a primitive village or in a strange peasant community becomes involved in a complex set of human relations, just as he would be at home in his own society. Some of the individuals with whom he works, lives, and encounters daily are highly intelligent, some mentally slow, some friendly and overt, some dour, some placid, and some quick to become irritated. And then, each anthropologist is himself a distinctive personality who handles, in his own way, his dual role as an objective scientific observer of a society and culture not his own, and as a human being forced to maintain relations with the people among whom he lives for a time. Here I hope to summarize for the reader my relationship to four individuals whom I knew rather well during my sojourn with the Tapirapé. I shall also attempt to tell how each taught me some aspect of the local culture. To achieve this end, I have had to project myself into the picture, to insert my own feelings about people and places, and to tell of my personal experiences in the course of my research.

The sketches that follow tell something of these four: their background, their place in their society, and my relations with them. Above all, I hope that the reader will come to understand something of their way of life in the same way that they made it known to me within the context of life situations. None of these individuals could be called average citizens. The girl Antanchowi, who was looked down upon by her fellow men and women, was about seventeen years of age when I knew her in 1939. Both Champukwi and Kamairaho were especially admired men whom I met in 1939-40; Champukwi was about twenty-five and Kamairaho approximately forty-five. I knew Cantidio first in 1939, when he was about twelve or thirteen years of age, but I came to know him best as a "modern Tapirapé" of thirty-eight or thirty-nine in 1965. Anthropologists must build their knowledge of a culture from a variety of people, but it would be impossible to portray the whole gamut of individuals and personalities found among the Tapirapé. I have selected out of my notebooks and my memory these individuals with different roles in their society about whom I knew more than I did about others. I have not tried to provide a full life history for any of them, nor have I told a chronological story of their lives. I have merely described and analyzed my own relationship with each and discussed certain events in their lives.[117]

As an anthropologist, and as a human being, I have learned much from these four individuals and from many other Tapirapé. Both Champukwi and Kamairaho were my teachers overtly and consciously. They were "key informants" in my study of the Tapirapé culture. Although an anthropologist gathers information from a wide variety of people, there are generally a few individuals who provide him with his basic picture of a particular society and culture. It seems that in all human cultures there are individuals who might be called "natural observers," people with a particular interest in the human scene and a tendency to speculate about it. Part of the struggle to penetrate a strange culture is to discover such natural observers. But I have never found this to be difficult. Such people seem as much attracted to an anthropologist as the anthropologist is to them. It often appears that they have been waiting for the anthropologist to appear, and they seem to find considerable satisfaction in attempting to explain their culture to the outsider. With such "key informants," an anthropologist may spend literally hundreds of hours in intensive interviews. In

---

117. I hope that the reader will forgive the repetition of some facts about Tapirapé culture already described in this volume. It is necessary to recall some descriptive data in order to place events and people in their social and cultural context.

the course of time, a close relationship inevitably grows between the anthropologist and such an informant. Often, a sympathetic friendship takes form. In some respects, this relationship is similar to that between a psychotherapist and his patient; for in the course of many long interviews, such people reveal (and perhaps discover) much about themselves. Champukwi was perhaps my most important key informant in 1939-40, and Kamairaho not only taught me much about his culture but was also the key person in establishing my network of Tapirapé friends and kinsmen.

Other individuals who are mentioned in this volume were not, strictly speaking, my informants. They were but my friends and acquaintances in the Tapirapé village in which I lived and studied. Yet, in their own way, these friends equally taught me about their culture. Anthropologists learn about a culture not only from interviews with key informants, but also by observing the behavior of people around them and by participating as far as is possible in the life of the community. Among the people of any community, there seem always to be a few whom the anthropologist comes to know and to like better than others—just as it would be in a community within our own culture. These people become one's friends. They are the children next door from whom one learns much about children—that is, what games they play, how they are punished, and how they learn the rules of conduct of their culture. The native woman who comes to sweep the house of the anthropologist may become a friend, and from frequent conversations with her one may learn much of what is expected of women in that society. A hunting companion may not become one's key informant, but on a long day's hunt he provides the anthropologist with much to be written in his notebook. Such observations of the behavior, the problems, and the opinions of one's friends in a strange culture must be checked again and again with others in similar roles within the same society. But in the end, one's friends provide the life situations from which anthropological knowledge is drawn.

CHAMPUKWI: a Tapirapé Teacher*

I must have seen Champukwi as soon as I arrived in Tampiitawa, for presents were distributed to the whole population on the day of my arrival. But I did not then distinguish him as an individual, nor did he

---

224 * An earlier version of this sketch was published in Casagrande: *In the Company of Man* (Harper & Row, 1960).

stand out in any way from the other men of his village. His name does not appear in the notes taken during my first month among the Tapirapé.

For me, and even more for Valentim Gomes, the first weeks in the Tapirapé village were a period of grappling with a strange and often confusing world. Three Tapirapé youths had spent a few months at mission stations and thus spoke a rudimentary form of Portuguese with a vocabulary limited to a few basic nouns and verbs. Our main problem at first was communication, but those youths were able to help us. Aside from them, the only individuals we knew by name during the first two weeks were the "captains," the older men who were the heads of the nine large longhouses in the village. But even the names of these men, such as Opronunchwi, Wantanamu, Kamanaré, Mariapawungo, and Okane, who appear so often in this book, were hard to remember at that time.

During the first weeks in Tampiitawa, I began to study intensively the Tapirapé language. Until I could use the language at least passably, I was limited to observing and recording only those overt forms of Tapirapé culture which the eye could see, and even they usually needed explaining. I visited their gardens. I watched the women making flour from both the poisonous and the "sweet" varieties of manioc and making pots out of clay. I watched the men weave baskets out of palm fiber and manufacture their bows and arrows as they sat in hammocks in the men's house. These and many other overt aspects of Tapirapé culture could be recorded in notes and photographs while I studied their language.

The Tapirapé are a friendly and humorous people, and they seemed rather pleased by the curious strangers in their midst. They found our antics amusing; the gales of laughter which accompanied the conversations we could hear but not understand seemed stimulated by tales of our strange behavior. Then, of course, our presence was materially valuable because the salt, knives, needles, beads, mirrors, and other presents we brought were greatly appreciated. Within a very short time, some of these people began to emerge as individuals. There was Kamairaho, the household leader, who received us so well. Then there was a small boy of about six, named Awanchowa, who followed me about and literally haunted our little house, staring at the large bag of salt, which he ate in the same way children in our culture might eat sweets. There was Tanui, a woman of middle age (whose hair was cropped short, indicating that a near relative had recently died); she often brought us presents of food. Gradually, most of the villagers emerged as distinctive personalities. Among them was Champukwi. I cannot remember when I first came to know him as an individual, but his name begins to appear regularly in my field notes about one month after our arrival. Soon he became my best informant, and, after a time, an inseparable companion.

Champukwi must have been about twenty-five in 1939. He was tall for a Tapirapé male, measuring perhaps five feet six inches, strongly built but lean, weighing about 150 pounds. Like all Tapirapé men, he wore his hair in bangs across his forehead with a pigtail tied at the back of his neck. He was something of a dandy, for his feet and the calves of his legs were painted in an intricate design, and he wore the crocheted disc-like wrist ornaments of cotton string dyed red. He was obviously a man of some prestige among men of his age, for youths and younger men treated him with deference, always finding him a seat on the bench that was built against one wall of our house. I learned soon that he, too, had spent a short period at a mission station several years earlier and that he knew a few words of Portuguese. He was married and had a daughter about two years of age. His wife, hardly attractive according to Tapirapé tastes, appeared to be some-what older than he and was pregnant when we first met.

Champukwi seemed more patient than other Tapirapé with my attempts to use his language and to seek information. He would repeat a word, a phrase, or a sentence several times so that I might write it phonetically. He resorted to his meager Portuguese and even to mimicry to explain what was meant. Of course, his patience was tempered by gifts of beads, hardware, and salt which I provided from time to time. After a few days I began noting questions to be asked of Champukwi in the late afternoon, when he habitually visited our house. But that was the time of day when others liked to visit also. Often our house was crowded with men, women, children, and even Tapirapé pets—a situation which was hardly conducive to an ethnological interview or even to the systematical recording of vocabulary.

So I asked Champukwi if I might go with him to his garden. There, alternating between helping him cut brush from his garden site and sitting in the shade, I was able to have something that resembled an interview. Often, while he worked, I formulated questions in my halting Tapirapé, and I was able by repetition to understand his answers. Although the Tapirapé villagers began to joke about Champukwi's new garden site as belonging to the two of us, those days were very

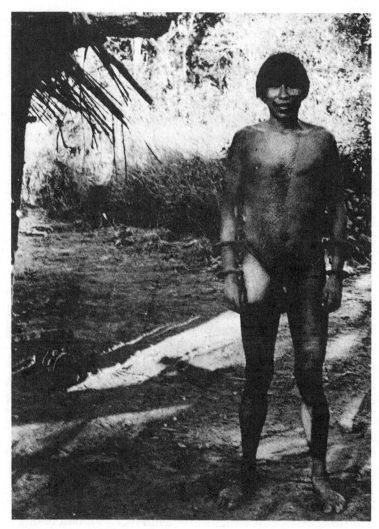

Champukwi in 1940.

valuable for my research. He taught me the rudiments of Tapirapé culture. It was the dry season and he was felling the large trees and clearing the underbrush for his garden site. I did not see him burn the site in late October but I was present in late November when he planted maize, beans, peppers, yams, bananas, and manioc sprouts. Champukwi's wife came to plant cotton. It was like a maze without order—nothing like a European garden, planted in orderly rows.

Walking through the forest to and from Champukwi's garden, we often hunted for jacu. I attempted to teach Champukwi how to use my .22-calibre rifle, but he had difficulty understanding the gunsights and missed continually. He attempted to show me how to "see" the jacu hidden in the thick of the trees, but I seldom caught sight of the birds until they had flown. So our hunting in the tropical forest was not very productive, and in disgust Champukwi often resorted to his bow and arrow. Only later in the year, after he had practiced shooting at tin cans, did Champukwi master the use of the rifle, and his newly found skill added to his prestige among the Tapirapé.

But perhaps my friendship with Champukwi really began when I came down with malaria about two months after our arrival. During the first few days of my illness I knew little or nothing of my surroundings. I am told that while one shaman predicted my death, another tried to cure me by massage, by blowing tobacco smoke over my body, and by attempting to suck out the "object" that caused the fever. Evidently his efforts, plus the Atabrine tablets administered later by Valentim Gomes, were successful, for my fever abated. I realized, however, that convalescence would be slow. Unable to leave the house for almost three weeks, I spent my days and evenings reclining in a large Brazilian hammock. After people realized that I was recovering and would not die, our house became, each late afternoon, a gathering place for the Tapirapé villagers, who came not only to visit with me (communication was still difficult) but also with each other, and to gaze upon the belongings of the torí. This was good for ethnographic research. They told stories not only for my benefit, but also to entertain each other. In attempting to explain a myth to me, a man would find himself telling the myth to the attending audience. In this setting I heard (and saw) Tapirapé stories told as they should be—as dramatic forms spoken with vivacity and considerable mimicry of the animals that are so often characters in the stories. But I usually lost the thread of the story and had to be told more slowly.

Champukwi was a frequent visitor during the days of my convalescence. He came each morning on the way to his garden and he became accustomed to drinking morning coffee with us. And, each late afternoon after he had returned from his garden, he came "to talk"—often slowly retelling the stories and incidents which I had had difficulty understanding the evening before. Several days during this period he did not work in his garden and sat for two or three hours talking. He learned that he had to pause and often repeat, so that I might take notes. He came to understand what writing meant, for what I wrote in my notebook could be repeated back to him later. He understood that I was not so much interested in learning to speak and understand the Tapirapé language as in comprehending the Tapirapé way of life. As so often is the case when a person understands and speaks a foreign language poorly, communication is possible only with one person who is accustomed to the alien's particular mistakes and limited vocabulary. I could understand and make myself understood to Champukwi better than to any other Tapirapé. But also, because he spent long hours in our house, he was learning Portuguese from Valentim Gomes—and this was an aid in helping me translate newly learned words and phrases in Tapirapé and even in his explanations of Tapirapé custom. So, Champukwi became consciously my teacher and others came to realize that he was teaching me. During the next two months we had daily sessions, some very brief and some lasting two or more hours.

In October of 1939 I found it necessary to leave Tampiitawa to go to Furo de Pedra for supplies and to collect mail that was being held for me there. Valentim and I had come up the Tapirapé River pulled by the outboard motor of my anthropological colleague. Now we had to paddle ourselves downstream and the river was low, so that it might be necessary to haul our canoe through shallows. Malaria had left me weak, but several Tapirapé men, including Champukwi, offered to accompany us. Having Indians with us in Furo de Pedra was not advisable. First, there was their well-known susceptibility to common colds and other diseases. Second, unaccustomed to clothes, money, and many foods, as well as Brazilian customs and forms of etiquette, they would be totally dependent upon us during our stay in the frontier community. But the temptation to have my best informant with me during the trip and during our stay in Furo de Pedra was great, and we agreed to take Champukwi. The trip was made slowly; two good frontiersmen in a light canoe could have made it in three days, but we took eight. Champukwi was of little help in the canoe, for the Tapirapé were then a forest people knowing little about the water and few had ever traveled by canoe. Champukwi was unusual in that he could swim. Although he had more endurance than I, his efforts at paddling endangered the equilibrium of our canoe. Only Valentim was adept at paddling. Champukwi, however, could shoot fish with his bow and arrow. The late dry season had driven game from the open savanna that borders the Tapirapé River, and we were   229 able to kill deer, mutum, and a wild goose. Each night we camped on a beach from which we were able to collect tracajá (turtle) eggs. Only the mosquitoes which swarmed at sundown and in the early evening marred our trip. They were memorable days, and my appreciation of them was shared, I believe, by Valentim Gomes and Champukwi.

In Furo de Pedra, Champukwi adjusted with amazing rapidity. His short visit to the mission station as a youth undoubtedly contributed to his quick adaptation, although there were minor problems and incidents. The Brazilians of Furo de Pedra were accustomed to Indians, for near by there was a village of semi-civilized Carajá Indians who frequently visited and traded in the settlement. Yet Champukwi was a bit of a curiosity—they had seen only one other Tapirapé. The local Brazilians invited him into their homes and offered him coffee and sweets. Both Valentim Gomes and I attempted to control his movements for fear that he might be exposed to a respiratory infection (he did not contract any) or that the hospitality of the local Brazilians might persuade him to drink cachaça, for unlike many South American Indians, the Tapirapé were not familiar with any alcoholic beverage. According to Champukwi's own report, he tried chachaça only once in Furo de Pedra and, quite understandably, found it distasteful and unpleasant. Yet there were moments which felt awkward at the time, although today they do seem humorous. One day, when I bought several dozen oranges in the street, Champukwi calmly removed his trousers, which had been provided him, to make a sack by tying the legs to carry home the oranges. In Furo de Pedra, he often went nude in the house. Even the Brazilian female cook, who came to prepare our meals, became more or less accustomed to that; however, sometimes Champukwi forgot to dress before sallying forth into the streets. The rural Brazilian foods, which are derived in many instances from Indian foods, seemed to please Champukwi, but he could not be comfortable eating at a table. He preferred to sit across the room on a low stool during meals.

Champukwi's reaction to this rural form of Brazilian civilization was not, however, a childlike one in any way. He in turn became an ethnologist. He wanted to see the gardens which provided the food for so many people (Furo de Pedra, remember, had hardly more than two hundred inhabitants). He was fascinated by the sewing machines at which he saw the women working. He attended the Catholic ceremonies held in the little chapel. He saw men and women dance in pairs. About these and other strange customs he had many questions. But

230

like the anthropologist who had lived in his village, his curiosity sometimes became inconvenient. He peered into people's homes and sometimes entered uninvited. And he followed the Brazilian women to their rather isolated bathing spot in the Araguaia River to discover if there were any anatomical differences between these women and those in his village. He even made sexual advances to Brazilian women, which was very dangerous in view of the norms of behavior of the Brazilian males, who protect the honor of their wives and daughters. But, on the whole, Champukwi became quite a favorite of the local Brazilians during his two-week visit to Furo de Pedra. His Portuguese improved as he visited in their homes, and he collected simple presents such as fishhooks, bottles, and tin cans to take home with him. During this short period away from the village, my work with him continued. He told me of antagonisms, gossips, and schisms in the Tapirapé village which he would have hesitated to relate on the spot. He told me of adulterous affairs in progress and of the growing determination among one group of kinsmen to assassinate Urukumu, the powerful shaman, because they suspected him of performing death-dealing sorcery.

After two weeks in Furo de Pedra, I found that it would be necessary to travel up the Araguaia River to the motor road and on to Rio de Janeiro. I arranged for two Brazilian frontiersmen to return Champukwi to a point on the Tapirapé River from which he could easily hike to his village in a day. Valentim Gomes and I began our slow trip upriver. Two months later, when I had recovered from malaria and we had a new stock of supplies, we returned down the Araguaia and up the Tapirapé River to spend the long rainy season from early December until June with the Tapirapé. Champukwi was there to welcome us, and he helped each day to repair and enlarge our house. We easily fell into our former friendly relationship, which was now strengthened by the common experience of the trip to Furo de Pedra and by the feeling which many anthropologists have shared with the people of their communities—that anyone who returns is an "old friend."

But my return in early December marks, in a sense, the end of what might be called the first phase of my relationship with Champukwi as a friend and as an anthropological informant. During the course of at least two hundred hours of conversation (many of which qualified as formal interviews), I had learned much about Champukwi as a person as well as about Tapirapé culture. I knew that as a small boy he   *231* had come from the Village of Fish, where his parents had died, to live in Tampiitawa. He lived with his father's younger brother, Kamairá, who was the leader of a large household. He even told me his boyhood name—as I have said, the Tapirapé change their names several times during their lifetimes, and their first name is usually that of a fish, some other animal, or else is simply descriptive (i.e. Mankai, "mango"; or Aneuna, "black one"). The mention of a person's childhood name causes laughter among the audience and considerable embarrassment to the individual. I knew that Champukwi had been married before and that his first wife had died in childbirth. He revealed that her kinsmen had gossiped that her death was caused by his lack of respect for the food taboos imposed upon an expectant father. This same set of taboos bothered him now and again. On two excursions to the savanna, which then abounded in deer, Champukwi had eaten venison. He had broken the food taboo several times during the visit to Furo de Pedra. The rather scrawny condition of his two-year-old daughter, he feared, resulted from his faults. Just after my arrival in early December, his wife gave birth to a second daughter. She had a difficult delivery, and he remembered his transgressions of the taboos. Several village gossips, without any basis of knowledge, had accused him of his peccadillos.

Champukwi's home life was not a happy one. He was frequently in conflict with his second wife, who had considerable basis for complaint. She could not claim that he was a poor provider, for Champukwi was a good hunter and worked hard in his garden. But he did confide to me that he did not find her attractive, at least not as attractive as other women in the village. Champukwi had a lusty sense of humor and enjoyed joking with Valentim and me. He also told of his many extramarital affairs, which were only slightly veiled, for I would have heard of them anyway. He gave his paramours beads, which everyone in the village knew I had given him as a present. This caused trouble for the women themselves, because their husbands could readily identify the source. It also caused trouble for Champukwi at home. His wife complained of his affairs and on one occasion, according to Champukwi, she fought him, grabbing him by his pigtail and squeezing his exposed testicles until he fell helpless into the hammock. On other occasions, she retaliated in a more usual manner for a Tapirapé woman—she simply refused to carry drinking water from the creek, to cook food for him, or to allow him to sleep in the hammock (which they ordinarily shared). For a Tapirapé man to carry

232

drinking water, to cook, or to sleep on a mat is considered ridiculously funny. Without his foreign friends in the village, Champukwi would have had to seek recourse with a female relative and all the village would have known, causing considerable merriment and jest. Champukwi would come to our house quietly at night to drink water, to ask for something to eat, and even to sleep in an extra hammock we had for visitors. His affairs were evidently numerous, for once he listed all of the adult women of the village in two categories—those "I know how to talk with" (to seduce) and those "I do not know how to talk with." His list of those with whom he could "talk" was extensive.

By late December 1939, unfortunately, I knew too much about Champukwi's affairs either for his comfort or for mine. His wife sometimes came to my house to ask if I knew where he had gone (I could easily guess), and once an irate husband even came to inquire of his whereabouts. His Don Juan activities evidently increased. And his friendship with me caused him troubles with other Tapirapé, as they were jealous of the presents he received. The story was circulated that he had stolen the pair of scissors which in fact I had given to him. Several people caught colds and he was accused of bringing the infection from Furo de Pedra (actually, it was probably transmitted by a frontiersman who had helped us to the village early in December). Champukwi sought revenge by cutting down one of the main supports of the takana, which promptly caved in. No one died and the destruction of the takana was soon forgotten since it was normally repaired or even rebuilt each year. But people continued to criticize Champukwi and much of their criticism revolved around his relationship with me. There are no realms of esoteric secrets in Tapirapé culture (as there are in many cultures) that should not be revealed to an outsider; there is only the "secret" kept by the men from the women that the masked dancers are not supernaturals, but masquerading men. But then I had been fully brought into this "secret." I was exceedingly careful not to refer to any personal bit of information which any informant, Champukwi or another, had told me. But in the small village, rumors were rife—that I was angry and would soon leave (I was by then a valuable asset), that Champukwi had told me lies about others, that I had refused to give a bushknife to a household leader because Champukwi had urged me not to do so (I did refuse, but it was because I had already given him one bushknife).

Champukwi reacted moodily and often angrily to this situation. I could no longer count on his visits nor on our research interviews. He 233 would visit us with a dour look on his face, and when he was not offered coffee at once he left, offended. But the very next day, he might return gay and joking, yet without the same patience for teaching or explaining Tapirapé culture. Once he returned from a hunting trip tired; irritated by his wife, he beat her with the flat side of his bush-knife and marched off in anger, thoughtfully taking the family hammock and a basket of manioc flour, to sleep four nights in the forest near his garden. Soon afterward he left his wife, taking the wife of a younger man. This was not a major scandal in the village. After some tense but calm words between the two men, it seemed rather clear that the young woman preferred Champukwi as a husband, and the abandoned husband moved to the takana. Champukwi's former wife and their two young daughters continued to live with her relatives, which is the Tapirapé rule. But the switch of spouses caused tension between Champukwi and his former wife's kinsmen and between Champukwi and the abandoned husband's kinsmen; and he now had a new set of in-laws to satisfy. For about a month, I rarely saw him; he obviously was avoiding our house. When we met in the village or in the takana, he simply mentioned that he was busy repairing his house or hunting. Discussing emotions with someone of such a widely different culture as Tapirapé was from my own is difficult, and language always continued to be a barrier. Although my Tapirapé vocabulary was increasing, it was hardly adequate to probe deeply into emotional responses; nor was Champukwi addicted to introspection. I shall probably never fully understand Champukwi's temporary rejection of Valentim and me, but there were probably several causes. First, his apparent influence with me and our close friendship had attracted antagonism from other villagers. By rejecting the outsider, he hoped to reintegrate himself into his society. Second, deeper and more personal reasons probably caused his rejection, for he had told me too much about himself and feared that he had lost face in the process. Also, it was obvious that I was growing less dependent on him as my facility with the language improved and my knowledge of Tapirapé culture grew. The rejection was not one-sided. Now additional informants were desirable for my research. Also, if I remember correctly (it is not stated in my notebooks), I was annoyed by Champukwi's neglect and disappointed by his lack of loyalty.

As the heavy rains of January set in, all of us were more or less confined to the village when the rivers and streams rose to flood the savanna. What had been brooks in the tropical forest became wide streams—difficult and sometimes dangerous to ford. It rained many hours each day. The Tapirapé women and children remained most of the time in their dwellings, and the men and older boys lounged in the takana. Again, our house became a meeting place, and this was an opportune time for interviewing; so I joined the men in the takana and entertained visitors at home. And again I began to see more of Champukwi—first in the takana, then when he became again a steady visitor at our house. Now he brought his new (and younger) wife along with him. He liked to sit late at night after other Tapirapé visitors had retired to their dwellings or to the takana for the night-long sings that are customary at this time of year. Under the light of our kerosene lamp, we again took up our study of Tapirapé culture. Not once did he mention his period of antagonism, except to complain that the Tapirapé gossip too much.

Thus, sometime late in January began what might be considered the second phase of my relationship with Champukwi. Our friendship was no less intimate, but our conversations and interviews were no longer as frequent. Throughout the next months, Champukwi became almost a research assistant. He continued to provide invaluable information and data, but when I became interested in a subject of which he knew little, he would recommend that I talk to someone else with more knowledge. He directed me to Urukumu on the subject of shamans, yet Champukwi himself related dreams he had heard other shamans tell. He explained that he himself did not want to become a shaman, for he had seen grieved relatives beat out the brains of Tapirapé shamans whom they suspected of causing death by sorcery. He was not certain, he said, whether such shamans had actually performed sorcery; any shaman might come to such an end, he reasoned. But Champukwi did have frequent dreams, which, the reader will recall, the Tapirapé consider indicative of powers to become a shaman—and in some of his dreams he saw anchunga spirits. He had told only one or two of his kinsmen about this, and he did not want it to be known throughout the village—lest there be pressure upon him to train for shamanism.

Champukwi sketched the stories of Petura, the Tapirapé ancestral hero who stole fire from the King Vulture, daylight from the night owl, genipap from the monkeys, and some other items for the Tapirapé. But he also persuaded Maeuma, an elder famous for his knowl-   235 edge of mythology, to relate the details, although Champukwi helped considerably to clarify the meaning of native phrases and to make me understand more fully the stories told by Maeuma.

Champukwi also forewarned me of events which I might want to witness and which without his warning I might have missed, such as the wrestling matches that took place upon the return of a hunting party between those men who had gone and those who had remained at home. He explained that the men who had been away hunting suspected those who remained behind of sexual misbehavior with their wives. He told me of a particularly handsome basket which a man had made and which I might want to purchase for the collection I was making for the Brazilian National Museum. He came to tell me that a young woman in a neighboring house was about to give birth. I attended the birth of a child and was able to get a photograph of the newborn infant being washed in the stream. At that time Champukwi urged the men to celebrate a ceremony, which might easily have been omitted, for my benefit. He became more than an informant; he was a participant in ethnographic research, although, of course, he never thought of it in these terms. He seemed somehow to understand the anthropologist's task in studying his culture, and in the process he gained considerable objectivity about his own culture and society.

Yet it must be said that Champukwi did not discredit the norms, institutions, and beliefs of his people. Although he saw Valentim and me walk down the path through the forest late at night, he steadfastly refused to do the same; for the path was a favorite haunt for the lonely ghosts of deceased Tapirapé who might harm the living. He reasoned that perhaps the torí were immune to this danger. When he was ill he took the pills we urged upon him, but he called the shaman also. His curiosity about airplanes, automobiles, and "gigantic canoes" (passenger ships) which he saw in the magazines we had brought with us was great; but he countered that the Tapirapé could walk farther and faster than any torí or even the Carajá. In fact, his interest and enthusiasm for certain Tapirapé activities seemed to be heightened by our presence. Almost all Tapirapé ceremonials involved choral singing, and Champukwi was one of the best singers of his Bird Society. He was always pleased when we came to listen, and particularly if we made the motions of joining. He was an excellent wrestler in Tapirapé style. Our wrestling match was brief (he won, although I was much taller than he); and his match with Valentim Gomes, who outweighed him by more than forty pounds, was a draw. Unlike so many people who get a glimpse of a seemingly "superior" cultural world, Champukwi never became dissatisfied with his own way of life.

In June 1940, my period of residence among the Tapirapé ended. The waters on the savanna, which had to be crossed afoot to get to the Tapirapé River where our canoe was moored, had not completely receded. Many Tapirapé friends, among them Champukwi, offered to carry our baggage, which was made lighter after a final distribution of gifts, down to the river. On the night preceding our departure there was a festival with the usual songfest to celebrate the final phase of the ceremony during which a youth "ties his hair." Champukwi led the singing most of the night, but at dawn he came to our house to supervise the packing of our belongings into basket-like cases made of palm which are used for carrying loads of any kind. He divided the baggage among the younger men; even some of the older household leaders decided to accompany us, but they, of course, did not carry anything. Our trip was slow because everyone was tired after the all-night festival and because of the water through which we had to wade. At one point, rafts had to be made to transport our baggage across a still swollen stream. Since most Tapirapé did not swim—or like Champukwi, swam poorly—it was the job of the torí to swim pushing the rafts. I had the honor of swimming across the stream pushing Kamai-raho on a raft. (How he got back I never knew.) After a day and a half, we reached the landing on the Tapirapé River; the next morning we embarked downriver. My last memory of Champukwi was his standing on the bank waving in torí style as our boat made the curve of the river.

I did not return to visit the Tapirapé until 1953, but news of them came at intervals. Valentim Gomes returned to the region in 1941 as an Indian Officer of the Brazilian Indian Service, and he was entrusted with the protection of the Tapirapé. In his first year in that capacity, he wrote me: "I report that I was in the village of the Tapirapé on the 26th of July (1941). They were in good health and there were plenty of garden products such as manioc, yams, peanuts, and the like. There were plenty of bananas. But I am sorry to say that after we left them, twenty-nine adults and a few children died. Fifteen women and fourteen men died. Among those who died was Champukwi, the best Informant in the village, and our best friend." Several slow exchanges of letters brought further details from Valentim. In some manner, perhaps through a visit by some Brazilian frontiersmen, several Tapirapé had contracted common colds. So, following 237 so many deaths, including that of a young man like Champukwi, who had prestige and many kinsmen, I was not surprised also to learn from Valentim Gomes that Urukumu, the powerful shaman, had been assassinated. As Champukwi had told me, suspicion had been growing even during my residence in the village. After the death of Champukwi, one of his many "brothers" (actually a cousin, but called by the same term as "brother" in Tapirapé) had entered Urukumu's house late at night and clubbed him to death.[118]

I have already recorded that in 1953, when I returned to the Araguaia River, I found only fifty-one people, the remnants of the Tapirapé tribe, settled in a small village near the mouth of the Tapirapé River under the protection of the Brazilian Indian Service. Champukwi was but one of the many victims of this disintegration of Tapirapé society. Upon my arrival several of Champukwi's surviving relatives met me with the traditional "Welcome of Tears"; to the Tapirapé, such a return mixes emotions of joy at seeing an old friend with the sadness of the memory of those who died during the interim. Both the sadness and the joy are expressed ritually by crying. People spoke sympathetically to me of the loss of my friend and they introduced me to a young man who had been only a small boy in 1940 but who was now known as Champukwi. This boy had visited for many months, even studied a little, with the Dominican missionaries on the lower Araguaia River; thus, he spoke Portuguese well. He remembered my friendship with his namesake and perhaps felt, as I did, some strange bond between us. So for a few days the name of Champukwi was again entered into my notebooks as my source of information on Tapirapé culture.

KAMAIRAHO: a Tapirapé Leader

In 1939, Kamairaho was the man of greatest prestige in Tampiitawa. I had heard his name in the faraway city of São Paulo from Herbert Baldus, the anthropologist who had previously visited the Tapirapé, and I heard it again from Brazilians living along the Araguaia River who spoke of him as the "capitão" of the Tapirapé. Then in late April, when I entered the village for the first time, the men, women and chil-

---

118. During this same epidemic, the shaman and household leader Wantanamu also died. Urukumu's assassin Irawú was also Wantanamu's "younger brother" (see Chapter 6).

dren who crowded around me kept pointing to one of the large dwellings saying, "Kamairaho! Kamairaho!" And, I understood that I was
expected to go to the house of this "chieftain."

As I approached his house, several horribly emaciated dogs broke
forth, to be driven off with sticks by the villagers. Then, through the
door emerged a man of about forty-five years of age, short, as are most
Tapirapé, but strongly built. He came to shake hands and embrace
me in Brazilian style (he had learned this from the Dominican
priests) and motioned me into the house. I was exhausted by the fifty-
kilometer hike across the plains and through the forest, and everything was confused at first. But I sat in a hammock, drank water from
a cup made of half a gourd, and then ate the piece of wild pork and
some of the rancid manioc flour offered by a woman whom I learned
was Kamairaho's wife, Kantuowa. Kamairaho stood silently near by.
He could speak only a few words of Portuguese, but I felt that he had
welcomed me. He invited me into the plaza to watch the lines of
dancers, for I had arrived in the midst of kawió, the major Tapirapé
ceremony marking the end of the rains and the beginning of the dry
season. Kamairaho and I stood back from the dancers in the shade of
the takana—almost as honored guests.

As the afternoon wore along, I wandered about the village. At each
house, people motioned me to enter and in each I met a mature
man—Wantanamu, Urukumu, Kamanaré, Maeuma, and Kanchiwanio—who were obviously men of high prestige. In each house, people pressed bananas, peanuts, yams, and other foods upon me. But I
soon returned to Kamairaho's house, where I had left my belongings.
I was still under the impression that Kamairaho was the chieftain of
the village and I aimed at working within the hiearchy of power.

My impression that Kamairaho was the single powerful chieftain
continued for several months. It was he to whom our first presents
were extended. Kamairaho made the arrangements for men to return
to the river port to carry in the remainder of my baggage. I selected a
site to build my house (no more than a shelter at first) just behind
his dwelling, and he seemed to have ordered the young men to cut the
broad wild banana leaves to cover it. Each evening when the sun went
down I came to visit Kamairaho, sitting behind him on a low bench
in front of his dwelling—talking very little, but at least being seen by
the villagers in the company of their leader. Through the young men
who spoke Portuguese I learned that Kamairaho had decided to call   239

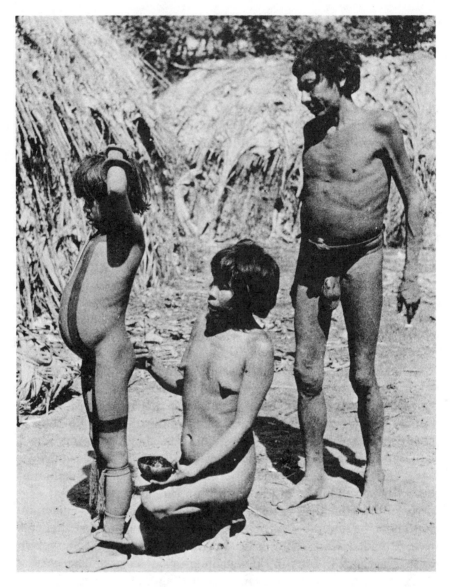

Kamairaho and his wife, Kantuowa, decorating the son of Urukumu in 1940.

me cheriwura ("my younger brother") and, an eager field anthropologist, I learned that he was my cherikeura ("older brother"). Little did I realize the difficulties that would entail!

As I learned more of the workings of Tapirapé culture and something of the language, I became more aware of Kamairaho and his

240

position in his society, both from others and from Kamairaho himself. Kamairaho had had two wives before he married Kantuowa. The small girl of about eight years old called Ampitanya, whom I had taken to be his daughter, was his wife's daughter by a previous husband. The adolescent youngster called Kanchinapio whom I had believed to be his son was his deceased sister's son. In fact, Kamairaho had no children of his own—or to put it in terms of the Tapirapé, none of his wives had conceived by him. But it was publicly known that he was the "father" of three boys in the village since he had sexual intercourse with their mothers during their pregnancy.

Kamairaho's wife, Kantuowa, was at least ten years his junior. Although gossips assured me that she had had many lovers in the past, she was known as one of the few women in the village who granted her favors only to her husband. There was certainly a queenly air about her. She carried herself erect and proudly, as the wife of an important man. She treated Kamairaho with respect, covering his body with coconut oil mixed with red annatto dye and searching his hair for lice. Kamairaho no longer wore wrist ornaments nor painted his body with elaborate designs. Kantuowa publicly entwined her arms about her husband, for Tapirapé couples show affection openly. Her daughter, Kamairaho's stepdaughter, was treated with special care, and I was told that she was "A beautiful child"—one selected for special attention—who would be a "captain" later.

Kamairaho seldom left the village to hunt or make gardens, yet he spoke of his gardens and suggested we visit them. In his multi-family longhouse, he and his wife and their daughter hung their hammocks in front of the only door—a favored spot—where they were less apt to be bothered by the smoke from the many cooking fires. In the eaves above their hammocks was his property—many strings of beads, gifts from the missionaries and from expeditions; several bushknives; and bamboo tubes filled with tail feathers of the red macaw, which were used to fabricate headdresses for ceremonials. His property multiplied as our kinship was solidified—he received from us an axe, scissors, another bushknife, a blanket, a woman's dress, trousers, several mirrors, salt, and many more strings of beads. There was no doubt that Kamairaho was an important man, and he looked and played that role. He was calm, serene, and dignified, and I found he had thorough knowledge of his people.

In time, however, I came to realize that Kamairaho was not the head chieftain, but rather that each household had its own leader. *241*

And while these men might be considered to form some loose sort of a village council, they actually never met as a formal body. And all was not well between them. Between Kamairaho and Wantanamu, whose household was every bit as large as Kamairaho's, there was a long-term rivalry. The two leaders seemed to differ in their "policy" toward the torí. Wantanamu was reserved, almost sulky or sullen with Valentim and me—and he had evidently been so with Herbert Baldus and the Protestant missionary who had lived for a time in the village. He came to visit us when we were installed in our house and he accepted our gifts. But he avoided coming to our house when Kamairaho was present, and he was sensitive to insults. He left our house in anger when he was asked not to sit on a bag containing photographic equipment. Kamairaho, on the other hand, was known to like the torí, and he sought us out. It was because the villagers knew of his attitude that we had been directed to his house at once upon our arrival. So, unwittingly, we had become attached to his household, to his kinship group, and, in a sense, to his faction of the community.

Likewise, Kamairaho was at odds with Kamairá, a quiet and rather stolid leader of another large household. The basis of this antagonism was that in his youth Kamairá had killed Kantuowa's father, a famous shaman who had been suspected of working evil sorcery. Kantuowa fed the rivalry and antagonism between the two men. She gossiped about Kuchinantu, Kamairá's wife, and on days when Kamairá and his male kinsmen were away hunting or clearing garden sites, Kantuowa sent the younger women of her household to taunt Kuchinantu openly. One day Kuchinantu was driven to violence, and she attacked and pulled the hair of one of these women. Then she broke into tears. Despite these difficulties, the relations between the two men remained controlled and ceremonious. If thrown together, they would converse politely, but they took care seldom to be in the same group. Kamairaho, when shown a basket manufactured by Kamairá, looked at it with some disdain and said, "I will make a good one for you." The reputation of Kamairá as a leader with many younger kinsmen and as a man of action who had actually killed demanded that their rivalry be subdued.

This lack of central leadership and the antagonism and rivalry between the household leaders made any cohesive action on the part of the community very difficult. Kamairaho, for example, gave orders to the young men of the village to carry my baggage to the river port when I left for Furo de Pedra in September, but the men of other households complied only after consulting their own household leaders. Again, in November, at the end of the dry season, when the roof of the men's house had to be renewed, no one leader seemed willing to give orders for an apachirú. Kamairaho ordered the young men of his own household to work, and they were joined by the young men of Kamairá's household—and then by those of another household (or other households) until finally, one day, in an all-out effort, a true apachirú took form. Throughout, Kamairaho, among all the leaders, was the one who had the pose of a strong leader whose orders were respected.

Although Kamairaho was not, as I had supposed, the supreme chieftain of his village, he was probably considered by all the Tapirapé as the man of highest prestige. His position, I learned, was derived from several important roles which he held in his society—as the patriarch of a large household, as a leader of a Bird Society, as a member of an illustrious family, and, finally, as a panché, or shaman. Because of the cumulative effect of all those roles, his social position was high.

It was clear that Kamairaho's most powerful role was that of the leader of his household. Kamairaho was the patriarch of a group of related females and their spouses and children. He had no daughters, but his deceased brother had two. Since a man calls the children of any brother or any male cousin "my daughter" or "my son." In this way, Kamairaho had taken several women under his care—daughters of deceased "brothers" whom he called "daughter." Thus, in Kamairaho's longhouse lived his wife, her daughter, his sister's son, and five other women with their husbands and children. The men were Kamairaho's "sons-in-law." They were the men who cut away the forest for gardens; Kamairaho went only to plant the plot which they assigned to him. He showed us "his gardens" and offered us manioc and yams from the gardens of his whole group. I saw him dig manioc roots and collect yams and beans, but I never saw him do any of the heavy work, such as clearing a garden site.

Kamairaho told me that his father and his father's father before him were called Kamairaho. Of course, he had carried several names during his life—a child's name, a name during adolescence, a name as a young man, and finally Kamairaho. And, he said, since he had no son, this famous name would pass to his sister's son when he himself was very old. All of his names were inherited from his father, but he might have received them from his maternal uncle. Such names brought prestige, and as a child he was treated accordingly, since, he   *243* said, he had been a anchirikantu. During childhood such children were not supposed to play with others. They were waited upon, and they were decorated with elaborate body paint so that they would be beautiful. They were told stories, and, if Kamairaho could be believed, water was carried to the house to bathe them so they would not have to walk to the stream. They were truly destined to be people of high status; thus Kamairaho's pose as a man of dignity and importance was something he had been trained to perform. His stepdaughter was being treated as a "beautiful child" as well, for both men and women could be placed in such a role. Trained as he was for high status, Kamairaho had had a fine coming of age ceremony.

Kamairaho belonged to the Tanawe Bird Society. Champukwi had explained to me what this meant, so when Kamairaho told me of it I was not surprised. Since Kamairaho was a member of Tanawe and I was his "younger brother," I became an Anachá (the mature male society of the Parrot moiety), the group with whom I danced during festivals and with whom I went on communal hunts. As a younger man, Kamairaho had been a leader of the Ananchá, for he could sing well and was a good hunter.

In addition, Kamairaho belonged to Chankanepera ("the place of the alligator"), one of the eight Feast Groups which were still functioning during my residence in Tampiitawa. Again, I was assigned to Kamairaho's Tantanopao, or Feast Group, since I called him my older brother. And, less than three weeks after my arrival in Tampiitawa, a feast for all groups was held. I brought rapadura as my contribution to the Chankanepera meal. It was much appreciated, for the only other source of sweetening was the rather acid wild honey. Others brought a piece of roasted wild pork, as well as manioc flour, boiled yams, and lima beans recently harvested from their gardens. In an effort to ingratiate myself, I sent a cake of rapadura to each Feast Group. Then my own group demanded more, which Valentim begrudgingly provided from our larder. A total of fifteen to sixteen large cakes of rapadura, each weighing about one pound, were consumed. Some two months later Valentim remembered the feast bitterly as we drank coffee without sweetening, for we had run short of both refined sugar and rapadura. Chankanepera was a strong Feast Group with many members, and Kamairaho's generous contributions to their meetings brought him prestige.

Finally, Kamairaho owed his high prestige, in part, to the fact that he was a panché. He was not the most powerful shaman in the village,

244

for Urukumu, Wantanamu, and Panterí were more famous for their cures and their relationships with the supernatural. Still, Kamairaho had performed many cures and he was able to enter into relationships with the supernatural. Kamairaho had learned to be a panché from his present wife's father, who had been killed by Kamairá. His period of apprenticeship had lasted only "one moon," he explained, but the other young men might spend several moons learning. During this time as a novice shaman, Kamairaho had learned to "eat smoke." He explained that as a neophyte he had become ill and had vomited violently. Finally, Kamairaho said, he was helped into his hammock and in his sleep he dreamed. In his dreams he encountered supernaturals— demons of the forest and ghosts of the dead who became his familiar helpers in curing. Some men, and, in the past, a few women, showed natural talent to dream like panchés while still small children. But Kamairaho had had to learn how, and during his period of apprenticeship he had observed the taboos against bathing, sexual relations (he was already married), and eating animals that "walk at night," such as the tortoise and the monkey. He was rewarded by dreams in which he saw anchunga and several demons of the forest.

But Kamairaho explained to me, "I learned to dream only on the level of the earth," indicating that he was not a powerful shaman such as Panterí, who had visited in his dreams the Pleiades and the Jaguar of the Skies, places where the most powerful supernaturals are found. But even so, some of Kamairaho's dreams related to me late in my period of residence were dramatic enough. After treating a young man by the name of Aneí, who was ill with fever, he retired to his hammock and in his sleep traveled far away, to a former village site. There he saw the old houses (which had long since fallen down) and the ghosts of many Tapirapé. He saw and recognized one ghost as that of a man who had died six or seven years earlier; the ghost carried an animal over his shoulder which he had just killed; he was all white and scattered a white dust as he walked. And, in his dream, Kamairaho saw Aneí. He knew when he "returned" from his dream travel that Aneí suffered from an encounter with a ghost. I watched Kamairaho treat the youth the next evening. He knelt by Aneí's hammock and began to blow smoke over the patient's body, massaging his body toward the extremities as if ridding the entire body of a substance that coated it. Bystanders said that this was the "white dust" (invisible to us) which the ghost had cast upon the young man. Then Kamairaho staggered off to his hammock to dream again, and his dream predicted 245 the recovery of Aneí. And in time this came about and Aneí was well.

Kamairaho was one of the shamans who tried to cure me when I suffered from malaria. According to his diagnosis my illness was caused not by a ghost, but by another shaman (he hinted that perhaps it was Wantanamu) who had sent a fishbone into my body. Although I did not see it, he massaged my body working upward toward the forehead and then sucking with his mouth he withdrew the fishbone, spewing it forth in one of the attacks of vomiting induced by tobacco.

Another success of Kamairaho as a shaman had to do with "calling a child" for the wife of Maeuma. Maeuma's wife, who wanted a child, brought wild honey as a present to Kamairaho. This would induce him to dream, and, so he said, it did. Sometime later the woman conceived and she had a small daughter.

But Kamairaho played down his shamanistic abilities, rather than making a display of them. He was fully aware of the danger of being a powerful shaman—he had known several shamans who had been murdered during his own lifetime. During the ceremonies of "fighting" Thunder, Kamairaho was struck down sooner than others by the "arrows" of topu, the small beings which Thunder sends down against shamans. As a result he was rigid in a trance until one of the more powerful shamans brought him around by blowing smoke over his body and massaging him. And when his sister's son, Kanchinapio, was ill, Kamairaho sent for two shamans to cure the youth. He said that he did not have the powerful supernatural aids to allow him to make the cure himself. Then, when he himself was ill, three shamans took turns treating him during most of one night. It was characteristic of Kamairaho that he knew well how to draw the line between using the role of shamanism for prestige and power and allowing shamanistic power to carry over into the realm of growing suspicion—as it did for Urukumu.

Kamairaho's story was not, however, entirely a successful one. He had difficulties in his society. Among the Tapirapé, he had many detractors, especially among the kinsmen of his rivals, Wantanamu and Kamairá. People complained, but seldom in my presence, that he was ankantaum—stingy. They pointed out his behavior during the annual kawió ceremonies, when men of prestige must give gifts to those of lower status who drink of "bad kawi." But if the first leader to be so invited to drink this brew should refuse the challenge (i.e. not take a mouthful and then spit it out), the pot is overturned and no more challenges will be made that year. In 1940, Kamairaho, who had accumulated considerable merchandise, mainly from me, was offered the brew first, but he refused the challenge, thus ending the challenging and gift-giving that year. Frankly, I was rather glad, for as a young man of some prestige, I was highly vulnerable and my stock of gifts was running low. Kamairaho, however, lost status in the eyes of his people by his "stingy" behavior.

On the whole, I came to agree, as the months went by, with some of the critics who thought of him as ankantaum. Perhaps by then I had come to think somewhat like a Tapirapé. Also, it seemed to both Valentim and me that we had been rather steadily exploited by Kamairaho and especially by his wife Kantuowa. Both of us came to look upon her as a veritable shrew. She would come to our house with Kamairaho, survey our belongings, and surreptitiously attempt to look into our packing cases. Then she would send back women and younger men to beg. She kept a mental account of what gifts we gave to each Tapirapé, and she knew exactly who brought us maize or manioc, and how much. Sometimes it seemed as if she were stimulated in her behavior by Kamairaho and it is certain that he schemed to relay the beads and hardware we brought as presents into his hands or those of his close kinsmen. As the months went by both Valentim and I came to resent Kamairaho and his apparent control over us. We became more friendly with Kamairá, one of his rivals. Even Champukwi became openly critical of Kamairaho; after all, he had been raised by Kamairá and perhaps fed our irritation. It could be that our irritation was just the result of mal de forêt—of being cut off from people of our own culture for so long.

But as the time for us to leave approached, Kamairaho planned the initiation ceremonies of Kanchinapio, his sister's son. For him this was a big occasion. He restrung his numerous beads, he fabricated the enormous headdress of red parrot feathers, brought out the long, white quartz lip plug, and his wife and daughters spun cotton for wrist and arm ornaments—all this for Kanchinapio's initiation. His household was very busy for days preparing food for the occasion. Then, on the day that Kanchinapio danced in all his finery, I stood by Kamairaho's side proud of his accomplishments. My irritation at Kamairaho, even at his wife, Kantuowa, vanished. I realized that he was a man who understood his own society and culture. And he had exploited me to achieve the means to give prestige to his sister's son. After all, it was as if a naïve member of the Rockefeller Foundation staff, rich   247

Antanchowa, Kamairaho's daughter, and her husband, Chawankatu, in 1965. In 1939-40 I knew her by her childhood name, Ampitanya.

in grants and other funds, had suddenly appeared in the midst of a group of college presidents. Kamairaho had protected my interests; yet, gracefully, and with dignity, he had manipulated the strange torí for his own purposes.

Kamairaho had taught me much about Tapirapé life, for while he was never as patient as Champukwi or as wise about shamanism as Urukumu, he made a point of consciously instructing his "younger brother." But more important, he had given me a position in the social structure. As Kamairaho's younger brother, I had kinsmen, was a member of associations, and was, by extension, a member of a household. So with my new-found objectivity, I made presents to Kanchinapio, who, after all, was also my "sister's son" and had always treated me with great respect and deference. For, as the Tapirapé have it, "a boy never lets wind that his mother's brother does not smell." The next day, when I left for New York, Kamairaho accompanied me as far as the river port and Kanchinapio carried my personal belongings.

In 1953, when I returned to visit briefly with the Tapirapé, I found only Ampitanya and Kanchinapio—my "elder brother's daughter" and

248

my "sister's son." Kamairaho had died several years before.[119] His wife had survived him, but after the savage Kayapó had attacked and the Tapirapé had been driven to the Indian post, she too had died. Ampitanya and Kanchinapio and their spouses lived in a large dwelling with the few of their kinsmen who had survived. They had carried on the tradition of friendliness to outsiders, for they spent much time with the Little Sisters of Jesus, who had come to live with the Tapirapé.

ANTANCHOWI: a Scapegoat

Antanchowi was the antithesis of the "ideal" young Tapirapé woman. She was about sixteen or seventeen years of age when I lived with the Tapirapé in 1939 and 1940. She was not ugly; in fact, she was rather well formed, yet the Tapirapé found her unattractive and often showed their dislike for her. She was not a person who stood out first in any way. But soon after we had established our residence in Tampiitawa, we came to know her. Lacking anything better to do, she came to our house whenever there were other Tapirapé present, just to sit, watch and listen. And the little boys, who often played near our house, hoping for a handout of salt, obviously teased her. She took their teasing rather placidly, and she seemed pleased when we included her in passing out salt or candy to the children. Gradually, from Champukwi, I learned much of Antanchowi and the reasons for her low status in Tapirapé society.

Antanchowi was perhaps somewhat slow-witted, but she did not seem to either Valentim or myself to be mentally defective. On rare occasions she did converse with us, and what she had to say made good sense. She was, however, without any of the skills that Tapirapé women were expected to possess. She had never learned to make pottery out of clay, a feminine occupation which was, in 1939, in sharp decline. But more important, she did not know how to spin cotton into string, to crochet the string into wrist ornaments and leg ornaments worn by the men, nor how to fabricate a hammock—all of which women must do for their families. Antanchowi could, of course, do the rather unskilled women's work of manufacturing manioc flour, pounding maize into a flour in the large wooden mortar, and carrying drinking water, but she tended to be lazy and to shirk those duties.

---

119. His testicles became enormous, I was told, and at the end he could not walk.

She was far from a hard worker, which Tapirapé men admire so much in a woman. For it was the women on a trip who carried the heaviest loads so that men would have their arms free to use their clubs and bows and arrows in case of an enemy attack. And, although men helped their wives dig up the large manioc tubers, a man and his wife each carried a large load on their backs to the village. The arduous task of reducing manioc to flour was entirely that of the women. Antanchowi was evidently not too careful and not too skillful in this work, for her hands were often bleeding from cuts as a result of a mistake in grating manioc tubers in the process of making flour. This was a time-consuming task which any Tapirapé wife spent most of her time doing. Antanchowi apparently tried to avoid working with her female relatives in preparing the flour.

Not only was Antanchowi looked down upon for her lack of industry and abilities in the work normally assigned to women in Tapirapé culture, but she lacked those personal qualities admired in women by the Tapirapé men. And, as so often is the case, from the explanations of her negative qualities I learned what positive qualities to look for in a Tapirapé woman. First, Antanchowi lacked personal cleanliness. Without clothes and involved in considerable manual labor, Tapirapé women were often dirty, but a woman with pride bathed often—at least once a day, sometimes several times. All women had their bodies anointed with palm oil mixed with a red annatto paste, which made them glisten in the sun. They kept their jet black hair neat with combs made of thin spines taken from a tree which grows in the forest, and female relatives spent time picking lice from each other's heads. Young women of Antanchowi's age often had their bodies painted with the black genigap juice in intricate gemoetrical designs. Like the men, women kept all body hair carefully plucked—even eyebrows and eyelashes were considered ugly. A woman had to help her husband remove his body hair, and often the husband would perform this service for his wife. Without a husband, Antanchowi had to depend upon other women to aid her in her toilet.

Antanchowi had none of these fine points of feminine cultivation. The Tapirapé pointed out that she was often dirty and bathed too infrequently. During her menstrual period she was known to have appeared in public with blood on her legs; any self-respecting woman would have bathed several times, or at least kept out of sight, for menstrual blood is considered ugly and unclean. Furthermore, perhaps because she was lazy and often unwashed, Antanchowi's female relatives were seldom willing to spend the time giving her beauty treatments. She was seldom covered with palm oil and practically never was her body painted. She combed her hair herself and it was said by other Tapirapé that she had trouble with head lice. Once she left a gathering abruptly, evidently much embarrassed. Noting her behavior, I asked for an explanation. A small girl, it seems, had commented that Antanchowi had allowed several strands of pubic hair to grow and she had hair under her arms.

Furthermore, Antanchowi had reached the age when all women should have their faces scarified. As I have said, all women, after their marriage but generally before they bore children, had a permanent black design cut into their faces. Antanchowi had witnessed this operation, and she cried, saying that she would never submit to it. Again, people taunted her, saying that she would always be ugly and—unlike all other women—without the facial design.

But Antanchowi's greatest drawback as a woman was the fact that she suffered from occasional epilectic seizures, as several people explained to me. Eanwurup, or epilepsy, according to the Tapirapé, was caused by small supernatural beings which are white. They live in the clouds. They select certain individuals to attack, striking them down during either day or night. Kamairaho explained that a child who was subject to epilepsy might be treated with baths of water in which manioc leaves were soaked. This might be successful and the attacks would not recur. But after an individual became an adult, no remedy would help and eanwurup might be expected to recur throughout one's life. Although I was assured that both men and women were subject to such attacks, the only people who had suffered epileptic attacks in 1939-40 were women.[120] Children of such women were never allowed to live but were buried immediately after birth. Thus, Antanchowi knew and the men knew that she could never have a child of her own. This made her less interesting as a potential spouse. Although the Tapirapé limited the size of their families, all men wanted to have children.

I never saw Antanchowi in the midst of an epilectic seizure. I was told, however, of the consequences of one of her attacks of epilepsy. One day late in the evening, while I was away from the village, Antanchowi suddenly fell to the ground, writhing. According to Champukwi, and his account was verified by others, the young men loiter-

---

120. In 1965, I was told that the small boy, Carlo, named after me was epileptic. He died by drowning when he was ten or twelve years old.

ing near by quickly carried her into the brush. While she was still in the throes of the attack, several of them, each in turn, had sexual intercourse with her while others held her. Just how many did was difficult to discover. Champukwi named six men, and among them even Panterí, a well-known shaman. But those who had been named laughed when I asked about it. They said, "No, the others copulated with her. I did not. She smelled bad." They told me that she did not resist for she was weak, beaten down by eanwurup. Her elder brother came on the run as soon as he heard what was happening, and carried her back to his house. He did not remonstrate with her rapists. This, it seems, was their traditional right. He was sad and asked Valentim one day if he would not take Antanchowi far away so she could live with the torí. No one ever explained why men had this sexual privilege at the time of an epileptic attack, but later events indicated that perhaps it was considered a punishment.

Despite all her disabilities and faults as a woman, Antanchowi had gone through several quick marriages. In 1939 there was a shortage of women in Tampiitawa, and several young men of marriageable age were without wives. One or two had even resorted to a traditional Tapirapé custom of marriage with a child bride. As a girl, Antanchowi had had several husbands who had abandoned her as soon as they could find an older woman. Even Tanuí, a middle-aged and rather ill-formed woman, had a husband, despite the fact that she was subject, on rare occasions, to epileptic attacks. Like Antanchowi, Tanuí had been sexually attacked by a group of men during a seizure. Tanuí, however, had a gay personality and was a hard worker. In 1939 her husband died, but within less than a month she had another mate. But Antanchowi had too many strikes against her, and despite the shortage of women she could not keep a man.

During our residence in Tampiitawa, several young men "married" her—they moved into her household and made presents to her elder brother, thus publicly announcing their betrothal. Such unions lasted, however, only a few days. Once Antanchowi seemed to make an effort to keep one of these men. She was seen working hard in preparing manioc flour and went with her husband to the gardens to harvest manioc tubers. But she was ill-kempt and not a skillful worker, and he left her after two weeks. Her husbands were vulnerable to teasing, and people would ask them if their new wife was making a hammock (she did not know how). Soon they gave up. They quarreled with Antanchowi, leaving her, perhaps with a few blows, and moved back

252

to the takana or into the house of a female relative. Antanchowi thus remained unmarried.

Antanchowi's day-to-day life among her relatives was not difficult. Her parents, I was told, had died when she was young. She had been adopted by Kamairá, who was her father's younger brother. In addition, two men in the village called her "sister"—they were actually her first cousins. She lived in Kamairá's household and Kamairá and his wife treated her well, at least it seemed so to me. She worked, when she would, with the women of the household. She had an old but adequate hammock and she had food. Often she seemed almost happy in the security of her household, talking with the women and playing with the children. And she often participated in community affairs. Early in the dry season, when the men's Bird Societies danced monikanchi, during which the women select a man with whom to dance, Antanchowi selected Champukwi as her partner. There was much laughter, for he was a well-known dandy, and it was known that Antanchowi would have but a few peanuts, if any, to give him as a present. For traditionally, peanuts, a crop planted and harvested only by women, are given by a woman to the man with whom she dances on this occasion. The man, in turn, must kill a forest fowl, a monkey, or even a wild pig as a return gift for the woman who has invited him to dance. Antanchowi danced well, and her brother's wife provided her with a bowl of shelled peanuts to give Champukwi. Another night during the same ceremonial she selected me as her dance companion, and my gift, in return for her peanuts, was several strings of beads, which all Tapirapé prized highly. Antanchowi did not live an isolated life, nor did she avoid people; but she was often vulnerable to ridicule.

In fact, it was clear that she often had casual sexual affairs. No man would easily admit that he had sexual relations with Antanchowi, for he would be ridiculed by his fellows. But Champukwi assured me that several young men often sought her out, making a rendezvous with her in the forest near the stream or stealing unseen at night to her hammock. This must have been so, for Antanchowi came into possession of beads I had given in payment to several younger men for baskets, bows and arrows, and other artifacts they had given me for the collection I was making for the Brazilian museum. Panterí, the shaman, was said to have had several amorous encounters with her, for he often was at odds with his wife. Such adventures had to be secret, because, according to Tapirapé custom, her brothers and her father's brother would have been angry—it was their protection, so to   253 speak, that prevented Antanchowi from being open prey to the young men of the village.

Nothing more dramatically brought home to me this protective force of kinsmen in Tapirapé society than the events in March of 1940. The end of the rainy season was not far away and the men of the White Bird Society were planning a group hunt, hoping to kill wild pigs. The women of Kamairá's household were busy throughout each day preparing manioc flour for the men to take with them on their trip to the flooded savanna country. But Antanchowi worked only lackadaisically. The other women of Kamairá's household complained bitterly of her lack of cooperation. When he spoke to her, she refused outright to work and for a whole day she lolled about the house while the other women grated manioc for flour. The villagers knew that Kamairá was intensely angry and they told me so, but they did not prepare me for the form that his punishment took.

Suddenly I heard a loud voice issuing from Kamairá's longhouse. My house was too far away for me to understand what was being said, but it was clear that he was threatening her and that the women were backing him up. Then he emerged from his house and began to make an announcement to the whole village. I did not know what he said until later, for events took a quick turn. Antanchowi burst out of the longhouse on the run and disappeared quickly down a path into the forest. Within a minute or two, she was pursued by a group of men. Very curious as to what was taking place, I followed along through the forest, tripping over vines and falling behind. But I could hear the characteristic hunting cries of the Tapirapé men ahead, so I soon found them. They had caught Antanchowi. She was struggling, but not desperately, for she was being held by several men. Wild banana leaves were cut from the forest to make a pallet on the ground. Antanchowi was forced to the ground and held by two men. As we all watched from a not-too-respectful distance she was raped by at least twelve men. At first she struggled, then became passive. But as each mounted her, her legs had to be pulled apart by others. There was considerable laughter among the men as this proceeded and discussion as to who would be next. When they finished, they left her behind in the forest crying and evidently too weak to walk. Sometime later, an older woman from her household came to fetch her, helping her back to the household and to her hammock.

Then the discussion of the event began. I learned that Kamairá had simply announced to the village that Antanchowi was without brothers (i.e. disowned by her relatives) and this was a signal for the amu-chino (literally, "together to eat"), or mass rape, that followed. Without the protection of relatives she was fair prey for any and all who wished to have her. This was not an isolated case among the Tapirapé, I was assured. Many years before, Kamairaho told me, when there were more unmarried women, it had been resorted to with more frequency. He remembered a young woman who ran from the painful scarification operation on her face and had been subjected to this punishment. Then, just a few years before, Mariampi, one of Kamai-raho's "daughters" (i.e. adopted daughters) had continually refused to have intercourse with any of the several men who entered the household as her husband. She also refused to work. Irritated at the loss of these sons-in-law, Kamairaho denounced her in the same way, and with the same result. She now seemed happily married and was the mother of one son.

But Kamairaho seemed somewhat angry and shocked with Kamai-rá's action and a bit worried about my reaction to the event. He asked me not to tell Frederico, the Scottish missionary who had lived on at least two occasions with the Tapirapé, what I had seen. He said that "Frederico would be angry with the Tapirapé," for the missionary had been rather protective of the women and shocked by the far less bi-zarre wife-beating which now and then occurred. But Kamairaho learned that I never intervened in Tapirapé life and that, at least overtly, I never passed judgment on anything I saw or heard. Valen-tim felt differently, not having the "benefit" of anthropological train-ing. He would have liked to lecture the Tapirapé on what they had done. With some difficulty I restrained him, for I needed to know more about what I had witnessed.

The young men did not share Kamairaho's reticence or fear that I would tell the missionary about the rape of Antanchowi. They dis-cussed the event with great gusto. They kidded me for not participat-ing. Yet all denied they had taken part themselves, although I had witnessed several in the act and, like any assiduous anthropologist, I had written down their names in my notebook soon afterward. Each was happy to provide a list of the others that had participated—to which they added names of men, particularly of older married men, who had not even been near the scene. Two or three middle-aged mar-ried men had taken part, but I was assured that their wives would not be angry as they would have been had they indulged in an extramarital sex affair. "When many go to eat a woman, wives do not quarrel. All

255

Tapirapé do this; women are not angry. Our grandfathers did this often," said Champukwi.

Antanchowi did not emerge from the longhouse for two days. During this time people often talked about the event, and the list of men who were supposed to have copulated with her grew at each retelling. Finally, on the third day, Antanchowi left her hammock and walked slowly down to the stream to bathe. In the afternoon she came to our house where a group of her relatives had gathered. She seemed to be accepted again by the women folk in her household; no one molested her. She sat on a bench listening to the conversation and then returned to her dwelling. As soon as she had left, several women inspected the bench on which she had sat. They professed to see spots of semen on the bench and floor. Everyone began to spit, which is what the Tapirapé do when they smell something bad. One woman threw dirt over a spot of "semen" that had dropped on the earthen floor (I could see nothing except marks of perspiration). When Valentim suggested that someone wash off the bench with water, men and women turned away in disgust. No one would sit on the bench for the rest of the day.

Several days went by and the incident faded into the past. No one talked of it any longer. The men of the White Bird Society went off on their hunt as planned. Antanchowi began working alongside the women in her father's brother's house. She seemed no more energetic now, however, than before. As time went by, she took to spending hours at our house, and Valentim, out of sympathy for her, often offered her food—he purposely cooked more than we needed to offer our inevitable guests. She became somewhat of a fixture, appearing whenever there were others in the house. She said little but would sometimes go for water when our five-gallon can was empty. She was teased continually by the children and youths, but she reacted apathetically. When the going got rough—when too much attention was turned toward her—she would calmly stand up and return to the house of her kinsmen and protectors. In May of 1940, when I left Tampiitawa, Antanchowi was much the same. She watched calmly and silently as our baggage was organized for the trip to the river port. I often wondered how Antanchowi filled her days after the torí had gone away.

In 1953, revisiting the Tapirapé, I was having dinner one evening served by Juana, Valentim's wife, at the Indian post. Several Indians were sitting on the benches against the wall. Now the men wore trousers, or at least underwear shorts, when they came visiting Valentim—and the women had been taught to wear wraparound skirts. The few remaining Tapirapé held Valentim in great affection and trusted him as they had thirteen years before. Everyone was at ease and I had been asking about old Tapirapé friends. Suddenly, a young man asked in clear Portuguese, "Don't you want to know about Antanchowi?" Then, slowly, knowing, I think, the impact of his story, he told me the horrible tale of her end. Antanchowi had survived the epidemic of colds that had caused the death of twenty-nine Tapirapé men and women in 1941. However, she had been very ill and never fully recovered. After her fever subsided, she developed open sores, infected, undoubtedly, through scratching and then by the flies and gnats. Without anyone to care for her, she became very dirty and, if the Tapirapé could be believed, she smelled. She lost weight. She lay all day in her hammock. Her sores were "filled with worms." She became so weak she could not walk and she could hardly talk. So one day it was decided that she was dead. A grave was dug in the house floor, as was customary among the Tapirapé, and Antanchowi was lowered into the tomb-like grave in her hammock, strung between two supports. Then, as the women cried, they covered over the tomb with earth, a handful at a time. Perhaps Antanchowi was too weak to know what was happening to her. But my young storyteller, who remembered the scene clearly, said, "We could hear her cry for awhile, there under the floor. But then she stopped and everything was quiet." The Indians laughed at the expression of horror that must have come over my face. They knew that Valentim was angry, and when I asked an older Tapirapé for added details of the event he was evasive.

CANTIDIO: a Modern Tapirapé

In April of 1965, when my wife and I emerged from the small plane at the landing strip about one kilometer from New Village, one of the first Tapirapé to greet us was Cantidio. We had just been flown from Brasília in the "Spirit of Philadelphia" by a missionary pilot of the Summer Institute of Linguistics. The plane, of German manufacture, was designed to land on short runways and it had received its name in honor of the Protestant groups of the "city of peace" who had provided the funds to purchase it. Our pilot, anxious to arrive before the afternoon rains in Macauba on the Araguaia River where he was to pick up a colleague working among the Carajá, unloaded our   257

Cantidio, a village leader in 1965.

baggage rapidly. Within ten minutes he was airborne again. We remained surrounded by about ten or more Tapirapé Indians and over 200 kilograms (440 pounds) of baggage. Despite my previous experience, I was confused, and Cecilia, my wife, was even more so, for this was her first visit to the Tapirapé. The transition from twentieth-century Brasília to the Araguaia River and Indians in a matter of about four hours involved considerable culture shock. It was Cantidio who took charge. "Wait," he said in Portuguese, "I will go bring the tractor."

His words only added to my confusion. What in the world did he mean? A tractor in a Tapirapé village? In any case, we settled ourselves in the shade of a tree to wait. Soon the Little Sisters of Jesus arrived; they said they had been expecting us, for their colleagues, who worked in a slum in Rio de Janeiro and whom I had seen over a month before, had written that we were coming. Then, about a half-

Cantidio at the wheel of Padre Francois' tractor in 1965.

hour later, a tractor pulling a platform-like trailer arrived. Cantidio was at the wheel and the trailer was loaded with men, women, and children from the village. Cantidio loaded our baggage on the trailer and we rode triumphantly to New Village, to the house of the Little Sisters. En route the Little Sisters explained that the tractor belonged to Padre François, the resident missionary priest, and that he had trained Cantidio to drive it. It was used, they said, to haul produce from the gardens to the village. Cantidio was an excellent *motorista*, they said, but, unfortunately, on that same day the gears of the tractor locked while he was parking it in a shed and it was out of order for more than a month.

After taking coffee and lunch with the Little Sisters the question of where we might live came up. I had purchased a large tent in Brasilia, but it had proven too heavy for the small plane and we had left it behind to be sent by commercial plane to Santa Terezinha (it never arrived). We could not stay in the takana, for obvious reasons, and the Little Sisters did not have a room in their house for a couple. I had been married since 1941, but this was the first time that Cecilia had accompanied me to the Tapirapé. They had seen her picture in 1953 and in 1957, but now she was the center of attention. They were anxious to find family quarters for us. Again, it was Cantidio who solved   259

The Little Sisters of Jesus with Cecilia Wagley in New Village in 1965.

our problem. His brother-in-law, Chawankatu (also named Manero), who was married to Antanchowa (whom I had known as Ampitanya, the daughter of Kantuowa and wife of Kamairaho), was building a house into which they had not yet moved. Cantidio took me to see the house. It had a roof, and the upright poles, ready for taipa (wattle and daub), were in place. We went to talk with Chawankatu and Antanchowa, who immediately gave us permission to stay in their incomplete house. I promised to pay them "rent," which we later did in the form of trade goods. Cantidio then called women to sweep out the house, and he began to build a platform to hold our baggage. By the time the rains came that afternoon we had a roof over our heads, thanks to Cantidio's energy and efficiency.

For the first few days I had a hard time placing my Tapirapé friends, connecting their faces to names and trying to remember who was who. I had seen them during very short visits in 1953 and 1957, but I had known them best in 1939-40. Many of them had been children then; those who had been young adults were now twenty-five years older, as was I. Almost everyone had changed their Tapirapé names; and, to add to the confusion, many of them used Brazilian names now. I quickly recognized such people as Opronunchwi, Tampirí, Kanchiwanio, and others whom I had known very well in 1939-40, but I called them by names they had abandoned. As I recognized people who had been children (they helped me by telling me the names of their parents), I called them by their childhood names—much to everyone else's delight and their own embarrassment. Although Cantidio, whose Tapirapé name was now Ipawungí, seemed to think that I remembered him well, I had a hard time placing him in my memory even with the help of my field notes. I found references to him in my notes taken in 1953, when his Tapirapé name was Okanchowa, and I remembered him from my 1957 visit when I already called him Cantidio, but my notes indicate that his Tapirapé name at that time was Anawuo. Every time I asked him his konomí-wera (boy's name), he laughed and said, "You know because you wrote it down in your notebook." He told me that he had been an orphan when I first came to the Tapirapé and that he had been raised by Wantanamu. I found from my notes that three small boys had lived in Wantanamu's longhouse in 1940. I rather think that Cantidio was called either Toripuku or Champeí. I easily identified him in a group photograph. I remembered the boy of about twelve to thirteen years old who had often visited at our house. Then he was still konomí, wearing a long lip plug and as yet not painted black as churangí.

If my estimation of his age in 1939-40 is correct, then Cantidio must have been about thirty-seven to thirty-eight in 1965. As far back as 1953 he had been married to Tanchowai, and by 1965 they had five children. The notes taken by my wife from the records of deaths kept by the Little Sisters indicate that two additional children of the couple had died, probably in their infancy. In 1965 their eldest child was Kuchanrawa, a girl about thirteen or fourteen years old; and there were two other daughters, Choikatu, about four, and Maranchowa, an infant of about eight months. There were two sons: Tamora, who was of churangí age (about twelve or thirteen), and Wanakani, who was about six. Cantidio and his wife were not the first couple to have broken the taboo of having a family larger than three living children. Nor was theirs the largest family in 1965. Imanawungo (also called José) and his wife had seven children. Cantidio and his family occupied a separate dwelling without any extended kinsmen, but it was located near his older brother's house (Okaniwa) and near that of his brother-in-law (Tampirí). Most Tapirapé houses in 1965 contained only one nuclear family.

As soon as we had settled in our borrowed house we saw Cantidio and members of his family daily. We learned to call Cantidio by his Brazilian name, for the nuns and the priest used that name for him. It also seemed to me that the Tapirapé called him Cantidio more often than Ipawungí; at least they did when speaking with us. We also spoke Portuguese with Cantidio because my wife did not know the Tapirapé language at all and my rather rudimentary knowledge of that language was very rusty. Cantidio spoke Portuguese fluently, although with poor grammar and a limited vocabulary. In fact, most of the youths and middle-aged men spoke a sort of pidgin Portuguese when speaking with torí or with the Carajá. In my own rather extensive conversations with Cantidio we often mixed Tapirapé words with Portuguese. Cantidio took on a similar role to that which Kamairaho had had in 1939-40 in regard to my relations with the Tapirapé. Although he laid no claim to being the village "captain," he was a man of considerable prestige and was often referred to as such. He soon became a central figure of my network of friends and without doubt my best informant. In 1939-40, Kamairaho had wanted the trade goods I had brought with me to increase his prestige; in 1965, Cantidio, with a wife and five children to support, needed my presents in trade goods and needed to earn money to support his wife and children.

It soon became obvious to my wife and me that we needed some help in our daily chores if we were not to spend all of our time hunting for firewood, washing clothes, cooking, and washing dishes. We had hired a young man from Santa Terezinha, an illiterate Brazilian caboclo, to work for us, but there were certain tasks that Clarindo (that was his name), refused to do. He complained about washing clothes and would not carry water except under duress. Cantidio suggested that his own elder daughter might also work for us; so Kuchanrawa came to be our employee for a time at a daily salary of 600 cruzeiros (about $1.00 at that time). She worked hard at first, washing clothes (rather badly) in the river, sweeping out our house from time to time, washing pots and pans, and carrying water from the village well. Cantidio came with her to collect her salary about once each week. He insisted that the money was hers and in fact she did buy some cloth for a dress and asked for some objects which we had brought for trade rather than cash. It was obvious, however, that Cantidio was in control, for he and his wife quarreled with the girl when she did not go to our house to work and they may have used some of the money to buy manioc flour, of which there was a shortage at that time. Kuchanrawa worked with us about one month. She obviously did not like to be confined to such obligations. She told my wife that she would never want to be married and have to work for a husband. She liked to play soccer with the younger boys in the plaza and to play with small children. After a month she did not come any longer to help us, and we hired Manoya, who was called Cecilia in Portuguese, to take her place. Cecilia was one of the seven living children of Imanawungo and his wife. She was more mature, if not in years, at least in her ways, than Kuchanrawa. She enjoyed sewing, and talking with my wife. She had been strongly influenced by the Little Sisters and she could sing simple songs in Portuguese and French. Cantidio was somewhat upset about his daughter, but it did not change our good relationship.

If I were asked to describe Cantidio in purely American terms, I would have to state that he was "a guy out to make a buck." He was illiterate, of course, but he could recognize the value of different units of Brazilian paper currency. In 1953 I had written in my notebook that Cantidio had come to me with a 20 cruzeiro note (about 50 cents at that time) asking me what it was worth. By 1965 he was handling money with ease and some security. He had learned, for example, that Indian artifacts were being sought by traders. He had taken over 14,000 cruzeiros as an advance for artifacts from Antonio Pereira Machado, the son of the guide who had worked for my colleague William Lipkind in 1939. Cantidio worked steadily in the takana making upé masks and small benches to pay off his debt and to have a surplus to sell when the traders came with their boat. He was one of the few men who knew how to weave baskets in the traditional Tapirapé style, and he had several to sell which he had decorated with bunches of macaw feathers. When the trader did arrive in late April of 1965, Cantidio had enough artifacts to pay off his debt and have a surplus. The trader paid about $5.00 (3000 cruzeiros) for a small Tapirapé bench carved out of wood and stained with annatto and genipap dye, about the same for a ceremonial bow with arrows decorated with tassels of bright feathers; and as much as $40 (approximately 25,000 cruzeiros) for a well-made upé mask.

After deducting the amount owed and receiving the money owed to him, Cantidio then made several purchases from the trader's stock. He bought a pair of bathing trunks, a piece of cloth for his wife to make a shirt, and an imitation leather jacket for himself. He had a small amount of cash left over. Cantidio was well aware of prices then

263

Tapirapé boys playing soccer in the plaza in 1965.

By 1976 the Tapirapé had a uniformed tribal soccer team. They compete against the Carajá and neighboring Brazilian teams. (Photo courtesy J. Lisanky)

A Tapirapé house in New Village in 1965. This is Cantidio's home; it is typical.

being charged by the stores in Santa Terezinha and by the passing trading boats that stopped briefly at the port of the Tapirapé village. Cantidio and Timoteo (Awanao) gave me a list of prices for a bush-knife, an axe, a small kitchen knife, kerosene by the liter, scissors, manioc flour by the liter, sugar, beans, and shells for a .22-calibre rifle. Their estimates of prices proved remarkably accurate when I checked them with the small stores in Santa Terezinha. In 1965 many Tapirapé men were well aware of the monetary value of the artifacts they manufactured, and even of the pelts of wild pigs and ocelot (*gato de mato*) which they sold and of the prices of manufactured articles and foodstuffs which they often bought.

Cantidio's house was a mixture of the traditional and modern frontier style. There was one room in which the whole family slept, and an open veranda which served as a kitchen and a place to sit during the daytime. The walls of the bedroom were of clay wattle and daub construction. The whole house was covered by a thatched roof made of palm leaves. The family slept in hammocks, but only one was made in the traditional Tapirapé style; the others had been purchased from 265 passing traders or in a store in Santa Terezinha. Cantidio owned a large handbag of imitation leather in which he kept his extra clothes and valued objects. One day he opened his handbag to show us his beads. From among several shirts, pants, and other garments he took out a plastic bag containing more than fifty strands of the porcelain beads which the Tapirapé had valued so highly in 1939-40. The package must have weighed at least three kilograms. We asked him about the value of such beads, and he estimated that they were worth about 3000 cruzeiros a strand; if so, he owned almost $200 worth of beads, although he could not have sold them to any Brazilian trader. Only the Tapirapé and some Carajá still put much value on such beads. Cantidio's outdoor kitchen, with its fireplace of several stones on the floor, had utensils of mixed origin—gourds and tin plates, pottery purchased from the Carajá (the Tapirapé no longer made pottery), iron pots for cooking, carved wooden spoons and metal spoons, gourd containers, and tin boxes which had once held cream crackers. There was also a native mortar used to crush maize and palm nuts.

Cantidio owned a .22-calibre rifle and a small revolver and he was particularly anxious to purchase—or receive as a gift from me—ammunition. At least ten men in the village owned .22-calibre rifles. Everyone still owned bows and arrows, but they were used mainly for shooting fish. Almost all hunting was done with .22-calibre rifles. Cantidio became enamored of the shotgun which I had borrowed in Brasília. He borrowed it from me several times, and he even kept it well oiled and clean. But he seemed to have little interest in owning one, particularly after he heard the cost of a shell. His rifle was far less expensive both in original cost and in ammunition—and, as Cantidio pointed out, .22-calibre bullets could be purchased from any traveling trader, but shells for a shotgun were not easily found.

In front of Cantidio's house there was the framework of a small house which had never been completed. He told us that this was the house of the sewing machine. Padre François had purchased a sewing machine some time before, and, under the tutelage of the Little Sisters, several women, including Cantidio's wife, had learned to use it. Because he feared that it would be broken or coveted by only one family, the padre said that the sewing machine must be installed in its own workshop. Cantidio, with the help of several other men, had started to build the sewing-machine house, but as yet they had not completed it. The machine remained in the padre's storehouse and was never used, at least during our visit, by anyone. Cantidio's wife

In 1965 Tapirapé boys still practiced with the bow and arrow.

and other women, could, however, sew by hand, and they were able to make simple sack dresses for themselves and their daughters. Tanchowai, Cantido's wife, was delighted when my wife made a small dress for their baby daughter. But men's trousers seemed beyond the women's sewing skills, and there was a great demand for men's underpants and ready-made trousers. Cantidio had pants made for him by a Brazilian woman who lived near the SPI post, and he paid her in cash for her work.

Cantidio never appeared nude in 1965; he always dressed in trousers and often a shirt. Most Tapirapé men had given up wearing the penis band and they were thus much embarrassed to appear without trousers of some kind. Yet several of the older men, among them Opronunchwi, Kanchiwanio, and Kuriwa (Julião), would return from their gardens or from hunting and sit in the evenings nude (wearing a penis band) with their feet and calves painted with red annatto. Likewise, in the privacy of their homes some older Tapirapé women wore no clothes, but Cantidio's wife and daughter seemed always to be dressed, as did almost all of the younger women in the village. Their modesty seemed to be connected with the rather frequent visits of Brazilians to the village. Clothes demanded washing; thus, bars of crude washing 267

Kanchiwanio, the oldest Tapirapé male in 1965. He still wore the penis band and painted himself with red annatto.

soap made by local Brazilians were much in demand. But the Tapirapé had few changes of clothing, and their clothes were often filthy. Cantidio and his family were notable in being among the cleanest people in the village.

Cantidio was one of the best adapted men to the new conditions of New Village. He told me that after Tampiitawa had been abandoned he went to live on the ranch of Sr. Lucio da Luz at Porto Velho on the Tapirapé River. Before that he had started on the trek with several Tapirapé families to Chichutawa, several days to the north, where Kamairá had settled; but after two days of walking he had turned back because one of his companions had a thorn in his foot. He did not witness the Kayapó attack on Tampiitawa because he was camped with several families on the savanna at the time. He was one of the first Tapirapé to move to the SPI post when Valentim Gomes began to reunite them in New Village. When I saw Cantidio in 1953 he was already an expert canoeman, and in 1965 he told me that he knew how to construct a dugout canoe, but that "it is better to buy canoes from the Carajá." He owned a good canoe which he used from time to time for fishing. I walked one day with Cantidio to his gardens. They were located about two hours' walk from the village (about six

268

or seven kilometers). By pacing off the width and length of his garden I estimated it to be about 45,000 square meters in size. He was then beginning to clear another site alongside the old garden to be planted during the early rains in 1965. In April of 1965 his garden had little to offer except for manioc, peanuts, some dried maize, and some bananas. During our trip to the garden he showed me a cleared path over which the tractor could pass across low bush country (campo cerrado) to a point about a half-hour's walk from the garden. Next year, he said, he hoped to clear a wide path through the forest so that the tractor might reach his garden and transport his garden products more easily to the village. Now, he explained, he usually came to stay a few days with his family on the field in an open shed built for that purpose. Sometimes, Tampirí (Marcos) and his family came with them, for his gardens were near by. Cantidio was a very hard worker, energetic and intelligent.

Cantidio was very aware of the rather precarious situation of the Tapirapé in regard to land. He told me when we visited his gardens that the area in which they were situated belonged to the land company. He knew that Brazilians had been there demarcating the area and he feared that the Tapirapé would lose all of the forest region where they planted their gardens. He told me that Padre François had made several trips to try to resolve the land problem, but he said the torí kept on coming and they wanted "to leave us just some campo which is good for nothing." He told me that he had little confidence in the SPI. "They will do nothing for us." He pointed out, correctly, that there was not even an Indian officer in charge at the SPI post. In fact, Sr. José Auce had been transferred and the post was in the hands of a local Brazilian frontiersman. Cantidio had not traveled, as a few other Tapirapé had, to other parts of Brazil, including Rio de Janeiro and São Paulo; even so, he told me that it was important for the Tapirapé children to learn to speak and write Portuguese. The Tapirapé had, in fact, built a house for a school under the direction of Padre François. For a short time a young Brazilian couple lived in the village as teachers, but now they had gone away and the school was being used to house a carpenter who was working on the chapel. Cantidio was well aware of the problems which his people faced as a result of the rapidly encroaching frontier. Although he was not recognized as the village "chief," he was looked upon by his fellow villagers as one who could deal with the problem of their contact with Brazilians.

Yet Cantidio was also a traditionalist interested in things of the   269 past and Tapirapé custom. He did not approve of the Tapirapé dancing in Brazilian style and had ordered his daughter not to participate. He admitted trying Brazilian cachaça once in Santa Terezinha, but he found it distasteful; he criticized Timoteo (Awanao), whom he said drank frequently, and he joined with the Little Sisters in trying to keep alcohol out of the village. Cantidio liked to come to my house in 1965 to see the collection of photographs from the 1939-40 period which I had brought with me.[121] He identified people, anchunga masked dancers, the shamans fighting Thunder, and other scenes. The photographs stimulated him to talk about the past (but it also led him to ask me questions about that past, many of which I could not answer). One evening after looking for perhaps the fifth time at the photographs, he told my wife in considerable detail of the travels of Chankanepera, the ancestor of the Feast Group which carries that name. Another evening he began to tell stories of Opossum, and how he sought a son-in-law among the various birds and other animals. I had never before heard the Tapirapé tell these stories, which were almost identical with those which I had recorded among the Tupí-speaking Tenetehara Indians in 1942 (Wagley and Galvão, 1949: 151-54). Such stories are purely recreational. They tell of how Opossum tries to imitate each of the animals who, in succession, marry his daughter. In one incident his daughter marries Kingfisher. Opossum tries to fly like his son-in-law to catch fish, but he almost drowns. In another, his daughter marries Hawk, and Opossum again tries to imitate the hunting techniques of his son-in-law, but, of course, he fails. Hawk hunts by swooping down upon his prey, but Opossum lacks wings. Opossum tries to swoop down to seize animals but each time falls heavily to the ground. Cantidio regaled us with a series of these charming stories.

Cantidio also respected the Tapirapé food taboos, though in an attenuated form. He was the father of a small infant; thus he refrained from eating venison and other foods. Several times he brought forest fowls, traditionally prohibited to women and to men with small children, to our house as gifts after hunting. He did eat beef and allowed his wife and daughters to eat it. He reasoned that it was torí food and thus exempt from the food taboos. Unlike some Tapirapé, he did not identify beef with venison and thus include it in their system of taboo

---

121. These photographs were an excellent aid to field work in 1965. People, both young and old, came to our house to look at them, and in the process gave us information about the past and present.

foods. Cantidio participated in the few kaó songfests which took place during our visit in 1965. He was not, however, a "song leader"; those roles were filled by Marcos (Tampirí) and Julião (Karuwa), who led the singing for Ananchá and Wuranchingió. Although Cantidio said that he had the right to make and wear a upé mask (the spirit of an enemy), it was Timoteo (Awanao) who sponsored the upé masked dancer and provided the kawi for the Bird Societies to drink in the takana in 1965. Cantidio begged off, explaining that he did not have enough sweet manioc in his garden, and "my family is hungry."

In May of 1965 my wife came down with a fever which I feared might be malaria (it was not); I urged her to travel to Brasilia, where she could receive medical attention. She left, loaded with gifts from Cantidio and his family. Then, just ten days later, when I traveled to Santa Terezinha to catch the commercial DC-3 which landed there each week en route to Goiânia and Brasilia, Cantidio and Marcos accompanied me. They carried my bags to the airport and waited through a whole morning until the plane arrived. Both urged me to return again soon. Since then I have had only occasional bits of information from Cantidio in letters from the Little Sisters of Jesus; from Judith Shapiro, who returned for a brief visit in 1974; and in a dictated tape which a graduate student delivered in 1976. In their last letter, dated December 30, 1975, the Little Sisters wrote that the Tapirapé now have a school where a young Brazilian couple teach. According to a FUNAI report, forty-two students are registered and the teachers were attempting to teach reading and writing in Tapirapé and Portuguese. The Little Sisters said in their letter that "young men and women are studying. Of the older ones who have attempted to study, only Cantidio has persevered." As I read of the Tapirapé sending representatives to a meeting of Indian chiefs in Mato Grosso in 1975 and, even more recently, of a mission of Tapirapé chiefs who traveled to Brasilia in 1976 to plead their case with the director of FUNAI for guarantees for additional lands (Judith Lisansky, personal communication), I feel certain that Cantidio is among them. It seems to me that Cantidio, among all the Tapirapé I knew in 1965, had the clearest vision of the contemporary problems of his people and the greatest commitment to help solve them.

8
The Tragedy
of the Brazilian Indians

The Tapirapé are the descendants of only one of hundreds of independent tribal groups which once inhabited the immense lowlands of the Amazon Valley. The societies of the South American lowlands differed profoundly from those of the highland regions of the Andes and Central America. The highlands were inhabited by millions of American aborigines who were organized into complex native states. There intensive agriculture provided the basis for high population density, and even for cities as large as those of contemporaneous Europe. But the lowland tribes of South America were hunters and gatherers, or, as in the Amazon basin, they supported themselves by swidden cultivation or slash-and-burn horticulture supplemented by fishing in the rivers and hunting in the tropical forest. There were probably no more than two or three million people throughout lowland South America and no more than one million in the whole Amazon basin when the Europeans arrived in Brazil in 1500. It is possible that some tribes were organized, led by chieftains who united several villages or more into social units, but generally these Amazonian peoples were without any socio-political unit larger than an individual village.

These two factors—population density and socio-political organization—were important in determining the different reactions of the highland and lowland Indian societies to conquest by the Europeans and later to integration under colonial rule. Everywhere the first contact between American Indians and Europeans was generally marked by armed violence. The Spanish *conquistadores* waged war in the highlands of America to subdue such highly civilized peoples as the Aztecs of Mexico, the Mayas of Yucatan and highland Guatemala, and the Incas of Andean South America. In Brazil, the Dutch, French, and Portuguese penetrated into the interior seeking Indian slaves, laying waste to small Indian villages and massacring whole groups in the process. As in North America, not only did the Europeans wage war against Indian tribes, they used them as warriors in their own struggles for territory. New diseases such as the common cold, measles, smallpox, and whooping cough were also brought to the New World by Europeans. In both the highlands and the lowlands, as the result of war, enslavement, and disease, there was a rapid population decline among the aboriginal peoples in the years immediately following the arrival of the Europeans. By the end of the sixteenth century, for example, the Indians of the islands of the Caribbean were reduced to a handful, living in isolated groups. The population of the Mexican plateau, which may have been as great as 11 million or more, was reduced to 4,400,000 by 1565 and to only 2 million by 1700 (Cook and Simpson, 1948: 38ff.). The population of Peru is thought to have declined by at least 50 per cent between 1531 and 1561 (Kubler, 1946: 334-38).

Likewise, the population of the Amazon lowlands suffered in the first years of contact with the European invaders. We cannot be precise about the rapidity of population decline in the first years, but it is known that during the first century of Brazilian colonial history epidemics were common and the Portuguese and French involved the coastal peoples in their internecine struggles. In 1562 and 1563, smallpox epidemics were recorded in the vicinity of Bahia (Brazil); the first is said to have killed one-third of the Indians in the region and the second from one-fourth to three-fifths of the remainder. Epidemics so disorganized these native groups that gardens were neglected and hunger followed (Marchant, 1942: 116-17). By the end of the sixteenth century the coastal tribes of Brazil were either totally extinct or had fled to the hinterlands.

In 1621, smallpox ravaged the tribes on the lower Amazon (the city of Belém was established in 1616) and by 1651 the disease had reached the main upriver tributaries. By the end of the seventeenth century most of the Tupinambá tribes of the Brazilian coast were extinct or their remnants had fled inland. But Brazilian colonial expansion did not move steadily westward. For the most part, the Portu- 273 guese colonists stuck "like crabs" to the coast. Into the nineteenth and twentieth centuries vast regions of central Brazil remained unexplored or so isolated that no Brazilians inhabited them. There, a thousand miles from the colonial cities of the coast, in the Amazon valley but above the rapids and falls, where navigation was impossible or very difficult, Indian tribes continued to live, most of them unknown to Brazilians. Their time would come in the twentieth century.

The final outcome of European contact with the highland and lowland aboriginal populations was not the same. They reacted differently to the wars of conquest and to the economic exploitation which followed. In the highlands, the Spaniards were able to conquer and dominate the native rulers. In Peru, Guatemala, and Mexico a handful of European soldiers thus successfully conquered and set out to rule millions of American Indians. In the lowlands of Amazonia, however, each chieftainship, each village or band, had to be conquered or destroyed. Even when the "treaties of peace" were made with the local *caciques*, or chieftains, these treaties were never understood by the lowland Indians, whose societies lacked political unity. Thus, wars broke out again and again with the same tribes, and tribes that had been conquered once had to be conquered again. Often the wars ended only with the complete extermination of the aboriginal group. Likewise, differences in indigenous social and political organization resulted in different methods of control by Europeans. The settled populations of the highlands could be governed and taxed, as they had been before by their own rulers, and they could be made to work by systems of forced labor. The small village populations of the lowlands, on the other hand, were not easily governed. They often simply faded deeper into the forest as the Europeans advanced. They could be induced to work only by outright slavery or by a system of trade, exchanging firearms and steel tools for products of the forest. On the whole, the wars of conquest and the later exploitation were probably much more destructive to the tribes of the lowlands than to the highland peoples.

Although imported diseases undoubtedly killed a larger number of people in the highlands than in the lowlands, there was a greater demographic reserve in the densely populated highland areas. By the middle of the eighteenth century the aboriginal population along the coast and along the mainstreams of the Amazon River basin had been either exterminated or driven into the interriverine areas or into inaccessible regions of the Amazon headwaters. It is doubtful whether a single lowland tribe, despite their isolation from European contact, had not already felt the impact of the European presence, directly or indirectly. Most lowland tribes that persisted were in total or partial disarray. And yet, by the same date, the Indian populations of the highlands had recovered from the first shocks of conquest. The people who survived had acquired some immunity to the Old World diseases, and new tools, new crops, and relative peace under their new rulers made it possible for the population not only to increase rapidly, but actually to exceed the number present in 1500. Today the descendants of the aboriginal population, although they may not call themselves "Indians," form the majority of the population in the highland areas of South America. On the other hand, the Indian population of the lowlands is insignificant in relation to non-Indian peoples of the region. In all of Brazil, there are perhaps less than a hundred thousand Indians, and in the Brazilian Amazon the number of Indians probably does not exceed fifty thousand.

The Tapirapé are one of those Indian groups which simply faded deeper into the interior as the European advanced from the coast. The main body of people who shared their Tupian language once inhabited the Brazilian coast from the mouth of the Amazon to as far south as São Paulo. The Tapirapé are an isolated group of Tupí-speakers surrounded by tribes which speak languages of the Gê family. In all probability, the Tapirapé were a refugee tribe that moved west from the coast after 1500 (Metraux, 1927). They were probably not driven out of their original territory by direct contact with Europeans, for they seem not to have known Europeans until early in the twentieth century. They were probably forced indirectly to migrate westward by other aboriginal tribes even nearer the coast who fled from the Europeans (Metraux, 1927). This drove them into the territory of the Gê-speakers; and Tapirapé social structure and culture reflects their close association with Gê-speakers. They may have been in peaceful contact with the Sherente or the Shavante, whose original territory was east of the Araguaia River, or one of the Kayapó groups, who lived to the north. Tapirapé oral history or mythology has it that for a time in the past they lived near or even with people of the Javahé division of the Carajá tribe, which today inhabits the western branch of the Araguaia River where it divides to form the large island of Bananal.

The Tapirapé, perhaps because of their western migration into the heartland of Brazil, were spared the first impact of European contact 275 during which many tribes totally disappeared. They also escaped the horrors of the Amazonian rubber boom which attracted so many Brazilians to the Amazon area during the late nineteenth and early twentieth centuries. During that period, which lasted until 1910, numerous tribal groups were driven out of their territories, decimated, or brought into peonage or outright slavery.

The Tapirapé met their first western man at about the time a new era began in Brazil in regard to Brazilian Indians. In 1910 the Serviço de Proteção aos Indios (SPI) was founded. The creation of the SPI, however, was a reaction to a scandal involving Indian wars—not deep in central Brazil, where the Tapirapé lived, but just inland from the coastal strip which had been occupied during the first wave of European colonization. Then, in a second surge of occupation, Brazilians again encountered hostile Indians. The Kaingang tribe, for example, spread terror along 300 kilometers of the Northeast Railroad, which was being constructed inland from the growing city of São Paulo. In the Rio Doce Valley, in the states of Minas Gerais and Espírito Santo, where the rich iron deposits of Itabira are located, the Aimoré resisted with arms as Brazilians penetrated their tribal domain. The Italian immigrant colony which had been established in that area was in danger of being abandoned because of Indian attacks. And in the pine forests of Paraná and Santa Catarina states, the Xokleng Indians were being hunted by professional Indian hunters, who were being paid with public funds to drive Indians out of lands destined to be colonized by Italian and German immigrants.

Newspapers of Rio de Janeiro, São Paulo, and other principal cities were filled with stories of Indian wars at the very doorstep of civilization, wars which were interrupting the economic progress of the country. The problem was discussed in the Legislative Assembly, and the President of the Republic called meetings of ministers to study the possibility of sending federal troops to wipe out the hostile savages. All were eager to complete the railroads (the construction of which had been suspended by Indian hostility), to extract the riches of the Itabira iron deposits, and to guarantee the lives of Brazilians and European immigrant farmers who were clearing the forests to plant coffee. Only a few philanthropic and scientific organizations and a few idealists raised their voices in defense of the Indians and against the horrors of Indian hunts and massacres. The Indians were driven from their lands or forced to make peace with the encroaching Brazilians.

This was disastrous to them despite the efforts of the newly created Indian service.

Perhaps the story can best be told through the dramatic example of the Kaingang of São Paulo state, one of the tribal groups which in 1910 was impeding the march of Brazilian civilization. The Kaingang were seminomads inhabiting the São Paulo forests, which were soon to become some of the world's richest coffee lands. In 1910 they were at war with Brazilians. They not only attacked the railroad workers as the railroad was being built, but they also impeded the settlement of European immigrants eager to clear the forest and plant coffee. The pacification of the Kaingang became of national interest to Brazil. It was clear to the idealists of the SPI that either the Kaingang must be pacified or troops would be ordered to wipe them out in a one-sided battle of machine guns against bows and arrows. In 1912 Dr. Bruno Horta Barbosa, one of the early officers of the SPI, established peaceful contact with a band of Kaingang comprising 200 people and led by an Indian named Vauhim. This was but one of six wandering Kaingang bands, and the band led by Vauhim was at war with the other five. The other bands, certain that Vauhim had made peace with the Brazilians in order to secure allies in his battles with them, fled deeper into the forest. It was not until 1915 that the SPI was able to pacify these other bands, and by then the hostile groups had been reduced to only one remaining band.

By the time peaceful relations had been fully established with the Kaingang, the ravages attending contact with the western world had already taken their toll. In 1912, according to Dr. Barbosa, the six bands numbered at least seven hundred people in all. In 1916, just one year after the last band had been pacified, less than two hundred were left. Influenza and measles wiped out not only the first band to be pacified, but were also transmitted by casual contacts between Indians to the bands still at war. On one occasion, Dr. Barbosa received news that a hostile band of Kaingang were starving because so many had fallen ill from the new diseases. But when the men of the SPI arrived to give aid to them, there was no one left; they found only bones at the campsite (Barbosa, 1954). While the Kaingang were still at war with the Brazilians, the land they occupied was the legal property of one man, Sr. Luis Piza. But while the Indians remained hostile, the land was almost worthless. As soon as the first band of Kaingang were pacified, however, the land became worth 100 milreis (the Brazilian 277 currency at the time) per alqueire (24,000 square meters). Soon afterward it was bringing 1000 milreis per alqueire. Sr. Piza became a rich man and a senator from the state of São Paulo, and the Kaingang who once had inhabited an enormous area were left with about 1000 alqueires. Settled upon this small patrimony, they were induced with difficulty to become agriculturalists (they had practiced only some shifting cultivation before). In 1917, their pacifier described their economic condition:

> They have clothes which they absolutely do not use; houses which are better constructed and protected than their primitive huts; platforms as beds substitute for those which they made out of palm leaves on the floor next to their fires: food with salt and fat; and they use food unknown before such as rice, sugar and beans. (Barbosa, 1954: 73).

Yet despite these dubious advantages of reservation life, the Kaingang were totally disorganized due to the clash of their aboriginal values and customs with those of the national culture. In 1910 the average Brazilian frontiersman considered the Indians as savages and brutes and were suspicious of them, just as they are today. The Kaingang were ferocious warriors, but they saw early that they were outnumbered and that they would have to make peace with the new "white tribe" which was penetrating their territory. From their point of view, it was the Brazilians who had to be pacified. On one occasion, before they came into contact with the SPI, the leader of the band decided to "pacify" a group of Brazilian railroad workers. This warrior, leaving his arms behind and taking his small son with him, approached a "band of men from the new tribe." But the railroad workers, frightened by the sudden appearance of the "savage," received him with a volley of bullets. The Indian child was killed but the father escaped, wounded.

In 1910 this same Kaingang leader again tried to pacify the hostile "tribe," this time with greater success, for he encountered a party sent out by the SPI. Until 1914, the Kaingang believed that it was they who had pacified the whites; or, to put it another way, the Kaingang and the Brazilians each believed that they had pacified the other. But in 1914 a group of Kaingang was taken by Indian Service officers to the city of São Paulo by railroad. At each station the Kaingang became more and more amazed at the number of the Brazilians, and by the time they reached the city they finally realized that this "new tribe" so vastly outnumbered them that it was they, not the Brazilians, who had been pacified. It is said that after they returned to their reservation they seemed disheartened and their pride in their songs, dances, and customs diminished. They saw now that they had been conquered. Previously they had been proud before Brazilians; now they were humble.

The new situation which the Kaingang and other simple groups like them had come to face called for difficult adjustments in tribal values, customs, and institutions. The Kaingang marriage rules are a case in point (as is the Tapirapé population policy). In aboriginal times, the Kaingang of São Paulo were divided into two hereditary groups, or exogamous moieties. Each individual of the tribe belonged to the moiety of his or her father and had to seek a spouse in certain clans of the opposite moiety. Marriage, or even extramarital sexual relations, with a fellow moiety member—or with a member of the wrong clan in the opposite moiety—was considered to be incest. The offending pair were severely punished, and sometimes killed. The number of potential marital or sexual partners was always very limited, but in the days when the Kaingang had several bands, a partner of the proper clan of the opposite moiety could be found with little difficulty. By 1916, however, when the whole Kaingang tribe had been reduced to a mere two hundred individuals, some clans were represented only by a few people. Several clans had died out altogether. Under those circumstances, some people were denied all rights to marriage, since there were no individuals of the opposite sex belonging to the moiety and clans into which they were allowed to marry. Faced with this situation, a few couples broke the rules of exogamy and incest. They did not do so publicly by open marriage, but by occasion and furtive sexual relations. The first couples to do so were executed when apprehended, according to the tribal rule. Dr. Barbosa, the SPI Indian officer, on learning of the marriage regulations and the tradition of enforcing them, had to intervene. Thereafter, when he noticed a young couple who seemed to be attracted to one another, he inquired of their moiety and clan. If they were not of the proper moieties and clans, he tried to persuade them to run away to live on the reservation of a group of Guaraní Indians, whose ideas of a proper marriage were different. Several couples thus escaped, and only after many months did they dare return to their own people.

It took almost a generation for the Indian officers to persuade the Kaingang to modify their strict marriage regulations. This seems to 279 have been accomplished finally by Sr. Eurico Sampaio, who was in charge of the Kaingang Post for more than twenty years. Sr. Sampaio, in whom the Kaingang had great confidence, married a woman whom he introduced as his father's brother's daughter and thus of his own moiety and his own clan from the Kaingang point of view. Only after they saw this much-trusted Brazilian fly in the face of danger by marrying a woman of his own moiety and his own clan were they convinced that it was not wrong for "kin" to marry and have children. But it was already too late. By clinging so long to their old marriage rules, the Kaingang had accelerated the rate of depopulation, thus hastening their own demise. Adherence to the old marriage regulations evidently contributed to a sharp decline of the birth rate; in fact, Dr. Barbosa reported that from 1912 to 1916 there were only three live births among the Kaingang and that all three infants had died during the first year of life. In the 1950's it was reported that only sixty-five Kaingang remained despite the special efforts of the SPI to save them.[122]

The SPI, which was created in 1910, was led by a highly idealistic group of men, all of whom had had early experience in the Brazilian backlands. At the head of the SPI was Cândido Mariano da Silva Rondon, an unusual man in any country at any time, who has by now become a Brazilian national hero. By 1910 Rondon already had considerable experience with Indian problems. As early as 1890, soon after he graduated from the military academy, he was sent to serve as an army officer in his home state of Mato Grosso. He was charged with the mission of stringing a telegraph line from the state capital of Cuiabá to the more eastern state of Goiás. The line crossed the territory of the Bororo Indians, who were then hostile to the Brazilian settlers in the area.[123] Rondon's commanding officer, General Gomes Carneiro, issued an order stating that any act of hostility on the part of civilian or military personnel directed against these Indians would be punished. Later, when Rondon himself assumed command of the expedition, he placed the Indians under the protection of the troops. When the telegraph line was completed, the Bororo tribe was living in peace with settlers and soldiers. Rondon thought that he had found a strategy for the protection of such Indian groups, and he established,

---

122. The history of the Kaingang of São Paulo is related in some detail by Darcy Ribeiro (1970). It is based upon SPI reports.

123. It is said that Rondon was, on one side of his family, a descendant of a Bororo.

at least for his military mission, an Indian policy which he later used in the SPI.

Rondon was afterward charged with extending telegraph lines to the borders of Paraguay and Bolivia. During these activities, Rondon met with Indians already in contact and living with Brazilian settlers. Such tribes as the Terena, the Kadiweu, the Guato, and the Guaraní were settled in this zone. They already had been despoiled of their lands; many of them lived as peons on ranches. Rondon could see the results of economic exploitation of tribal groups already living within the network of Brazilian national culture. Then, in 1906, he was charged with his most difficult task—not only to extend the telegraph line across a thousand miles of arid country and two thousand miles of Amazon jungle between Cuiabá and the newly acquired District of Acre, but also to carry out scientific studies of this unknown region of Brazil. Over a period of eight years Rondon lived mainly in the Brazilian hinterlands; his expedition made important contributions in the fields of zoology, botany, geography, ethnography, and other natural sciences for which he is justly famous. But it is just as important that during these years, Rondon began to put into practice his Indian policy.

During that expedition, innumerable tribes came into contact for the first time with western man. Rondon made every effort to avoid the calamity and cruelty suffered by the Indian inhabitants of other regions where railroads, roads, navigation systems, and even simple geographical explorations had penetrated into Indian territories. Furthermore, he attempted to protect the Indians' right to their lands. Rondon found in his explorations large areas of Brazil where no civilized man had ever trod already registered as the property of individuals who lived far away in São Paulo and Rio de Janeiro. He saw Indians expelled from such lands at the will of those "proprietors." During the expedition, Rondon and his associates developed their techniques for pacification of warring tribes. Their famous motto, which was adopted by the SPI, was "Die if you must, but never kill." Their technique involved patience and waiting, allowing the Indian to attack without reprisal; and setting out trade goods where they would be found by the Indians as offerings of their good will.

The territory between Cuiabá and Acre was inhabited by several tribes who were in a state of constant war with Brazilians. In the same area there were tribes totally unknown to civilization. Among the 281 known tribes were the Nambikuara, who were famous for their ferocity. The telegraph line had to pass directly through their territory. Rondon was determined that somehow it should be done peacefully. He recognized that the men of his Commission constituted encroachers into the land of the Nambikuara and that inevitably the Indians would attack. But he also knew that any reprisal would mean that the telegraph line could only be completed at the cost of many human lives, both among the Indians and the Brazilians. And the Nambikuara did attack the expedition. Rondon, rather than ordering armed reprisal, had his soldiers leave presents of iron tools and other articles much sought after by the Indians in places where he knew they would find them. Such behavior was hardly comprehensible to either the Indians or the soldiers and guides of the expedition. From the Nambikuara point of view, here was a curious group of enemies who, rather than counterattack, left valued presents. This was also against the accepted code of conduct of Brazilian soldiers, who thought of the Nambikuara as savages to be eliminated. Furthermore, among the guides of the expedition were Paressí Indians, traditional enemies of the Nambikuara. Perhaps Rondon's most difficult task was to restrain his own men.

Finally, in 1910, his methods proved successful. After numerous Indian attacks, a small group of Nambikuara met with Rondon's mission on peaceful terms. They left burdened with presents which had been saved for the occasion. Then, just a few months later, hundreds of Nambikuara Indians—men, women, and children—came to see the strange men who had entered their territory and had sought peace. During the years that followed, other tribes, such as the Kepkiruwat and the Rama-Rama, Tupí-speaking groups on the Gy-Paraná River, were pacified by the Rondon Commission by similar means.

These same methods are being used today along the frontiers of Brazil to pacify tribal groups that are just now being discovered for the first time. In 1947, the SPI was able to pacify the Shavante living along the Rio das Mortes between the Araguaia and the Xingú Rivers, although, in the process, one entire pacification team was killed by the Shavante in 1941. Since 1950, pacification teams have entered into contact with such tribes as the Xikrin and Kubenkrankren, the Parakanã, the Assuriní, and the Gaviões—tribes until then either at war with Brazilians or totally unknown. And in the 1960's, the famous Villas Boas brothers, who founded the Indian Park of the Xingú as a refuge for Indian groups, used essentially the same techniques in entering into peaceful contact with hitherto unknown tribes of the upper Xingú River and the basin of the Teles Pires River.

Rondon also learned about what we might call "directed culture change" during the years of the telegraph line missions. The first tribe to be encountered by the Rondon Commission between Cuiabá and Acre were the Paressí. For centuries the Paressí had been exploited by Brazilians: first by the early bandeirante expeditions, then by miners who found their women attractive, and then by rubber gatherers. Those who lived close to frontier settlements were fully involved in regional extractive industries. Rondon placed the Paressí under the protection of the Commission. He made every attempt to see to it that they were no longer torn from their villages by force, robbed of their lands, or introduced to cachaça by frontiersmen and rubber gatherers. He was able to convince the Paressí chiefs to move their people to better village sites where the Commission might guarantee their lands and where the men might work as line keepers on the telegraph lines. Schools were established among them and many were taught to read and write Portuguese. Many became artisans of one kind or another and a few became telegraph operators, taking charge of the telegraph stations in their area. Rondon was able to rehabilitate the Paressí by retraining them as a people and by respecting their institutions and authorities.

Rondon's experience provided him with the basis for framing an idealistic and humanitarian policy for the Brazilian Indian Service. But, unfortunately, these policies formulated by Rondon and his early followers were difficult to put into practice for various reasons. First was the difficulty implicit in the great variety of tribal cultures and languages with which the SPI had to deal. Second was the great difference in contact situations, since the Brazilians involved varied from the rubber gatherers eager for Indian labor to cattle ranchers anxious to remove the Indian from their pasture lands. Any policy which the SPI adopted, whether it tried to guarantee an honest wage for the Indian or attempted to set aside lands as Indian reservations, always seemed to run counter to economic interests of either the local Brazilian frontiersmen or the businessman in faraway São Paulo or Rio de Janeiro. And third, this economic pressure meant that the SPI suffered politically. It soon was shunted off to the side in the bureaucratic struggle and it was always without sufficient funds to realize its proper task. As time went on, the early leaders of the SPI disappeared and the Indian posts were manned by appointees of local politicians who were often far from well-educated. And, finally, the SPI was faced with the fact that, whether peaceful or not, contact with modern Brazilians continued to bring new diseases to Indians, as European contact had in the past, and with the same deadly result. The unknown tribes which have been pacified within the last few years such as the Parakanã and those encountered while building the Amazon highway system are already reduced to only a handful. Rondon died in 1959 at the age of ninety-three, a Marshal in the Brazilian Army and a national hero—fortunately, before 1968, when the SPI became a national scandal. Before his death, however, it was already clear that his idealistic policies had lost out to Brazilian realities.

Sometime ago Darcy Ribeiro, the well-known Brazilian anthropologist, brought together data that clearly indicated that the SPI had failed in its mission to "protect" the Indians during the first half of this century. He was able to collect information on 230 tribes known to be in existence in 1900. From the information which he was able to bring together from the archives of the SPI and other sources, he classified those tribes by the degree of their contacts with Brazilian civilization as of that time.

He classified the tribes which still inhabited zones outside the orbit of Brazilian society, which rarely had contact with civilized people, which were either withdrawn peacefully or hostile to Brazilians, and which still retained lands and their cultural autonomy as *Isolated*.

Those tribes which lived in regions in the process of being swallowed by Brazil's pioneer expansion and thus had more often had contacts with Brazilians he classified as in *Intermittent* contact. Such tribes often retained some cultural autonomy and they often continued to gain their subsistence through traditional means, but they already had acquired needs which could be satisfied only through economic relations with civilized peoples.

Then there were tribes which he spoke of as being in *Permanent* contact. Those tribes maintained direct and permanent communications with different representatives of civilization. The greater part of their sense of cultural autonomy had been lost, and they were totally dependent upon outsiders for such necessities as salt, medicine, cloth, and industrial products. Some cultural autochthonous traits may have been retained by groups in permanent contact with Brazilian civilization which were compatible with the new situation and were modified by them. Most tribesmen in this degree of contact with civilization were able to speak Portuguese, which was a necessity in their day-today life. The population of such tribes might actually be in the process of increase since they had survived and by this time had some immunity to foreign diseases.

Finally, there were tribes which he classified as *Integrated*. These were groups which had survived until the turn of the century as "islands" in the midst of the national populace. Their economic role was that of reserve labor employed in the production of certain marketable products. Most of them had forgotten their aboriginal language, but in some cases it had been retained to some degree as a symbol of their tribal identity. Some of these groups which were fully integrated into Brazilian life were held together (and sometimes distinguished from the surrounding population) only by the fact that at some time or another they had received a land grant or had been settled on a small reservation (Ribeiro, 1967: 86-87).

Of the 230 tribes on which Darcy Ribeiro had good information for the year 1900, he classified 105 as Isolated, 57 as Intermittent, 39 as Permanent and 29 as Integrated. By 1957, the year that he completed his study, the picture had changed drastically. Of the same 230 tribes, 33 could be classified as Isolated, 27 as Intermittent, 45 as Permanent and 38 as Integrated. And 87 of those 230 tribes were extinct. This classification, which Darcy Ribeiro has used in showing the various degrees of contact with Brazilian national society, must not be mistaken for a set of stages through which tribes pass in the inevitable process toward integration or assimilation. Under the worst circumstances, an isolated tribe might suddenly enter into intermittent or sporadic relations with Brazilians and within a few years be extinct. It is interesting to see what happened to the 105 tribes which Dr. Ribeiro classified as Isolated in 1900. By 1957, 33 of them remained Isolated, 23 had entered into Intermittent contact, 13 were in Permanent contact, 3 had become Integrated, and 33 were extinct (Ribeiro, 1967: 84-94).[124]

Although I have cited Darcy Ribeiro's statistics as evidence of the

---

124. "Virulent epidemics alone cannot explain so high a rate of extinction. Various factors appear to have acted cumulatively, among them the docility with which some tribes spontaneously approached civilized men who came to them with the all-powerful attraction of metal instruments, porcelain beads, guns and other marvels. After this first meeting with officials of the Rondon Commission, many tribes, entranced by their prodigal welcome, sought contact with rubber collectors in the belief that the latter were the same people. The consequences were fatal; within a few years one tribe after another was exterminated, and those who survived suffered such substantial reductions in numbers that today their ranks constitute infinitesimal fractions of the former population." (Ribeiro, 1967: 97-98).

failure of the SPI to protect the Indian tribes between 1900 and 1957, he points out that the situation might have been even worse. As he wrote:

> The essential differences from 1900 to our times in the conditions of life synthesized in each of these categories reflect the presence of a new factor, the protective intervention exercised by the Serviço de Proteção aos Indios. By virtue of their interference, the process of contact, integration or extinction no longer operates spontaneously, as it did in the past; on the contrary, it is in a large measure artificially controlled. For this reason, the contemporary condition of isolation, or of intermittent or permanent contact, or of integration does not correspond precisely to the stage earlier designated in the same terms. (Ribeiro, 1967: 90.)

When we apply Ribeiro's scheme to Tapirapé history, certain factors stand out and we can understand better some of the special, sometimes almost fortuitous, circumstances which any single tribe might well experience. In 1900, the Tapirapé were certainly an isolated tribe; in fact, they are listed as one of the 230 by Dr. Ribeiro. The upper Araguaia River and especially its tributaries were seldom traveled by Brazilians. Diamond deposits have been discovered on the lower Araguaia River near the present city of Marabá, but there were no known mineral lodes along the middle reaches of the river which divides to form the inland island of Bananal. And wild rubber trees and Brazil nut trees did grow in the forests just to the west of the island of Bananal. The Tapirapé with their five villages intact were, as yet, out of touch with civilized Brazilians, who only knew of their existence by hearsay. The Brazilian frontier had not reached the Araguaia River in any force, and the region to the west of the river was beyond the edge of the frontier.

Around 1912, however, the isolation of the Tapirapé was broken when they entered into intermittent contact with the Dominican missionaries and with occasional backwoodsmen who penetrated their territory. It was in this period, between about 1912 and 1939-40, when they made only occasional and intermittent contact with outsiders, that they suffered severe depopulation. The contagion which caused that depopulation may not have been derived only from contact with Brazilians; it may well have been received indirectly from their casual contacts with other Indian groups such as the Carajá, who encoun-

286

tered Brazilians more frequently since they lived along the mainstream of the Araguaia River.

By the time I visited the Tapirapé in 1939-40, they were in intermittent contact with Brazilians; visits or contacts with outsiders were rare, being limited to seasonal meetings with the Catholic missionaries, a few visits to their village by a single Protestant missionary, and visits by adventurers and anthropologists. It must be noted that despite intermittent or sporadic contacts' with Brazilians, they retained their aboriginal culture and cultural autonomy almost intact. Yet they had come to depend upon iron instruments in making their gardens, and for these they depended upon outsiders. Porcelain beads had become highly valued objects. Otherwise, their aboriginal subsistence and economic system seems to have been little changed, except for the lack of manpower which depopulation had brought about. Certainly there was no lack of land.

In 1942, a post of the SPI was established to "protect" the Tapirapé at the confluence of that river with the Araguaia. As I have said, it was manned by Valentim Gomes, who had been my companion during my 1939-40 residence among the Tapirapé. The post was much too far away to keep in permanent contact with the remaining Tapirapé village. In addition, it was located near a village of Carajá Indians (which it also was supposed to serve), whom the Tapirapé feared. Valentim Gomes wrote that several Tapirapé men visited the post during the first two or three years of its existence, but that there was an unfortunate accidental death of one Tapirapé youth at the post and an encounter with a group of drunken Brazilian men which thoroughly frightened the small group of Tapirapé visitors. Valentim was only able to keep in contact with the Tapirapé by occasional trips up the Tapirapé River. But in 1947 a small group of Tapirapé refugees appeared at the post to tell him of the attack on their village by the Kayapó. After that the Tapirapé dispersed—some moving to a ranch on the Tapirapé River, others moving to the SPI post, and still others returning to Chichutawa under the leadership of Kamairá to begin their twenty-five years of isolation in the forest.

The Tapirapé did not exist as an organized society between 1947-1950, except for the small group far to the north in the forest of Chichutawa. During these years they could easily have joined the long list of extinct tribes of Brazil. Perhaps it is due to one man that they did not. It seems almost unbelievable that Valentim Gomes, as an   287 agent of the SPI, was able to gather the Tapirapé Indians into a single, new village established near the Indian post. It is equally admirable that Valentim was able to help them survive until their gardens were growing and there was enough to eat. In 1953, Valentim told me of the hardships of the first two years. He had little support from the regional office of the SPI in Goiânia. His own meager salary was usually months late in arriving, and he wrote the regional office asking not only for payment of his own salary but for extra funds to feed the Tapirapé gathered into their new village near the post. He told me that he personally went into debt to buy manioc flour and other necessities for the Indians. He made several long and laborious trips upriver to Goiânia (it took ten days by riverboat and two by truck) to beg his superiors for help before he finally secured funds to repay his debts. In my experience, this was often the situation of the "Chefes de Posto" (Indian agents) of the SPI, who were located far away from the bureaucratic centers without any supervision or support from the regional offices or from the headquarters. It is no wonder that many of them, forced to make a living in some way, resorted to exploitation of their Indian charges. Somehow the Tapirapé survived those crucial years. In 1953, I found only fifty-one individuals in New Village.

By that time the Tapirapé were without doubt in permanent contact with Brazilian society in terms of Ribeiro's categories. Brazilians had established themselves along the Tapirapé River, and by 1953 there were three cattle ranches at localities along the river where Indians had often come during the dry season to hunt and fish. The vast campos along the Tapirapé River which formerly teemed with game now provided grazing lands for cattle. In addition, although the Brazilian settlement of Furo de Pedra had actually declined in size, the little settlement (once but a few houses) called Santa Terezinha, which was only thirty kilometers from the SPI post, was now a small but thriving Brazilian settlement. It had an airport (landing strip is perhaps a better phrase) and a commercial airline landed there once each week. The Tapirapé were not visited daily by Brazilians, but hardly a week went by that visitors did not arrive or that a Tapirapé did not visit Santa Terezinha. By 1953 Tapirapé women wore skirts, mainly, I think, because of the gaping Brazilians at nude women. And the Tapirapé men were anxious to acquire men's undershorts to be used when visiting Santa Terezinha and to don when visitors arrived in their village.

Their survival as a distinct tribal group was still very precarious in

1953. They had reunited and they had weathered the dangerous years of heavy depopulation during intermittent contact, but they could have easily been swallowed up by the expanding frontier, as ranch hands or as miserable loafers in Santa Terezinha. In my opinion, it was the arrival of the Little Sisters of Jesus and of Padre François Jentel and their residence in New Village that saved the Tapirapé from total disorganization and, probably, extinction. Neither the missionary priest nor the Little Sisters did anything really heroic. The intervention of the Little Sisters in persuading the Tapirapé to give up their practice of infanticide was crucial, but both the padre and the nuns tried to intervene as little as possible in Tapirapé life. Nor did the missionaries have any power to prevent Brazilians from intruding upon the Indians. One of the nuns had some training as a nurse and offered some medical assistance, but her supply of drugs was meager and she was not aggressive in trying to attract Indian patients. Never did I hear these missionaries attempt religious proselytism. Following the ideology of Charles de Foucault, the founder of their order, they hope to influence "by living example," and not by persuasion. Thus, the Little Sisters built their house with some help from the Tapirapé and each year they cleared and planted their own gardens, again with occasional help from Indian friends. Each evening they held prayers in a small chapel within their house, and the Indians often watched out of sheer curiosity. Several times in the 1960's Padre François traveled to Brasília, where he lobbied with the SPI and with its successors, the FUNAI, for lands for the Tapirapé. And he extended his efforts beyond the village, helping the people of Santa Terezinha and vicinity to organize cooperatives. The Little Sisters and Padre François were able to persuade the Tapirapé to continue their subsistence activities; they sometimes supervised barter transactions with itinerant Brazilian traders who came to the village seeking animal skins and "Indian" artifacts; they urged the Tapirapé not to travel to "see the city"; and, above all, they gave them pride in their own customs and ceremonials. By 1957, the Tapirapé numbered 57; by 1965 there were 80; and, according to reports I received in 1976, there are now over 130 people in New Village.

Perhaps the Tapirapé were fortunate to escape the full "protection" of the SPI and also to have a friend, Valentim Gomes, as their protector. For in 1968 an enormous scandal broke in Brazil regarding the conduct of the SPI throughout the country. In March of that year General Alburquerque Lima, Minister of the Interior, announced to   289 the press that the "SPI had become an instrument of the Indian's oppression," and therefore he had to dissolve the Service. I have never been able to secure the full report that was issued at the time, but numerous newspaper articles made much of it known to the public. The SPI was accused of conniving with rich landowners and land companies located in Rio de Janeiro and São Paulo in the virtual extermination of many tribes. A judicial inquiry was initiated into the conduct of 134 SPI functionaries, and the head of the service, Major Luis Neves, was accused of 42 crimes, including collusion in several murders, the illegal sale of lands, and the embezzlement of $300,000. The Attorney General informed newspapermen that the documentary evidence collected during 58 days of visiting SPI posts all over the country amounted to 5115 pages. Evidently, the document contained accusations of pioneers and Indian service employees in league with corrupt politicians to usurp Indian lands, the destruction of whole tribes by issuing clothing impregnated with smallpox virus, the poisoning of food to be given to Indians, the bombing of an Indian village, the abduction of Indian children, and the teaching of sexual perversions to Indians (Lewis, 1974). It is amazing that the military government of Brazil would allow such a document to become public, and understandable why during my frequent visits to Brazil I have never been able to secure a copy.

In time, local interest in the SPI scandal cooled. I have no idea how many of the individuals named and indicted were ever convicted. But the report did alert the world to the tragedy of the Brazilian Indians. International humanitarian organizations sent commissions to investigate the plight of the remaining tribes. The international press continued to print articles, many of which were shrill, exaggerated, and even erroneous. Almost all of them lacked historical understanding—that is, that they were dealing with a process which had begun in 1500. The Brazilian government was accused of "genocide" and "ethnocide" and the whole scheme was viewed as an international conspiracy to rid the frontier of Brazil of its remaining inhabitants so that multinational corporations could more easily exploit mineral reserves, establish enormous ranches, and agribusiness enterprises.

Late in 1968, the Brazilian government created a new organization, FUNAI (National Indian Foundation), to replace the defunct SPI with more liberal funds and with statutes that endorsed the United Nations and the International Labor Organization statements as regards human and minority rights. The statutes of FUNAI promised respect for tribal institutions and communities; guarantee of permanent possession of lands which the Indian inhabit and the exclusive use of natural resources therein according to the Brazilian constitution; preservation of biological and cultural equilibrium of the Indian communities in contact with national society; and defense of the spontaneous acculturation of Indian communities, rather than their rapid and enforced acculturation.

But by 1974 FUNAI was already under attack. A group of Brazilian anthropologists presented a document to the XLI International Congress of Americanists, held in Mexico City, accusing FUNAI of deviating from its charter and giving in to the pressures of economic groups from the south of the country—large landowners and national and foreign corporations. That document quoted a decree signed by the president of FUNAI which read: "Assistance to the Indian will be as complete as possible, but cannot obstruct national development nor block the various axes of penetration into the Amazon region." The report then proceeded to detail instances where FUNAI seemed to have served economic interests rather than those of the Indians. In particular, it criticized FUNAI for condoning construction of a highway through the Xingú National Indian Park which would necessitate the moving of at least one Indian tribal group, and it condemned the policy of rapid integration which ignores the history of indigenous experience in Brazil. Most of the complaints in the document revolve around the question of Indian lands. About the Tapirapé the document has this to say:

The Tapirapé Indians live near the town of "Santa Teresita" [sic] along the Mato Grosso side of the Araguaia River. Protected over the last decade [sic] by a religious mission, their population nearly doubled, reaching 104 persons in 1972. The Tapirapé territory, however, was included in the immense landholdings bought by the Tapiraraguaia Colonization Company, a São Paulo real estate firm supported by incentives from SUDAM [a government organization for development of the Amazon]. Typically FUNAI did not come to the defense of the Indians but rather decided to relocate them to the Araguaia Park on the Island of Bananal.

This decision to move the Tapirapé village to Bananal island has been revoked by FUNAI. The question of the size of the Tapirapé reservation still is in doubt. The Tapiraraguaia Company has ceded some land to the Tapirapé and the Indian Foundation has promised to es-   *291* tablish a forest reserve contiguous to this land. The land ceded to the Tapirapé, however, seems to be mainly in campo cerrado and thus not arable in terms of their slash-and-burn system, which requires forest land. It is my understanding that their present gardens do not fall within this meager area.[125] The Tapirapé are still demanding that FUNAI enlarge and demarcate a larger reservation which would guarantee their future survival against the steady encroachment of the frontier.

In fact, the problem of land seems to be the most serious one faced by any tribal group that survives the first trauma of contact with civilization. It is the foremost problem faced by FUNAI in its efforts to be of assistance to the Brazilian Indians, especially those whose isolation has been broken and are now in intermittent or permanent contact with the national life of the country.

FUNAI has promised the creation of five indigenous parks similar to the Xingú National Park. It has plans for the Tumucumaque Park situated in the extreme north of the state of Pará, the Aripuana Park in the district of Rondônia and in the extreme west of Mato Grosso, the Araguaia Park on the island of Bananal, the Ianomani Park in the extreme north of Amazonas, and the Atalaia Park of the North in the west of Amazonas. As of 1975, however, these Indian parks (except for the Xingú Park) seemed but vague marks on maps rather than living realities. The so-called Araguaia Park is really misleading, because for years a large part of the Island of Bananal has been occupied by privately owned cattle ranches, and, if, indeed, the whole island were actually to be transformed into an Indian park, hundreds of Brazilian peasant settlers who live on the land as squatters would have to be removed. In addition, the Xingú National Park, where fifteen tribes now live, seems to be threatened by encroaching Brazilians. And the creation of any of these parks would probably mean the moving of numerous tribes from their traditional lands to new areas. It is doubtful whether the plans for these parks will be carried out any time in the near future. In the meanwhile, the President of Brazil has, by decree, granted reservations to several Indian groups on the recommendation of FUNAI.

---

125. Approximately 24,000 acres may seem like a large plot to the European or North American reader. It is, however, small for a system of swidden farming, or if compared with land concessions made in Amazonia such as 500,000 acres granted to Bruynzeel Corporation (Dutch lumber) and 1,250,000 acres to Georgia Pacific Company, to cite but two examples.

Land is the crucial problem on the Brazilian frontier, not only for the Indians but also for the Brazilian frontiersmen. The situation of the people who inhabit Santa Terezinha and its vicinity is a case in point. They too have a land problem, and it is as serious for them as it is for the Indians. In 1967, Santa Terezinha had a population of about a hundred and forty families, but perhaps three times that number live in the vicinity. These people are simple backwoodsmen and most of them are illiterate. They live by slash-and-burn farming, much as do the Tapirapé. The farmers of Santa Terezinha are squatters; none of them have titles or deeds for the land they use. However, since many of them have been living in the area for many years, they have acquired rights to the land by virtue of squatter's rights' provisions of the civil code.[126] Padre François Jentel, the missionary priest of the Tapirapé, was also the parish priest in Santa Terezinha, and every Sunday he came by outboard motorboat to perform mass. In addition to his religious duties, Padre François managed to found a school in Santa Terezinha and arrange for a trained nurse (a missionary) to provide some medical care for these settlers. He also directed the building of a road running inland from the river so that the farmers might transport their products to the village, and bought a jeep to provide transportation.

One of the padre's major efforts, however, was the founding of a farmers' cooperative among the people of Santa Terezinha. He organized meetings among the farmers to make them aware of advantages of forming a cooperative, to help raise as much of the initial necessary capital, and to set in motion all the official procedures to give their cooperative legal existence. The cooperative came into formal existence in May of 1962 with an original membership of 40 families, but it had grown to 92 families by 1967. Its aims were simply to buy and sell necessary goods such as coffee, sugar, macaroni, and kerosene to its members and to market their produce at the best prices that could

---

126. The civil code concerning squatters' rights is complex. In cases where the land had not been purchased by written deed, the land becomes the property of any individual who has cultivated it for twenty years. It is doubtful whether many of the farmers of Santa Terezinha could prove twenty years of continuous cultivation of any plot, since they move their garden sites frequently in keeping with the methods of slash-and-burn farming. Furthermore, the settlers along the Araguaia River move frequently, always seeking to better their condition. However, the civil code provides that, in case of eviction, the squatter is entitled to payment for any improvements made upon the land during his period of residence. All of them had built homes upon the land, and in a sense they had built Santa Terezinha, the small chapel, the school, and other public buildings.

be secured. The cooperative relieved many of the families of exploitation by itinerant or local merchants.

But the land on which Santa Terezinha was built is owned by the Araguaia Development Company (Companhia de Desenvolvimento do Araguaia). In 1960, a total of 1.2 million hectares (3 million acres) were sold by the state of Mato Grosso to a large investment firm based in São Paulo. This large area was sold without any investigation as to whether it might already be inhabited. It was then split up and bought by a series of other companies. The Araguaia Development Company is said to own 320,000 hectares (800,000 acres), including the land on which the little village of Santa Terezinha stands. It is the company's plan to turn the area over to cattle raising, and to that end they began to clear certain forested areas. Out of the total area it is estimated that the little farms of the Santa Terezinha settlers occupy a mere 1000 hectares. But the company claims ownership of these lands and of the village itself. One possible solution—to sell the 1000 hectares to the farmers' cooperative—was ignored by the company and the government. Unable to secure local labor to clear the land, the company imported laborers from the arid Northeast. There were strikes among the imported laborers because of their working conditions (they worked from 6 a.m. to 6 p.m. for a little over $1.00 per day, and had poor food and lodging). Even the settlers at Santa Terezinha, themselves extremely poor and accustomed to a difficult life, were moved by the spectacle of exhaustion and undernourishment among these peons.

The company claimed that the people of Santa Terezinha interfered with its work, and it tried to mobilize the imported laborers to force the people of Santa Terezinha off their lands. Padre François traveled to Brasília hoping to get aid from the federal government, not only to prevent the eviction of the people of Santa Terezinha, but also to maintain peace in the area. Incidents between company agents and local settlers became almost daily occurrences and the cooperative was a focus of irritation to the company. It was reported that twice the company actually destroyed the cooperative's headquarters with bulldozers. Finally, the government sent in troops to maintain order (Shapiro, n.d.).

The outcome was a sad one. Padre François Jentel was denounced to the Minister of the Interior, to the Minister of Justice, and to various state authorities as a "communist agitator." Despite the support of his bishop and other Catholic authorities, he was tried and sentenced to ten years in prison. He served part of this term in a prison in Mato Grosso, and it was not until 1974 that he was released and exiled from Brazil. By then his case had been widely reported by the press in the United States and in Europe.

Thus, the problem of land for the Indians differs little from the problem of land for the poor settlers along the Brazilian frontier. If anything, the Indians have some advantage. The Indians are charges of FUNAI; theoretically, lands on which Indians are settled, once they are registered by FUNAI as Indian lands, are legally inalienable except by consent of that organization. The Indian, unlike the illiterate backwoodsman, does not have to prove squatter's rights, and, in fact, FUNAI has the legal right to establish and hold rights over lands belonging to the Indians. The problem, however, is to demarcate the traditional lands of each tribe and to secure those lands against intruders. That is more easily said than done, for there are powerful forces in modern Brazil eager for land. Some land for the Tapirapé has been vaguely demarcated and mapped and it has been registered with FUNAI, I am told. But a huge land development company still lays claim to enormous tracts, just as it does to the lands of the poor settlers in Santa Terezinha.

Today, FUNAI, which has greater knowledge and skill than its predecessor SPI did, has formed pacification teams, and in the last few years they have pacified several newly discovered tribes. Fully aware of the dangers of pacification for such people, FUNAI has tried, with mixed success, to protect them from the contamination of new diseases. Of the 200 Arara Indians first contacted in 1972, for example, no more than 50 were alive in 1974, according to one report, and within six months after the first Parakanã Indians were pacified in 1970, 40 were reported to have died of influenza. FUNAI has a greater number of Indian agents than the SPI ever could support. Their salaries are better and they are paid on time (sometimes an airplane is dispatched to posts to meet paydays), they have better communications than in the past, and in the FUNAI headquarters are specialists trained in Indian affairs and fully cognizant of the history of Indian-Brazilian relations. But FUNAI is faced with the last great surge of expansion of the Brazilian frontier. It is also faced with the awful dilemma which faces anyone, idealist or cynic, who first pacifies a Brazilian tribe. Should one go through the slow process of locating a hostile or withdrawn tribe, patiently offering them presents and promises of peace with the white stranger, and finally draw them into relations with the outside world, when one knows that the fate which generally awaits such people is death from western disease or at least the loss of their traditional territory? Years ago I heard Curt Nimuendajú, the great expert on Brazilian Indians, curse himself for having so pacified the Parintinin tribe in Amazonia in 1922 (Ribeiro, 1970: 165-75): "It would have been better if I had encouraged them to resist and to have died fighting rather than to have died of disease and hunger." If those were not his exact words, it was certainly the way he reasoned almost twenty years after he had pacified them. And the famous Villas Boas brothers, Claudio and Orlando, who have appeared worldwide on television in the act of pacifying "new" tribes, are often plagued by the same question.

Neither FUNAI nor any other organization, even with the highest intentions, can ever really solve the problem of the initial period of contact with Indian tribal groups. They cannot completely isolate small tribal groups which have recently come into contact with Brazilians unless they construct large air-tight hospitals or some kind of air-tight reservations where these few Indians might be kept like animals in the zoo. Once Indians come into contact with outsiders they are as curious about these so-called civilized people as the Brazilians are about the strange Indians. The legendary and hostile Cranhacacore (Kreen-Akarore) tribe, which were first contacted by the Villas Boas brothers in February of 1973, is an example. Both brothers are said to have lamented their pacification efforts, for they knew well the fate that awaited the tribe. But the Cuiabá-Santarém highway, a segment of the new Amazonian highway system, was planned to pass within a few kilometers of Cranhacacore territory and cattle ranches were beginning to surround the tribe. At once, in March of the same year, the President of Brazil signed a decree establishing a Cranhacacore reservation (critics pointed out that it did not include their traditional domains). Throughout the year following their pacification, Cranhacacore Indians began to visit the highway, where Brazilian construction crews were at work. They were probably attracted by curiosity, and by the possibility of receiving gifts in exchange for bows and arrows and other artifacts. Wild accusations reached the Brazilian press that the fault was that of FUNAI and that the Indians were already addicted to alcohol and dying from disease. In 1974, the Cranhacacore were still reported to be dispersed along the highway, fraternizing with workmen and begging for food. FUNAI and the Villas Boas brothers hope that they will be persuaded to settle within the confines of the Xingú Park, which is near by, but more pessimistic observers predict that they will either disappear, be taken as workers to surrounding cattle ranches, or be forced to relocate into the confines of the Xingú National Park (Document Report in Supysana, 1974: 27).[127]

The Tapirapé have already weathered these early years of intermittent and sporadic contact with the Brazilian frontier. They are no longer filled with curiosity and awe of the Brazilians around them, and they have learned that the Brazilian frontiersmen often live in worse conditions than they do and are often less capable of coping with the natural environment. As of today, it would seem as if the Tapirapé have successfully survived and will continue to form an ethnic enclave within Brazilian society. Around 1947 the Tapirapé population reached a low point of forty-seven people, from which it seemed dubious whether they could recuperate. But now, with over one hundred and thirty people, the majority of whom are children or young adults, the trend is toward rapid population growth. If this population increase continues unchecked, the Tapirapé will more than double their number in another generation.

Their continued population growth as well as their persistence as a distinct ethnic group is, however, predicated upon certain conditions. First, FUNAI must not only secure for them a land grant or reservation large enough for them to make a living by slash-and-burn techniques,[128] but also see to it that land is secure against encroachment.

Second, the Tapirapé must continue their informal rule of tribal endogamy. As of now, only four or five young men have married Carajá wives, and thus, following the rule of matrilocal or uxorilocal residence, they have gone to live with their wife's family. If Tapirapé women should, by chance, form a stable union with Carajá men or even with Brazilians, their husbands would be forced by the same rule to live with the Tapirapé and their children would be raised as Tapirapé. If the rule of tribal endogamy and matrilocal residence were to be ignored, then the Tapirapé might well be assimilated into the surrounding Brazilian population.

Third, the Tapirapé must retain some elements of their native cul-

---

127. On January 22, 1975, a band of Cranhacacore were transferred to the Xingú National Park. (Personal communication from Dr. George Zarur and Dr. Roberto Baruzzi.)
128. It has now been shown that swidden, or slash-and-burn, agriculture provides a relatively efficient use of tropical soils.

ture to provide them with a sense of tribal identity *vis-à-vis* the national culture they face. Their native Tupian language, which they continue to speak, could easily provide this symbolic identity. It is hoped that they will maintain some of their ceremonial life and native custom to provide them with tribal identity. Other Brazilian tribes, such as the Fulnio of Pernambuco state, who are completely surrounded by a rather dense population of Brazilian peasants, have kept their identity, in spite of two hundred years of contact with rural Brazilian society, through the continuation of the *ourikuri* festival, a ceremony from which outsiders have always been excluded (Kietzman, 1972: 204ff.). The Maxakali tribe, who also have continued to maintain their tribal identity, live in a heavily populated region in the state of Minas Gerais, halfway between the large city of Salvador (Bahia) and the new capital at Brasília. The Maxakali not only have a relatively small reservation, but they continue to speak their native tongue and maintain a religious ceremony limited to tribal members (Kietzman, 1972: 246ff.). In fact, Kietzman maintains that "after four and a half centuries of unremitted pressures from advanced civilization, there are at least 130 tribal groups in Brazil with populations large enough to make survival a possibility. Some, in fact, are growing in size, and their indefinite continuation as distinct ethnic units appears a certainty" (1972: 1). The Tapirapé are one example of these surviving tribal groups.

There is no doubt that in the future, as the population along the frontier increases, Tapirapé individuals will leave the group to become incorporated in the surrounding society. It is also certain that the Tapirapé in their village will become acculturated in the direction of the demographically and politically dominant national society. They will imitate and borrow Brazilian culture and Brazilian artifacts and technology. A large number of Tapirapé will become bilingual (many men now speak very passable frontier Portuguese) and even literate in Portuguese. This is to be expected. But acculturation need not result in assimilation or total incorporation. Over the centuries ethnic groups have kept their separate identity within powerful nations even though they have come to live in most respects like the dominant culture that surrounds them. Brazil, a nation which prides itself on racial tolerance, can well afford to extend that same tolerance of cultural difference to those native societies which somehow have survived the ravages of the expansion of Brazilian civilization.

298   Modern Brazil has an obligation to provide lands for its remaining

aboriginal population and to provide the necessary protection for them until such time that they are full citizens of the nation and are able to protect themselves. One can sympathize with the national policy of Brazil to fully occupy its immense territory and incorporate its internal frontiers into the economic life of the country. On the other hand, one cannot be sympathetic to national development at the expense of native Brazilian tribesmen. Any country able to construct such a modern city as Brasília, and able to build a new system of highways, including the dramatic Trans-Amazonian system, can carry out a sensible plan for Indian parks and reservations and provide for adequate protection for tribal groups forced into contact with the modern world. The cost to Brazil in energy and financial outlay would be small in relation to other programs such as those mentioned above. Furthermore, the cost of a sound program to provide conditions for the survival of these Indian societies cannot be calculated in utilitarian terms (i.e. the number of people benefited per cruzeiro or per dollar), but only in humanitarian and moral terms.

At this point, I must confess that I feel most vulnerable and most uncomfortable in making such *pronunciamentos*. After all, I am a citizen of a great nation whose history is marked by unsavory policies and treatment of its own Indians. Nor can I say that the United States has even today solved its own "Indian problems," as the violent events at Wounded Knee, South Dakota, on the Oglala Sioux Reservation in 1973 attest.[129] Nor can I avoid criticism by claiming that I express the so-called objective point of view of anthropology. Anthropology, as a science and as a profession, has been under fire in recent years from critics (often Indians, and often anthropologists themselves). Such critics have accused anthropologists of being agents of colonialism. It has been pointed out, and not entirely without some justification, that anthropological studies have often been used to control native groups rather than to improve their condition. Furthermore, I would be the first to admit that anthropologists who have attempted to intervene in policy or action programs aimed at improving the lot of the people they have studied seldom have been successful.[130] Anthropolo-

---

129. In response to an interview which I gave to *Veja* (Mar. 10, 1976), a widely read Brazilian weekly periodical, concerning the development of the Amazon region and Indian policy, a letter to the editor suggested that I "go home and tend to my own Indians."

130. This statement will certainly be contested by colleagues who are more impressed than I have been with such programs as the Vicos project, carried out in Peru by Cornell University, which has been an important influence on the direction of highland Indian policy in recent years. (*Cf.* Holmberg, 1960; Dobyns and Doughty, 1971.)

gists have been able to explain in retrospect why and how such people have suffered or have been exploited. On occasion, they (or individuals and groups influenced by them) have been able to alleviate conditions of so-called primitive peoples and to interrupt the course of a dreadful process which would have led to extinction. Such is the case, for example, of the lifetime work of Claudio and Orlando Villas Boas, who were able to negotiate the creation and administration of the Xingú National Park in central Brazil, where a dozen or more small tribes have found it possible to survive. Neither of these men would say that they are professional anthropologists; indeed, they have called upon many anthropologists for advice. Yet most programs to protect, to integrate, or to incorporate small primitive enclaves into our complex, modern societies have been at best palliatives and at worst outright failures, for the forces of the modern technological and industrial world are powerful.

Yet anthropologists do have something to say, and they have an obligation to make themselves heard in regard to the plight of the pre-literate peoples they have studied. After all, it is the anthropologist who has made himself a repository of the history and the way of life of a tribal group or a community and who is able to communicate with the institutions, the governments, and the people who have the power to establish policy and instigate action. This is particularly true during the first crucial years of contact with the civilized world. One of my principal reasons for writing this book is to make known the complexities of the culture and society and the problems of one small Brazilian tribe with the hope that such information will be heard by those responsible for Indian policy and by the public in general. The Tapirapé are but one example out of many; numerous other tribal groups in the Amazon Valley in Brazil, Peru, Bolivia, Ecuador, Colombia, and Venezuela share their problems and have a way of life as distinct as that of the Tapirapé from the national society to which they must now accommodate themselves. To a large extent, the difficulty in contact between such societies and their own complex civilization derives from us, not from them. This is best expressed in a statement attributed to Orlando and Claudio Villas Boas:

> In our modest opinion, the true defense of the Indian is to respect him and to guarantee his existence according to his own values. Until we, the "civilized" ones, create the proper conditions among ourselves for the future integration of the Indians, any attempt to integrate them is the same as introducing a plan for their destruction. We are

not yet sufficiently prepared. (Quoted in *Supysaua*, p. 41; italics in original.)

It is the obligation of the anthropologist to attempt to educate the "civilized ones."

As an anthropologist, I feel called upon to warn of the dangers of two points of view too often implicit in our policies and programs toward primitive societies. The first of these is a "Social Darwinism" view of primitive societies. According to that point of view, the Tapi-rapé, and many tribes similar to them which have been reduced in numbers or have entirely disappeared during the last four and a half centuries since the Europeans arrived, could be considered as "dead ends" in the whole process of cultural evolution. It is reasoned that, when viewed from the long range of cultural evolution, these small groups did not contribute to the mainstream of the evolutionary process which led men from simple hunting and gathering bands of the Paleolithic to the settled villages of the Neolithic and finally to cities and the formation of nations. It is also argued that such small tribes were too highly specialized and maladaptive in evolutionary terms. They were vulnerable, not only biologically, but also socially and culturally, to the change in the total environment brought about by the presence of the European. Such an explanation has helped salve the guilt of "civilized" men who, through armed warfare, transfer of disease, forced labor, and other gifts of progress have brought about their destruction. Such a point of view has been and still is being used by those who state that such small groups cannot be allowed to stand in the way of "progress" and economic development.[131]

The second dangerous view might be called the romantic, or "natural man," concept of such primitive groups. This point of view may not be so vicious in its immediate implications as Social Darwinism, but it is wrongheaded, and ultimately leads to bad policy. Ever since the sixteenth century, the Brazilian Indians have been pictured as "natural men," innocent and without vices. Because they were nude and lived in a colorful "tropical paradise," they caught the European

---

131. This point of view was expressed in Desmond Morris's widely read, popular book, *The Naked Ape* (Dell edition, New York, 1969). He characterizes such so-called primitive societies as "remote cultural backwaters so atypical and unsuccessful that they are nearly extinct." And his old-fashioned Social Darwinism is clear when he states that "The simple tribal groups that are living today are not primitive, they are stultified." Furthermore, he says, "any society that has failed to advance has in some sense failed, 'gone wrong.' " (Pp. 9-10.)

imagination. Despite the indisputable fact that the Indians were cannibals, seventeenth-century chroniclers such as Claude d'Abbeville and Jean de Léry painted an idyllic picture of the Tupinambá character and way of life. Many Tupinambá of the Brazilian coast were transported to Europe for display in various courts, and in 1550 there was a famous re-creation of a Tupinambá village in Rouen, France, in which at least 50 Tupinambá (and over 200 "false" Indians, who were said to have been sailors from Brittany and Normandy) were paraded nude to imitate village life as it was said to be in Brazil. And Montaigne, in his famous essay *On Cannibals*, based much of his material on data obtained from reading earlier chronicles on Brazil and from his interviews with three Tupinambá in 1562. Much later, in the eighteenth century, Jean Jacques Rousseau derived much of his concept of "natural man," uncontaminated by civilization, from accounts of Brazilian Indians (see Mello Franco, 1937). Even today, Brazilians in the large cities of the coast, Europeans, and North Americans retain this romantic view of the Indian as a simple and pure "natural man." Such groups as the Tapirapé are apt to be viewed as man in his pristine state—well-adapted and especially sensitive to the natural world around them. Such a view, I hope, will be dispelled by this book; for it is, of course, unrealistic and romantic.

Such a view leads to thinking of primitive people as children. It also results in the collecting of so-called primitive art, a harmless pleasure which even provides tribes such as the Tapirapé with some income. But more important, it leads to government policies which make such people legal minors and charges of the state. It also justifies paternalistic policies established by those who are alien to native customs and values, without allowing the peoples themselves any voice in determining their future. It can lead to government policies which isolate such people on reservations, almost as endangered species, or living fossils. The Tapirapé whom I have known and who are depicted in this book are not "natural men." They have human vices just as we do, although their vices may not be our vices. Some of them are intelligent, some ambitious, some conniving, some honest, and some humble—just as people are in any human society. They do not live "in tune" with nature any more than I do; in fact, they can often be as destructive of their environment, within their limitations, as some civilized men. The Tapirapé are not innocent or childlike in any way. At present they may not be fully aware of the economic and political

302

complexities of modern Brazilian society, but in time they will learn to make decisions for themselves—if they are allowed to do so.

Brazilians must learn that "incorporation," a word used frequently by FUNAI and other institutions of Brazil in reference to the future of Brazilian Indians, does not mean total acculturation to national culture or assimilation into national society. It can mean, as one Brazilian anthropologist defines the term, the "effective participation of the tribal group within national society, with the adoption of some customs and technological practices but without losing those aspects of their own culture which they consider important, and without losing their ethnic identity. That is, even as the group considers itself a part of national society, they continue to consider themselves as Indians. . . ." (Laraia, 1976: 13). However, that same anthropologist calls the possibility of the Brazilian Indians achieving "integration in these terms as 'utopian.' " He doubts whether FUNAI will receive from the government

the necessary force which will impede the large financial groups, the gigantic agricultural and cattle ranching firms from continuing their dispute with the Indians, in an unequal battle, over the possession of lands which in accordance with the Constitution belong to them. If this is not the case, the ideal of integration so many times formulated by Marshal Rondon will continue to be a utopia. (Laraia, 1976: 13; translation mine.)

Yet the Brazilian government guaranteed these policies by signing the statement known as the Declaration of Brasília at the Seventh Inter-American Indigenous Congress held in Brasília in 1972. The Declaration recognized that in the process of integration proper respect will be shown for the Indian and his tribal institutions, that the ethnic identity of each group shall be respected, and that each group shall have inalienable rights to its territory.

But we are all aware of the difference between the best intentions and the realities of modern political and economic systems. The Brazilian Indian problem is basically a political problem. The future of the remaining Indian tribes depends upon political decisions and political support above and beyond the efforts of anthropologists, Indian officers, or idealistic "indigenistas." Given the enormous problems which Brazil as a nation faces today, among them illiteracy, transportation, sources of energy, the sprawl of great cities, the production of basic foodstuffs, and the unequal distribution of income between the poverty-stricken and the middle and upper classes, it is doubtful whether the Brazilian government will give the Indian cause the support that it deserves. I shall never forget being chided by an idealistic Brazilian educator and leader about my concern for the Brazilian Indian: "How can you spend your time worrying about less than a hundred thousand people, when before your eyes over fifty million Brazilians are illiterate and hungry?" He was, of course, partially correct, for the rural Brazilian caboclo and the urban masses suffer duress similar to that of the enclaves of Indians. Yet as "civilized" men and women, we cannot ignore the plight of the many simple societies which have somehow survived into the modern world. Such small societies as the Tapirapé and other Brazilian tribes caught up in the process of an increasingly changing world are especially vulnerable. They lack the skills, and often lack the biological immunity, to cope with the situations with which they are confronted and which at first they cannot understand. As human beings trapped in such circumstances, they deserve special consideration and the aid of other human beings better equipped to comprehend the complexities of the modern world. The loss of these myriad of small societies would rob the world of a wide range of human cultures. Each human culture, in its own way, has a view of the world in its own terms and each has much to offer. And each of these small societies represents a solution by an organized human society and culture to the fundamental problems of man—human reproduction, understanding the real and imaginary forces of the universe, and achieving some measure of human well-being. Each of these small societies is composed of that unique animal, *Homo sapiens*, who speaks and uses symbolic thought and who speculates about the past, the present, and the future. The disappearance of societies such as that described in this book would be an irreplaceable loss to the world. Their survival depends upon decisions by "civilized" men and the urgent actions of the nation states which have engulfed them.

Glossary

agouti: (Eng.) (S. *Dasyprocta aguti*) a small rodent about the size of a rabbit. In Port. *cutia*

aiuma anchunga: (Tapirapé) water spirits without eyes who dance around a pot of boiling water

aiwiró anchunga: (Tapirapé) the spirits that come to live in the dance house after Thunder has gone

aiwo anchunga: (Tapirapé) spirits stolen from the Kayapó; also, a masked dancer

alqueire: (Port.) land measure; about 24,000 square meters in São Paulo

ampí: (Tapirapé) vocative term for mother and for mother's sister: man and woman speaking

Ampirampé: (Tapirapé) one of the Feast Groups: "those of the first people"

ampukáya anchunga: (Tapirapé) crying spirits; also the masked dancers who represent these spirits

amuchino: (Tapirapé) a mass rape (lit. "together to eat")

amumaia: (Tapirapé) an unidentified herb

anachowa: (Tapirapé) a mythological giant red parrot

anajá: (Port.) (*Maximiliana regia*) a palm with edible fruit which also provides fiber for the manufacture of baskets and mats

Ananchá: (Tapirapé) a Bird Society in the "Parrot" moiety for mature men of 16-35 years

anawe: (Tapirapé) (*Blatella germanica*) cockroaches

Ancheriko: (Tapirapé) the sun

anchirikakantu: (Tapirapé) "a beautiful child," that is, a child given special treatment during its early years

anchiwawa: (Tapirapé) a special friend; a system of formalized friendship

Anchopeterí: (Tapirapé) a legendary culture hero who married the moon, brought firewood and tobacco to the Tapirapé, and was the discoverer of the Bird Societies

anchunga: (Tapirapé) the generic term for shadows; souls; spirits of game animals and fish; also the masked dancers representing those spirits who visit the takana. See also *aiuma, aiwiro, aiwo, ampukáya, anapí, irancha, iranchaho, iranwuré, iriwe, jakaconya, manupi, anka, tachaho, tampanchi*

anchunga anapí: (Tapirapé) spirits with huge penes

ankantaum: (Tapirapé) stingy; an important Tapirapé negative value

ankungitána: (Tapirapé) large headdress made of the tail feathers of the red macaw and worn during the Thunder ceremonial

annato: (Eng.) (*Bixa orellana*) a bush from whose pod-like fruit is extracted a red dye. In Tapirapé *uruku*

anteater: (Eng.) (*Myrmecophaga jubata*). In Port. *tamanduá*

apachirú: (Tapirapé) a Tapirapé communal work party

Apuwenonu: (Tapirapé) a legendary culture hero who brought cultivated plants to the Tapirapé

anta-uwa: (Tapirapé) a leader of a Bird Society

Arara: (Port.) an Indian tribe first contacted in 1872 (lit. macaw)

awachewete: (Tapirapé) the mature male age period

Awaikú: (Tapirapé) one of the Feast Groups ("those of the sweet manioc people")

awampena: (Tapirapé) spirit messengers

awauahu: (Tapirapé) age period of a young boy about to undergo initiation, or "coming of age"

bacaba: (Port.) (*Oenocarpus bacaba*) a palm with edible nuts

bandeirante: (Port.) an explorer; early explorers in Brazil

beiju: (Port.) a pancake made of manioc dough; a flat cake of two feet in diameter, which is the basic bread of the Indians of the upper Xingú River

boto: (Port.) (*Inia geoffroyensis*) the freshwater dolphin

buriti: (Port.) (*Mauritia*, sp.) a type of palm used extensively by the Tapirapé

caboclo: (Port.) a term widely used for anyone of lower social status living in the Brazilian interior, regardless of racial appearance

cachaça: (Port.) raw sugar rum

caititú: (Port.) (*Pecari tajacu*) a type of wild pig which runs in pairs or in small bands. In Eng. the white-collared peccary

caja: (Port.) (*Spondrias lutea*) a yellow plum-like wild fruit which ripens during the dry season

campo cerrado: (Port.) a type of savanna characterized by a mixture of tall grasses and clumps of low contorted trees and palms

campo limpo: (Port.) a type of savanna characterized by low bunch grasses

capitão: (Port.) captain. A word used by the Tapirapé for men of prestige

capitão monika: (Tapirapé) singing captain, combining a Portuguese word with a Tapirapé word; a leader of a men's moiety

capivara: (Port.) (*Hydrochoerus capybara*) the largest living rodent, weighing about 100 pounds. In Eng. *capybara*

capuchin monkey: (Eng.) (*Cebus capucinus*)

cara grande: (Port.) word used for Tapirapé wooden masks

Carajá: (Port.) Indians on the Araguaia River, east of Tapirapé territory; traditional enemies of the Tapirapé

chanche: (Tapirapé) my father's sister: man or woman speaking

champií: (Tapirapé) a type of hawk

champoó: (Tapirapé) (*Ostinops, sp.*) a big bird. In Port. *japu*

Chanetawa: (Tapirapé) one of the Feast Groups: "our village people"

Chankanepera: (Tapirapé) one of the Feast Groups: "those of the alligator people"; also, the name of the ancestor of the group

chanuya: (Tapirapé) my grandmother: man or woman speaking

charanúra: (Tapirapé) my son and my male cousin's son; man speaking

chawana: (Tapirapé) jaguar; the name of one style of body painting

chawanamu: (Tapirapé) long song sang by men

chekochamemura: (Tapirapé) my sister's daughter and my female cousin's daughter: man speaking

chekupu ura: (Tapirapé) my younger sister and younger female cousin: woman speaking

chekuwura: (Tapirapé) my brother or male cousin: woman speaking

chememura: (Tapirapé) my son and sister's son: woman speaking

chepena: (Tapirapé) my brother's son and daughter: woman speaking

cheramuya: (Tapirapé) my grandfather: man or woman speaking

cheranchura: (Tapirapé) my daughter and my male cousin's daughter: man speaking

cheranura: (Tapirapé) my sister and my female cousin: man speaking

cherekawiana: (Tapirapé) my sister's son and my female cousin's son: man speaking

cheremamino: (Tapirapé) my grandchild: man speaking

cheremianiro: (Tapirapé) my grandchild: woman speaking

cherikera: (Tapirapé) my older sister and older female cousin: woman speaking

cherike ura: (Tapirapé) vocative term for older brother and older male cousin: man speaking

cherikeurangi: (Tapirapé) older brother and older male cousins: man speaking

cheriwura: (Tapirapé) vocative term for younger brother and younger male cousin: man speaking

cheriwurangi: (Tapirapé) my younger brother and my younger male cousin: man speaking

cheropu: (Tapirapé) my father: man or woman speaking

cheropuí: (Tapirapé) my father's brother: woman speaking

cherowurani: (Tapirapé) my father's brother: man speaking

chetotura: (Tapirapé) vocative term for mother's brother: man or woman speaking

chetoturangi: (Tapirapé) my mother's brother: man speaking

cheu: (Tapirapé) my mother: man or woman speaking

cheu ura: (Tapirapé) my mother's sister: woman speaking

cheu urani: (Tapirapé) my mother's sister: man speaking

chipampu: (Tapirapé) wrist ornaments

chirankonya-chiwawa: (Tapirapé) penis band

churangí: (Tapirapé) the young adolescent boys' age period

chureni: (Tapirapé) an ancestral spirit connected to the electric eel. His spirit, in the form of two masked dancers, appears in the takana each year

coati: (Eng.) (*Nasua*, sp.) an animal related to the raccoon, but with a longer body and tail and a long flexible snout. In Port. *quati*

dog fish: (Eng.) (*Cynodon vulpinus*) a specie of fish with long sharp teeth. In Port. *peixe-cachorro*

eanwurup: (Tapirapé) epilepsy

é é chu: (Tarirapé) the Pleiades

embira: (Port.) (*Daphnopsis*) any of the various trees which yield a bast fiber (also called *embira*) used for cordage

été: (Tapirapé) "the body"

galeria (Port.) a narrow strip of forest found along the course of a river

garças: (Port. pl.) a generic term for a variety of herons and egrets

gato-do-mato: (Port.) (*Felis tigrina*) the margay or spotted cat

Gê: a language family spoken by numerous tribes of Northeastern and Central Brazil

genipap: (Eng.) (*Genipa americana*) a tree with a small, edible fruit from which a black dye is made; In Port. *genipapo*

Gorotire: a Gê-speaking branch of the Kayapó who attacked Tampiitawa in late 1947

Guaraní: people speaking the Tupí-Guaraní language family in southern Brazil and Paraguay

guariba: (Port.) (*Alouatta*) a howling monkey

ipion: (Tapirapé) the color blue or black

ipira kunya: (Tapirapé) fishbone extracted by a shaman from an ill person

irancha anchunga: (Tapirapé) the spirit of a fish; also the masked dancers who represent the spirits

iranwuré anchunga: (Tapirapé) a wild pig spirit; also the masked dancers who represent the spirits

iriwe anchunga: (Tapirapé) electric eel spirits; also the masked dancers who represent the spirits

Iriwehe: (Tapirapé) the Javahé branch of the Carajá

iunga: (Tapirapé) generic term for his or their soul or spirit

Iungwera: (Tapirapé) place of spirits

iwuterahu: (Tapirapé) angry, sad; the Tapirapé experience these feelings after the death of a relative

jaburus: (Port.) pl. (*Jabiru mycteria*) jabiru storks; giant water birds

jabuti: (Port.) (*Testudo tabulata*) fruit-eating land turtle

jacamim: (Port.) (*Psophia crepitans*) the agami or trumpeter and other birds with long necks which are easily domesticated

jacaré: (Port.) (*Caiman*, sp.) alligator or cayman

jacu: (Port.) (*Penelope*, sp.) any guan; a fowl almost as large as a chicken which lives high in branches of the tropical forest *jaguar:* (Eng.) (*Felis onca*) the largest of the Amazon wildcats, equivalent to the panther or cougar. In Port. also called *onça-pintada*

jakaconya anchunga: (Tapirapé) masked dancers with enormous penes, said to be related to the spirit of the howler monkey

jakui: (Tapirapé) the spirit of the *jacu* fowl

Javahé: (Port.) a branch of the Carajá tribe

kaí: (Tapirapé) (*Cebus capucinus*) the capuchin monkey

Kaingang: (Port.) an Indian tribe of south Brazil

Kanawana: (Tapirapé) Thunder; a powerful supernatural

kaó: "Big Garden," planted in the dry season; a songfest and festival

kara: (Tapirapé) (*Dioscorea*, sp.) the name of several varieties of tubers, similar to yams. In Port. *cará*

Karajuntu wera: (Tapirapé) ancient, pre-Tapirapé people, in their mythology

Karanchahó: (Tapirapé) large Carajá

kawa: (Tapirapé) wasp with edible larva

Kawano: (Tapirapé) one of the Feast Groups: "those of the wasp people"

kawi: (Tapirapé) a liquid drink made from peanuts, manioc, tapioca, or maize; a soup-like beverage

kawió: (Tapirapé) ceremonies; literally, "big soup" ceremonial; also, a nauseous beverage

Kayapó: (Port.) Indians north of the Tapirapé divided into various bands such as Gorotire, Xikrin, and others

kocha: (Tapirapé) vocative term for sister and female cousin: man speaking

konomí: (Tapirapé) the small-boy age period

konomi-wera: (Tapirapé) a boy's name

kopia chawana: (Tapirapé) the "Jaguar of the Skies"; a figure seen in the Milky Way

kotantaní: (Tapirapé) the small-girl age period

kucha moko: (Tapirapé) the adolescent-girl age period

kuchan: (Tapirapé) the mature-woman age period

Kuchananché: (Tapirapé) women shamans, from *kuchan*, "woman," and *panché*, "shaman"

kuchanwete: (Tapirapé) the somewhat-older-woman age period

kururu: (Tapirapé) (*Bufo*, sp.) a large toad. In Port. *cururú*

kwanchiana: (Tapirapé) a geometric pattern of body painting; it is also incised upon gourds

macaw: (Eng.) (*Ara*, sp.) the largest South American parrot. There are two varieties, one red, the other blue. The former is much sought after for its tail feathers by the Tapirapé

maguari: (Port.) (*Euxenura moguari*) the American stork; a large fish-eating water bird related to the *jaburu*

mamupi ank anchunga: (Tapirapé) spirits who killed the Tapirapé and drank their blood

mandiaga: (Tapirapé) (*Manihot utilissima*) a variety of manioc

mandiagete: (Tapirapé) large manioc

mandiakaw: (Tapirapé) manioc used for *kawi* beverage

mandiunchinga: (Tapirapé) a white manioc

manioc: (Eng.) (*Manihot*, sp.) several varieties of edible tuber, also called cassava and yucca

Maniutawera: (Tapirapé) one of the Feast Groups: "those of the manioc people"

Maratawa: (Tapirapé) the village, far to the west, of the panchés (or shamans) after death and of the ancestral culture heroes. Also called *panché iungwera*

marikeura: (Tapirapé) the old-man age period

maxixe: (Port.) (*Cucumis anguria*) a vegetable-fruit similar to a small cucumber, but with a spiny skin

monikahuya: (Tapirapé) songs with a quick rhythm

monikanchi: (Tapirapé) a dance

motorista: (Port.) a driver—e.g. of a truck or tractor

Mukwura: (Tapirapé) ancestral culture hero who gave the bow and arrow to the Tapirapé and the gun to the Europeans

município: (Port.) "county"-like subdivision of a Brazilian state

munpí anká: (Tapirapé) a breed of forest spirits, or *anchunga*

mutum: (Port.) (*Crax*, sp.) a curassow, a forest bird about the size of a small turkey

nameí: (Tapirapé) the male-infant age period

Omagua: (Port.) a Tupí-speaking tribe in the upper Amazon River

ó ochinga: (Tapirapé) savanna deer

oreya: (Tapirapé) forest spirits with long hair wound in a mass on top of their heads

ourikuri: (Port.) a festival celebrated by the Fulnio Indians of Pernambuco state. From ouricuri palm (*urycury palm*)

paca: (Port.) (*Agouti paca*) the spotted cavy, much appreciated for its meat

Pananiwana: (Tapirapé) one of the Feast Groups: "Those of the river people"

panché: (Tapirapé) a shaman. This word is obviously related to the Portuguese term *pagé*, which is of Tupi origin

panché-iúnwera: (Tapirapé) the souls of deceased Tapirapé shamans

Paressí: (Port.) an Indian tribe of Southern Mato Grosso; traditional enemies of the Nambikuara

pehura: (Tapirapé) a palm basket to carry loads, supported by arm straps and a band across the forehead

pensão: (Port.) boardinghouse

peropí awa: (Tapirapé) forest demons who can send fevers to the Tapirapé

Petura: (Tapirapé) a legendary hero who brought many cultural gifts to the Tapirapé and transformed the world

piau: (Port.) (*Leporinus*, sp.) a small spotted fish; also known as *piaba* and *lambarí* in Portuguese

pequi: (Port.) (*Caryocar villosum*) a wild fruit from the souari nut tree, which grows on the savanna

piranha: (Port. and Eng.) (*Serrasalmo*, sp.) a carnivorous fish

310 *pirarara:* (Port.) (*Phratocephalus hemiliopterns*) a large freshwater fish

pirarucú: (Port.) (*Arapaima gigas*) one of the largest freshwater fish, often weighing 200 pounds or more

posseiros: (Port.) a Brazilian term for squatters, meaning "people who occupy the land"

quati: (Port.) (*Nasua narica*) brown coati; also, the ring-tailed coati (*Nasua rufa*)

queixada: (Port.) (*Tayassus pecari*) the white-lipped peccary; they rove in large bands. In Tapirapé *Tachaho*

rapadura: (Port.) brown sugar in blocks

regatões: (Port.) pl. sing. *Regatão;* Brazilian ambulatory traders

rhea Americana: (Eng.) The three-toed American ostrich

saudade: (Port.) a longing, yearning feeling

socó: (Port.) (*Butorides*, sp.) any of various herons and bitterns

squash: (Eng.) (*Curbita*, sp.) any fruits of a plant or vine of the gourd family

sweet potato: (Eng.) (*Ipomoema batatas*) a native American plant which has large, thick, mealy, tuberous roots

tachaho anchunga: (Tapirapé) wild pigs' spirits

taipa: (Port.) wattle and daub, used in house construction

takana: (Tapirapé) the men's house

tampanchi: (Tapirapé) wild pigs' spirits; also the masked dancers representing these spirits

Tamparawa: (Tapirapé) the moon

tamungó: (Tapirapé) (*Polyborus plancus brasilliensis*) a type of hawk

Tanawe: (Tapirapé) a Bird Society in the "Parrot" moiety for older men of 35-55 years

tantaní: (Tapirapé) the female-infant age period

Tantanopao: (Tapirapé) Feast Groups; from *tantan,* "fire" and *opao* "to eat around"; lit. "the place of the fire"

tapir: (Eng.) (*Tapirus terrestris*) one of the largest mammals of South America, weighing up to 400 pounds. It lives in forests near lakes and rivers. In Tapirapé *tampi*

taquara: (Port.) (*Bambusa*, sp.) a bamboo type of plant used with *buriti* palm in the making of sieves to remove manioc fiber

tartaruga: (Port.) (*Podocmenis expansa*) a large river turtle

tawa: (Tapirapé) village

Tawaupera: (Tapirapé) one of the Feast Groups: "those of the village people"

timbó: (Port.) (*Paullinia pinnata*) an Amazon woody vine; its bitter bark contains a fish poison

Tomatochiri: (Tapirapé) ancestral hero who is twin son of Mukwura and brother to Mukwura-ura

topu: (Tapirapé) small anthropomorphic beings, creatures of Thunder

tori: (Tapirapé) term used both by Carajá and Tapirapé for non-Indians

tracajá: (Port.) (*Podocnemis*, sp.) any small dark freshwater semi-aquatic turtle with a reddish head

tucum: (Port.) the fiber of the *Tucumã* palm; it is used for ropes

tucumã: (Port.) (*Astrocaryum tucuma*) the tucuma palm, which has long thorns used to grate manioc. It also produces nuts, the oil of which is used for personal decoration

tucunaré: (Port.) (*Cichla ocellaris*) a large trout-like fish weighing from 5 to 10 pounds

tuhawa: (Tapirapé) friend

Tupã: (Port.) supernatural being who caused thunder and lightning; word used by early missionaries for God

Tupí: (Port.) in Brazil, the name for the Tupí-Guaraní language family

Tupí-Guaraní: (Port.) a language family

Tupinambá: (Port.) a generic name for Tupí-speaking peoples who lived along the Brazilian coast in 1500

ubá: (Port.) a primitive dugout canoe

umbaúba: (Port.) (*Cecropia palmata*) a silver leaf pumpwood or trumpet tree; its light wood is easy to carve

upé: (Tapirapé) wooden masks representing the spirits of enemies killed in battle; also called *upé tawa*

upuhawáwa: (Tapirapé) body design made with genipap in horizontal lines resembling a fish

uuáka or *áwai:* (Tapirapé) gnawing worms thrown by a shaman at his victims

urucu: (Port.) (*Bixa orellana*) the fruit of the annatto tree; also the red dye extracted from the seeds. In Tapirapé *uruku*

urupema: (Tapirapé) in the Tapirapé universe, a world above; (lit. a sieve)

uwu chinga: (Tapirapé) a white clay

uwurantana: (Tapirapé) an insect, "that which lives in the wood"

waikura: (Tapirapé) (*Manihot dulcis*) a variety of manioc

waikurona: (Tapirapé) black sweet manioc

waikurão: (Tapirapé) large wet manioc

waiwí: (Tapirapé) the old-woman age period

Waré (Tapirapé) a great shaman or *panché* who lived in the distant past. He killed many spirits

wetepe: (Tapirapé) "many," any number over 20

Wuran: (Tapirapé) "birds"; men's Bird Societies. See also *Tanawe, Ananchá, Wurankura, Wuranchingó, Wuranchingió, Wuranchinga*

wuran champokaiya: (Tapirapé) "the birds which cry," chickens

Wuranchinga: (Tapirapé) a Bird Society in the "White Bird" moiety for youths of 10-16 years

Wuranchingió: (Tapirapé) a Bird Society in the "White Bird" moiety for mature men of 16 -35 years

Wuranchingó: (Tapirapé) a Bird Society in the "White Bird" moiety for older men of 35-55 years

wurankane: (Tapirapé) the kingfisher bird; the name of a style of body painting with genipap dye

Wurankura: (Tapirapé) a Bird Society in the "Parrot" moiety for youths of 10-16 years

yams: (Eng.) (*Dioscorea*, sp.). In Port. *Inhame*

Appendix I:
Kinship Charts

The kinship terms used in these charts are transcribed using the simplified orthography described in the Preface. Anyone desiring a more precise transcription is referred to the charts with terms published by Judith Shapiro (1978a), Wagley and Galvão (1947), and Baldus (1970: 308). Shapiro, however, warns that Wagley and Galvão (1947) do not consistently separate referential forms from terms of address. I have tried to correct this error in the following list of kinship terms. Following the system used by Shapiro, the terms which appear in parentheses are terms of reference only. It should be noted that in same cases alternate terms of address exist and often the term of address is the same as that of reference. The prefix "che-" which appears before most terms denotes the first person singular possessive "my."

TAPIRAPÉ KINSHIP

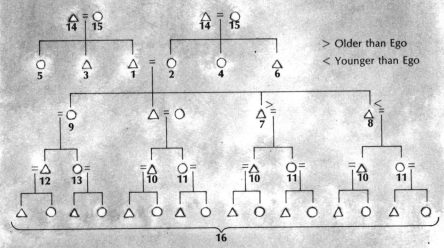

> Older than Ego
< Younger than Ego

CONSANGUINAL TERMS, MALE SPEAKERS:

1 cheropu
2 ampí (cheu)
3 cherowurani (cherowura)
4 cheu urani, ampí (cheu ura)
5 chanche
6 chetoturangi (chetotura)

7 cherikeurangi (cherike ura)
8 cheriwurangi (cheriwura)
9 cheranura, kocha
10 charanúra
11 cheranchura

12 cherekawiana
13 chekochamemura
14 cheramuya
15 chanuya
16 cheremamino

note: sibling terms are extended to all cousins, both cross and parallel, with distinction made by males for older and younger "brother."

TAPIRAPÉ KINSHIP

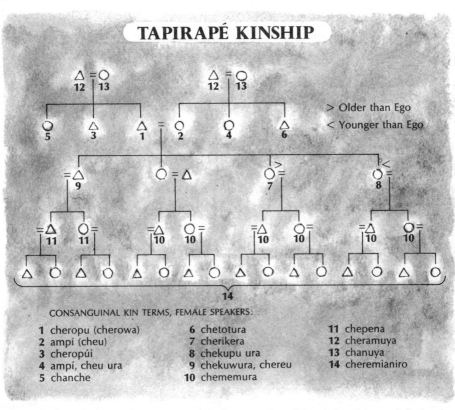

> Older than Ego
< Younger than Ego

CONSANGUINAL KIN TERMS, FEMALE SPEAKERS:

1 cheropu (cherowa)
2 ampí (cheu)
3 cheropúi
4 ampí, cheu ura
5 chanche
6 chetotura
7 cherikera
8 chekupu ura
9 chekuwura, chereu
10 chememura
11 chepena
12 cheramuya
13 chanuya
14 cheremianiro

note: sibling terms are extended to all cousins, both cross and parallel, with distinction made by females for older and younger "sister."

References Cited

Abbeville, Claude d'
  1614 *História da Missão dos Padres Capuchinhos na Ilha do Maranhão,*
        trans. Sergio Millet. São Paulo: Livraria Martins Editora (n.d.;
        originally published 1614).

Baldus, Herbert
  1937 *Ensaios de Etnologia Brasileira.* São Paulo: Companhia Editora
        Nacional, Série Brasiliana, No. 101.
  1948 "Tribos da Bacia do Araguaia e o Serviço de Proteção aos Indios,"
        Revista do Museu Paulista, vol. II. São Paulo.
  1970 *Tapirapé: Tribo Tupí no Brasil Central.* São Paulo: Editora da
        Universidade de São Paulo, Companhia Editora Nacional.
  n.d. "Some Aspects of Tapirapé Morals." In Vegilus Ferm (ed.), *En-*
        cyclopedia of Morals. New York. Pp. 604-605.

Carneiro, Robert
  1961 "Slash and Burn Cultivation Among the Kuikuru and Its Implica-
        tions for Cultural Developments in the Amazon Basin." In *The*
        Evolution of Horticultural Systems in Native South America, edited
        by Johannes Wilbert, *Anthropologica:* Supplement #2, pp. 47-67.
        Caracas.

Cook, Sherburne, and L. B. Simpson
  1948 *The Population of Central Mexico in the Sixteenth Century.*
        Berkeley: University of California Press.

Cardoso de Oliveira, Roberto
  1959 "A Situação Atual dos Tapirapé." *Boletim do Museu Paraense*
        Emílio Goeldi, Antropologia, no. 3. Belém.
  1964 *O Índio e o Mundo dos Brancos: A Situação dos Tukúna do Alto*

Solimões. Corpo e Alma do Brasil, XII. São Paulo: Difusão Européia do Livro.

Document by a Group of Brazilian Anthropologists
   1974   "The Politics of Genocide Against the Indians of Brazil." In *Supysaua: A Documentary Report on the Conditions of the Indian Peoples in Brazil.* Berkeley, Calif.: Indigena, Inc., and American Friends of Brazil. November.

Dobyns, Henry F., and Paul Doughty (eds.)
   1971   *Peasants, Power and Applied Social Change: Vicos as a Model.* Beverly Hills, Calif.: Sage Publications.

Dominican Missionaries
   1933   *Mensageiro do Rosário.* Uberaba and Rio de Janeiro.

Fernandes, Florestan
   1949   *Organização Social dos Tupinambá.* São Paulo: Instituto Progresso Editorial S.A.
   1970   *A Função da Guerra na Sociedade Tupinambá,* 2nd ed. São Paulo: Livraria Pioneira Editora.

Fleming, Peter
   1933   *Brazilian Adventure.* New York: Scribners.

Galvão, Eduardo
   1949   *Apontamentos sobre os Índios Kamaiurá.* Pub. Avulsas do Museu Nacional. No. 5. Rio de Janeiro.
   1967   "Indigenous Culture Areas of Brazil, 1900-1950." In Janice H. Hopper (ed.), *Indians of Brazil in the Twentieth Century.* Washington, D.C.: Institute for Cross-Cultural Research.

Hohenthal, D., and Thomas McCorkle
   1955   "The Problems of Aboriginal Persistence." *Southwest Journal of Anthropology,* vol. 2, no. 3, pp. 228-300.

Holmberg, Allan R.
   1960   "Changing Community Attitudes and Values in Peru: A Case Study in Guided Change." In *Social Change in Latin America Today.* New York: Vintage Books.

Horta Barbosa, L. B.
   1954   "Relatório dos Trabalhos Realizados pela Inspectoria do S.P.I. durante o Ano de 1916." *Revista do Museu Paulista,* vol. VIII, pp. 59-77. São Paulo.

Kietzman, Dale Walter
   1972   *Indian Survival in Brazil.* Ann Arbor, Mich.: University Microfilms.

Kubler, George
   1946   "The Quechua in the Colonial World." In Julian Steward (ed.), *Handbook of South American Indians,* vol. 2. Washington, D.C.: Bureau of American Ethnology.

Laraia, Roque de Barros
   1976   "Integração e Utopia." *Revista de Cultura,* vol. LXX, no. 3, pp. 5-13. Rio de Janeiro: Vozes.

318   Laraia, Roque de Barros, and Roberto da Matta

1967   *Índios e Castanheiros.* Rio de Janeiro: Difusão Européia do Livro.
Lévi-Strauss, Claude
1969   *The Elementary Structures of Kinship.* Trans. J. H. Bell and I. R. von Sturmer; ed. R. Needham, rev. ed. Boston: Beacon Press.
Lewis, Norman
1974   "Genocide." In *Supysaua: A Documentary Report on the Conditions of the Indian Peoples in Brazil.* Berkeley, Calif.: Indigena, Inc., and American Friends of Brazil. (Article originally published in Sunday *Times*, London, Feb. 23, 1969.)
McDonald, Frederick J.
1965   "Some Considerations about Tupí-Guaraní Kinship Structures." *Boletim do Museu Paraense Emílio Goeldi,* Antropologia, no. 26. Belém.
Marchant, Alexander
1942   *From Barter to Slavery: The Economic Relations of Portuguese and Indians in the Settlement of Brazil.* Baltimore: Johns Hopkins University Press.
Maybury-Lewis, David
1967   *Akwé-Shavante Society.* London: Oxford University Press.
Mello, Franco, Alfonso Arinos de
1937   *O Índio Brasileiro e a Revolução Francesa.* Rio de Janeiro: Livraria José Olympio.
Métraux, Alfred
1927   "Migrations Historiques des Tupí-Guaraní." *Journal de la Société des Americanistes.* N.S., vol. XIX, pp. 1-45. Paris.
1928a   *La Civilization Matérielle des Tribus Tupí-Guaraní.* Paris: Librairie Orientaliste Paul Geuthner.
1928b   *La Réligion des Tupinambá et ses Rapports avec celle des autres Tribu Tupí-Guaraní.* Paris: Librairie Ernest Lerou.
Murphy, Yolanda, and Robert F. Murphy
1974   *Women of the Forest.* New York: Columbia University Press.
Nimuendajú, Curt
1946   *The Eastern Timbira.* Berkeley: University of California Press.
Oberg, Kalervo
1957   "Types of Social Structure among the Lowland Tribes of South America." *American Anthropologist,* vol. 57, no. 3, pp. 472-487.
Ribeiro, Darcy
1956   "Convívio e Contaminação." *Sociologia,* vol. XVIII, no. 1, pp. 97-103. São Paulo.
1967   "Indigenous Cultures and Languages of Brazil." In Janice H. Hopper (ed.), *Indians of Brazil in the Twentieth Century.* Washington, D.C.: Institute for Cross-Cultural Research. Pp. 77-167.
1970   *Os Índios e a Civilização.* Rio de Janeiro: Editora Civilização Brasileira.
Shapiro, Judith
1967   "Notes from Santa Terezinha." Unpublished MS.

1968a   "Tapirapé Kinship." *Boletim do Museu Paraense Emílio Goeldi,* Antropologia, no. 37. Belém.

1968b   "Ceremonial Distribution in Tapirapé Society." *Boletim do Museo Paraense Emílio Goeldi,* Antropologia, no. 38. Belém.

Supysaua

1974   A *Documentary Report on the Conditions of the Indian Peoples of Brazil.* Berkeley, Calif.: Indigena, Inc., and American Friends of Brazil. November.

Txibae Ewororo

1976   "A Voz dos que não tinha voz." *Revista de Cultura,* vol. LXX, no. 4, pp. 35-48. Rio de Janeiro: Vozes.

Wagley, Charles

1940a   "The Effects of Depopulation upon Social Organization as Illustrated by the Tapirapé Indians." *Transactions of the New York Academy of Sciences,* series II, vol. 3, no. 1, pp. 12-16.

1940b   "World View of the Tapirapé Indians." *The Journal of American Folklore,* vol. 53, no. 210, pp. 252-260.

1943   "Xamanismo Tapirapé." *Boletim do Museu Nacional.* Antropologia, no. 3. Rio de Janeiro.

1951a   "Cultural Influences on Population: A Comparison of Two Tupí Tribes." *Revista do Museu Paulista,* vol. V, pp. 95-104. São Paulo.

1951b   "The Indian Heritage of Brazil." In Alexander Marchant and T. Lynn Smith (eds.), *Brazil: Portrait of Half a Continent.* New York: Dryden Press. Pp. 104-124.

1955   "Tapirapé Social and Cultural Change, 1940-1953." *Anais do XXXI Congresso Internacional de Americanistas* (1954), vol. I, pp. 99-106. São Paulo.

1960   "Champukwi of the Village of Tapirs." In Joseph Casagrande (ed.), *In the Company of Man.* New York: Harper & Brothers. Pp. 397-415.

1970   "Kamairaho: A Tapirapé Indian Leader." *Universitas,* nos. 6-7, May-December, pp. 359-371. Salvador.

Wagley, Charles, and Eduardo Galvão

1946   "O Parentesco Tupí-Guaraní (Tupí-Guaraní Kinship)." *Boletim do Museu Nacional,* Antropologia, no. 6. Rio de Janeiro.

1948   "The Tapirapé." In *Handbook of South American Indians.* Washington, D.C.: Smithsonian Institution, Bureau of American Ethnology. Bulletin 143, vol. 3, pp. 167-178.

1949   *The Tenetehara Indians of Brazil.* New York: Columbia University Press.

Wagley, Charles, and Marvin Harris

1958   *Minorities in the New World: Six Case Studies.* New York: Columbia University Press.

Index

Abbeville, Claude d', 58-59*n*, 180*n*, 302
acculturation, 3-4, 298
adultery, 161-63
age grades of Bird Societies, 143-45, 149-53, 157, 168
age status terms, 105, 144
agriculture, *see* farming and gardening
Alberto Torres, Heloisa, 6, 17, 18
Amazon River and Basin, 26, 27, 50, 272-74
Anapatawa village, 32, 34
annatto pigment, 65, 129, 130, 132, 138, 140, 149, 155, 170, 182, 184, 188, 250, 263; source of, 57
Antanchowi, 223, 249-57; death, 257; epilepsy, 251-52; raped by group, 252, 254-56
anteater in myth, 177
Araguaia Development Company, 46, 294
Araguaia River, 8, 16, 17, 26-27, 30, 40, 43, 48, 78, 175, 176, 185, 194, 286, 287; frontier expansion on, 45-47, 80; rapids, 176-77; trading and tourists on, 80-81; voyage on, 9-12
armadillos, 52, 67
artifacts made for sale, 80-81, 114, 263, 265
Assuriní tribe, 27, 282

Awetí tribe, 27

Baldus, Herbert, 7-8, 16, 23, 29*n*, 31, 36, 37, 39, 51, 56, 57, 58*n*, 60, 64*n*, 66, 68, 75, 85, 87, 93-95, 106*n*, 107, 118, 139*n*, 142*n*, 145*n*, 151*n*, 169*n*, 171*n*, 242; Feast Groups described, 115-16; longhouse described, 89-90; on marital conflicts, 160-62
Bananal Island, 46, 47, 286, 291, 292
bananas, 57, 58, 139
beads, 5, 71-72, 73, 132-33, 154, 170, 266
beans, 57, 58
"beautiful child," 121, 241, 244
beef, 69, 79, 137, 270
Bird Societies, 77, 83, 85, 94, 101-8, 118, 122, 124, 244, 271; age grades, 102-6; boys in, 149, 150; in communal work parties, 56, 112-14, 119; in hunting, 61-62, 64, 112, 212; leaders, 107, 118; masked dancers, 108, 110-13; myth of origin, 103-4, 179, 214; names, 103-4; old men relinquish membership, 106; patrilineal descent in membership, 104-5; songs and dances, 212-14, 217, 253; wrestling contest, 63-64